Amidst Mass Atrocity and the Rubble of Theology

Amidst Mass Atrocity and the Rubble of Theology

Searching for a Viable Theodicy

PETER ADMIRAND

Foreword by
DAVID B. BURRELL, CSC

CASCADE *Books* · Eugene, Oregon

AMIDST MASS ATROCITY AND THE RUBBLE OF THEOLOGY
Searching for a Viable Theodicy

Cascade Books
An Imprint of Wipf and Stock Publishers
199 W. 8th Ave., Suite 3
Eugene, OR 97401

www.wipfandstock.com

ISBN 13: 978-1-61097-306-9

Cataloging-in-Publication data:

Admirand, Peter.

Amidst mass atrocity and the rubble of theology : searching for a viable theodicy / Peter Admirand ; foreword by David B. Burrell.

xxvi + 366 p. ; 23 cm. —Includes bibliographical references and indexes.

ISBN 13: 978-1-61097-306-9

1. Theodicy. 2. Holocaust (Christian theology). 3. Holocaust, Jewish (1939–1945) — Influence. 4. Liberation theology. 5. Genocide — Religious aspects — Christianity. I. Burrell, David B. II. Title.

BT160 .A36 2012

Manufactured in the U.S.A.

For the Drowned and the Forgotten

"Lord, even the dogs under the table eat the children's crumbs."
(Mark 7:28)

Contents

Foreword

David B. Burrell, CSC

In this demanding study, Peter Admirand sets himself a formidable task: proposing "a theodicy of humility and circumspection that acknowledges its limits and failures." This will elicit a prose at once enticing and captivating, both descriptively and philosophically. Citing Charles Taylor in *A Secular Age*: "Naïveté is now unavailable to anyone, believer or unbeliever," he reminds us that theodicy is not alchemy:

> in the sense of *aurum et stecore—gold from filth*. It cannot turn all mutilation and senseless destruction into intrinsic meaning and purpose. The question is whether it can provide a framework and philosophy to examine honestly this world, the lives and actions of human beings, and the God that is believed to be a theist's source and ultimate hope, while orienting a person to prevent or combat injustice and horrors. In such a candid examination, questions and failures will remain, but, perhaps, a viable position can still be reached.

As in any theological inquiry, everything turns on the way it is carried out; there can be no "conclusion" apart from the mode of inquiry which arrives at it. For therein lies the test—the exercise which readers and critics can examine to determine whether what emerges is worth the effort. The effort demanded in this case is considerable: from enduring horrendous descriptions of the plight of human beings at the hands of others who claim to be human, to negotiating theological argument whose very vocabulary can be annoyingly arcane. Yet amazingly enough, Admirand manages to parse theological argument deftly, so those less accustomed to it can find their way.

Yet he spares no one as he forges ahead to execute a venture which many (myself included) would have thought quite vain. Indeed, what could be more pretentious than attempting to "justify the ways of God to us," as theodicy has classically been described? Yet what saves this attempt is the way he presses to have something to say—however broken or inarticulate. And to learn to say it to ourselves in an age which has so starkly experienced human beings' manifest disdain for others' dignity, whether in a frenzied paroxysm of destructive behavior or in chilling inattention to the plight of victims. The result will necessarily be expressed in fragmented, fractured language, for the theodicy he begins to articulate cannot result in answers given, but rather in asking the questions correctly.

In the face of the previous century, most of us have been tempted to dismiss the enterprise itself, and the evidence of human malice that Admirand amasses is cannily organized towards that end. Yet he insists we must go on. But how? With a pervasive intellectual humility that never presumes to speak on behalf of a creator who "saw that everything was [not only] good, but very good," yet cannot not let go of that very insistence. What results is a relentless inquiry which defies summation, for no closure is possible, not simply due to the magnitude of the evil perpetrated, but also to the reality of that creator with the ensuing relation to creatures. Such daunting challenges to undertaking theology at all must show readers how that mode of inquiry can be carried out in the teeth of a human reality which beggars any shred of decency. Readers already initiated into these challenges will find his analyses of formidable thinkers illuminating, while others who dare undertake the journey will learn how this apparently arcane mode of inquiry proceeds, and why he contends it to be unavoidable. By directing us to witness and trauma studies, assisted by post-Shoah Jewish thought, the thicket into which he leads us bears a distinctively human face. Those who are enticed to follow his argument will assess its success, if "success" be the term for an inherently broken inquiry elegantly executed. Nor is this a critical observation, for the complaints he himself raises against standard theodicy keep him from attempting anything like a seamless "explanation" of divine activity in our parlous world. Moreover, the work's intricate structure, organization, and development will lead us to appreciate that the best one can settle for is a fractured faith built on a fractured theodicy, expressed in a language explicitly fragmented, pluralist, and broken.

(Fractured) Preface and Acknowledgment

How should one be grateful when so many others cry out in anguish? It is a disconcerting question that coerces thankfulness with guilt, but demands gratitude nonetheless. In saying "thank you" one is cognizant of one's privilege, one's fortune not to be rootless or abandoned, to be endured and loved despite one's ineptness and pettiness. In rendering thanks, one acknowledges one's frailty and weakness: one's inevitable nothingness without those Others, known or unknown, who sustain and feed and heal one's body and soul.

The book you are about to read is over thirteen years in the making, but its seeds linger much deeper, though like the birds in the parable, a poor or inadequate memory lurks and devours whatever is unprotected on the path.

I first thank my wife, Kelly, who sometimes sees more aspects of me than God, for good or for bad, and whose testimony before God about me would send shivers down my spine. Such is an inevitable curse and blessing for those privileged to have another know them while they are exposed, ungraceful, and frail—and still find the means to love. Know that I love and appreciate you despite your seeing the real me.

To my three, beautiful children, miraculously quiet now as I write these words: thank you, and I am sorry for the ways I have, and inevitably will, fail you, sometimes through misguided love, sometimes simply because we all hope and yearn for too much, perhaps the root of much evil and suffering.

To my parents, Margaret and Peter: I know having a son with wanderlust has not been easy with the grandchildren in a different continent. Know that I am both sorry and grateful for your love and support. Similar sentiments are expressed towards my sisters, Mary and Kathleen, and their respective husbands, Vincent and Gerard.

I thank Chris Love who challenges and accepts me like all best friends are ideally supposed to. I also thank my in-laws, Tom and Cathy Scanlon, along with Mary, TJ, and Matt Scanlon. To Dar Shiang and Ching Huang: "Sen-moon."

Academically, too many people deserve credit for whatever worth there is that follows. Some I have only met in dreams or thoughts or in reflecting on their words and ideas. Where would any of us be without them? At The Catholic University of America, I especially thank Professor Ingrid Merkel and the Senior Honors seminar that impacted me. I also thank Dr. John Feneley of the Centre for Medieval and Renaissance Studies at Oxford University, where I grew and learned during my semester abroad. To my Jesuit Volunteer Corps housemates in our year of service: thank you. At Georgetown, a belated thanks to Dr. Anne Cubillé, whose course "Women's Testimonial Literature" made its mark on me. I also cannot express sufficient gratitude towards Professor Jason Rosenblatt for his advising of my MA thesis in English on testimonial literature, and his devoted, humble presence linked with an acute, wide-ranging mind: the perfect combination for any teacher.

At Boston College, I thank Dr. Colleen Griffith and Dr. Thomas Groome. I also thank Professor Elie Wiesel, whose class at Boston University still remains with me. At Trinity College, Dublin, I thank my PhD advisor, Professor Nigel Biggar (now Regius Professor of Pastoral and Moral Divinity at Oxford University). I also thank Dr. Kieran Flynn, a true friend who has become a part of my family.

Not enough praise can be expressed for Professor John D'Arcy May, who retired from Trinity College Dublin in 2007 after teaching for twenty years at the Irish School of Ecumenics and is currently a research fellow at the ISE, Monash University, Australian Catholic University, and the Melbourne College of Divinity; and Didier Pollefeyt, Professor in Pastoral Theology, Theology of Jewish-Christian Relations, and Post-Holocaust Theology, and Vice-Dean for Education at the Faculty of Theology and Religious Studies at the Katholieke Universiteit Leuven. I am also deeply blessed and humbled with the support of Professor David Burrell, Hesburgh Professor Emeritus in Philosophy and Theology at the University of

Notre Dame and Professor of Ethics and Development at the Uganda Martyrs University in Nkozi, Uganda.

After graduating from Trinity, I found an almost immediate home at the Irish School of Ecumenics. I want to particularly thank Dr. Andrew Pierce and Professor Linda Hogan. Only space prevents me from listing my gratitude to everyone on the staff. At St. Patrick's College I am also greatly appreciative of Dr. Caroline Renehan.

In January 2011, I joined the staff in the School of Theology at Mater Dei Institute, Dublin City University. I could not have found a more supportive and collegial environment and want particularly to thank the Institute's President, Dr Dermot Lane; the Director, Dr. Andrew McGrady; the Head of the School of Theology, Dr. Ethna Regan; and all my other colleagues. I am also grateful for the grant I received from the Institute's Research Committee that paid for the index in this book.

I also thank my editor, Dr. Charles Collier, for having faith in my project; Jacob Martin, for his devoted and meticulous copyediting; Ian Creeger for his openness and flexibility while typesetting the book; and for all the staff at Cascade/Wipf and Stock.

Lastly, should I—can I—thank God? How can I not? And yet, moving from the joy expressed above to the often despairing scenes that follow in this work, my personal gratitude must be tempered by all those whose "acknowledgment page" is unwritten; or written in thorns and hopelessness; or is never allowed to be written; or has little to acknowledge or be grateful for; for whom no seeds were scattered, or nurtured, or allowed to grow; for whom prayers were choked and "yielded no grain"; and for whom we, and perhaps God, failed in unforgivable ways. Here again, thankfulness and guilt uncomfortably unite; an awkward break seems to linger, a silence that jars and discomforts. One wants to return above and linger by one's wife and one's children now slumbering peacefully. The outside world, the one of periodic violence and horror, like the earthquake and tsunami that struck Japan, unleashing further suffering as I now write, can be momentarily quelled. But not for long: and that is the key and calling for so much of what will follow in these pages: the first sprouts of a faith as fractured as it is flourishing, whose seeds must learn to grow, even on rocky and thorny ground, amidst ravenous birds, little soil, and a scorching sun.

Introduction: Theology in an Age of Genocide

Who do you think you are, anyway, to imagine yourself so high and mighty as to want to understand the ways of the Blessed name? You are but mortal human beings . . . And you want to understand the ways of God? . . . Who do you think you are?[1]

DESPAIR

It is hubris to claim to have answers to unanswerable questions. But such questions—as part of their burden and worth—must still be asked, investigated, and contemplated. How can there be a loving, all-powerful God and a world stymied by suffering and evil? This is one of the unanswerable questions we must all struggle to answer, even as our responses are closer to gasps, silences, and further questions. More importantly, how and whether one articulates a response will have deep, lasting repercussions for any belief in God and in our judgments upon one another.

The title of this work refers to the "rubble of theology." Such a term is meant to invoke reflection upon the violence and injustice that buries so many individuals in this world and the theological (and secular) explanations and systems that have ultimately failed to address

---

1. Rabbi Unsdorfer, leader of the Bratislav Orthodoxy, was later murdered at Auschwitz. The quotation is from Greenberg, "Between Holocaust and Redemption," 114–15. In a similar vein, David Burrell writes: "And what could be more pretentious than attempting to 'justify the ways of God to us,' as the venture of theodicy has classically been described?" (*Deconstructing Theodicy*, 13).

or admit their loss, as loss. One salient aim of this work is to uncover whether and how faith in God can still be meaningful and integral while facing the reality of appalling loss and affliction that crushes lives, hopes, and prayers.

In *A Long Way Gone*, a former child soldier of Sierra Leone, Ishmael Beah, depicts the moment he was given an AK-47. A child trying to flee war, he had already experienced acts of brutality and violence. Soon, of course, he would partake in them. In describing the moment he is given a gun, Beah writes: "I hesitated for a bit, but [the colonel] pushed the gun against my chest. With trembling hands, I took the gun, saluted him, and ran to the back of the line, still holding the gun but afraid to look at it. I had never held a gun that long before and it frightened me. The closest thing to it had been a toy gun made out of bamboo when I was seven."[2] The repetition of the word *gun* and the apt details—his hands "tremble," and the gun reminds him of a toy (yet he is "afraid to look at it")—begin to paint the story of the metamorphosis of a child into a murderer. Beah's world is one rife with violation, hopelessness, and moral decay.[3]

Similarly, in *Gulag: A History*, Anne Applebaum quotes Hava Volovich, a political prisoner of the Stalinist regime, who gave birth to "Little Eleanora" while in the gulag: "Every night for a whole year, I stood at my child's cot, picking off the bed bugs and praying. I prayed that God would prolong my torment for a hundred years if it meant that I wouldn't be parted from my daughter . . . But God did not answer my prayer . . ."[4] After working all day at a small mill, Volovich would return to the mother's camp to see her daughter. She continues:

> Little Eleanora, who was now fifteen months old, soon realized that her pleas for "home" were in vain . . . She stopped reaching out for me when I visited her . . . On the last day of her life, when I picked her up (they allowed me to breast-feed her) she stared wide-eyed somewhere off into the distance, then started

---

2. Beah, *Long Way Gone*, 111. For a similar depiction by a former child soldier, see Jal, *War Child*, 90–94. Jal, a seven-year-old boy forced to take part in Sudan's bloody civil war, was told by his new commander: "Always remember: the gun is your father and mother now" (94).

3. For inspiring accounts of mothers' acts of healing in the context of child soldiers, see Lederarch and Lederarch, "When Mothers Speak."

4. Applebaum, *Gulag*, 320.

to beat her weak little fists on my face, clawing at my breast, and biting it. Then she pointed down at her bed.

In the evening, when I came back with my bundle of firewood, her cot was empty. I found her lying naked in the morgue among the corpses of the adult prisoners. She had spent one year and four months in this world, and died on 3 March 1944 . . . That is the story of how, in giving birth to my only child, I committed the worst crime there is.[5]

Both these stories reek with despair: a child is forced to murder, while the birth of a baby is the "worst crime," and a mother's desperate prayers to God are met only with silence. These are not the only voices in our world, but they are many and vast, and their clamor neither diminishes nor fades with the passing of time.

In *The Brothers Karamazov*, Ivan challenges Alyosha to answer whether he would construct a world that ultimately provides peace and happiness but requires the torture of one child: "'No, I wouldn't consent,' said Alyosha softly."[6] The stories above are also of individual loss, but consider these statistics. Timothy Snyder estimates that "between them, the Nazi and Stalinist regimes murdered more than fourteen million people in the bloodlands."[7] Jung Chang and Jon Holiday begin *Mao: The Unknown Story* by stating: "Mao Tse-tung, who for decades held absolute power over the lives of one-quarter of the world's population, was responsible for well over 70 million deaths in peacetime."[8] In turning back to Africa, how many individuals have been lost through colonialism, slavery, genocide, starvation, disease, and wars? Here one must weigh not only the notion of millions of lives that have been brutally tortured and murdered, but one must also remember the individual lives like Little Eleanora's.[9] Despair, followed by a stubborn resilience, seems the only candid response if life is still to be endured.

5. Ibid., 320–21.

6. Dostoyevsky, *Brothers Karamazov*, 239. Alyosha, however, wants to substitute the boy with Christ, "who gave His innocent blood for all and everything" (239). Ivan then tells his "poem" of "The Grand Inquisitor" in which the Grand Inquisitor rebukes Christ for expanding human freedom (247) and asking too much of humanity (249).

7. Snyder, *Bloodlands*, 379.

8. Chang and Halliday, *Mao*, 3.

9. See Snyder, *Bloodlands*, 407–48. For a more hopeful view, see Pinker, *Better Angels*, 295–97.

THEODICY

Classical theodicy entails an attempt to justify or make coherent the existence of evil and a loving, omnipotent God. Etymologically, we can connect *theos* (God) and *dike* (justice).[10] In Lars Svendsen's words: "[T]he function of theodicy might be described not as justification of evil but as a means of explaining how God *can be found innocent* when the world contains so much suffering . . ."[11]

For this current undertaking, a theodicist is one who attempts to analyze the conditions of this world primarily in the context of one's faith tradition and presents a picture or argument for why belief in a loving God can be justified or viewed as a reasonable undertaking. If a theodicist traditionally sought to justify God's innocence despite the rubble and desperation, theodicists today must be situated at the margins and among the forgotten where justice, let alone so-called innocence, is in short supply. Cognizant of the suffering and frailty of this world, a theodicist seeks to locate or advocate a fragmented, but still viable meaning within and beyond it.[12]

In this quest for a viable theodicy, I endeavor to formulate a pastorally sensitive approach that is theologically acute for our contemporary, post-Holocaust age. A key to this approach will be a sustained engagement with testimonies of mass atrocity to test and challenge various theodicies and antitheodicies. From this testing, I aim to highlight salient features that a theodicy needs to incorporate for any hope of being viable. Such a position, while "living" (and even, at times, dynamic), will not be bereft of loss, discontinuity, or doubt. The epigraph above, however, from a rabbi murdered at Auschwitz, undermines the possibility to develop any theodicy—for how can a human being understand any purpose and meaning behind God's

---

10. For an explanation of the difference between a theodicy and a defense, see Van Inwagen, "Argument from Evil," 62–73.

11. Svendsen, *Philosophy of Evil*, 44.

12. An anonymous reviewer has labeled me a post-theodicist "who attempts a practical-theoretical response that affirms divine providence in the face of evils." The reviewer continues: "Theodicies . . . are *not* responses to the anguished cries of the victims, but to the philosophical questions that the evils, often presented very much in the abstract . . . serve to engender for the questioners or skeptics [of theodicy]." Theodicy, however, limited to philosophical questions without any performative, pragmatic, apologetic, or theological response, has dire consequences for any fractured but still viable religious faith.

creation of this world? While such questions can disarm a theist, they pale in comparison to whether one should even desire to understand or acknowledge a God who is said to create a world brimming with goodness and beauty, but one also steeped in agony and misery.

It is not difficult, therefore, to understand the growing support for antitheodic approaches. Richard Swinburne writes that the antitheodicist "denies [the claim that it is 'not morally wrong for God to create or permit the various evils'] by putting forward moral principles which have as consequences that a good God would not under any circumstances cause or permit the evils in question."[13] An antitheodicist, then, refuses to provide or accede to any claim, argument, or position that seems to reconcile the existence of God and the existence of evil. Such a position is particularly robust in light of what are termed mass, unjust, or senseless evils. As Sarah Pinnock writes in *Beyond Theodicy*: "In the intellectual space of twentieth-century thought, the term 'theodicy' has accumulated pejorative connotations among some analytic and continental philosophers . . . In particular, post-Holocaust thinkers widely reject theodicy as morally scandalous."[14] As Levinas writes: "Perhaps the most revolutionary fact of our twentieth-century consciousness—but it is also an event in Sacred History—is that of the destruction of all balance between the explicit and implicit theodicy of Western thought and the forms which suffering and evil take in the very unfolding of this century."[15] Giorgio Agamben, moreover, refers to "the conciliatory vice of every theodicy . . ."[16]

Many theists also try to bypass theodicy. Though his position "is not grounded in a theodicy of any kind,"[17] Brian Davies, in *The Reality of God and the Problem of Evil*, examines (and aims to uphold) belief

---

13. Swinburne, "Evil Does Not Show," 600.

14. Pinnock focuses on thinkers who "eschew theodicy": Gabriel Marcel, Martin Buber, Johann Baptist Metz, and Ernst Bloch (*Beyond Theodicy*, 7). Dorothee Sölle, furthermore, writes: "I suspect that fixing on the problem of theodicy is a way of avoiding or denying suffering" ("God's Pain and Our Pain," 111). See also Laato and de Moor, *Theodicy in the World of the Bible*, vi.

15. Levinas, "Useless Suffering," 452. Elsewhere, he remarks how "indecent" all theodicy "probably" is (*Nine Talmudic Readings*, 187). For analysis of Levinas' rejection of theodicy, see Davies, "Sincerity and the End of Theodicy," 161–78; Bernstein, "Evil and the Temptation of Theodicy," 252–67. See also Welz, "Reasons for Having No Reasons to Defend God," 167–86.

16. Agamben, *Remnants of Auschwitz*, 20.

17. Davies, *Reality of God*, 229.

in God despite the dilemma of evil. John Roth adds: "Most theodicies have a fatal flaw: they legitimate evil. They do so by saying too much or too little as they answer questions posed by waste."[18]

Others voice more acerbic remarks about theodicy.[19] Peter Berger "has argued that theodicy is a type of social masochism that legitimates social institutions at the expense of suffering individuals."[20] Amos Funkenstein deems theodicies "offensive."[21] For Lars Svendsen, "theodicies are themselves evil."[22]

Disillusionment with theodicy hovers around various causes. Some theodic attempts, it is argued, often prevent an honest appraisal of blame and responsibility; seek to muffle the voices of the victims whose sobering words or jarring screams do not neatly fit into any "easy" system of beliefs; or posit unethical, if not harmful, justifications that (unwittingly) collude with the perpetrators and leave the victim doubly violated—abused and shamed.[23] In *The Evils of Theodicy*, for example, Terrence Tilley analyzes the social situation of speech acts in theodic texts to prove how "engaging in the discourse of theodicy *creates* evil."[24]

While one may also turn to a title like Michael Stoeber's *Reclaiming Theodicy*,[25] the challenges and accusations against theodicy are wide and diverse. Yet, key questions still remain: Does denying the discourse of theodicy thwart evil or entail a denial of God's existence? Contra the antitheodicists, can theodicy still be viable today, especially in the face of catastrophic suffering, and if so, how? Lastly, why would turning to survivor testimonies from various mass atroci-

18. Roth, "Rejoinder," 17.

19. For Gabriel Marcel, theodicy is "sacrilegious, dogmatic." Quoted in Pinnock, *Beyond Theodicy*, 27.

20. Braiterman, *(God) after Auschwitz*, 25.

21. Funkenstein, "Theological Interpretations of the Holocaust," 641.

22. Svendsen, *Philosophy of Evil*, 231.

23. Sarah Pinnock writes that "after Auschwitz, theodicy is exposed as perpetrating amoral justifications of evil and rationalistic caricatures of practical faith struggles" (*Beyond Theodicy*, xi).

24. Tilley, *Evils of Theodicy*, 3.

25. See also Queiruga, "From 'Ponerology' to Theodicy," 80–89. Queiruga coins the term "*Pisteodicy* (from *pistis*, 'faith' in its broad cosmovisional sense)" and writes that "theodicy then appears as the Christian pisteodicy . . ." (82). While I do not use the term in this work, I will often speak of a theodic faith, which also resonates with Queriuga's term.

ties be a possible means to argue for a theodicy's relevance? When the Baluchistan poet Balach Khan talks of the sadness of "children who dream of more light / than the sun can spare,"[26] can any theodicy provide such ample light to victims like these?

HOPE

In light of such tragedy and horrors, it is legitimate to ask why another attempt at theodicy is needed or even what right one has to engage in theodicy, but it is more legitimate to ask why another child is forced to murder, why another landslide buries forty-five people, and why the world ignores another genocide. So long as these other questions proliferate and the reverberating torrent of "Why, O Lord?" rings in the hearts and minds of many human beings, the search for answers and explanations will never cease. Attempts at theodicy extend deep into our past. As Joel Burnett writes: "In the ancient world, reflection on the problem of evil and unjust suffering did not begin with Israel, nor is it peculiar to monotheism."[27] Paleoanthropologists' work on Neanderthals and other protohumans may even push such possible theodic reflections back further.[28] For a theist, when prayer and questioning are interlocked and a God of love and justice is invoked, the love of such a God stirs the search to respond to those eternal questions. It is when silence and resignation follow such losses that spiritual desolation seems to unfurl all about us.

And yet, theodicy can be a messy, often unsatisfying venture. How does one, for example, respond to this question by Élie Mizinge, convicted of crimes of genocide in Rwanda: "Why did [God] not stab our murderous eyes with His wrath? Or show some sign of disapproval to save more lucky ones? In those horrible moments, who could hear His silence? We were abandoned by all words of rebuke."[29] When victims and perpetrators of genocide claim abandonment by God, which approach to theodicy remains meaningful? The choices, indeed, often seem to be stark: one can read a theodicy of hubris or naïveté that claims to leave little room for doubt or questioning, or a theodicy of humility and circumspection that acknowledges its limits and fail-

---

26. Harlow, *Resistance Literature*, 41.

27. Burnett, *Where Is God?* 107.

28. See Finlayson, *Humans Who Went Extinct*.

29. As interviewed by Hatzfeld, *Machete Season*, 145.

ures. In this work I will argue that only the latter approach is the most sound and fruitful. As Charles Taylor writes in *A Secular Age*: "Näiveté is now unavailable to anyone, believer or unbeliever."[30] Theodicy is not alchemy "in the sense of *aurum et stecore—gold from filth*."[31] It cannot turn all mutilation and senseless destruction into intrinsic meaning and purpose. The question is whether it can provide a framework and philosophy to examine honestly this world, the lives and actions of human beings, and the God that is believed to be a theist's source and ultimate hope while orienting a person to prevent or combat injustice and horrors. In such a candid examination, questions and failures will remain, but, perhaps, a viable position can still be reached.

My evaluation of the relevance of theodicy is based on two major presuppositions that I want to test:

1. Theistic belief cannot bypass theodicy.[32]

2. How a theodicy addresses and incorporates its theoretical limitations—or what I refer to as the fissures, gaps, and caesuras of a faith stance—are the fundamental criteria of whether a theodicy can be considered viable.

Similar to antitheodicists, I am skeptical that any theoretical theodicy will categorically succeed in providing an argument that justifies the existence of mass atrocity or a devastating earthquake. However, I argue that a theist must still aim to develop a viable theodicy, although to do so entails a recognition and incorporation of those fissures, gaps, and caesuras and the need to articulate why one can still believe and hope where the "evidence" calls for total silence or radical doubt. This stance is based on my conviction that jettisoning theodicy has dire consequences for any possibility of a meaningful, enduring theodic-faith. For if one advocates the failure of all theodicy, one may as well

---

30. Taylor, *Secular Age*, 21. For my analysis of this work, see my "Embodying an 'Age of Doubt, Solitude, and Revolt,'" 905–20.

31. Forbes, *Dazzled and Deceived*, 46. Forbes' context is mimicry and camouflage by plant and animal species and refers to the ancient alchemical hope of "the rose emerging from rotted manure, the pure lotus flower casting off mud in murky waters" (46). The analogy is useful for our current investigation of theodicy.

32. In ch. 3, we will see D. Z. Phillips describe what has been called "theism without theodicy" ("Theism without Theodicy.") In "Useless Suffering," Emmanuel Levinas (analyzing Emil Fackenheim) writes of a "faith without theodicy." It would seem that much depends on one's definition of theodicy (and the incorporation of my second presupposition, above) for any hope of salvaging a reasonable theodic position.

remove God completely from the locus of one's thoughts and conceptions. There can be no theism without theodicy, as such theism still has evil and suffering hovering about it, and eventually, a type of theodicy emerges if traditional belief in God is maintained. If the theodicy enterprise is deemed obscene or impossible, then one believes against all reason or sense. If one wants to worship and be in relationship with God, I do not see how "a theodicy without religion" will ultimately lead to a faith that perseveres and heals. Moreover, without belief in God redeeming and healing the suffering of so many in this world, the possibility for worshipping such a God is also dubious.

Worship of God is fundamental for a relationship with God and to orient ourselves to assess our own worth properly—a value that ultimately springs from our being created by God in God's image and likeness. Such worship also demands a love and care for the Other, whose being calls us to see God's image within all of us and to treat that Other with dignity, respect, and love.

In this work I will argue that these witness testimonies must be given sufficient authority to place all of one's theological doctrine, traditions, and beliefs into question. However, I remain suspicious of Christian theologies that radically alter seemingly foundational components of theological belief, especially in regards to God's moral goodness, God's power to redeem, God's mercy, God's connection with human suffering, and God's relation to this world and humanity. Without these aspects, I cannot fathom a viable faith or theodicy, though I also acknowledge that even these core elements may not withstand a sustained turning to the victims of atrocities of our world.

Thus, I want to advocate a fractured (but still viable, even dynamic) faith that is reflected in a fractured (but still viable) theodic position.[33] Through the three parts in this work, we will see how and whether this approach can be sustained.

To ensure that the most searing questions are asked, Part 1 analyzes what I call "the testimonies of mass atrocity" in order to be confronted by and listen to those victims of trauma and horrific affliction. Their words of witness and interpretation will depict a world where God and the goodness of humanity are predominantly absent and where theological statements seem irrelevant and inapplicable.

---

33. See, for example, my "Amidst Fractured Faith and the Fragility of Reason."

Where pertinent I will also turn to various perpetrators or bystanders in these events.

Seeking a constructive approach to theodicy in Part 2, I will examine key theodic or antitheodic texts within Christian philosophical theodicy, Catholic Latin American liberation theology, and Jewish post-Shoah theology. Because Catholic Latin American liberation theology is formulated in the context of the poor and voiceless of Latin America, and post-Shoah Jewish theology after the desolation of Treblinka and Majdanek, I anticipate that approaches within those particular fields will address some of the main challenges posed by many testimonies of mass atrocity. While there is much diverse thought and interpretation among and within all three fields, I will also argue why they are particularly useful for a Christian theodicist attempting to locate and form a viable theodic position.

In Part 3 I will aim to incorporate the key insights and questions posed by the witnesses of mass atrocity from Part 1 and the theodicists and antitheodicists of Part 2 and underscore how these groups respond to and confront one another. Drawing from this encounter between these varied texts and approaches to the problem of evil, I will end the work with my five criteria that any viable Christian theodicy needs to integrate, especially when grappling with mass atrocity, genocidal destruction, and other devastating ruptures that challenge one's religious faith and striving for meaningful existence.

Not all problems are solved, and not every story has a happy ending. Nor, however, is every ending tragic, for a theodicist must also promote the holy and sublime of this world, what Dostoyevsky termed the "sticky little leaves as they open in the spring."[34] Like sticky little leaves, human beings can also bloom, even after so many winters of discontent[35] and horror. Recall Ishmael Beah, the child soldier who had

---

34. Dostoyevsky, *Brothers Karamazov*, 224. For a penetrating reading of the major works of Dostoyevsky, especially on the issues of suffering, love, and responsibility for the Other, see Williams, *Dostoevsky*.

35. Shakespeare, *Tragedy of Richard III*, I.i.30 (712). Recall how Shakespeare's hunchbacked Richard III is "determined to prove a villain," but still has moments of doubt, a catharsis on the horizon that never fully comes. Despite some of Richard's horrific crimes, he is, arguably, the most appealing and pitiable of all of Shakespeare's villains. His determination for villainy is in part a reaction against "dissembling" nature that created him "deform'd, unfinish'd" and a society that constrains and condemns him because of his physical defect, a society whose dogs even bark at him. Because Richard's words above are from a soliloquy, he intends to speak with-

been given an AK-47 and who writes in one troubling passage: "Every time I stopped shooting to change magazines and saw my two young lifeless friends, I angrily pointed my gun into the swamp and killed more people."[36] Beah's subsequent success story as college graduate, author, and activist is well known. While Gabriele Schwab comments that Beah is "being commodified like a poster-child soldier,"[37] one can also look to less heralded cases of other former child soldiers being rehabilitated.[38] We know, however, that such stories do not solve the problem of evil nor annul those cases where happy endings are illusive and seemingly unattainable. The loss of Little Eleanora still remains, as do Beah's victims. In many ways, Beah's tale further complicates one's moral horizon where the line separating the "good" from the "bad" is often inaccurate or blurry. For a theodicy still to be considered meaningful and relevant, however, it must immerse itself within this conflicting, often ambiguous world where suffering and horrific tragedy may strike without warning or reason and where individuals will risk everything to save a stranger or to implement policies to murder an entire people. This work aims to develop a viable theodic position that is formed through such an immersion.

One final note on where I situate my position: I am a post-Vatican II (post-Medellín) Roman Catholic, which is to acknowledge the pervasive (or festering) anti-Judaic element in much pre-Vatican II theology, the requirement for theology to be guided by the option for the poor, and the call to acknowledge and overcome a general failure of accepting, listening, and seeking to learn from the Other.[39] Failure to recognize the gifts and talents of the Other has led, inexorably, to the Catholic Christian perpetrator slaughtering and defiling millions throughout history, either by intention or neglect. Failure to heed and listen to the victims of mass atrocity and injustice has led to immoral theodicies and so immoral theologies. Much of this work seeks to

---

out duplicity (even if rationalizing the evil he is about to unleash). Thus, he says he will become a villain because nature (and society) will not let him "play the lover." Interestingly, the historical Richard III still has his supporters who claim he has been unduly slandered.

36. Beah, *Long Way Gone*, 119.

37. Schwab, *Haunting Legacies*, 181.

38. See Dunson, *Child, Victim, Soldier*, 121–35.

39. Waldenfels, "Ecclesia in Asia," 196. See also my "Overcoming 'Mere Oblivion.'"

address these failures even if it means my own Christian faith becomes further fragmented, questioned, and possibly, silenced.

Lastly, I began this work because it is foundational to my development as a theologian and teacher, and more importantly, as a believer in God who passes on his faith to his children. If such religious faith is to bear any fruit, it must be deeply aware of its bitterness, toxicity, and hoped-for ripeness. Again: if theodicy (and so theology) is meaningless to those who suffer, then theism is neither moral nor viable.

Within this work, therefore, are the fundamental and foundational starting points if one is to maintain a viable belief in and relationship with God in a world in which happiness and goodness collide with anguish and debilitating loss. I can now say this in hindsight and amidst subsequent projects I have since been engaged by in the realm of interreligious theology and intercultural dialogue: recognizing the gaps, fragments, and failures within my own Catholic tradition and in theistic belief more generally impels me to dialogue, partnering and learning from the Other—whoever he or she may be.

Most of us deeply want to know we are right and have certitude in our faith and path. Few of us cherish unanswered or only partially answered questions. And yet, such unanswered questions spur the need for openness, searching, and faith. Even as this work exposes potentially faith-shattering themes and stories, my hope is that it helps secure one's faith in an embrace of questions, fragments, hope, and interreligious partnership.

PART 1

Trauma, Memory, and Truth: Testimonies of Mass Atrocity

People, seeing only its baldness, tend to think that it never had any trees. But can this possibly be the nature of a mountain? Can what is in man be completely lacking in moral inclinations?[1]

We became more and more cruel, more and more calm, more and more bloody. But we did not see that we were becoming more and more killers. The more we cut, the more cutting became children's play to us.[2]

The two epigraphs above inhabit and represent the themes of hope and despair highlighted in the introduction to this work. While Mencius' parable points to humanity's original goodness, the second quote, from a perpetrator of the genocide in Rwanda, reveals the extent of the depravity of which humankind is capable. Part 1 of this work will seem dominated by despair as I analyze testimonies of mass atrocity.

In chapter 1, "Traumatic Witnessing: Depicting and Interpreting Mass Atrocity," I will first highlight some key questions studied in this work by examining Irving Greenberg's "working principle." I will then

---

1. Mencius, *Mencius*, 145. For a discussion of Mencius in the context of the Axial Age, see Armstrong, *Great Transformation*, 301–6.

2. Spoken by Fulgence Bunani, a Hutu (and fervent Catholic) convicted of crimes of genocide and crimes against humanity. Quoted in Hatzfeld, *Machete Season*, 50.

1

address whether the scope and magnitude of evil cause particularly acute problems for a theodicy. Because many of the witnesses and their harrowing accounts are questioned due to the deleterious effects of traumatized memory, I briefly unpack the meaning of *trauma*, an often confused, but integral term. As Fassin and Rechtman write: "Trauma has become a major signifier of our age. It is our normal means of relating present suffering to the past."[3] To examine how trauma affects testimonies, I will then divide the experience of trauma into four stages, analyzing the process of experiencing, remembering, writing, and critiquing (the depiction of) the traumatic event. Thus, I will trace the often-unreliable nature of memory in such cases, as the moment of trauma, the preponderance of misinformation, the conditions in the camp or prison, the elapse of time, and the tendency for one's memories to become conflated with others, all lead to the potential for such memories to be doubted, if not cursorily refuted. If these testimonies are to challenge theodicy, I must evince how and why their truth claims and interpretations remain reliable and valuable and how to assess these works fairly and accurately.

In chapter 2, "Testimonies of Mass Atrocity," I will examine three texts of atrocity from non-Christian sources followed by the story of a Catholic martyr from the Nazi camps. Part 1 will conclude with a reflection on the life of Jesus of Nazareth as a fellow witness and sufferer of atrocity. Many of the Christian theodicists in Part 2 will highlight Christ's life as the answer to the problem of evil. Does presenting Christ as a fellow sufferer in solidarity provide the theological ground for potential meaning and value to suffering, even that endured by non-Christians? Additionally, I will probe the argument that because Jesus's life reflects a merciful God of the oppressed, God will redeem and heal all who endure unjust evil and suffering. Witness testimony, however, also challenges these assertions and so becomes another issue I must grapple with in this work.

---

3. Fassin and Rechtman, *Empire of Trauma*, xi. On the question of trauma's impact "on the relationship between self, human freedom, and divine grace," see Beste, "Challenges of Interpersonal Harm," 8.

1

Traumatic Witnessing: Depicting and Interpreting Mass Atrocity

I therefore concluded that it would constitute a criminal neglect of my duty to remain silent about the enormous loss of life . . .[1]

Bartolomé de Las Casas, once awakened to the evils that the European conquistadors were unleashing upon the native peoples of the Americas, devoted the remainder of his life to combating such injustice. For my context, Las Casas's words challenge one's theology and theodicy to "sit" at the feet of such victims[2] and to listen to the horrors and outrages that subsume so many.

---

1. Las Casas, *Destruction of the Indies*, 6.

2. In Jincy Willett's "Under the Bed," the middle-aged protagonist has been raped but is adamant against being called a victim and allowing that act of violation to define her (654–61). Similarly, using the term *survivor* is problematic, as many of the individuals we will be discussing were murdered, or even if physically alive, feel like Charlotte Delbo: "As far as I'm concerned / I'm still there / dying there / a little more each day / dying over again" (*Auschwitz and After*, 224). While agreeing with Claudia Card that victims "are also, often, capable of agency," I will predominantly use the term *victim* (*Atrocity Paradigm*, 11). As will be discussed below, the language of "victim" and "perpetrator" can also be problematic, as the terms are not always indistinguishable in every instance, or a perpetrator in one context may have been a victim in another, but as Card acknowledges: "The less than saintly (or even cruel) character of victims does not negate the evils done to them. That Aztecs cut out the hearts of masses of live slaves in sacrifice to their gods does not imply that the conquest of the Aztecs by Hernan Cortes was not evil" (209).

3

How to interpret and incorporate witness testimony of atrocity, however, can be divisive. Critiquing Alexander Donat's remarks that Auschwitz proves there is no God, Moshe Unna, for example, writes: "There is no basis for us to accept such a personal, subjective testimony as objective truth, no matter how horrifying it may be and no matter how reliable it is as an expression of what took place within the consciousness of the writer . . . Would we accept as minister of foreign affairs a person who suffered trauma and therefore judges war and peace from that personal perspective?"[3]

This chapter will underscore the flaws in this type of discourse that seeks to dismiss these survivor-testimonies on account of the trauma they endured in the "swirl of tragic events."[4] At the same time, in light of the world's initial unquestioning embrace of a fraudulent work like Binjamin Wilkomirski's *Fragments: Memories of a Wartime Childhood*, a proper balance needs to be struck to evaluate witness testimony. As Lawrence Langer writes: "The attitude of reverential silence that still greets public presentations of survivor testimony . . . does not discredit the teller or the tale, but it reveals how unprepared modern audiences remain to find a niche in consciousness for the horrific substance of such narratives."[5]

While acknowledging some of the methodological problems in relying upon these texts as "evidence" and an outsider's difficulties in examining these works "objectively,"[6] I will argue that witness testimonies should pervade any attempt to develop and test a theodicy. Therefore, despite the conflicting, multivalent voices among testimonies, I will need to assess how such voices challenge, and perhaps undermine (if not annul), certain theological positions and doctrines. Are there aspects of one's faith and tradition that are sacrosanct? If so, does this mean that no matter what victims may testify or claim, certain doctrines or aspects of one's theological tradition are impervious to any criticism or challenge? If this is so, what are the consequences of adhering to a doctrine or aspect of tradition that offers

---

For a sustained discussion of what Lawrence Langer calls "deathlife" (in response to remarks like Delbo's above) see his *Using and Abusing the Holocaust*.

3. Unna, "Who Can Heal You?" 288–89.

4. Ibid., 289.

5. Langer, *Using and Abusing the Holocaust*, 55. See also Ozick, "Rights of History and Imagination," 3–18; Suleiman, "Do Facts Matter in Holocaust Memoirs?" 21–42.

6. See Hirsch, "Gray Zone," 93.

neither comfort nor relevance to some of the most marginalized and victimized?[7] Again, how does one weigh the authority of victims and the authority of one's religious tradition? In order to listen to the full scope of a victim's testimony, it would seem that believers need to accept the fragility and vulnerability of all of their religious doctrine, including its central and most sacred aspects. This practice touches on a fundamental problem facing a theist's encounter with the non-believing or religiously-different other. As John D'Arcy May writes: "We are thus confronted with an unsettling dissymmetry: in the realm of *gnôsis*, the religions assume their own superiority based on the certainty that they possess definitive truth; in that of *êthos*, however, they refer to the prior demand of the Other as Stranger, in extreme cases even as Enemy, to be treated with respect and love."[8]

When facing and listening to the victims of mass atrocity, should such a dissymmetry always be overcome? If so, individuals and communities must gauge how, and whether one's foundational views and doctrines are applicable to such victims. The consequences of such reflection must also be studied (and enacted).

In turning to witness testimony, I will examine the process of experiencing, remembering, writing, and reading the traumatic event. As Miller and Tougaw write: "If every age has its symptoms, ours appear to be the age of trauma."[9] To accentuate fundamental issues at stake in my investigation, I will now commence my wrestling with Irving Greenberg's "working principle" and then delve into whether the magnitude of mass atrocity poses particularly new or more acute problems for a theodicy in this age of trauma. I will then discuss the term "testimonies of mass atrocity" and the trauma that is at the root of re-inscribing and enduring such affliction.

PRELIMINARY UNDERPINNINGS

Theological Litmus-Test: Greenberg's "Working Principle"

After arriving at Birkenau, the reception center for Auschwitz, one prisoner told Elie Wiesel and those with him: "Poor devils, you are heading for the crematorium." Wiesel thought this man was telling

---

7. See my "Healing the Distorted Face," 302–17.

8. May, "Catholic Fundamentalism?" 131.

9. Miller and Tougaw, "Extremities," 1.

the truth, for "not far from us, flames, huge flames, were rising from a ditch. Something was being burned there. A truck drew close and unloaded its hold: small children. Babies! Yes, I did see this with my own eyes . . . [children] thrown into the flames. (Is it any wonder that ever since then, sleep tends to elude me?)"[10]

In response to such examples of terrifying suffering, Irving Greenberg has written, "No statement, theological or otherwise, should be made that would not be credible in the presence of the burning children."[11] It is a phrase often invoked at the beginning of many examinations of radical evil,[12] and one that seems to share many affinities with my more general (but, I will argue, more useful) turning to the diversity of witness testimonies. What can be said among burning children? Do not all words get consumed as well? In Greenberg's seminal essay "Cloud of Smoke, Pillar of Fire: Judaism, Christianity and Modernity after the Holocaust," he seems to dismiss any talk of theodicy in the call for praxis: "To talk of love and of a God who cares in the presence of the burning children is obscene and incredible; to leap in and pull a child out of a pit, to clean its face and heal its body, is to make the most powerful statement—the only statement that counts."[13] Echoing these assertions, Kenneth Surin remarks: "No attempted justification of God on the part of human beings can aspire to meet this test; indeed, the thought that it is possible for someone to say, with the sufferings of these children in mind, that God is justified, is a blasphemy."[14]

Contra Surin, I will argue that witness testimonies ultimately support the basis and need to develop a viable theodicy. One way of doing so is through a closer analysis of the strengths and weaknesses of Greenberg's principle and its context within Greenberg's other writings.[15] The salient questions to remember for now are:

1. What is the purpose of invoking such a principle at the beginning of any examination of radical evil?

---

10. Wiesel, *Night*, 32.

11. Greenberg, "Cloud of Smoke," 506.

12. See Knight, "Face of Forgiveness," 29; Steele, *Christianity, Tragedy, and Holocaust Literature*, 1.

13. Greenberg, "Cloud of Smoke," 514.

14. Surin, *Theology and the Problem of Evil*, 147–48.

15. I will return to the working principle in chs. 5 and 9.

2. Does such a stance ultimately silence anything one can say about God and the problem of evil? If so, what are the theological and moral repercussions?

3. What does it mean to be in the presence of the burning children, and who or what determines "credibility?"

4. Who are theodicies meant for, and what is implied in seeking a theodicy despite such evils?

5. What does a call to silence imply about a victim's needs or desires? What about victims who are (or were murdered as) theists?

For my purposes, repeated reminders from witnesses of atrocity (or challenges like Greenberg's working principle) are meant to question, critique, and possibly invalidate any subsequent theological statement or point. That is the risk in not only seeking to do theology after Kolyma or Rwanda, but amidst Kolyma and Rwanda. Through the course of this work, we will see how possible or realistic this is, particularly with the scope and magnitude of some evils, an issue I will now address.

Magnitude and Scope

Eliezer Berkovits writes: "With God the quantity of injustice must be immaterial. To think otherwise is a sign of callous indifference toward injustice and human suffering."[16] Contra Berkovits, I have chosen accounts from mass atrocities because I believe these evils pose particularly grave problems for the theodicist. Distinguishing the "severity" or "degrees" of evil, as Claudia Card argues, "is more complex than one might initially expect. For harm has many aspects and 'degrees' is a metaphor . . ."[17] Despite these difficulties, both Card and I still focus on "atrocities," though naming or disclaiming certain events as such can still be a matter of debate.

My theodic approach is a post-Auschwitz one.[18] After Auschwitz and the global condemnation of its sytem of technological but human-

16. Berkovits, *Essential Essays*, 482.

17. Card, *Atrocity Paradigm*, 14.

18. Understandably, someone else may accentuate a similarly paradigmatic and epochal event. For a detailed discussion of my use of the term *post-Holocaust*, see ch. 10 and my first criterion for a theodicy in ch. 12.

devised brutality—after other atrocities in Cambodia, the gulags of Russia or North Korea, the *laogai* ("reform through labor" camps) in China, the genocide in Rwanda and the (sometimes genocidal) wars in Sierra Leone, the Congo, Liberia, and the Sudan—one cannot help reading the Bible and one's core secular and religious traditions in a different light. Other devastating events like the destruction of the Jerusalem temple, the Lisbon earthquake, or the plague have been the cause of faith crises in the past for many, but two paradigm shifts have complicated the contemporary theodic position.

The first is the spread of universal human rights and the universal application of the dignity of humanity. This means that wherever there is injustice, one (eventually) acknowledges that fellow humans are being maltreated. During war (or another crisis), belligerent factions try to conceal this truth. In the past, whether it was the Aristotelian concept of natural slavery or the European judgment of African slaves or Aboriginal Australians, one could insulate oneself from a majority of other people's misery. This is not a valid option for anyone today.

The second shift is our ability to hear and see, often instantaneously, images of suffering, war, and devastation from all over the world. We are thus now in a better position to gauge this world's vastness and interconnectedness. As Jonathan Glover writes: "Because we live in the first period in history in which there is such full awareness of cruelty and killing as they happen, our response is particularly important."[19] We are continually reminded of affliction and depravity in the world, though often without instances and evidence of the concomitant good. Of major import is the impact such evils have on how one perceives the value and goodness of our world.

Thus, in these cases, the theodicist must address the extent of harm and suffering, the intention of the perpetrator, and the complicity of the political, civic, and religious institutions in those killings. First, to illustrate a perpetrator's intentions, consider: a murderer kills an individual; a serial killer destroys a number of individuals based on some pattern or shared characteristic; a government purge or persecution targets a high number of individuals, either with a veiled or purported criteria[20] or to spread havoc and fear but not to exterminate

19. Glover, *Humanity*, 42.

20. Soon Ok Lee, a then-committed communist, was sentenced to the North Korean gulags based on a personal grudge with the local commissar. She escaped as

systematically any group; while genocide aims to wipe out a whole group "as such." I am tempted to claim the existence of Auschwitz or the Armenian genocide does not raise a substantially deeper moral or philosophical difficulty than the murder of an individual, as all involve senseless losses and horrors, wastes of individual human lives by human beings.

However, probing into the differing intentions of those acts reveals important distinctions. As Natan Lerner clarifies: "What typifies the crime of genocide is the intent to destroy the group. Since a group consists of individuals, its destruction can only be achieved by steps taken against individuals. But the object of the crime of genocide is the group . . ."[21] Note that the individual loss gets interred within the group's destruction, inflicting another invidious violation of the victim by the culprit. This act does not simply seek to erase the individual person, but that person's identity and culture without any hope of "living on" through collective memory or through one's progeny. The crime of genocide is particularly reprehensible because of the aims behind those acts. At the same time, I am not disagreeing with Daniel Goldhagen's contention that "discussions of genocide often founder over definitions . . . The problem with these debates is that genocide's common definitions exclude both elimination's nonlethal forms and the many instances of lethal eliminationist assaults deemed too small or partial."[22] Take, for example, the well-known passage from the Talmudic tractate *Sanhedrin 37a*: "Adam was created alone to teach you that if anyone destroys one life, Scripture reckons it is as if he had destroyed a whole world; conversely, if anyone preserves one life, Scripture reckons it as if he had preserved a whole world."[23] Any time there is such a loss there is a travesty, but scale and scope contribute to the heinousness of the crime.

---

a committed Christian. See her *Eyes of the Tailless Animals.*

21. Lerner, *Religion, Beliefs, and International Human Rights*, 70. How one defines genocide becomes crucial here (I have used the more flexible term *mass atrocity*, though it, too, needs clarification, as will be noted below). For a thorough examination of the term *genocide*, and for a history of genocide and genocidal "massacres" or "moments," see Kiernan, *Blood and Soil.*

22. Goldhagen, *Worse than War*, 26. See also Snyder, *Bloodlands*, 412–13, for his preferred term *mass killing.*

23. See Solomon, *Talmud*, 503.

When vast portions of the world go awry, theodicists are more acutely constrained in trying to argue for the goodness of God's creation than in cases of isolated murders outlawed by the State and condemned by the population at large. As Gerald Gahima, Deputy Justice Minister of Rwanda, remarked, "It was as if there was a kind of collective insanity."[24] What makes the genocide in Rwanda so morally debilitating is not only the virtual silence and indifference of most of the world to those massacres, but how nearly every religious and political institution within Rwanda (a traditionally Catholic country) was complicit in the genocide.[25] As Alphonse, a Hutu convicted of genocide, claims: "There is no one who can say to God, eyes closed in prayer, that he never went hunting."[26] By "hunting," he is referring to murdering Tutsis.

Similarly, and also well documented, almost every facet of German society participated in or benefited from the establishment and implementation of the Final Solution, from "postal officials [who] delivered mail about definition and expropriation, denaturalization, and deportation . . . [to] stockholders [who] made profits from firms that supplied Zyklon B to gas people and built crematoriums to burn the corpses."[27] In reading witness accounts, culpability and trauma are spread far and wide; it is intergenerational.[28] That reality paints a picture of our world that is far more challenging to justify than an isolated series of murders or, arguably, even an outbreak of the plague or other disease, as devastating as some outbreaks of plague have been.[29]

This claim is in part based on hindsight from those events: we now know how to prevent the spread of those diseases to a greater extent. We can apply a similar logic and confidence towards viruses we

24. Quoted in Neuffer, *Key to My Neighbor's House*, 259.

25. See Rittner et al., *Genocide in Rwanda*.

26. Hatzfeld, *Machete Season*, 72.

27. Roth, *Ethics during and after the Holocaust*, 29.

28. Hatzfeld, *Machete Season*, 40. See also Schwab, *Haunting Legacies*, 3.

29. Charles Mann, in *1491: New Revelations of the Americas before Columbus*, includes estimates by one researcher that "disease claimed the lives of 80 to 100 million [Native Americans] by the first third of the seventeenth century," 105. In regards to the term *Native American* and other "loaded words" see ibid., 387–92. Maria Kelly, in *The Great Dying: The Black Death in Dublin*, states that plagues wiped out "some 50 million Europeans between the fourteenth and the eighteenth centuries," 9.

are still struggling to contain (Ebola and AIDS, for example). While a world without mass violence and genocide is a goal and dream worth striving for, a world without a case of smallpox, for example, is proven, or certainly highly plausible.[30]

Regardless, a theodicist not only is challenged to avoid justifying the unjustifiable, but must name what cannot be justified, thus acknowledging a theodicy's limitations or failures. Dominican John Tauler, who lived during "natural disasters, endemic warfare, persecutions of the Jews, and the Black Death that killed almost half the population in large parts of Europe,"[31] could "reasonably" utter in a sermon: "Whatever might happen to cause you distress—all this molds you and serves to make you a noble and joyful person. It has been completely ordained by God that this should happen to you."[32] Such claims are not applicable in the contemporary context of mass atrocity. According to Filip Müller (survivor of the Auschwitz-Birkenau *Sonderkommando*), twenty-year old Menachem, while in the crematoria, "flung these hard words in his former religious teacher's face: . . . '[N]ot once have I felt divine justice here. Absolutely everything that you stuffed into my head in school was just nonsense. There is no God, and if there is one, he is an ox and a bastard!'"[33] A viable theodic position uncomfortably inhabits a space between these two poles, as the magnitude of evil demands theological humility, caution, and a greater capacity to listen and learn.

Turning to how to analyze witness testimonies, I now need to address the issue of what to call these texts that will serve as challengers

30. For an account supporting the above contentions, but with a twist, see Brown, "Noncommunicable Diseases." In *The Better Angels of Our Nature*, Steven Pinker contends that the world is becoming less violent and credits Enlightenment humanism and reason (183 and 668); expansion of sympathy, especially through literature (690, 177); feminization (527); and democratic states that promote international free trade and "gentle commerce" (288, 682) and are prepared to play the Leviathan to enforce legal behavior (35, 680). The Bible is "blood-soaked" (87) and religion is given little, if any, positive role (677). While Pinker notes how theists may want to smuggle in some higher power as a cause, he claims he "can easily resist the temptation" (694). He should have left the question open. In short, theists can reveal great hubris when proclaiming theodic phrases amidst devastating evils; atheists when dismissing the possibility of the Transcendent amidst the tenacity of goodness and holiness, let alone a systemic decline in violence.

31. McGinn, *Christian Mysticism*, 379.

32. Tauler, "Sermon 3," 381.

33. Müller, *Eyewitness Auschwitz*, 66.

and refiners to the project of theodicy. In the next two sections, therefore, I will examine various classifications of texts that depict these traumatic ruptures and will address the issue of incorporating heterogenous historical atrocities in this work and how that bears on the question of uniqueness.

The Politics of Naming: How to Read Genre

Classifying any work is an act of interpretation that can persuade others how to read or analyze it. The debate of whether Elie Wiesel's *Night* is deemed fiction or nonfiction is but one of sundry examples on the difficulties of classifying a text. Hybrid texts in particular challenge rigid classifications, and some of the works I will examine, like Alicia Partnoy's *The Little School*, embody this hybridity. Despite these acknowledged difficulties, I will refer to these texts as testimonies of mass atrocity.

As a general category, texts depicting atrocity have gone by many names beyond memoir or autobiography: *testimonio*,[34] testimonial literature, witness testimony and literature,[35] literature of freedom, literature of survival,[36] resistance literature,[37] literature of atrocity,[38] testimony of atrocity,[39] and literature of trauma[40]—along with specific titles such as Holocaust literature, gulag literature, and so on. The literary critic John Beverley asks: "Do social struggles give rise to new forms of literature, or is it more a question of the adequacy of their representation in existing narrative forms such as the short story or the novel?"[41] As an answer to this type of question, Wiesel

---

34. For a concise history of the *testimonio*, see Nance, *Can Literature Promote Justice?* 1. See also Sklodowska, "Spanish American Testimonial Novel," 84; Beverley, "Margin," 25.

35. Langer, *Using and Abusing the Holocaust*, xii.

36. Steele, *Christianity, Tragedy, and Holocaust Literature*, 57. He also refers to the "literature of victims" (65).

37. See Harlow, *Resistance Literature*.

38. Steele also refers to the "literature of mass atrocity" (9, 66) and quotes Langer's term for "literature of atrocity" (*Christianity, Tragedy, and Holocaust Literature*, 42).

39. Cubilié, *Women Witnessing Terror*, 145.

40. See Tal, *Worlds of Hurt*, 17.

41. Beverley, "Margin," 23. For further discussion on the *testimonio*, see Yúdice, "*Testimonio* and Postmodernism." For contrary views on the definition, see Sklodowska, "Spanish American Testimonial Novel," 84.

writes: "If the Greeks invented tragedy, the Romans the epistle, and the Renaissance the sonnet, our generation invented a new literature, that of testimony."[42] Agreeing with Wiesel, I will employ the term *testimony* for these texts, though such a term still needs clarification and definition, as debates remain on whether to distinguish oral and written testimony and where testimony diverges from autobiography. Other distinctions involve debates on whether testimonies are predominantly an individual or communal witness[43] and whether the literature of testimony is a different sub-group.[44]

Zoë Vania Waxman in *Writing the Holocaust: Identity, Testimony, Representation* has also argued for a greater need to understand that Holocaust testimony in particular is not a homogenous literary or historical field, and to misunderstand is to diminish crucial distinctions that can help us gain greater comprehension of the Holocaust.[45] She writes: "Life in the concentration camps was very different from that in the ghettos . . . Also, the brutality of the *Kapos* in the concentration camp attests to the heterogeneity of Holocaust experiences."[46]

Anne Cubilié also highlights the important role of "gendered survival" in these historical mass atrocities.[47] This key distinction is particularly neglected in many philosophical and theological accounts of the Holocaust.[48] Cubilié notes how "the women's literature discusses

42. Wiesel, "Holocaust Literary Imagination," 9. Quoted from Felman and Laub, *Testimony*, 6. Annette Wieviorka titles her work *L'ère du témoin* (*The Era of the Witness*). Georg Gugelberger, on the other hand, asserts that the *testimonio's* inclusion in the canon has been a sign of betrayal and is another "form of colonialization" (13). See also Agamben, *Remnants of Auschwitz*, 17–18, 54, and 120.

43. This difference is also evident in the multiple forces that influence a testimony. Zoë Vania Waxman writes: "Testimony is mediated by both the concerns of collective memory and the concerns of the individual survivor, the latter often writing as an act of atonement or even exorcism in an attempt to assimilate overwhelming memories" (*Writing the Holocaust*, 158). See also Lubin, "Holocaust Testimony," 130–41.

44. Works of fiction that incorporate testimonies from actual survivors or historical documents straddle a fine line between fiction and nonfiction. See, for example, Traba, *Mothers and Shadows*; Rahimi, *Earth and Ashes*. See also Young, "Holocaust Documentary Fiction," 212.

45. Waxman, *Writing the Holocaust*, 188.

46. Ibid., 87.

47. Cubilié, *Women Witnessing Terror*, 83–90. On gendered violence against undocumented women, see Marrujo, "Gender of Risk."

48. A major exception is Melissa Raphael's *The Female Face of God in Auschwitz*,

specific problems faced by women in the camps—for example, pregnancy, menstruation, rape, abortion, and enforced prostitution—that the men's narratives often not only do not address, but also sometimes condemn as instances of promiscuity, collaboration, or amorality."[49] Thus, there needs to be distinctions within the distinctions.

Despite some of these tensions, the term *testimony* is specific and comprehensive enough to represent a wide range of works. It also connotes some key features unique to the genre. As Paul Ricoeur notes, "when the test of conviction becomes the price of life, the witness changes his name. *Martus* in Greek means 'witness.' Such a connection slightly shifts the grounds of testimony from what only occurs in the court room to one's living out one's life as a means of testifying— as if one's whole life is a part of a trial—or witnessing to a cause or truth."[50] As W. James Booth aptly summarizes: "To bear witness, then, is to remember, to guard the past, to ask others to do likewise, and to illuminate the traces of the past and their meaning."[51]

Thus, calling these works "testimonies of mass atrocity" seems appropriate, especially in drawing upon its etymology in witnessing (and consequently, as martyr) with its strong legal connection to testify in court, to call forth the truth; and in religious language, to bear witness to God. As Nancy Miller and Jason Tougaw write: "Testimony attempts to bridge the gap between suffering individuals and ultimately communities of listeners, whose empathic response can be palliative, if not curative."[52] Theodicy is also preoccupied with (and mired in) bridging gaps (for what greater abyss can there seem to be than between the existence of genocide or the devastation of an earthquake and the argument for an omnipotent, omnibenevolent God?). Therefore, pairing witness testimony and theodicy may help bridge certain caesuras, or at the least, come to better acknowledge and face such gaps.

---

which I will examine in ch. 9.

49. Cubilié, *Women Witnessing Terror*, 83.

50. Ricoeur also writes: "Testimony is the action itself as it attests outside of himself, to the interior man, to his conviction, to his faith" (*Biblical Interpretation*, 129–30).

51. Booth, *Communities of Memory*, 73. See also Tuhabonye, *Voice in My Heart*, 153.

52. Miller and Tougaw, "Extremities," 11.

Adding the term *atrocity* remains somewhat problematic. What is atrocious to one may not be so to another, but the underlying premise here is that suffering and death are an indelible part of this world. We all suffer and we all will die, but some types of suffering and some types of deaths because of their brazen attack on the dignity of the human person (and it can be argued, the well-being of other sentient life) are deemed particularly tragic and cruel. In *The Atrocity Paradigm*, Claudia Card asks: "Why take atrocities as paradigms? Many evils lack the scale of an atrocity . . . I choose them for three reasons: (1) because they are uncontroversially evil, (2) because they deserve priority of attention, . . . and (3) because the core features of evils tend to be writ large in the case of atrocities . . ."[53]

Card correctly points to why atrocities demand a specified focus. The Oxford English Dictionary, for example, defines an atrocity as "1. savage enormity; horrible or heinous wickedness. . . 3. an atrocious deed, an act of extreme cruelty and heinousness." While helpful, the definition still does not necessarily place clear, uncontroversial limits to what may and may not be deemed an atrocity. Are the deaths of children from disease or starvation an atrocity? Is it callous, for example, to say a child's death from SIDS[54] is not shockingly wicked, but sadly, perhaps even more tragically, a fairly "common" occurrence? Because Card "does not define evil by motive," she contends that her "atrocity paradigm encourages a focus first on suffering. Harm is what is most salient about atrocities."[55] She is pointing to the fact that some "perpetrators commonly do not understand their deeds as atrocities."[56] Regardless of whether an atrocity can be clearly deemed an intentional act or not by human beings, its assault on lives and the meaning of this world still challenges the aims of any theodicy. Moreover, while circumstances are always crucial, if the death of a child from SIDS is not deemed an atrocity, one can still ask whether such a death is also a valid reason to question the existence of a loving God.[57] Atrocities make such questions more pointed, but they are not the only grounds for such doubt and recriminations.

53. Card, *Atrocity Paradigm*, 9.

54. Sudden infant death syndrome.

55. Card, *Atrocity Paradigm*, 9.

56. Ibid., 9.

57. While I will touch upon the problems raised by so-called natural evil in ch. 6,

Returning to the issue of magnitude, how significant is the adjective *mass* before atrocity?[58] Does this addition cause any further moral or philosophical problems for the theodicist, particularly based on the limitations of human justice? If it is true that the death of one innocent child is enough reason to question the entire purpose and role of God and creation (á la Ivan Karamazov), then what further value comes from discussion of the genocide in the Sudan or the Srebrenica massacre?

The magnitude of these evils is often cited by antitheodicists as reason to disavow any theodicy. Geoffrey Hartman, for example, writes of the "impossibility of theodicy,"[59] while Primo Levi remarks: "There is Auschwitz, so there cannot be God."[60] While focusing on heinous acts of evil, my aim is to include all forms of evil, though differentiating the scale, intent, and destruction of the acts. Thus, by asking how one can speak of a loving God despite the killing fields of Cambodia, one utters similar types of questions when a child dies in a car accident or a father of young children succumbs to cancer. It is questioning simultaneously the tragic suffering of Little Eleanora and the other twelve to twenty million people who died "unnecessarily" from the Stalin and post-Stalin regimes.[61] Therefore, where an individual tragedy may cause the theodicist sufficient difficulty, how much more so a mass atrocity?

As Anne Cubilié pithily states:

> . . . testimonial witnessing cuts across literary genres and disciplinary categories in its engagement with trauma as destabilizing narrative, memory, identity, and history, its performances of the fragmentation of identity, effected by atrocity, its demand for a performative witnessing engagement with the survivor's interlocutor as witness, and its enactment of an ethical community of humans across difference as those people

---

see also my "Dirt, Collapse, and Eco-responsibility."

58. See Evans, *Responsibility to Protect*, 11–13.

59. Hartman, "Elie Wiesel and the Morality of Fiction," 109.

60. Quoted in Clendinnen, *Reading the Holocaust*, 44. For a discussion of this quote and Levi's subsequent modification of it, see Roth, *Ethics during and after the Holocaust*, 145.

61. Applebaum, *Gulag*, 584.

who resist violence and their effacement from judicial and cultural fields.[62]

Thus, for the above reasons, I name these texts "testimonies of mass atrocity."

Because this work will weave testimonies from various historical "monstrosities" (to paraphrase Ignaz Maybaum's term[63]), I now need to address the extant debate on the "uniqueness" of the Holocaust and other mass atrocities.

The Dilemma of Uniqueness

In his historical examination of genocide, Ben Kiernan identifies shared patterns and features that have often caused various genocides, genocide "moments" or "genocide atrocities," but still maintains the possibility for uniqueness.[64] While Steven Katz highlights Nazi Germany's unique state-wide implementation of genocide against the Jews,[65] Kiernan concurs but adds that the "Nazi killing machine also had a more antiquated power source. It was operated by interlocking ideological levers that celebrated race, territory, cultivation, and history."[66]

As Kiernan, Runblom, Fasching, and others have argued, comparing the causes, scope, and magnitude of various atrocities means to increase our knowledge of these often impenetrable events and to develop ways to identify potential future genocides in order to stop them.[67] As Markusen also clarifies: "*comparing* two events is not the same as *equating* them or considering them as equivalent."[68] In his essay "Faith and the Holocaust," Michael Wyschogrod astutely remarks: "It is necessary to recognize that, from any universally humanistic

62. Cubilié, *Women Witnessing Terror*, xv–xvi.

63. Maybaum, *Ignaz Maybaum*, 160. Maybaum uses the word *monstrosity* to distinguish from *tragedy* and to underline the actions of humanity in causing such suffering.

64. Kiernan, *Blood and Soil*, 5, 35.

65. Katz, "Introduction," 367. For Roth's argument that the 1994 Rwandan genocide was ultimately intended to extirpate all Tutsis within and beyond the Rwandan border, see *Ethics during and after the Holocaust*, 154.

66. Kiernan, *Blood and Soil*, 454.

67. See Runblom, "Foreword," xii; Fasching, "Ethics after Auschwitz and Hiroshima," 5; and Kiernan, *Blood and Soil*, 6.

68. Markusen, "Reflections on the Holocaust and Hiroshima," 27.

framework, the destruction of European Jewry is one notable chapter in the long record of man's inhumanity against man, a record which compels the Holocaust to resign itself to being, at most, a first among equals."[69]

While the purpose of this work is to incorporate a wide variety of witness testimony to examine theodicy, we will also encounter penetrating insights from testimonies that provide useful means to compare and contrast the methods and aims of the perpetrators and the interpretations and survival tactics of victims from otherwise diverse and unique historical tragedies. I still need, however, to justify why these texts are pieces of "evidence" and to elucidate why we should assess these texts with respect, but not gratuitous piety. As noted above, some critics question the truth and factual accuracy of witness testimonies because of the traumatic residue that can expunge or limit the reliability of memory and one's sense of a stable identity. I need, therefore, to establish the methodological criteria for how and why we can still trust certain witnesses' interpretations of these traumatic events without relinquishing the need for critical engagement with their accounts. I also need to address why many of us revere witness testimonies, but may not integrate their warnings and truths within our spiritual practices, philosophies, and worldviews—often with negative (if not catastrophic) consequences.

TRAUMA

To begin to address the above methodological issues, I will turn to Fassin and Rechtman's *The Empire of Trauma* and Leys's *Trauma: A Genealogy* to encounter some of the different meanings of this contested but important term.[70] I will then examine the issue of traumatized memory, the process of forming a coherent depiction of these horrific experiences, and the difficulties a critic has in analyzing these interpretations of raw, often devastating events.

---

69. Wyschogrod, "Faith and the Holocaust," 460. For a discussion of uniqueness in the context of the Palestinian-Israeli Conflict, see Locke, "The Holocaust, Israel, and Jewish-Christian Relations," 191–200. Locke writes: "A serious examination of anti-Semitism, however, if it is to occur among other than Jewish people themselves, requires abandoning the notion of its uniqueness" (198).

70. Richard McNally writes: "How victims remember trauma is the most divisive issue facing psychology today" ("Politics of Trauma," 1).

Bearing the Wound with the Scar[71]

The traumatized—and those deemed as such—are often determined by inadequate cultural, scientific, and political criteria. As Fassin and Rechtman write: "the history of trauma appears as a series of appropriations and dispossessions, with some people being included, on an unequal basis, and others being excluded."[72] Much remains to be learned.

In "Our Children are Killing Us," Elizabeth Rubin details the trauma of children who were abducted by members of the Lord's Resistance Army in Uganda.[73] These children were forced to serve as "wives" and fighters, resulting in torture and death if they disobeyed and tried to escape, reinforced by having to "hack to death, with hoes, axes, and branches, a recently kidnapped girl who had been caught trying to escape."

A trauma center for surviving children teaches group therapy through "reenactments of life in the Bush . . . all designed to teach the children to forget. It is a challenging concept: remembering to forget."[74] Few would discount these experiences as traumatic, and yet as Ruth Leys notes, the word *trauma* is often used indiscriminately so that "it is hard not to feel that the concept of trauma has become debased currency."[75]

Cathy Caruth has written that "the orginary meaning of trauma itself (in both English and German), the Greek *trauma*, or 'wound,' originally referred to an injury inflicted on a body,"[76] while Leys notes that "trauma was originally the term for a surgical wound, conceived on the model of a rupture of the skin or protective envelope of the body resulting in a catastrophic global reaction in the entire organism."[77] However, the locus of the wound—whether the mind or body—has been a continual area of disagreement among psycholo-

71. In *The Tremendum*, Arthur Cohen writes that those of us who come after the Holocaust, "bear the scar without the wound" (20).

72. Fassin and Rechtman, *Empire of Trauma*, 152.

73. For a memoir of a child soldier from Uganda, see McDonnell and Akallo, *Girl Soldier*.

74. Leys, *Trauma*, 1.

75. Ibid., 2.

76. Caruth, *Unclaimed Experience*, 3.

77. Leys, *Trauma*, 19.

gists. According to Fassin, Rechtman, and Leys, the shell-shocked soldier of World War I, the combat fatigue associated with World War II, and the "chronic concentration camp syndrome or survivor's syndrome" in the post-Holocaust (and gulag) era were documented, but trauma was not widespread and accepted until a number of influential social workers, psychologists, and activists responded to the high number of American soldiers returning traumatized from Vietnam.

Post-traumatic stress disorder (PTSD) was first recognized as an ailment by the American Psychiatric Association in 1980. Writing seventeen years later, psychiatrist Judith Herman contends: "The fundamental question of the existence of PTSD is no longer in dispute."[78] According to Leys, PTSD was defined as "fundamentally a disorder of memory . . . the victim is unable to recollect and integrate the hurtful experience in normal consciousness; instead she is haunted or possessed by intrusive traumatic memories. The experience of the trauma, fixed or frozen in time, refuses to be represented *as* past, but is perpetually experienced in a painful, disassociated traumatic present."[79] Symptoms characteristic of PTSD include flashbacks, nightmares, and other re-experiences, emotional numbing, depression, guilt, autonomic arousal (what can often be called psychosomatic symptoms), explosive violence or the tendency to be hypervigilant (overly sensitive to sights or sounds).[80]

In short, as Fassin and Rechtman contend: "Trauma, and the traces of it identified by mental health specialists, bear witness to the unspeakable."[81] This sense of the unspeakable is also linked to trauma's attack upon identity and reflection. As Gabriele Schwab writes: "Trauma disrupts relationality . . . and [is] ultimately an attack on thought itself."[82] Because many victims rely upon their memory to reconstruct or interpret what has happened to them, how reliable is this memory, which, like the body and the self, are also traumatized? Can these memories be trusted?[83] And if not, how can they be considered

78. Herman, "Dialectic of Trauma Continues," 238.

79. Leys, *Trauma*, 2.

80. Ibid. Since this definition, the application and terminology has extended to fields beyond war in adopting the best approaches for treatment, as seen, for example, in cases with child abuse or victims of natural disasters (ibid., 4–5).

81. Fassin and Rechtman, *Empire of Trauma*, 273.

82. Schwab, *Haunting Legacies*, 2.

83. Critiquing the assertion of a mechanism of repression, Richard McNally

reliable indicators as evidence against a loving God or proof of a loving God amidst evil?

Re-inscribing the Self: Traumatized Memory

Memory is indispensable for the project of witnessing—but it is also the domain that trauma seems to attack mercilessly, leaving a victim fraught with mnemonic fissures, gaps, and irreparable damage. Memory is depended upon to testify to what was experienced as well as blamed for its variable dependability, a characteristic that deniers and doubters are quick to raise. In this section, I will examine the conflicting interpretations of the reliability of memories among survivors of the camps, and how various genocidal regimes implemented policies to control or block the memories of victims and perpetrators. Such attempts sought to determine how any survivors could then interpret what they experienced or enacted.

"We are the sum of our memories," Diane Ackerman writes. "They provide a continuous private sense of one's self. Change your memory and you change your identity."[84] A nightmare scenario coalesces when words and thoughts cannot be trusted or seem inapplicable to what has happened—or there are no witnesses left to remember. Many despotic regimes anticipate such doubt and skepticism, trying to raze memory by annihilating a victim's identity. In *Gulag*, Anne Appelbaum documents how "many former prisoners believe that their first few hours in captivity were deliberately designed to shock them, to render them incapable of coherent thought."[85]

Such a process often had another practical cause. Franz Stangl, commander of Treblinka, admitted to Gitta Sereny that camp inmates' treatment was designed to "condition those who actually had to carry out the policies. To make it possible for them to do what they did."[86] Further incentive for the guards to act includes patriotic or even benevolent motivation, often linked to what Peter Haas calls a "Nazi ethic."[87] In reference to the mass killings, Himmler infamously

---

writes that "people remember horrific experiences all too well. Victims are seldom incapable of remembering their trauma" ("Politics of Trauma," 2).

84. Ackerman, *Alchemy of the Mind*, 76.

85. Applebaum, *Gulag*, 131.

86. Ibid., xxxvii.

87. See Haas, "Science and the Determination of the Good," 49–59.

acknowledged to members of the SS: "We have accomplished the most difficult task out of love for our people. And we have not suffered any damage to our inner self, our soul, and our character."[88] Notice the co-option of moral and religious terms in order to conceal genocidal acts.

Such brazen words are spoken with the conviction that no intended victims will survive these "difficult tasks" and that the world will be indifferent or disavow the survivor's story. The primary aim is to destroy the memory of the victim's present to prevent any mobilization for action in the future while controlling how the guards interpret such acts for their enduring sanity and well-being. These regimes aim to possess the totality of memory—past, present, and future.

While Inga Clendinnen notes how "even honest eyewitnesses can get things wrong, and not all eyewitnesses are honest, or not all the time,"[89] Aharon Appelfeld writes that in the camps "we would sit for hours and observe . . . Rather than the murderers, we observed their victims, in their weaknesses and in their heroism. Those tortured faces on the brink of the chasm will not be forgotten. To 'be forgotten' is not the correct expression. They were stamped upon us the way childhood is stamped upon the matrix of one's flesh."[90]

In *The Story of a Life*, however, Appelfeld also acknowledges that articulating such experiences remains a lifelong challenge, though one that has "even achieved some level of meaning."[91] So, too, Primo Levi, despite asserting the factors in the camps that obliterate memories, insists: "I conserve pathologically precise memories of my encounters in that now remote world."[92] Thus, many of the same survivors can be cited to support or question the reliability of memory.[93] However, that

88. Quoted from Clendinnen, *Reading the Holocaust*, 84.

89. Ibid., 23. In her *Dangerous Games*, historian Margaret MacMillan refers to "the director of the Yad Vashem Memorial to the Holocaust in Israel who once said sadly that most of the oral histories that had been collected were unreliable. Holocaust survivors thought, for example, that they remembered witnessing well-known atrocities when in fact they were nowhere near the place where the events happened" (47). See also Wieviorka, *Era of the Witness*, 145–49.

90. Appelfeld, "After the Holocaust," 91.

91. Appelfeld, *Story of a Life*, ix.

92. Quoted in Clendinnen, *Reading the Holocaust*, 48. See also Him, *When Broken Glass Floats*, 21. Him calls herself "a human recorder" while growing up under the Khmer Rouge (21).

93. See the essays about Holocaust survivor Helen "Zippi" Spitzer Tichauer and the transcription and translation of her 1965 interview in Matthäus, *Approaching an*

some instances may be forgotten or misrepresented does not belie the fact that some memories remain irrefutable and factual even if they are only bodily felt. While Emmanuel Jai was fleeing the ravages of Sudan with his mother and sister, his mother told them not to look at an image of a dead mother and baby just shot in a battle by SLA and government troops. "But it was too late," Jal writes. "My sister and I had seen the woman and would never forget. Her memory was carved into us. The stench of this place was inside us. Death was part of us now."[94] Soon separated from his mother and forced to become a child soldier, Jal found that death would take an even greater part of him until he was freed.

In such contexts, Appelfeld, Levi, and Jal assert the truth and inviolability of some of their memories, while Holocaust survivor Bruno Bettelheim underscores how difficult it was to remember in the camps, as one was malnourished, exhausted, and emotionally, mentally, and physically barraged from the daily onslaught of concentration camp existence. Though Bettelheim repeated events to himself every day so he wouldn't forget, "concentration camp life clearly had a detrimental effect on the memory."[95]

Memory was also hampered by the unwritten camp rule "thou shalt not look." As Douwe Draaisma writes: "The situation had a perverse logic: to know what you may not see you have to look, and in order to know what you must pretend you must know what you actually saw."[96] These observations, in addition to statements of survivors such as Ellie Cohen in his *The Abyss* that in the camps "you couldn't recognize anyone anymore" and that "I should be quite unable to testify at a trial of SS-men,"[97] make subsequent retellings always, at the least, questionable, especially if these memories are thirty, forty, or fifty years old.[98] Such a description of memory's failings would seem

---

Auschwitz Survivor. Over the years Zippi has adamantly maintained that "there are a group of people [in the camps] who could not think, who had no time to think and there are people who had the time, or a chance to think. They are the people who could memorize" (Lower, "Distant Encounter," 109).

94. Jal, *Warchild*, 19.

95. Quoted in Draaisma, *Why Life Speeds Up*, 119.

96. Ibid., 119.

97. Ibid., 121.

98. For an argument on the benefits of writing about these experiences after sufficient time has elapsed see, Breznitz, "Advantages of Delay," 43–51.

to render these accounts completely unreliable, but as we saw above, while one person's memory may be weak, another's may be unerringly accurate. One cannot discount all such memories.

To account for these conditions and minimize criticism about the reliability of Holocaust testimonies in particular, James Young argues that what Holocaust testimony offers us is "knowledge—not evidence—of events."[99] Thus, in these testimonies, there may be some discrepancy with parts of the historical record, but as an overall witness to the atrocities committed, the insights and descriptions of these memoirs illuminate and reveal otherwise unknown or contested historical ground. Contra Young, Vania Waxman highlights that there have been testimonies written in the midst of the atrocities that can be considered for factual content. She quotes Chaim Kaplan, a "teacher and diarist of the Warsaw ghetto,"[100] who writes that his testimonies "can guarantee the factualness of these manifestations because *I dwell among my people.*"[101]

These testimonies, therefore, are interpretations of historical and traumatic events whose veracity may not be entirely verifiable in every case by legal standards but which still can be considered as factual and experienced by the victim.[102] To doubt otherwise would be radically to question the basic underlying principle of trust that pervades our world.[103] As Eric Stover writes: "Both the records of the Yugoslav and Rwandan tribunals and numerous studies demonstrate that survivors of horrendous crimes can remember the essential facts about specific events vividly and with a wealth of detail."[104]

This approach seems rational and sufficient to argue for including these texts within the theodic discussion. Witnesses of mass atrocity, however, must not only disentangle key details from the blurry mass of their traumatic memories, but also must face the maelstrom of

---

99. Quoted from Tal, *Literature of Trauma*, 48.

100. Vania Waxman, *Writing the Holocaust*, 11.

101. Ibid., 48.

102. See ibid., 126–29. For an examination of legality and testimony in Rwanda's *Gacaca* Courts, see Thomson and Nagy, "Law, Power, and Justice."

103. For his discussion of the principles of credulity and testimony, see Swinburne, *Is There a God?* 134. See also Blustein, *Moral Demands of Memory*, 342; Regan, *Theology and the Boundary Discourse of Human Rights*, 100–142.

104. Stover, *Witnesses*, 9. See also Browning, *Remembering Survival*, 9.

violence and misery of the past to convey a meaning understandable to outsiders.

The Trauma of Re-creation: Depicting Atrocity

Articulating the meaning of these traumatic experiences often remains frustratingly elusive. Appelfeld writes: "Memory, it seems, has deep roots in the body. Sometimes just the smell of rotting straw, or the sharp call of a bird, is enough to take me back, piercing me deep inside. I say inside, although I still haven't found the words to give voice to those intense scars on my memory."[105] Regarding this dilemma, Lawrence Langer remarks: "One of the main problems of the Holocaust writer is to find a secure place, somewhere between memory and imagination, for all those corpses, who like the ghost of Hamlet's father, cry out against the injustice of their end, but for whom no act of vengeance or ritual of remembrance exists sufficient to bring them to a peaceful state of rest."[106] This secure place notwithstanding, the psychological and traumatic residue left from the experience is aggravated by the problem of language and the guilt of survival. Such a "crying out" can also be for that lost self now shattered, the "integrated" self that existed before the crime was perpetrated. This experience is exacerbated with the realization that the outside world is basically unchanged.

At the core of these testimonies is the vast void of the meaning of words before and after these traumatic events and how this gap complicates a witness's intention to interpret, describe, and report these atrocities to the outside world. As Wiesel writes: "Often I wonder: have I sufficiently emphasized my doubts on the capacity to transmit what we have endured or received, memories of fear and fire, in words, just in words?"[107] In this section, therefore, I will highlight examples of how language has been adulterated by various despotic regimes which in turn coerce many of their victims to adopt or adapt to this new, morally perverse language. I will also examine the relationship of many atrocities to literary, religious, or mythological texts. Lastly, I will test whether these "similarities" with mythical stories can situate and ground survivors' memories to help convey their experiences or heighten the searing isolation many victims endure. Langer opines

105. Appelfeld, *Story of a Life*, 50.
106. Quoted from Tal, *Literature of Trauma*, 82.
107. Wiesel, "Afterword," 157.

that the Holocaust survivor "must first invent a whole new mode of speaking in order to articulate his subject . . . to create a language and imagery that will transform mere language into vision and bear the reader beyond the realm of familiar imagining into the bizarre limbo of atrocity."[108] This creation of what seems a new language forms and intermingles at various levels, from the prisoners themselves to the authoritarian regime trying to forge their own ideology and conceal the atrocities they authorize. Here is a transcript from a monitored radio broadcast during the fall of Srebrenica:

> 14:17 P.M. Anonymous soldier: Legenda,[109] I have thirty pieces.
>
> Legenda: Finish with it. You know we are paid by the piece.
>
> 14:47 P.M. Anonymous soldier: Boss, the job is done.[110]

Similarly, the brother of Immaculée Ilibagiza told her how a group of Hutu killers were ordered: "This house is full of cockroaches—fumigate it! What are you waiting for? You have a job to do! It's time to stop these cockroaches!"[111] He was later murdered during the genocide. The prisons of North Korea, moreover, are places "where 'the animals that do not have tails' lived."[112] In Japanese-occupied Manchuria, Chinese individuals (including babies) who were brutally experimented upon to test the process of frostbite, were deemed "logs" because their frozen arms, when hit "with a short stick, emitted a sound resembling that of a boat when stuck."[113]

Such language and "truth" claims are indelibly intertwined with political power, as the victim loses all rights and has to contend against the so-called infallible State. This "State" then "determines" one's value and worth. Human beings are deemed "cockroaches" or "tailless animals" and are treated as such. James Baldwin writes: "Speech and language, however ceremonious, complex, and convoluted, are a way of revealing one's nakedness, and this revelation is really our only hope.

---

108. Quoted from Tal, *Literature of Trauma*, 81.

109. Legenda is Milan Jovović, head of the Drina Wolves, Bosnian Serbs reconnaissance unit. See Neuffer, *Key to My Neighbor's House*, 143.

110. Ibid., 206.

111. Ilibagiza, *Left to Tell*, 62.

112. Soon Ok Lee, *Eyes of the Tailless Animals*, 9.

113. Smith, *Secular Discourse*, 187.

But this hope is strangled if one, or both of us, is lying."[114] Such lying is routine in these systems of terror built into the fabric of its philosophy and ethos. Their pronouncements are lies that confiscate words of hope and goodness and rid them of all value until their old meanings are eclipsed by the new ones. Thus, a human being is a "piece" whose murder (deemed a commodity) is euphemized as a "job."

Alicia Partnoy, who had been kidnapped, imprisoned, and tortured at a "Little School" during Argentina's Dirty War, writes how one day "the guards told me they were taking me to 'see the radishes grow'—a euphemism for death and burial."[115] Notice that in these death worlds, life gets rewritten by death. A radish as potential nourishment and food now connotes murder and execution. A school is a site of torture and mutilation. The journalist Stanley Schanberg remarks: "With their cruelty, the Khmer Rouge brought a new language—words with a dehumanized ring, a mechanical robot-like quality, euphemism for atrocity, words that people had never heard before."[116]

Regarding the genocide in Rwanda, Philip Gourevitch similarly relates: "A councilwoman in one Kigali neighborhood was reported to have offered fifty Rwandan francs apiece (about thirty cents at the time) for severed Tutsi heads, a practice known as 'selling cabbages.'"[117] Here we see the same adulteration of the meaning for food as we saw in Partnoy's testimony from Argentina. Sometimes they are mere coincidences, but these regimes also share information or study what previous ones have implemented for their own perverse ends. Harry Wu, survivor of the Chinese *Laogai*, recounts the following story when he visited the concentration camp at Dachau in Germany and saw the slogan *arbeit macht frei*: "I asked somebody to translate it and was told, 'Labor makes (you) free.' I was stunned and I asked, 'Are you sure?' and my friend said yes. I said, 'In China, the slogan for our camps was 'Labor makes a new life.'"[118] Anyone who has read survivor testimonies from different despotic regimes or perpetrators of

---

114. Baldwin, *Evidence of Things Not Seen*, 43.

115. Partnoy, *Little School*, 15.

116. Schanberg, *Death and Life of Dith Pran*, 49.

117. Gourevitch, *We Wish to Inform You*, 115.

118. Wu, *Troublemaker*, 185.

injustice will attest to the eerily similar methods, rationalizations, and philosophy that undergird such systems.[119]

Moreover, such regimes force their victims to echo their perverse language to conceal various crimes and truths. Kang Chol-Hwan, a survivor of the North Korean gulag, quotes a fellow prisoner who had to address other gulag inmates prior to his release: "Due to the grace of our great leader, the comrade Kim Il-sung, we will be free in spite of our former crimes. We thank the party from the bottom of our hearts and will do all in our power to be worthy of its decision." Chol-Hwan notes the prisoner concealed any hint of hatred amid these obviously ingratiating lies.[120]

Prisoners also developed their own form of language. As Sara Nomberg-Przytyk writes: "To some extent all of us were drawn into a bizarre transformation of reality. We knew what those innocent words meant, such as 'gas,' 'selection,' but we uttered them, nevertheless, as though there was nothing hidden behind them."[121] As an example, she takes the word *organize*. She writes: "Usually it is associated with such positive values as political, social, and cultural order and well-being . . . In Auschwitz, however, 'to organize' meant to improve your own situation, very often at someone else's expense by taking advantage of that person's ignorance or inexperience."[122] Such new meanings and one's ability to adapt to the new language was often the difference between life and death. To survive, prisoners often employed this new language, inevitably reinforcing the regime's truth claims.[123]

Livia Bitton-Jackson was thirteen years old and momentarily elated after being transferred from a concentration camp to a German factory and given a warm, beautiful coat. She soon noticed the name stitched on the jacket and realized that it had belonged to another

119. For a brief historical sketch of the origin of concentration camps, see Applebaum, *Gulag*, xxxiv. For other similarities, such as the preponderance of "cold jokes" as torture by despotic regimes, see Glover, *Humanity*, 36–37.

120. Chol-Hwan testifies to their being forced to eat rats because they were so desperate to eat (*Aquariums of Pyongyang*, 157).

121. Nomberg-Przytyk, *Auschwitz*, 72.

122. Ibid., 72.

123. James Baldwin describes how African slaves in the United States were forced to adapt to a new language that "did not recognize them as human." He writes: "A language comes into existence by brutal necessity, and the rules of the language are dictated by what the language must convey" ("If Black Language Isn't a Language," 650).

Jewish girl. She writes: "I have become an accomplice to SS brutality and plunder by wearing these clothes . . . Leah Kohn, forgive me."[124]

Once a survivor reencounters the outside world, moreover, communicating what seems inexplicable raises further problems. "Notwithstanding my doubts about language," Wiesel admits, "and perhaps because of them, I plunge deeper and deeper into the whirlwind of the words. I try to capture and tame. And I go on writing because I cannot do otherwise."[125] To be silent and say nothing involves a great risk and hope that others can utter what one cannot; but it also means an antithetical account could be promulgated that aims to discredit or deny what one would have said. And so one testifies, though one is never completely satisfied.

Further complicating one's ability to articulate such horrors is their eerie but inadequate resonance to many of our foundational religious and mythological stories. Dith Pran, a survivor of the horrors of the Khmer Rouge, remarks: "In the water wells, the bodies were like soup bones in broth. And you could always tell the killing grounds because the grass grew taller and greener where the bodies were burned."[126] Again, we see that language from the peace-world ironically fills his description. Decaying bodies remind him of a usual pleasure—a warm, thick soup. But then the metaphor—even as conceit—is too jarring (bodies *cannot* be soup, can they?). And yet, such ridiculously violent stories fill our mythology and history—as in the tale of Thyestes and his brother Atreus[127]—and are steeped within

---

124. Bitton-Jackson, *I Have Lived a Thousand Years*, 156.

125. Wiesel, *And the Sea Is Never Full*, 5.

126. Schanberg, *Life and Death*, 53.

127. After Thyestes' extramarital affair with Atreus' wife, Atreus enacted revenge by chopping up his nephews and nieces, the children of Thyestes, and serving them to Thyestes in broth and feast. Ovid tells us Thyestes ate heartily, the solids filling his belly and satisfying his hunger. So, too, do we hear of such a thing in the story of Tereus, Procne, and Philomela: Tereus, descendent of Mars, and husband of Procne, raped his wife's sister, Philomela, "a virgin, all alone, and calling / For her father, for her sister, but most often / For the great gods. In vain" (146). Tereus was not finished, though: "He seized her tongue / With pincers, though it cried against the outrage, / Babbled and made a sound something like "father," / Till the sword cut it off . . . [Then he] took her, took her again, the injured body / Still giving satisfaction to his lust" (Ovid, *Metamorphoses*, 147).

biblical (and other religious) texts, from the bloody and problematic tale of Dinah[128] to God's order for genocidal killing.[129]

In the latter example, recall that for sparing King Agag of Amalek and the best of his livestock, Saul loses the Lord's favor and, for all intents and purposes, the kingdom. As explicated by the rabbinic authorities, Hamon is a descendent of Agag's son and therefore a product of Saul's disobedience. By sparing the son as well, Saul later jeopardized the existence of the Israelites until God saved the people through Esther. But do the ends justify the means? Regardless, it is imperative that the full story of the Bible is borne in mind as one prepares for some type of theodicy. As can already be judged, a theodicy based only on biblical passages is fraught with problems unless one treats contentious texts as radical metaphors, ignores them, or highlights them as exceptions or aberrations no longer morally relevant today.[130]

Perhaps it should not be shocking that such stories find their mirror image in reality, though there is no tidy metanarrative within which to place many of these survivor testimonies. Meaning and purpose often remain unknown and illusive. Martin Bormann relates that Himmler's mistress showed him and other children a room of their house with "tables and chairs made out of parts of human bodies."[131] Reality, torture, and the absurd uncomfortably mix.

Fictional works (and by analogy, despotic regimes) build and react upon their predecessors. In Shakespeare's *Titus Andronicus*, Ovid's stories (of Thyestes and Atreus and Tereus, Procne, and Philomela) are refashioned and made even more shocking, as Lavinia is raped, has her tongue cut out, her hands chopped off and is mocked: "So now go tell, and if thy tongue can speak, Who 'twas that cut thy tongue and ravish'd thee" and "Write down thy mind, bewray thy meaning so. And

128. Genesis 34.

129. 1 Sam 15:7.

130. For a biblical survey of types of suffering, see Laato and de Moor, *Theodicy in the World of the Bible*; McWilliams, *Where Is the God of Justice?*; and Burnett, *Where Is God?* For a volume that "considers the impact of the Holocaust . . . on the reading of the Hebrew Bible in both Judaism and Christianity," see Sweeney, *Reading the Hebrew Bible after the Shoah*. For the story of Dinah, see Sternberg, *Poetics of Biblical Narrative*, and Diamant's novel, *The Red Tent*.

131. Clendinnen, *Reading the Holocaust*, 94.

if thy stumps will let thee play the scribe."[132] Notice even this image cannot simply remain fiction, as one thinks of Sierra Leone[133] or this account from Etienne Niyonzima from Rwanda:

> "In my neighborhood they killed six hundred and forty-seven people. They tortured them, too . . . They had the number of everyone's house, and they went through with red paint and marked the homes[134] of all the Tutsis and the Hutu moderates. My wife was at a friend's, shot with two bullets. She is still alive, only"—he fell quiet for a moment—"she has no arms. The others with her were killed. The militia left her for dead. Her whole family of sixty-five in Gitarama were killed."[135]

From the mass killings of the Bible, to the mythology poetically retold by Ovid, to Shakespeare's retelling of Ovid, to the "furniture" at Himmler's mountain retreat near Hitler's Berghof, to the brutal acts committed against civilians in Rwanda and Sierra Leone, it is jarring how rich and various are the historical, biblical, literary, and mythological resources that one can compare, and yet words fail to convey the full truth and experiences of these atrocities. While such examples employ words that—at least by definition—the reader should understand, their new meanings or connotations remain resistant to comprehension and acceptance. Literary critic Kalí Tal writes: "Traumatic experience catalyzes a transformation of meaning in the signs individuals use to represent their experiences. Words such as *blood, terror, agony*, and *madness* gain new meaning within the context of the trauma, and survivors emerge from the traumatic environment with a new set of definitions."[136] This is an obstacle the survivor must constantly try to overcome. As Elie Wiesel acknowledges: "What can we do to share our visions? Our words can only evoke the incomprehensible. Hunger, thirst, fear, humiliation, waiting, death; for us these words hold different realities. That is the ultimate tragedy of the victims."[137]

132. Shakespeare, *Titus Andronicus*, II.iv.1–4.

133. See Beah, *Long Way Gone*.

134. Are the religious-minded condemned to see correlations between their holy scriptures and traditions (here, Passover) and the evil perpetrated in places like Rwanda? Recall again that innocent Egyptian children would have been killed in the Exodus tale.

135. Gourevitch, *We Wish to Inform You*, 22.

136. Tal, *Literature of Trauma*, 16.

137. Quoted from ibid., 16.

Thus, the completed or published memoir is a scion of darkness and confusion, misery and pain; it speaks coherent, even poetic phrases about events that for many seem a blur, a cacophonous nightmare. In many instances, these mere words are a funeral oration, our last link to individuals who were unjustly extinguished from this life. It employs a language that is a medley of the old and new and what had congealed from strange, uncomfortable combinations amidst desecration and loss.

Another problem then arises: are readers of these texts willing to accept the consequences of this new language upon their own worldview? Langer adds: "We use words to block our fears—liberation of camps means victory—not emaciated bodies."[138] Just as Nomberg-Przytyk criticizes herself for accepting the euphemisms of the Nazis—an acceptance of a limited and forced nature—Langer here condemns our own complicity in trying to protect our sensibilities and limit our own encounters with these brutal truths of desecration and anguish.

And so, one must ask, how and by what right does an outside critic, with no relevant experience in these matters, dare to analyze and critique such works?

Playing with Corpses: Reading (Dissecting) Texts of Atrocity

Once the survivors find the courage and the medium to tell their stories, how should their words be critiqued, especially in light of the difficulties in representing their experiences? Are such texts sacred and untouchable? Are there limits to how one should read and address such a text? As Jennifer Geddes writes: "Scholars also encounter the limitations of language, the fact that the series of events that constitute an atrocity and the extreme sufferings they result in far exceed our capacity to speak about them."[139]

Because I am arguing that theists must engage with and incorporate testimonies of mass atrocity within their theodic (and so theological) discourse, how to read such texts must be examined in some depth here. Michael Steele, for example, challenges: "[I]f readers make an authentic attempt to understand the message of the literature of atrocity, then it behooves them to do so from a perspective as close as possible to being within the value system used by the Jewish victims

138. Langer, *Holocaust Testimonies*, 8.

139. Geddes, "Religious Rhetoric in Responses to Atrocity," 25.

who have written about their life in the camps."[140] James Hatley, emphasizing a Levinasian priority of the ethical, states: "One must strive to be sincere in one's objectivity. But objectivity is not ultimately neutral, since it has already been commanded to speak as a mode of resistance against those who victimize."[141]

I take from Steele and from Hatley's Levinasian-infused approach the need to speak theologically from the vantage point of the poor and the oppressed.[142] And yet, even for the victims, there is no homogenous or infallible voice. As Didier Pollefeyt rightly cautions: "Ethicists need to listen to victims, scientists, and perpetrators, even if the ethical value of these perspectives is very different. Each of these viewpoints has its own contribution to offer, and *each* perspective also has its own limitations . . ."[143] Again citing Levinas, Hatley goes even further: because we are all responsible for one another—even the victim for the persecutor—this ethical obligation precedes and surmounts any interaction between one another.[144]

The vulnerability of witness testimony must be respected, and yet, to what degree? Ultimately, it is problematic to cede unquestioned, total authority to all witnesses of atrocity. Their words must be tested and analyzed so that some of their interpretations can be fully respected and acknowledged as penetrating truth, while others are held in less regard.

Is it, then, morally permissible to study a memoir about the Russian gulag as a literary text? When such victims are no longer alive, as Lawrence Langer asks, "To whom shall we entrust the custody of the public memory of the Holocaust? To the historian? To the survivor? To the critic? To the poet, novelist, or dramatist? . . . All of them re-create the details and images of the events through written texts, and in so doing, remind us that we are dealing with *represented* rather than unmediated reality."[145] Stressing how such texts are interpreta-

140. Steele, *Christianity, Tragedy, and Holocaust Literature*, 133.

141. Hatley, *Suffering Witness*, 114. In regards to Primo Levi's prologue to his *Survival in Auschwitz*, Hatley writes: "Faithfulness to the victim precedes any determination of the historical truth about the victim" (114).

142. This is also a fundamental step for liberation theology, as chs. 6 and 7 will make clear.

143. Pollefeyt, "Pollefeyt's Response to Critiques," 273.

144. Hatley, *Suffering Witness*, 160.

145. Langer, *Holocaust Testimonies*, 39.

tions of events does not necessarily detract from their truthfulness, but it exposes these works for scrutiny and critique. Concurrently, the exploitation of these stories then becomes a major issue, as these testimonies can be used for sundry themes and causes, an ethical issue that strikes at the heart of my work, for example.[146]

In the years immediately following the publication of Holocaust memoirs, the general trend was not to treat these texts as literary. However, critics such as James Young argued that it was time to renounce sacred guardianship while still maintaining sensitivity to the text in order to "explore both the plurality of meanings the Holocaust texts generate and the actions that issue from these meanings outside of the texts." Thus, he aimed to "legitimate discussion of the Holocaust as metaphor, force the recognition that representations of events are always already mediated . . . [that] even the Holocaust can never lie outside of literature, or understanding, or telling."[147] As Kalí Tal notes: "Critical reading can lead not only to further understanding of sacred and modern literary texts, but also a new understanding of the ways our lives and these texts are inextricably bound together."[148]

Because such critical reading can unlock incriminating truths, a politicized battle often results over the publication of these texts, as was the case with Peter Balakian's memoir about the Armenian genocide[149] or historian Jan Tomasz Gross's *Neighbors*, depicting a Polish massacre of Jews in the village of Jedwabne. The process of "demystification," while often illuminating, as it shines light on truth and a victim's experiences that were previously unknown, can often be disconcerting and feel morally ambiguous to the modern reader.

To illustrate this tension, Inga Clendinnen writes how "the Müller example brings into major focus a difficulty in reading witness testimony: how to assess it without piety."[150] She is referring to what Bauer calls "perhaps the most poignant story of any Holocaust testimony." As the oldest member of the Auschwitz and Birkenau *Sonderkommando* (or "Special Squad"),[151] and so witness to the op-

---

146. See also Raphael, *Female Face of God*, 15 n. 44 (170–71).

147. Tal, *Literature of Trauma*, 48.

148. Ibid., 49.

149. See Balakian, *Black Dog of Fate*.

150. Clendinnen, *Reading the Holocaust*, 25.

151. See Müller, *Eyewitness Auschwitz*.

eration of the crematoria, Filip Müller's accounts of the last moments of hundreds of thousands of lives inevitably invokes silence and awe. Regarding Müller's text, however, Clendinnen notes some discrepancies and suspects "the collaborator's hand in the use of the convention of dramatic direct speech reportage for long public speeches from the SS, and more remarkably and rather less plausibly, for the responses from the victims."[152] She writes that she does not think Müller was "'lying,' but rather that the story flowered in his mind, growing out of smaller actual moments in the undressing room, and his own terrible inability to intervene." Her questions should disarm us. Is it not a double violation to question the words of a victim of atrocity? Is not this in line with those who try to deny these actual events ever happened, deniers of the *Laogai* in China, the Shoah, or the Armenian genocide? To interrogate the person who was raped on whether it was by three or four men seems to smack of inhuman legality, void of all empathy and compassion.

Without undermining the need to practice discernment because of the subject matter, I contend that ignoring the literary, historical, or philosophical elements of these works reveals a failure to evaluate an author's words and intentions with proper respect. Not treating Primo Levi's *Survival in Auschwitz* as a literary text seems to render a judgment upon it as a work of art, even if aesthetic considerations are a secondary or tertiary objective of his reason for writing. At the same time, as Berel Lang notes: "it may be objected that to call attention to the *writing* in writing about the Holocaust must have the effect of distancing readers and writers from the subject of the Holocaust itself."[153] This objection would certainly be applied to a literary analysis of a testimony that inadequately addresses the malice and torment depicted within such a text.[154]

Yet when Wiesel includes the character of Moishe the Beadle in his autobiography *Night*, he is aware of his roles as a Cassandra-like foreshadower in predicting what catastrophe will spread, as a foil to the young protagonist's staunch faith, and as a dreaded mirror of the older Wiesel's worst fear—to be a witness to the horror and have no

---

152. Clendinnen, *Reading the Holocaust*, 23.

153. Lang, "Introduction," 3.

154. See Langer, *Holocaust Testimony*, xii, 19.

one believe you.[155] James Young argues how victims' use of metaphor in their writing fashions a way to understand the seemingly unspeakable trauma they had endured.[156] When Primo Levi, in his *Survival in Auschwitz*, alludes to Ulysses' odyssey, he is urging a comparison between Ulysses' imaginary journey and the Charon that led him (and later Aeneas and Dante) across the underworld. In short, Levi is asking if that hell is as terrifying as the Charon of the Nazi party[157] who ordered Levi and the others into the freight train and asked them "courteously, one by one, in German and in pidgin language, if [they] had] money or watches to give him?"[158]

Comparing his ordeal to the *Inferno* of Dante is the beginning of a movement towards understanding what otherwise seems unspeakable and unknowable.[159] If an analysis of Dante's *Inferno* sheds insight into the experiences Levi sought to convey in his texts, then such literary analysis becomes almost indispensable in the reading of his works.[160]

As seen above, even discussing the genre of these texts can reveal the pros and cons of ways of reading these testimonies. Such classification can also influence what type of truth or message a reader should seek. It may also uncover the different levels of interpretation that a reader should employ when grasping a text's multiple interpretations, its meanings unintentionally or mistakenly insinuated by the author, or ones illuminated by a critic or fellow survivor that divulge new possibilities of connection and analysis.[161] Such accounts can even aid those who might later endure similar ordeals. Irina Ratushinskaya writes in her gulag memoir: "Thank you, Aleksandr Solzhenitsyn, for your priceless counsels!"[162] Any reader may also, of course, distort an author's intentions and undermine what is, to the writers of testimonials, their main purpose: to bear witness to a truth of violence or

155. Wiesel, *Night*, 7.

156. Young, *Writing and Rewriting the Holocaust*, 50.

157. Levi, *Survival in Auschwitz*, 21.

158. Ibid., 21.

159. See Felman and Laub, *Testimony*.

160. See Shankman, *Other Others*, 23–36.

161. For a discussion of a contested phrase in Elie Wiesel's depiction of the deportation scene in *Night*, due to translation problems, insights from other survivors, and, perhaps, "repression," see Suleiman, "Do Facts Matter in Holocaust Memoirs?" 22–42.

162. Ratushinskaya, *Grey Is the Color of Hope*, 12.

injustice that the world at large has ignored, repressed, or doubted. Halima Bashir, a survivor of the Darfur tragedy, writes: "I hug my little boy close to my pounding, fearful heart. It is you who gave me . . . the spirit to go on. And because of you—and the countless other women and children who never made it through the horror alive—I am going to sit at this desk in our tiny apartment while you peacefully sleep, and I am going to start to write my story."[163] While Bashir's baby gives her the resolve to tell her story, tensions remain of how and whether the reader will respond.

Such agonic battles of meaning within and outside the text are not new, but more is at stake with these testimonies. As Tal writes: "No matter how empathetic the critic (if she is not herself a survivor) the trauma of the author becomes, upon translation into text, merely metaphor . . . Crucial then is the ability to consider the author as *survivor*, to bring to bear the tools of sociology, psychology, and psychiatry—an understanding of trauma—to the task of reading the literatures of survivors."[164]

While Tal rightly posits the need for critics to identify their social location and to view the authors of these texts as both writers and survivors, notice that she omits theology and philosophy, whose domains, in part, are to formulate, dissect, and respond to ultimate questions. An aim of my work is to bring together the voices of the theologian and the survivor of atrocity to examine the questions they both utter. Without losing sight of the ghastliness and torment these testimonies reveal, they must be critiqued to locate those truth claims that bear upon all academic fields.[165] To fail to do so may not only discredit some of these accounts but also may limit our ability to understand and respond to them.[166]

---

163. Bashir, *Tears of the Desert*, 5. Holocaust survivor Olga Lengyl similarly writes: "I had then two reasons to live: one, to work with the resistance movement and help as long as I could stand upon my feet; two, to dream and pray for the day when I could go free and tell the world, 'This is what I saw with my own eyes. It must never be allowed to happen again!'" (*Five Chimneys*, 89). There is no dearth of other examples.

164. Tal, *Literature of Trauma*, 131.

165. See Harrowitz, "Grey Zone," 83–103. Harrowitz analyzes Levi's complicated relationship as a scientist to the role science played in the Holocaust.

166. See Nance, *Can Literature Promote Justice?* 48–65.

CONCLUSION

This chapter outlined the problems of transmission from experiencing to writing about traumatic events, but argued that such depictions remain valid and are indispensable to test a theodicy's value and viability. Readers of these testimonies confront depictions of evils that seem too brutal, dehumanizing, random, and meaningless to develop any theodicy. They also highlight the scope and magnitude of accounts of suffering, as Little Eleanora is just one of millions of victims similarly brutalized and murdered by individuals within these various despotic regimes. Such scope poses particularly arduous impediments for a theodicy, problems that are exacerbated in our contemporary context. For Elie Wiesel, the magnitude of the Holocaust is in part why he questions whether Holocaust experiences, "like God's true Name . . . belong to the realm of the ineffable."[167]

Acknowledging this dilemma, I have argued that these texts, despite their limitations and an outsider's inability fully to comprehend their truths, provide an intrinsic means to critique and judge the relevance and viability of various projects of, or attempts at, theodicy. Or to put it another way, these texts become the canvass or evidence for a judgment and trial of a loving God. Failure to address and incorporate such testimonies will have dire repercussions on the viability and pastoral value of any theodicy, and so any theological enterprise. Most importantly, I also want to test whether these texts may actually support a fractured but still viable theodic faith. In the next chapter, though, I will examine the evidence presented by a group of survivors with the potential likelihood that their words alone are enough to silence or refute any such hope.

167. Wiesel, "Afterword," 159.

2

Testimonies of Mass Atrocity

See, O Lord, and behold, / To whom You have done this! / Alas, women eat their own fruit, / Their new-born babes![1]

In this chapter I will focus on three non-Christian testimonies of mass atrocity: Palden Gyatso's *Fire Under the Snow: Testimony of a Tibetan Prisoner*, Alicia Partnoy's *The Little School: Tales of Survival and Disappearance*, and Sara Nomberg-Przytyk's *Auschwitz: True Tales From a Grotesque Land*.

My aims are to examine how these witnesses manage to endure their afflictions, their portrayals of humanity, and the role, if any, that they render to God or religious belief. I include such accounts (which can never fully represent the diverse and seemingly limitless tales of horrific suffering) to ensure that voices sometimes silenced or not adequately represented in theodic and theological discourse constitute a prominent role.

None of the testimonies I will discuss in this chapter seeks to challenge or debunk anyone's belief in God or to defend or refute any theodic or antitheodic system. These witnesses want their stories to be remembered to prevent such monstrosities from happening again. Because such testimonies still endeavor to find or test any meaning within this world, they are, however, indispensible to the theodicist.

---

1. Lam 2:20.

Unfortunately, there is no paucity of applicable testimony. I chose authors who admit their inability to share theistic beliefs or who turn to their non-Christian resources and faith to survive or find meaning. They thus give a glimpse into some of the theological obstacles for any Christian theodicy, while standing on their own as captivating, deserving selections. Palden Gyatso's text is relevant because it is a story of a Tibetan monk who has suffered horrifically but radiates compassion and peace and so contests any exclusivist or unique Christian theodicy. Alicia Partnoy's work is an intricate and penetrating testimony in which Partnoy wishes she could believe in God but is unable to amidst a torture center in Argentina. Nomberg-Przytyk's poignant, pithy account raises numerous ethical quandaries that dispute belief in a world supposedly ordered by goodness and beauty. Her ability to craft a story of degradation and desolation so succinctly and powerfully is a further claim for the work's merit. In addition, reading about the Shoah is what spurred me to work in the area of theodicy, and for this reason I select one of the most memorable and gripping texts from its vast canon.

In addition, I will look briefly at the martyrdom of Karl Leisner and will sketch a picture of the life and death of Christ—His testimony, as it were—as a potential bridge between these witnesses to evil and the Christian theodic responses we will encounter in Part 2.

The road before us is difficult to traverse; the stories are often graphic and the accounts morally deflating. But as Elie Wiesel once mentioned in class in regards to Iris Chang's *The Rape of Nanking*, "If she had the courage to research and write about such things, we must have the courage to read them."[2] And so we must: it is the least we can do.

THREE TESTIMONIES AND THE ABSENCE OF GOD

Fire Under the Snow: *Palden Gyatso*

Palden Gyatso was arrested by the invading Chinese Communist forces during the Cultural Revolution while a young Tibetan monk at the age of twenty-eight and spent the next thirty-one years of his life in prison for seeking the freedom of the Tibetan people and refusing to

---

2. I took Elie Wiesel's course "The Literature of Memory: Hope and Despair," Fall 2001, Boston University.

relinquish his Buddhist values. According to the Dalai Lama, Gyatso "endured torture, virtual starvation, and endless sessions of 'thought reform.' Nevertheless, he refused to give in to his oppressors."[3]

Gyatso grew up in the village of Panam in Tibet. It seemed both his destiny and his desire to be a monk, which he soon became at the age of ten, beginning the process of severing his ties to the world. He took his final vow in 1952, but of the approximately twenty novices, only he is alive: "Some were to die in prison. Others were beaten to death during the Cultural Revolution."[4] In short, Gyatso's life and studies were soon torn asunder by China's invasion of Tibet and its planned and executed desecration of Tibetan culture and Buddhist religion. Temples were destroyed, holy books burned, and monks and nuns abused and murdered.

During one interrogation, Gyatso relates the torture he suffered because he refused to denounce one of his teachers:

> Before I could breathe in, Liao's open palm had caught me on the side of the face, knocking me backwards. The two guards who had been standing by the door came forward and grabbed my arms. I saw the interpreter, Gyaltsen, step back. He looked frightened. The guards began to kick me.
>
> "Do you confess?" asked Liao. "Do you?"
>
> "Do whatever you want with me!" I shouted. I was enraged. I'd lost my senses.
>
> The guards held my arms behind my back, tied them with a rope, then threw the end of the rope over a wooden beam. They pulled down on the rope, hoisting my arms up, wrenching them from their sockets. I screamed. I began to urinate uncontrollably.[5]

Gyatso passed out. When he awoke, the interrogation continued. He refused to betray his teacher.[6]

In another heart-wrenching scene, Gyatso is coerced to kneel before a group of condemned prisoners as a means to spur him to confess or be threatened with their fate. He stares at the face of one battered prisoner, whose name he remembers because she had stood

3. Dalai Lama, "Foreword." For an account of the Tibetan genocide, see Craig, *Tears of Blood.*

4. Gyatso, *Fire,* 34.

5. Ibid., 68.

6. Ibid., 69.

"up to the Chinese." The person before him though is that of an "old woman, deep-wrinkled and toothless . . .We stared at each other. Her eyes were red and misty and something in her face seemed to be asking for my prayers."[7] After an interminable meeting, the prisoners were then shot, fifteen in all that particular day. "Death," as Gyatso writes, "was our constant companion."[8]

The remainder of his thirty-one years of incarceration and torture show his similar resolve in the face of unrelenting brutality. The guards handcuffed him and "shackled his feet together with a chain"[9]—a punishment that he had to endure for six months in one case, unable to do anything without the help of fellow prisoners. At the age of sixty, an interrogator shoved an electric baton in his mouth and all over his body. It was so bad that one of the guards "ran out of the room in disgust."[10] Gyatso lost all of his teeth. Still more stories follow: of failed demonstrations and of witnessing young prisoners—the next generation—tortured and beaten. Throughout these ordeals, it was particularly harrowing to have to withstand a system that forced each person to be violent towards his fellow sufferers. During a *thamzing* (struggle session), "If they observed that your participation was not whole-hearted, they would accuse you of lacking revolutionary enthusiasm. You were expected to do harm to your fellow prisoners as if they were your worst enemies."[11]

After finally escaping and reaching the Dalai Lama at Dharamsala, Gyatso accepted the task to interview other arrivals and to record their testimonies: "I could not believe how many of us had the same story to tell. There was not a single individual without a story of horror and brutality, and I realized that all subjugated people share the common experience of bruised bodies, scattered lives and broken families."[12]

In his "Poem of Dedication," placed before the beginning of his prose account, Gyatso asks: "Is there any match for the suffering we endured, the losses we felt, the cries we made, even in the eighteenth

7. Ibid., 139.
8. Ibid., 140.
9. Ibid., 69.
10. Ibid., 195.
11. Ibid., 132.
12. Ibid., "Prologue."

layer of Hell?" These and similar questions get to the root of any theodicy and the role and purpose of God. They draw us into the classic questions raised by the notion of an omnipotent, omniscient, omnibenevolent God despite the reality of radical evil in the world. Are such questions applicable for Gyatso, though?

To address adequately Gyatso's remarks, one needs a deep and nuanced knowledge of Buddhism, or more specifically, its various traditions: Mahāyāna, Theravāda, Tibetan,[13] Zen, and so on. I am in no position to do so. My intention, however, is to sketch how Gyatso's account challenges a Christian theodicy, an issue that deserves its own separate treatment, but is a fundamental one that I must at least touch upon.

First, such an account testifies to the extreme debasement of torture and suffering inflicted upon Gyatso and his fellow Tibetans and seems to undermine any theodicy that alleges all suffering is deserved, didactic, or morally refining (note that the belief in karma and rebirth in Buddhism would be linked to the first explanation). Such accounts also seem to refute the grandiose claim that there is a purpose to all suffering, for what transcendent purpose can one argue for when a child is forced to murder his parents or a Tibetan nun is raped and brutalized? The horrific ordeal of Gyatso's trauma and suffering taught him no valuable lesson. If one tries to justify such evils because his life can inspire others, then individual lives become utilitarian tools, mere means to spur otherwise complacent people to act.

Secondly, notice that traditional theodic questions seem to be absent from Gyatso's memoir. This is not because the Chinese never brought the topic of God up in their interrogations, for they did. Other accounts from Tibetans who were tortured relate instances of the Chinese mocking their faith. One monk from Chamdo recalls how the "Chinese would also poke their fingers into the prisoners' eyes and throw dirt into their mouths so that it would choke and suffocate them. And then they would laugh in our faces and say, 'Now, where is your God? If he exists, call him.'"[14] This example, however, raises additional questions. What is the most authentic way for a Christian

13. According to Peter Harvey, "Buddhism was recognized as a state religion in Tibet in 779 . . .[It] was a mixture of monastically-based Mahāyāna, represented by Śāntarakṣita, and tantric mysticism and ritual, represented by the revered Padmasabhava: a mix which became typical for Tibet" (*Buddhism*, 145).

14. Quoted from Craig, *Tears of Blood*, 71.

theodicist to interpret how Tibetan victims or survivors viewed the presence of "God" amidst such evil when the victims may not share the same meaning ascribed of God or for whom such theodic questions are simply not relevant?

In addition, what type of God were the Chinese referring to above, and how would the Tibetan victim interpret such a question? Some scholars, for example, contend that Buddhism may not have a recognizable theodicy, in part, because the problems of theodicy for Christians, Jews, and Muslims are dependent upon belief in an all-loving creator God. According to the Buddhist scholar Peter Harvey, in Buddhism the closest being to a creator God, the Brahmā, is "a god of love who thinks he created the world but in fact did not. [Thus] there is no theological problem of evil in Buddhism."[15] This is not to say Buddhism ignores the problems of suffering, nor that a Christian theodicy would not benefit from such an encounter with Buddhism. The opposite is the case, as one can glean from the life of Gyatso, an embodiment of the "Buddhist way," as John D'Arcy May describes it: "The Buddhist way means practice in the present, not escape into a timeless realm removed from the transitoriness (*anicca*) and unsatisfactoriness (*dukkha*) of human existence. Buddhist practice, starting with the individual but radiating love and compassion (*metta-karuna*) to all living beings, is meant to make a difference to the world . . ."[16]

Gyatso's life testifies to this struggle and practice. For the Buddha, moreover, recognizing the ignorance that causes suffering and becoming aware that all aspects of life are connected with suffering, are a means for liberation. According to the Buddha, the summation of his teaching was: "Both formerly and now, it is only suffering and the stopping of suffering that I describe."[17] How to combat suffering is a key element of the Four Noble Truths and the Holy Eightfold Path.[18] Two famous stories help illustrate this outlook.

A mother, Kisa Gotami, had never seen death before. When her child dies, she insists on going from house to house in search of a

---

15. Harvey, *Buddhism*, 37. See also Southwold, "Buddhism and Evil," 128–41; Gira, "Buddhist Approach to the Question of 'Evil,'" 100–107. See also Schmidt-Leukel, "'Light and Darkness,'" 80–82.

16. May, *Transcendence and Violence*, 95.

17. Hallisey, "Buddhism," 55–56.

18. Vajiragnana, "Evil in Theravada Buddhism," 105.

cure. When she eventually reaches the Buddha, he tells her to go to a house where no child has died and to ask for "a pinch of white mustard seed." She can find no household where such a calamity has not occurred. She returns to the Buddha and is told, "You vainly imagined that you alone had lost a child. But all living things are subject to an unchanging law, and it is this: 'The Prince of Death, like a raging flood, sweeps away all living things into the sea of ruin; still their longings are unfulfilled.'"[19] When life is *dukkha*—burdened with "a sense of unsatisfactoriness or imperfection"[20]—one must expect such encounters and truths and know that overcoming them is a means for liberation.

A second story, which was particularly resonant with survivors of the Khmer Rouge,[21] but which many Tibetans could relate to, depicts a young woman, Patacara, who marries her servant in opposition to her parent's aims. She escapes with him and has two children under arduous circumstances, both times unsuccessfully trying to get home to her parents for the birth. During the birth of her second child outside during a rainstorm, her husband dies from snakebite. Then in trying to reach her parents' house, she encounters a wide riverbank that prevents crossing with both children. She carries the toddler over and then turns back to get the baby. When she is in midstream, a hawk grabs the newborn and carries him away. When the mother cries out to scare the bird, the toddler thinks she is calling him and subsequently falls into the river and drowns.[22] Seemingly cursed like the House of Atreus, she soon discards her clothes and goes mad after discovering her parents have died. Shunned by nearly everyone, she eventually comes to Gautama Buddha, who clothes her and "preache[s] to her about the nature of the world, whereupon she regain[s] her sanity and achieve[s] insight into the nature of suffering."[23]

Certain elements of these stories can resonate with a Christian: the emphasis on aiding the victim; the means for spiritual catharsis dormant within (some) suffering, or in the case of extreme affliction, the possibility of healing afterwards; and the need to view life honestly

---

19. Quoted from Hallisey, "Buddhism," 47.

20. Vajiragnana, "Theoretical Explanation," 101. The story is also recounted with some varied details in Him's Cambodian genocide memoir, *When Broken Glass Floats*, 38.

21. Hallisey, "Buddhism," 53.

22. Ibid., 53.

23. Ibid., 52.

and soberly. But the potential for individual redemption through a Redeeming Creator-God seems inapplicable here. Regardless, Gyatso practices the highest standards of Buddhist principles and is a testament to the beauty, value, and dignity of humanity despite unimaginable torture and pain. In looking at various theodicies in Part 2, we will see whether many theodicies are missing some key elements within Gyatso's reflections or if any insights from a Christian theodicy could have aided Gyatso.

The Little School: *Alicia Partnoy*

In *The Little School*,[24] Alicia Partnoy describes her arrest and kidnapping on January 12, 1977, and her subsequent disappearance and torture by the Argentine government for her involvement in the Peronist Youth Movement[25] and her advocating of human rights during Argentina's Dirty War. She was twenty-one, married, and had a nine-month-old daughter, Ruth. Her husband was also kidnapped. Partnoy opens her book with an excerpt from the *Final Document of the Military Junta on the War Against Subversion and Terrorism*, promulgated by the Argentine government, which denied that she and nearly thirty thousand others were kidnapped, tortured, and usually "desaparecido"—disappeared, killed: "There is also talk of 'disappeared' persons who are still held under arrest by the Argentine government in unknown places of our country. All of this is nothing but a falsehood stated with political purposes, since there are neither secret detention places in the Republic nor persons in clandestine detention in any penal institution."[26] Such deceitful lies by those in

---

24. In its structure and composition, *The Little School* blends numerous literary genres and alternates the story's time frame and narrative voice. Sometimes a chapter is told in the past tense; sometimes the present; sometimes the narrator is Partnoy as a prisoner; sometimes the narrator is a third-person omniscient one, describing Partnoy or other prisoners. In other chapters, the narrative voice is another prisoner's, such as Ruth's husband or Graciela, while he or she is beaten and interrogated. Partnoy's text is an example of hybridity as noted in the previous chapter.

25. Juan Peron was overthrown by a military coup in Argentina in 1955. Partnoy saw Peronism as a "very broad movement under the umbrella of economic independence, political sovereignty, and social justice . . . and thought the movement bore the seeds of change to socialism" (*Little School*, 12).

26. Ibid., 23.

power are all too common, a double violation of perpetrating and denying the crime.[27]

In this section I will first account for the role of identity and anonymity amidst Partnoy's ordeal. I will then concentrate on two relevant chapters for my aims: "Benja's First Night," which depicts Partnoy's helplessness in trying to mitigate her friend's torture, followed by "Ruth's Father," her account of her husband's thoughts while he is viciously interrogated. Lastly, I will discuss passages in the book where God is mentioned.

After being kidnapped, Partnoy and other prisoners were confined to a site "which the military ironically named the Little School (*La Escuelita*) . . . located behind the headquarters of the 5th Army Corps, fifteen blocks from the You and I Motel (*Tú y Yo*) on Carrindanga Road, a beltway. The house was near a railroad; one could hear trains . . . In the Little School there were two rooms where an average of fifteen prisoners remained prone, our hands bound."[28] The prisoners were always kept blindfolded. Partnoy writes: "The atmosphere of violence was constant. The guards put guns to our heads or mouths and pretended to pull the trigger."[29] Or they did, though the bodies were never found and the government denied any accountability.

The first chapter, "The One-Flower Slippers," opens: "That day, at noon, she was wearing her husband's slippers; it was hot and she had not felt like turning the closet upside down to find her own." As always in these stories, the enemies come unexpectedly, even catching unawares those who were "prepared." The narrator paints stark images of the capture: "She lost the first slipper in the corridor, before reaching the place where Ruth, her little girl, was standing. She lost the second slipper while leaping over the brick wall . . . Ruth burst into tears in the doorway. While squatting in the bushes, she heard the shot. She looked up and saw soldiers on every roof. She ran to the street through weeds as tall as she. Suddenly the sun stripped away her clothing; it

---

27. The Chinese government referring to their occupation of Tibet as "liberty" would be another example of institutional or governmental deceit. The document attesting to Gyatso's crimes, for example, states: "The above facts are clear and constitute irrefutable evidence of the crime for which the Defendant was arrested, facts that he does not deny" (*Fire*, Appendix, 234).

28. Partnoy, *Little School*, 14.

29. Ibid., 15.

caught her breath."[30] She, too, is caught by her attackers, though the chapter ends on that last line with its incongruous symbolism.

The story proceeds with this sense of detachment, maybe a necessary distance to describe her travails—or perhaps, the impossibility of believing the one now writing in relative comfort and peace is the same person being described. After agonizing interrogation, she is given a pair of slippers. One has a plastic flower on it, a sight worth peeking through the blindfold despite the punishment inflicted if caught because "that one-flowered slipper amid the dirt and fear, the screams and the torture, that flower so plastic, so unbelievable, so ridiculous, was like a stage prop, almost obscene, absurd, a joke."[31] It opposes everything these guards and their malicious acts represent: beauty, art, color. For weeks she conceals it—"blindly search[ing] for the flower under the bed . . . in-between the guards' shouts and blows." After being transferred to a prison, the guards decide that she needs a pair of tennis shoes. As the chapter ends, "The one-flowered slippers remained at the Little School, disappeared."[32] The woman, also disappeared, remains unnamed.

In "Latrine," the first-person narrator surreptitiously whispers to her fellow prisoners about how to beat the cure for constipation by thinking of the shift supervisor. Again the narrator is not named. When she asks for toilet paper, she is given sandpaper. She remarks: "I crouched above the latrine and I . . . spotted my slipper with its plastic daisy on the dirty floor caked with urine and excrement. There was a nice breeze, and if I didn't have my nose facing into the latrine I would have breathed deeply. Birds sang and I heard the sound of a train." This speaker, then, is the same person from the previous chapter. The unnamed narrator then depicts experiences of torture the guards forced on the prisoners as they walked to and from the latrine—hitting her twelve times for refusing to slap another prisoner—"If you don't hit him, I'll hit you!"[33] Like Gyatso, this still anonymous prisoner "doesn't sell [her] friends for five minutes of sunshine . . . not even for all the sunshine of the world."[34]

30. Ibid., 25.
31. Ibid., 28.
32. Ibid., 28.
33. Ibid., 32.
34. Ibid., 36.

Soon she is given a name. In the following chapter she is referred to as Skinny while lamenting the capture of her friends and waiting for their inevitable screams of torture. It was her birthday, as the chapter was called. Finally, in "My Names," through her interrogation session we learn her identity: "'Name?' 'Alicia Partnoy.'" Before being captured, she had numerous aliases. In the Little School, though, she has no name. "Only Vasca calls me by my name. The guards have repeatedly said that numbers will be used to call us, but so far that has just been a threat," she writes, as if she is talking to us while still confined, still being tortured.[35] However, two months into her kidnapping, the guards have taken to calling her Death. "Maybe that is why every day, when I wake up, I say to myself that I, Alicia Partnoy, am still alive." Just as the threat of impending anonymity looms, an identity emerges that both the government and the prison guards have tried to disappear and deny.

In "Benja's First Night," the guards celebrate the capture of a new prisoner by giving the other prisoners a special "treat." Partnoy had overheard the guards say: "'Hang them upside down.' It must have been the torture well where they dunk prisoners in putrid waters for hours on end . . . Poor little Benja!"[36] She recalls his childish face and "easy laughter" when he used to pass out leaflets "on the streets of Bahia Blanca," but he is now "helpless, naked, his ribs sticking out." She knows he is hungry and reasons that "by stretching my feet I can touch his frozen hands. I wish I could protect him . . . I have some cheese and a small end of bread saved for tomorrow . . . If I cut them into little pieces, then put them between my toes, I can pass the bread and cheese to Benja."[37] She manages to do so: a miracle in itself. But the guard is bored and wants to "box a little."[38] Benja, the newcomer, is the most likely target. With each blow to Benja, Partnoy's bed shakes. "My whole body contracts in rage and impotence." Then, desperate to delay the torture, she distracts the guard by asking for bread, and then goads him into an arm wrestling match—anything to give Benja a few

35. Ibid., 42.

36. Ibid., 46.

37. Ibid.

38. Ibid.

minutes of reprieve. She succeeds. Soon it is 7 a.m.: "A new day has just begun at the Little School."[39]

In "Ruth's Father," the narrator is Partnoy's husband, who is trying to remember the nursery song he sang to his daughter as a means to shield him from the torture the guards inflict upon him. The epigraph of the chapter is a translation of "*El Sapito Glo-glo-glo*"—"Ribbit Rib-bit, Little Frog"—in which the little frog has disappeared and "nobody knows where he hides / nobody's seen him at home." Like the lost flower, the lost frog is a fitting symbol and synecdoche for Partnoy and her husband. The reader is "transported" into the thoughts of Partnoy's husband as he is tortured:

> Daughter, dear, my tongue hurts and I can't say *rib-it rib-it*; even if I could, you wouldn't hear me. This little poem soothed you when you cried; you went to sleep listening to it . . . I've repeated it for a whole day but I still can't sleep. *Rib-it Rib-it he sings on the roof* . . . I won't see you again . . . The electric prods on my genitals . . . Trapped, like the little frog . . . *but we hear him all the time.* I told the torturers if they took me to the meeting place I would point to him; then, when I saw him I didn't do what I'd promised. Afterward, the electric prod again, and the blows . . . harder: "Where is he?" But my child . . . *Rib-it rib-it* . . . Where are you, my little girl?[40]

In a reversal of roles, in the further muddying of one's identity, the children's lullaby that had comforted the child is now sought by the parent for the same tranquillity. But while the child has difficulty pronouncing the words because of her age, the parent cannot say the words because of the torture inflicted upon him. And more tragically, even if he could say the words, she wouldn't hear them, not where he is, amidst the screams and the threat of murder. The interspersion of thoughts of the nursery rhyme, of life before the torture, amidst the torture, is a jarring juxtaposition for the reader. Here numerous lost items are merged into one: the lost frog, Partnoy's husband, his voice, the person the interrogators want him to reveal. But they are not all one: Partnoy's husband is found in a certain sense and he wishes he could be like the frog, truly lost so these guards could not continue

---

39. Ibid., 48.
40. Ibid., 95.

battering him. But then he has become an animal of sorts—or so his screams seem to reveal.[41]

The chapter ends mercilessly, hopelessly. It haunts the living. I quote it in its entirety:

> But when they come for me . . . to kill me next time . . . No, please don't come . . . I'm not an animal . . . don't make me believe I'm an animal . . . But that's not my scream . . . That's an animal's scream. Leave my body in peace. I'm a little frog for my daughter to play with; . . . she'll soon be two years old and she'll learn the whole poem . . . *We all hear him / Rib-bit rib-bit when it rains . . . rib-bit rib-bit.*[42]

Notice the repetition of certain phrases, just as a little child will often ask you to repeat what was funny. One can also hear the interrogators repeating the same questions: "Where is he? Where is your accomplice?"[43] Sadly, just as the father wishes he could be that little frog for his daughter to play with, it is the guards who "play" with him, tossing and poking and beating his body like a doll a child no longer wants.

Partnoy does not ask where God is. She simply tells these stories she has lived and seen, stories of what she has been forced to withstand without God or any hope of God. "Sometimes when I'm very scared, I wish I could believe in God: the Christian God, my family's God, any God. The truth is that I would like to believe in a God that protects and rescues me from here; I don't want a God that makes me a martyr."[44] Her fellow prisoners, many of them Christian, are awed by her stance. "'If you don't believe in God, how do you find strength to risk being killed by the military?' Néstor asked one day. He, Christian to the marrow of his bones, found the tools to fight injustice in the Theology of Liberation." But Partnoy cannot believe in such a God because she has only "encountered" him as a pretext, and, she writes, "I instinctively reject pretexts." For a woman blindfolded, beaten, and imprisoned, separated from her husband and daughter, how tempting a God of intervention would seem. Yet, while some Christian adherents have

41. Ibid., 94.

42. Ibid., 95.

43. See Scarry, *Body in Pain*, 28–29.

44. Partnoy, *Little School*, 62.

embraced or sought martyrdom,[45] for Partnoy, the idea of martyrdom is a metaphorical blindfold that augments the suffering caused from the literal one, tied firmly around her face. Like Auschwitz for Levi or Donat, Partnoy does not experience God while in the Little School, its lessons ones of cruelty and unmitigated evil. She feels no recourse but to rely on herself and the solidarity of others in order to bring some peace, some light into the depravity of her experiences. She will give no credence to what Kimberly Nance calls "testimonial hagiography—neither Jewish nor Christian nor even secular."[46]

Partnoy writes: "It is then time . . . [to] eat that piece of bread that reminds us that our present is a result of our fight—so that bread, our daily bread . . . that has been taken away from our people, will be given back because it is our right, no pleas to God needed, forever and ever. Amen."[47]

Auschwitz: True Tales from a Grotesque Land: Sara Nomberg-Przytyk

In Sara Nomberg-Przytyk's *Auschwitz: True Tales From a Grotesque Land*,[48] we have another account of humankind run amok. The Nazis shipped Nomberg-Przytyk to their death camps for being a Jew, but as a communist she views religious believers in Auschwitz with bewilderment and detachment. For Nomberg-Przytyk, as for Partnoy, God does not exist. In this section I will highlight a few memorable scenes that a theodicist must address.

Like *The Little School*, Nomberg-Przytyk's work depicts vignettes about the experiences of the author and other camp inmates. While all chapters are narrated in the past tense, like Partnoy's book, Nomberg-Przytyk's vivid descriptions of her surroundings and experiences give to

---

45. St. Thérèse of Lisieux, for example, writes: "Like you, my adorable Jesus, I want to be scourged and crucified. I want to be flayed like St. Bartholomew. Like St. John I want to be flung into boiling oil" (*Autobiography*, 154).

46. Nance, *Can Literature Promote Justice?* 41.

47. Partnoy, *Little School*, 86.

48. Interestingly, Nomberg-Przytyk's editor in Poland wanted her to remove all references to Jews. She refused, citing that "it would be very strange indeed to present a narrative of Auschwitz that contained no mention of Jews at all." She clandestinely took the manuscript with her out of Poland when she immigrated to Israel where the work was placed in an archive until the English translators discovered and published it (Hirsch, "Translator's Foreword," xii).

readers a creepy sense of voyeurism as if they, too, are now confined in the camp. The chapters are composed thematically—from the (variously depicted) story about the revenge of the dancer to an analysis of the new vocabulary that emerged in the camps. Still, there is a sense of linear progression. The book opens with her first night in Stutthof, described as if she wasn't in a concentration camp: "I lay on the lowest bunk of a three-decker bed, wrapped in a blanket. I was not cold. I was not hungry. I had drunk enough cold water to quench my thirst. I had gotten rid of the lice. You might say that I felt happy."[49] It ends with Nomberg-Przytyk on a civilian train after her liberation from Auschwitz, watching the Polish passengers who were living "normally."

Like previous examples, any chapter attempting to recreate the insanity and barbarity that was Auschwitz contains enough testimony of suffering to debunk all religious presuppositions. In one story, a doctor from the infirmary where Nomberg-Przytyk also "worked," tells her what happens to babies born in the camps: "It's very simple. We give the baby an injection. After that, the baby dies. The mother is told that the baby was born dead. After dark, the baby is thrown on a pile of corpses, and in that manner, we save the mother. I want so much for the babies to be born dead, but out of spite they are born healthy." Nomberg-Przytyk assists at one of these births—the mother in agony but unable to utter a sound. When the child is born—healthy—the doctor drowns him in a bucket of cold water and tells the mother the news. Nomberg-Przytyk later tries to warn Esther, an expectant mother. Esther, however, believes her baby will be spared. Indeed, the doctors take pity on Esther, who, after giving birth, nurses the baby for three days despite arguments from others to let the baby starve.[50] During selection, she holds the baby "high as though she wanted to show them what a beautiful and healthy son she had. Mengele slowly pushed the pencil into his clenched fist." The gesture was a signal to an SS man who "put down a cross next to the designated numbers."[51] Both Esther and her son were selected for the ovens.

49. Nomberg-Przytyk, *Auschwitz*, 3.

50. Ibid., 80.

51. Ibid., 71. For a case in which Dr. Mengele played a role in "saving" a life, see Bitton-Jackson, *I Have Lived a Thousand Years*. Bitton-Jackson writes that the "diabolical" Dr. Mengele "tenderly stroked my 'golden hair' and in a kindly voice advised me to double-cross his SS machinery and lie about my age to save my life" (78). She was thirteen at the time.

One of the prisoners told Nomberg-Przytyk that Mengele's rationalization for killing both the mother and the baby was for "humanitarian" reasons. Nomberg-Przytyk comments: "Imagine that cynical criminal justifying his hideous crimes in the name of humanitarianism, making a mockery of the tenderest of all feelings, a mother's love for her children."[52] Such crimes are also resistant to any fair punishment. Regarding the burning of the living children, she writes: "Living children burned like torches. What did these children do to suffer such a fate? Is there any punishment adequate to repay the criminals who perpetrated these crimes?"[53]

Such questions put the theodicist on the defensive. They seem to demand revered silence and praxis, as Greenberg argues. Yet such questions also invoke justice. In facing the imperfection of the reality of justice in this world, a theodicist tries to speak of hope of healing and redemption in the afterlife. For a Christian, Christ as victim and God is envisioned as the link between the need for justice and mercy and the possibility of such healing and redemption. And yet, camp images make formulating such statements an arduous and gruelling task: "Women and children got off the train. Often the little girls would be holding dolls in their arms, while the little boys in short pants were jumping and running after a ball."[54] Most would immediately be murdered and gassed.

While it is difficult for a theodicist to refrain from seeking some sign of God's presence,[55] Nomberg-Przytyk is unable to provide any hopeful glimpse of the divine. Instead, she expresses her irritation towards two Jewish girls who maintain their faith in the Jews as a chosen people.[56] What is religious heroism to the believer is a foolish hope for the nonbeliever.[57] Nomberg-Przytyk admits that it was "difficult" for her "to understand how they could maintain this belief in the face of the facts,"[58] which seem to render such faith madness, or at best, nonrational. A theodicy here would seem to be totally irrelevant or insensitive.

---

52. Nomberg-Przytyk, *Auschwitz*, 69.

53. Ibid., 82.

54. Ibid., 79.

55. Ibid., 106.

56. Ibid., 39.

57. Ibid., 39.

58. Ibid., 39.

Nomberg-Przytyk also relates how Dr. Mengele performed grue-some experiments on ten little people from Budapest who at first thought he was an angel. Their fellow prisoners said nothing to per-suade them otherwise. The little people eventually realized the truth after Mengele tortured one couple's three-year-old to death. Fellow prisoners then told the child's father that he could manage to slip through the wire and enter the women's camp to see his wife. "He took them seriously," the *kapo* Bubi told Nomberg-Przytyk. "But you know the guard wasn't one second late. When the midget got close enough to the wires the guard popped him. He never made it to his wife."[59] Bubi told the story while "laughing raucously." Nomberg-Przytyk sol-emnly remarks, "His fellow prisoners were as much to blame for his misfortune as the SS man who actually put the bullet into him. That was the tragedy of Auschwitz."[60]

BATTERED AND BROKEN BY THE "UNREAL"

The above are glimpses into mass atrocities. We will encounter other testimonies throughout the remaining chapters, all trying to recon-nect to their lost, often destroyed former homes. Inevitably, obstacles abound. As Nomberg-Przytyk writes: "Nothing was real. It was as if I were looking at a picture from another world."[61] This picture from another world, both real and unreal, she argues, could not be compre-hended with a normal mind.[62]

Other survivors have uttered similar statements.[63] Questions, doubt, fears, and moments of despair proliferate. As Nomberg-Przytyk writes: "It was dangerous to be too good in Auschwitz. As they say, in Auschwitz the pigs like to feed on good people."[64] Such statements do not rest easily when read in the supposedly "normal" world.

For someone seeking to defend or develop a theodicy, these ac-counts raise questions about the essence of human nature and the value of our free will that has inflicted such horror and evil. They

59. Ibid., 93.

60. Ibid., 90.

61. Ibid., 15.

62. Ibid., 59.

63. Soon Ok Lee writes: "The place where I was confined was not a place that normal people can imagine" (*Eyes of the Tailless Animals*, 7).

64. Nomberg-Przytyk, *Auschwitz*, 45.

challenge the role of prayer, the meaning of a personal relationship with God, and the role of a loving, omnipotent God who intervenes in history, to give a few examples.[65] None of these theological terms was explicit in these accounts, but they were all present, almost daring the reader to invoke them.

To what extent do these interpretations of God and life in these testimonies constrain what is permissible in a theodicy? Theologian Stephen Davis, for example, stresses that victims "are not in any more (or less) authoritative a position than . . . any other thoughtful person to rule on the theological implications of what they experienced."[66] And yet, they have witnessed and felt what most of us do not want to imagine. These survivors simply have seen more. This seeing more is not simply a quantitative asset. It deals with what can be hidden, subsumed, forgotten. These are facts and truths that make living—let alone believing anything—difficult once these voices are heeded. But then, what about those who have endured and witnessed such abasement and despair, and yet practice their faith to the end, enflamed with the love of God on their trembling, dying lips? This, too, is a crucial question that the theodicists and antitheodicists of Part 2 need to answer. We will read one case below.

TESTIMONIES OF ATROCITY AND THE GOD OF PRESENCE

There are prodigious numbers of witnesses who proclaim or despair at the absence of God, but their voices are not the only ones. Voices of theodic faith can still be heard, though perhaps with less frequency and vehemence. According to Langer, while moments of resilience and goodness exist in Holocaust accounts, they are infrequent and "often prompted by an anxious interviewer. But a resourceful, intrepid, and resolute audience will recognize that these moments are inseparable from their opposite—a genuine form of chiaroscuro."[67]

As noted above, theodicists must heed all perspectives. The pertinent issue is whether this approach is mired in ambiguity, whether this "chiaroscuro," or more negatively, clash of voices, conclusively proves that evil has overcome the good, or whether a credible argument can

65. See ch. 10 for further analysis.

66. Davis, *Encountering Evil,* 106.

67. Langer, *Holocaust Testimonies,* 36.

still be made for a fractured but still viable theodicy. If one thinks of the general malaise and despair when reading a thought-provoking but nearly hopeless work like Améry's *At the Mind's Limits*, how different a reaction occurs when reading Joseph Malham's *By Fire into Light: Four Catholic Martyrs of the Nazi Camps*.[68]

While Malham's accounts are biographies—and so are one step further removed from a survivor's interpretation of these raw events— they are valuable for depicting the moral and spiritual tenacity and witness of these individuals who testify that, despite the evil and death that engulfed them, their lived faith and presence of a loving God sustained them until the end. As Daniel O'Connell remarks: "To say that nothing is sacred anymore is to voice a commonplace. Hero worship is quaint and outmoded . . . [But] do we need a few heroes along the way? Very definitely!"[69] To admit there is no possibility for human beings to reach such heights of self-sacrifice, love, and kindness, even amidst trying and traumatic circumstances, is to deny the very pinnacle—and, some would say, essence—of what humankind is capable of.

While our media are often replete with wars and scandals, O'Connell affirms that "good people must be spotlighted somehow."[70] I am highlighting Malham's work because the stories of the Catholic martyrs he retells must also be presented in an argument of theodicy that looks to the victims of persecution and injustice for theological centering and grounding.[71]

These Catholic martyrs were not "better" than a Gyatso or Partnoy. Their singularity rests in their moral and theological interpretation of their plights. Here Christ's presence pervades the camps. This is a remotely different interpretation from a Partnoy or Nomberg-Przytyk. I will limit myself here to one incident in the lives of one of these martyrs. Deacon Karl Leisner had been seeking to become a priest before he was captured and imprisoned by the Nazis. While striving to live a holy and ethical life during his four years at Dachau, he nevertheless continued to pray and hope to be ordained. But the process of ordination, with its formalities and rules involving the right

68. Malham focuses on Titus Brandsma, Pére Jacques de Jésus, Karl Leisner, and Edith Stein.

69. O'Connell, "Foreword," 3.

70. Ibid., 4.

71. Ibid., 4.

vestments, books, and chrism (how would these be found?), the laying on of hands from a bishop (was there one in a camp?)—and approval from the bishop in Karl's diocese, Munich (how could word get to him?)—had to be followed. Looming over the whole process was the threat of execution if the Nazis discovered the planned ordination of a priest in the camps. Another problem was Karl's worsening health caused from the ravages of the camp and his own practice of seeking to help others even less fortunate than himself.

Despite these considerable barriers, the miraculous ordination happened because so many people sought to give to this dying deacon a gift that defied everything the Nazis represented. A Benedictine monk in the camp fashioned the crosier. A Russian communist "designed and executed a beautiful ring, and the silk for the vestments, pilfered by the SS from Jewish merchants in Warsaw." A young lady (her alias was Madi), who had lived at a convent nearby and who had already established herself as a regular at the camp sent by the Mother Superior "to buy seeds from the camp spice plantation," soon became a courier between Barracks 26 and Cardinal Faulhauber in Munich. Once all the materials were gathered and the ordination began, a Jewish prisoner played his violin to distract the Nazi guards. Such accounts of inspiring, collaborative, multifaith solidarity should be continually retold—as should the act of Partnoy trying to distract the Little School guard from battering Benja or Gyatso praying for the woman about to be executed. These stories may not extinguish the evil that surrounds them, but the fact that hope and light are present, and at times potent and bright, must be remembered. In our obligation to remember rightfully[72] the victims, such stories must be told. The life and death of Christ is one such story.

EMPHASIZING CHRIST AS VICTIM

In this chapter's final section, I will reflect upon a crucial step for any Christian theodicy: recognizing Jesus of Nazareth as a fellow victim in solidarity with the poor and oppressed. A fundamental issue is how and whether such analysis is relevant to non-Christians, particularly those who have suffered gross injustice.

Like Malham's account above, the gospels, though including the words of Christ, are also interpretations of his life and words, and so

72. See Volf, *End of Memory*, 11–16.

there is an additional step in the depiction and mediation of the horrific, raw events. As Martin Marty writes: "Not exactly biographies or histories, the gospels are narrative testimonies to what the early communities cherished and wanted preserved."[73] Nevertheless, the accounts of Jesus's life can still serve as his testimony, though one must take into account that unlike Partnoy, or Gyatso (who was also aided by a writer), Jesus did not write these gospels.[74]

My reflection is predominantly a means to examine further Gyatso's statement above: "I realized that all subjugated people share the common experience of bruised bodies, scattered lives and broken families."[75] If Christ's life attests to this solidarity with the suffering because he himself suffered, then the Christian's belief that this victim was God necessarily has a great and profound impact on any theodic attempt. Christ as redeemer will also be a reoccurring theme in later chapters of this work.

We do not know much of Jesus's early life,[76] but two details, though historically debated, offer tantalizing insights. First, Jesus's anticipated birth occasions the massacre of the innocents.[77] Thus, his life is marked from the outset by trauma, suffering, and mass atrocity. Secondly, if Jesus's family had to abscond for Egypt, and if he spent his early years there, then his status as an alien and refugee in a foreign land and the usual problems and hardships that arise from that situation resonates with many millions of refugees today and can be imaginatively constructed.[78]

While there were certainly moments of joy and insight in Jesus's life,[79] his ministry—not simply its egregious and embarrassing "end" on

73. Marty, *Christian World*, 5.

74. One thus has to trust that the traditions behind these stories are faithful to Jesus's original words or actions. See Cook, *Modern Jews Engage New Testament*, 49–57.

75. Gyatso, *Fire*, Prologue.

76. We also know little of Joseph and Mary's economic status save to interpret they were not affluent—and were possibly poor—if judged by their offering of the pair of turtledoves or two young pigeons (instead of a lamb) at Jesus's presentation in the temple (Luke 2:24, Lev 12:8), and Luke's version of Jesus's birth in a manger (2:7)—if they had money, room would have been found. For an illuminating interpretation of the birth narrative, see Bailey, *Jesus through Middle Eastern Eyes*, 25–37.

77. Matt 2:16–18. See also Bailey, *Jesus through Middle Eastern Eyes*, 56–59.

78. Matt 2:13. See also Senior, "Beloved Aliens and Exiles," 23.

79. Mark 5:24–34; Mark 15:40; Mark 10:13; Luke 19.

the cross—was fraught with failure and pain. He is surrounded by an inner core of disciples who remain utterly dumbfounded and oblivious to his mission and purpose. A moment of insight—"You are the Messiah"[80]—is immediately followed by "Get behind me, Satan!"[81] or the disciples' arguing among themselves as to who was the greatest.[82] At Gethsemane, his disciples' metaphorical blindness and their inability to stay awake had to be a sharp pain and disappointment for Jesus.[83]

Who is Jesus's real, intimate human connection in Mark's Gospel, for example? It is not his mother,[84] and there is no beloved disciple,[85] as there is in John (whether such a figure is John, Mary Magdalene, or some other). He seems isolated and alone, possibly only at peace when he tries to pray—which is often interrupted: "Now many saw them going and recognized them, and they hurried there on foot from all the towns and arrived ahead of them."[86]

From the murder of John the Baptist[87] to Jesus's cognizance of the Roman oppression of his people,[88] particularly the poor and the outcast, as evinced in his healing and table fellowship with the lepers, the lame, and prostitutes,[89] Jesus was not shielded from the misery and suffering of others but seemed to incorporate their ills into himself, or at the least, comfort those he could. This last seemingly innocuous statement has to be developed further: the gospels only reveal a few individuals who were healed. While there were other stories not told, he did not save everyone. With his own eyes, he saw desperate children, some perhaps malformed in some way, begging or abandoned; he heard the calls of the leper; he smelled the rank stench that alienation and poverty could bring.[90] He lived in a world where life expectancy was low, in a land of occupation, on the cusp of the destruction of the temple, of food short-

---

80. Mark 8:29.

81. Mark 8:33.

82. Mark 9:33.

83. Mark 14:40.

84. Mark 3:31–34.

85. There is much speculation, of course, as to who the "young man" is (Mark 16:5). See Myers, *Binding the Strong Man*, 397–99.

86. Mark 6:34–44; Mark 7:24.

87. Mark 6:14–29.

88. Mark 5:1–20.

89. Mark 2:16.

90. See the story of Legion: Mark 5:1–20.

ages and failed revolutions. While Paul could proclaim that through Christ, one can say, "Where, O death, is your Sting?"[91] the death of others stung Christ bitterly, as evinced in his weeping over Lazarus.[92] The failure to convince the majority in the Bread of Life discourse—"Do you also wish to go away?"[93]—may be the real culmination of his failure, a biting sense of loss. While the disciples remain—"Lord, to whom can we go? You have the words of eternal life"[94] (comfort and assurance indeed in that magnificent phrase)—the subsequent suffering of Jesus continues to reverberate through the ages: his betrayal by one of his own; his abandonment by nearly all of his followers save the women (and John); his own inner doubts in Gethsemane; the mocking; the insults; the spitting; the hitting; the slapping; the whipping; the scourging at the pillar; the piercing of the crown of thorns; the humiliation before the crowd; their choosing Barabbas; the carrying of the wooden cross; the heat that bore down on him; more insults and taunts; the falls—one, two, three times; aching of the legs and back and arms; sweat that burned the eyes; blood that trickled; the pounding of nails in the flesh; the crucifixion; the asphyxiation; more taunts and insults; the jeering; the sense, the *fear*, of abandonment on the cross—all dependent on how one reads those words from Psalm 22: "My God, my God, / Why have you abandoned me . . .?" In short, one can argue that the Incarnation of God did not end in suffering but incorporated suffering throughout Jesus's earthly ministry except for brief respites.

In Part 2, we will see how Christian theodicists argue why Christ is the answer to the problem of evil. Such a claim must be examined in the presence of the burning children, in the face of the holy but mercilessly tortured Tibetan monk, and in the example of the inspiring atheist who is beaten for striving to give all of us a more free and hopeful world. We thus await how these Christian theodicists portray Christ and how and whether they connect his suffering to others, particularly, non-Christians.

91. 1 Cor 15:55.
92. John 11:35.
93. John 6:66–67.
94. John 6:68–69.

CONCLUSION: IMAGINING THE OTHER

Regarding the value of literature, Amos Oz writes: "I believe that books that make us imagine the other, may turn us more immune to the ploys of the devil, including the inner devil, the Mephisto of the heart . . . Imagining the other is not only an aesthetic tool. It is, in my view, also a major moral imperative."[95]

These testimonies provide similar benefits. They are dangerous texts. They disturb and provoke and contain truths that can render the entire world fragile, amorphous, meaningless. Their voices are warnings that must be heeded; cacophonous screams that must be endured; voices that can instill doubt, questioning, and disquietude within almost any theological statement or belief. They are the specters hovering over every prayer and religious hope. They are the voices that are too often ignored, manipulated, or censored.

Theology, ethics, and spirituality can only benefit from sustained immersion with these texts, as they can be a catalyst for catharsis, a grounding in humility, and a means of reflection and self-analysis. For my purposes, they are a crucial resource to test and hone theodic and theological arguments and statements. And of course, a theodicist does not just imagine the Other, but *the* Other, the God who is said to create, love, and sustain us. It is imagining *par excellence*. Most of these testimonies—perhaps even ones sprinkled with an optimistic or hagiographic aura—hover about (and within) us. But it is the desultory depictions that we should most fear, whose potential may remain buried within us, only awaiting a circumstance (or pretext) for our reenacting them. This not-knowing demands honest, humble reflection and a just response.

And so, some voices who have experienced evil and suffering have testified. They have presented the truth of what they have seen. Are there any issues or questions asked here that a theologian is not able—or is ill-advised—to answer? Is there a specific theodic tradition that best reaches an answer? What are the values and the dangers of insisting on a specifically Christian theodicy? These and similar questions will be addressed in Part 2.

---

95. Oz, "Devil's Progress," 4–5; see also Pinker, *Better Angels*, 177.

PART 2

Theodicy amidst Doubt, Despair, and Destruction

"But the little sticky leaves, and the precious tombs and the blue sky, and the woman you love! How will you live? How will you love them?" Alyosha asked sorrowfully. "With such a hell in your heart, how can you?"[1]

In Part 2 I will present and analyze a select number of theodic and antitheodic attempts chosen from what I will contend are three essential fields for a Christian theodicist to draw from: Catholic Latin American liberation theology, post-Shoah Jewish theology, and Christian philosophical theodicy. Liberation theology's preferential option for the poor is a means to ensure that theology is centered on the marginalized and voiceless so that promoting the dignity of every human person, formed in the image and likeness of God, is a goal and presupposition. These aims share a great affinity with my project to include the voices of mass atrocity in any theodic attempt.

I turn to Jewish post-Shoah theology for three reasons: First, while Christians are culpable of a wide range of historical atrocities, the Holocaust is in many ways a culmination not only of an anti-Judaic bias and cancer within some of Christianity's key theological dogma and practitioners, but of Christianity's pervasive failure historically and doctrinally to embrace and love the Other. Tragically, Jesus's parable of the Good Samaritan, or even his grudging acceptance of the

1. Dostoyevsky, *Brothers Karamazov*, 256.

63

Syrophoenician woman, has largely fallen on Christian deaf ears. For my purposes, honest reflective study of Jewish post-Shoah thinkers will force a Christian theodicist to examine Christianity's complicity in evil and injustice, thus tempering any possibility for triumphant or self-righteous theodic language. Second, while not every aspect or interpretation of Jewish post-Shoah theology is applicable for Christians, its explicit focus on the tenability of belief in God amidst the devastating evils of the Holocaust stipulates that difficult questions are not avoided. My turning to testimonies of mass atrocity is to place Christian theodicists in a similar predicament, asking what it means to be a Christian theist in light of such mass atrocities. Thirdly, I believe that Christians need to study, listen, and learn from the entire Jewish faith and tradition, not only to overcome prejudice and bias in order to see that religion more clearly and honestly, but to have a greater understanding of how Christianity's own traditions developed in light of its original Jewish roots, the practices or traditions unfortunately lost, and any new, or recovered insights that Christianity has helped preserve.[2]

Philosophy of religion, despite some of its deserved criticisms, which I will treat, is an important discipline to test the rational and logical strengths of various theodic beliefs. Note that I have called this section "Christian Philosophical Theodicy" to acknowledge the fusion of theology and philosophy in early and medieval Christian thought and the reemergence of such a fusion in some contemporary figures. David Burrell has written that "the term 'philosphical theology' embraces many of the issues once considered under 'natural theology,' but with less concern to distinguish between the sources—reason or revelation—and no specific apologetic intent."[3] This is helpful, though the works of John Paul II and McCord Adams do not lack an apologetic tone, which is why John Paul II more often refers to Christian philosophy. Regardless of the exact term used, the line demarcating

---

2. In Bruteau, ed., *Jesus through Jewish Eyes,* a number of Jewish rabbis and scholars examine the life and thought of Jesus and contend that many Jewish people would benefit from studying the Gospels and the life of their ancient brother. A similar argument is made in Kogan, *Opening the Covenant.* See also Berger and Patterson, *Jewish-Christian Dialogue.* For my analysis of these works in the context of inter-religious dialogue, see my "The Other as Oneself within Judaism," 113–24.

3. Burrell, *Knowing the Unknowable God,* 10.

certain thinkers, historical periods, or academic disciplines is rarely tidy. This entire work is immersed in similar hybridity.

While I focus on three contemporary thinkers whose arguments and aims are quite distinct, they all are working within what I would call the shadow of the Christian tradition, so that, even if their own faiths are very different, foundational Christian thinkers and themes loom large.

The authors chosen are immersed in our contemporary age, writing in the context of a post-Holocaust perspective, and so should have in mind the experiences of a Nomberg-Przytyk or Little Eleanora. To repeat: the aim in Part 2 (barring a theodicy sufficiently adequate on its own) is for a close critique of texts within these diverse and stimulating fields—crossing boundaries of academic and religious spheres—to identify the most useful features that a Christian theodicy needs to incorporate to be sufficiently viable and pastorally meaningful.

Section 1

Christian Philosophical Theodicy:
In the Shadow of Christian Tradition

If He who in Himself can lack nothing chooses to need us, it is because we need to be needed.[1]

This section will focus on three texts grouped under the flexible heading of Christian Philosophical Theodicy. The first text I will analyze will be an antitheodicy, D. Z. Phillips's *The Problem of Evil and the Problem of God*, a challenging and moving work, with its dual, seemingly paradoxical components. The first part is written by a Wittgensteinian philosopher who highlights the failures of theodicy, while the end of the work echoes a religious mystic's outlook by advocating life as sacrifice and grace.

The second text will be Pope John Paul II's *Salvifici Doloris,* called "the first official Roman Catholic document that specifically treats the subject of suffering."[2] Like the text that follows it, I include John Paul II here as a contemporary figure who sought to bridge theology and philosophy. As Eduardo Echeverria writes: "The Pope not only accepts the concept of Christian philosophy as legitimate, but also boldly urges us to develop what he explicitly calls 'Christian philosophy.'"[3] In *Salvifici Doloris,* he will argue that the life, suffering, and redemption of Christ gives a salvific character unto suffering and opens the way

---

1. Lewis, *Problem of Pain*, 44.

2. Weinandy, *Does God Suffer?* 243.

3. Echeverria, "Gospel of Redemptive Suffering," 113. See also Kerr, *Twentieth-Century Catholic Theologians*, 163–82.

for individuals to respond to suffering as a means to participate in Christ's saving work and redemption.

Marilyn McCord Adams's *Horrendous Evils and the Goodness of God* also seeks to blur "the boundary between theology and philosophy."[4] In particular, she will argue for a God who has the creativity, imagination, and power to defeat all potential life-defeating horrors. According to McCord Adams, God will convince every individual that their lives were good and valuable on the whole. From what we have encountered through witness testimonies, this will be a crucial but almost insurmountable task.

---

4. McCord Adams writes: ". . . [M]y strategy for dealing with horrendous evils carries the corollary consequences of blurring the boundary between philosophy and theology and consequently between the roles of philosophers of religion, Christian philosophers, and philosophical theologians as well" (*Horrendous*, 206).

3

Phillips's Theism without Theodicy

If I was God, I would spit at Kuhn's prayer.[1]

I begin Part 2 with an antitheodicy. D. Z. Phillips rejects theodicy for its tendency to justify the unjustifiable.[2] He therefore aims to expose the faulty logic within various theodic arguments and contends (contra theodicists) that this life contains no sufficient order or rationale and that belief in an afterlife context for healing is "unintelligible."[3] Phillips's work will serve as a foil to subsequent theodic attempts in other chapters and will establish the type of arguments a theodicy will need to counter.

A brief note on Phillips: while a member of the Welsh Congregational Church, Phillips notoriously and enigmatically eschewed any intermingling of his personal belief into his philosophical writings. This chapter, then, assesses the argument within *The Problem of Evil and the Problem of God*. It does not enter into the muddle of what Phillips may have actually believed when not enacting the role of a philosopher.

While sharing many convictions with Partnoy and Nomberg-Przytyk, Phillips's work will also seem to agree with Greenberg's working principle, and so will contend to be a rational response to

1. Levi, *Survival in Auschwitz*, 130.

2. Phillips, *Problem of Evil*, xi.

3. Ibid., 85.

the problem of evil that still posits "meaning" and "God." The issue though is what type of God and meaning are conveyed.

THE FAILURE OF GOD AS A FELLOW MORAL AGENT

Phillips builds many of his criticisms of theodic arguments by highlighting the logical weaknesses of the premise (shared by some philosophers of religion) that God is a "moral agent who shares a moral community with us."[4] Holding such a premise requires that judgments of actions by human beings and the rationale behind them must be consistent when speaking of, and judging, God. Contra Phillips and McCord Adams, I want to maintain belief in a morally good God without sharing the erroneous presuppositions of many of Phillips's interlocutors who downplay the still-developing notions of human moral goodness reflected in the perfect moral goodness of God. In short, there is scant theological basis to limit God to a "fellow" human being, as if humanity and God are on an equal, ontological plane[5] and God is not transcendent as well as immanent.

Opposing the claim of moral goodness in God (as Adams and Brian Davies do) also has major pastoral repercussions for theodicy. While getting mired in the specifics of Phillips's argument here would lead me too far from my aims,[6] I will instead save the need for a morally good God when we encounter McCord Adams's claims in chapter 5. I will focus now on Phillips's analysis of divine goodness and omnipotence, his critique of redemption and the afterlife, and his support of a "disinterested faith" position, which views life as a grace and gift.

---

4. Ibid., 35.

5. As Aquinas also adds, what we say of God falls between what is univocal and equivocal. There is enough similarity to prevent comparisons being utterly opposed (equivocal) but the differences of our nature prevent statements referring to God and human beings to be taken in exactly the same sense. See Aquinas, "One Way of Understanding God Talk," 162–64; Davies, "Introduction [to The Problem of God Talk]," 135–40.

6. One of Phillips's aims is to employ words in their ordinary and not metaphysical use and so draws heavily on Wittgenstein where a word's meaning is dependent upon agreed-upon symbols and context in what is often called a language game (see Phillips, *Problem of Evil*, 9, and Wittgenstein's use of the word *slab* in Lycan, "'Use Theories,'" 92). Also note there is some disagreement as to whether Phillips's contention of a distinctive language-game of religion was ever clearly advocated by Wittgenstein. See Addis, "D. Z. Phillips's Fideism," 85–98.

God's Imperfect Goodness

According to Phillips, to maintain God's perfect goodness based on the premise that God is a fellow moral member of our community, one must claim that God "can only act freely with respect to any virtuous activity if God has within him the power to do its opposite."[7] Thus, if God "helps the innocent, he has it in his power not to do so."[8]

Remaining within the conceptual parameters of Phillips's protagonists inevitably results in a God who cannot be considered perfectly good or who cannot "exhibit the natural goodness we find, sometimes, in human beings."[9] In the latter example, Phillips includes the story of the Good Samaritan and claims that to leave the dying man was simply unthinkable to the Good Samaritan, which means he did not have the power within him to do otherwise.[10] Such a pure response to another's suffering would not be applicable of God if God must always have the possibility of refraining from committing a good act for that act to be morally good. If one removes this possibility, then Phillips claims a standard justification that evil is needed for there to be good subsequently fails. Moreover, if one maintains the above parameters for a free act to occur, then saying God allowed the evil with a second thought (i.e., of regret) ascribes evil to God in allowing the act, and if God had no second thought, then God is callous.[11] Otherwise, God is not omnipotent.

For Phillips, these arguments not only debunk the proposition that God is perfect goodness, but also highlight the problem of theodicy: the ends do not justify the means.[12] Even if all evil were somehow redeemed, or if we had to suffer in this world in order for good to be achieved, we could no longer maintain God's perfect goodness. What, for example, would we say of fellow humans who claim to allow an evil like the Shoah for some purported greater good?[13] Using our ethical and moral judgments against a human in a similar situation should

---

7. Phillips, *Problem of Evil*, 27.

8. Ibid., 27.

9. Ibid., 32.

10. Ibid., 32–33.

11. Ibid., 41.

12. Ibid., 46.

13. See Maybaum, *Ignaz Maybaum*, 156–57, 165, and 173; Katz, "Crucifixion of the Jews," 595.

not be altered if the principal actor is God. But if God is no longer Perfect Goodness, then God is flawed or becomes a mixture of good and evil. Thus, we have to maintain God's Perfect Goodness if such a God is still to be believed in, but we are still left with the magnitude of evil that challenges a theodicist's use of the term *omnipotent*. What type of God, then, does Phillips leave us with?

The Limitations of Omnipotence I

To avoid the conceptual trouble noted above, Phillips clarifies that we should not say that "God's will (understood as 'all power') is the grammar of God's nature, we should say that God's nature (in a sense of 'perfect goodness' yet to be explored) is the grammar of God's will."[14] This has some resonance with Aquinas, who writes: "[W]ith God, however, substance and power and understanding and willing and wisdom and justice are all identical. Therefore nothing can be within divine power which is not held in the wisdom and justice of his mind and will."[15] Phillips's pithy phrase, however, still maintains distinctions "within" God that Aquinas would not support (such as Phillips's conception of omnipotence[16]). While Phillips succinctly writes, "the only omnipotence God has is the omnipotence of love,"[17] his interpretation of the phrase has dire consequences, particularly in claiming that this love is powerless to resurrect people from the dead or heal any wrongs in an afterlife context. More specifically, he is adamant that

---

14. Phillips, *Problem of Evil*, 33.

15. Aquinas, "Why Think of God as Omnipotent?" 421. See also McCabe, *God and Evil*, 59.

16. Phillips erroneously follows Mackie's argument that those who do not assert that omnipotence means God can do anything, "depart from the traditional meaning of 'omnipotence'" (7). He then claims his protagonists fail to limit their discussion of divine omnipotence to a religious context, thus allowing someone to envision bodily acts that can be described without contradiction according to the traditional concept of God that God could not do (*Problem of Evil*, 12). The issue would seem to be resolved, however, if one turns to Aquinas, who writes: "things involving deficiencies or bodily changes are irrelevant, since ability to do such things is non-ability in God" and so would not be applicable to God being omnipotent. See Aquinas, *Selected Philosophical Writings*, 249. I will return to the issue of God's omnipotence in the section titled "The Limitations of Omnipotence II" in ch. 10.

17. Phillips, *Problem of Evil*, 272.

God could not "provide" these (supposedly) risen bodies "with the right memories."[18]

The (Guilty) God that Remains—A Purifying Atheism

By emphasizing that God cannot be a member of our moral community and still be absolved with inscrutable ways,[19] Phillips shares much affinity with Alicia Partnoy's remarks about the uselessness of martyrdom. In fact, he states that the God we are left with is not fit to plead his case.[20] He remarks that if "intellectually, at best, the divine is indifferent to us, we can afford to be equally indifferent to the divine."[21] He also contends that we cannot speak of a covenant ("understood in contractual terms")[22] with God because God is not an agent among agents. The covenantal partnership infused in the Hebrew and Christian Scriptures is therefore denied. Lastly, he also denies the possibility of God as pure consciousness because "there is nothing for God to be"[23]—God is not embodied. He calls his approach "a purifying atheism,"[24] which radically moves beyond any traditional, personal conception of God to a type of secular humanism.

THE REMNANT OF FAITH

From Purity of Atheism to Living in and through Grace

If Phillips's work concluded with purifying atheism, this would be an atheist's manifesto that demolished any attempt to speak about God, to God, for God, or of God. But just as Phillips brings us to a bottomless abyss, he reconstructs a spiritual possibility latent within all of us. This possibility renders the opportunity for an authentic life and response to the gift of life given to all. He identifies, but does not limit, his response within a Christian conception of human life, "that avoids

---

18. Ibid., 89. I instead agree with Aquinas' emphasis on the perfect unity within God so that God's being is identical with God's willing, understanding, power, and so on. In this sense, God is not tempted or able to do evil because there is no disunity or potential conflict between God's will and being.

19. Ibid., 122.

20. Ibid., 126.

21. Ibid., 130.

22. Ibid., 148.

23. Ibid., 156.

24. Ibid., 128.

the pitfalls of theodicy, but, at the same time, shows the possibility of a response to the contingencies of life that is other than celebration of the terrible, or a rebellious response to a God of caprice. It will involve showing how belief in a God of grace is possible."[25]

The Dying of the I

Turning to the writings of Simone Weil, Phillips advocates the dying of the I, as "suffering teaches us we are nothing, to recognize that one is not the center of the universe."[26] The question of course is, Why should one follow this seemingly Eckhartian sense of a denial of the self when the traditional motives of belief in God seem to have been swept away? For Phillips, however, debunking the flawed motivations and faulty conceptions of God are precisely what needs to be over-come: "In the religious response I am talking of, there is a requirement to love the fact that God has given life with its contingencies to human beings. This love is gratitude for existence."[27] We cannot link evil with God, he continues, because creation "was not an act of power and con-trol. God is seen as over against the world that is non-God, including human life. As such, in the granting of radical freedom to 'the other,' the essence of the Godhead is seen as a renunciation of possessiveness, a renunciation of the desire to control."[28]

According to Phillips, God's renunciation of control in creation and as later manifested at Calvary are pure examples of such self-sacrifice and detachment. This sacrifice, "in religious terms," strives for the dying of the "I" to become "a vehicle of grace"—which is not

---

25. Ibid., 141.

26. Ibid., 183. For an alternative reading of Weil, see Levinas, *Difficult Freedom*, 133–41. When reading the similarly provocative writings of Weil, affliction can sometimes seem raised to a level of meaningfulness and necessity. In Weil's defense, she is clear that such affliction should not be sought (*Simone Weil Reader*, 442). A key question for me is whether the radical detachment Weil and Phillips advocate—"We should ask nothing with regard to circumstances unless it be that they may conform to the will of God. We should not ask for earthly bread" (ibid., 496)—is crucial for a theodic position. Ultimately, radical detachment is a travesty against a God who has created this world for the goodness of all (especially humanity) and so calls all of us to enjoy the beauty and joys of life and to protest and strive against forms of injustice and affliction that continue to proliferate. See my second criterion for a viable theodicy in ch. 12.

27. Phillips, *Problem of Evil*, 184.

28. Ibid., 185.

the utter renunciation of the self (a complete dying would be a perfect love)—but paradoxically, a love of God that exemplifies the fulfillment and essence of what it means to be human. Rooted in disinterested religion, one's relationship with God in this light can be thought of as an eternal covenant because the relationship does not depend on what happens to an individual in this life.[29] The "acceptance of this grace in the soul involves a dying to the self. To see oneself as nothing, and grace as everything, is pure love of God. That is what loving God amounts to."[30] Here God is linked with love and grace and one participates in this love of God by accepting life for what it is and striving to embody this love for others.[31]

Life, for Phillips, is comprised of random violence and misery alongside times of goodness and beauty. We can see, therefore, why Phillips, seemingly embodying the language of a religious mystic, advocates self-denial. Certainly, the gospels are permeated with the language of renunciation: "If any want to become my followers, let them deny themselves and take up their cross, and follow me"[32]; and the more striking: "You lack one thing; go, sell what you own, and give the money to the poor, and you will have treasure in heaven; then come, follow me."[33] Phillips is simply echoing the more mystical and radical

29. See the dialogue between Levinas and Bishop Hemmerle in *In the Time of Nations*, 148–50. While Bishop Hemmerle stresses Jesus's kenotic love and defenselessness, Levinas responds that in the context of the Shoah, ". . . [K]enosis of powerlessness costs man too much! Christ without defense on the cross eventually found himself leading the armies of the Crusades! And he did not come down from the cross to stop the murderers" (150).

While Levinas's challenge is acute—and echoes one of the criminals crucified with Jesus (Luke 23:32)—I echo here what Moltmann writes (in response to Masao Abe's karmic interpretation of Auschwitz), ". . . I must see [the events of Auschwitz] from the point of view of God's justice. Then, on the one hand, I see a burden of guilt which can not be carried; and on the other hand, I see the God who will not allow the murderers to triumph over their victims" ("God Is Unselfish Love," 123). I will examine this issue further in ch. 10. Note that while many Christians will stress that judgment will come, Levinas's questioning of the kenosis of Christ leads to another question: in the light of the Shoah, will such justice come too late?

30. Phillips, *Problem of Evil*, 187.

31. Ibid., 183.

32. Mark 8:34.

33. Mark 10:21. The second quote as told to the rich man truly silences most of us, enmeshed in dramatic callings like the story of a St. Francis or St. Anthony, and puts many first-world concerns in perspective. The worst thing to be done with a quote like this is to succor the conscience by speaking of spiritual riches or say

elements within religion. Thus, the philosopher who seemed to gainsay any relation with God—or any means of conceiving of God—now seems to resonate with a Christian mystic like Catherine of Sienna, who writes: "Her beginning and end should be in the love of charity, and in this charity she should accept pleasure and its absence in terms of my will rather than her own. This is the way to avoid delusion and to receive all things in love from me."[34]

This delusion is also what Phillips seeks to prevent. If life is grace, and life is the beauty of the sticky leaves in spring but also the pain and suffering that can invade at any time—then acceptance of such a life given by God can become the means of a relationship with God. Loving God for the sake of God and nothing else is key. We are to die to expectations, for God is love. What still remains unclear is how life was a gift to those like Little Eleanora, who died in the gulag before she was two years of age, and what are the consequences of saying God is "seen as over against" human life?

Witness in Extremis

In regards to the first question above, Phillips turns briefly to survivors of the Holocaust (particularly Wiesel) to examine how they viewed faith and God to assess if the faith and concepts he has been writing about can still hold under such horrific situations. This is an admirable attempt to be true to his original aim in the beginning of the work. After analyzing Victor Frankl's contention that one could make moral choices even in the camps, along with Lawrence Langer's emphasis on choiceless choices, Phillips writes: "what we need is not a new language, different from our 'free' one, but a faithful depiction of the place of 'the unthinkable' in human experience. This can be done if the extremities of evil suffered are . . . allowed to be their horrendous selves."[35]

By juxtaposing Frankl and Langer and refusing to provide any one path, Phillips is acknowledging that from the vantage point of the sufferer, both conceptions may be equally affirmed: "One is conscious

---

this is not meant for everyone. Like all failings in faith one must confront, this is an especially important one.

34. Catherine of Sienna, *Dialogue*, 129–30.

35. Phillips, *Problem of Evil*, 206. Note his disagreement with Langer, who states that victims need a new language, as cited in ch. 1.

of walking on a tightrope. One is in constant danger of falling off."[36] Here, multiple truths exist, and there seems to be no ethical, lucid way to disentangle truth from falsity or the moral from the immoral. No ultimate good seems to transcend the concept of morality in the camps. Moreover, there is also no afterlife or hope for redemption for Phillips, although he wants to affirm the possibility that God is love.[37] I still need, however, to analyze what encompasses this love and how it is embodied by God in creating a world where the Holocaust is a reality that can never be justified and its suffering ever redeemed.[38]

Where Angels Fear to Tread

Because Phillips opposes arguments that contend that the afterlife context can heal or that try to justify the occurrence of atrocious suffering in this life, he asks: "What can be said from the perspective of eternity, of those who have been crushed by life's circumstances? Whatever is said *must respect the historical particularity of the lives concerned.*"[39] He is situating himself in the specific and the concrete by testing the logic of theodicy as it is applied to the distinctive horrendous evils suffered by individuals like Gyatso and Little Eleanora. Rejecting the possibility for any satisfactory redemption or healing, Phillips still, however, maintains the possibility for meaning. Because of belief in God, he writes, "the significance [of what has happened to the afflicted] is still exalted, raised on high. That is the judgment of eternity on these completed lives."[40] Phillips is claiming, therefore, that a God of love creates life as a gift, though for some this gift may be nothing but horror and suffering. The only potential "salve" is to know that such a God has renounced the power to control and will listen and "judge" such lives in eternity. Why, then, does Phillips reject any possibility of an afterlife but still maintain theism?

---

36. Phillips, *Problem of Evil*, 217.
37. Ibid., 216.
38. Ibid., 217.
39. Ibid., 270.
40. Ibid., 273.

Why Memory Minimizes the Beatific Vision

Phillips asserts that with the death of a body comes the final death of a particular self. There is no afterlife. Nevertheless, he wants to reveal further "logical difficulties *within* the general charge of unintelligibility" of afterlife conceptions and so spends considerable time on themes and ideas normally dealt with under eschatology or soteriology.[41] Phillips does not believe God can provide the resurrected body with what had been the memories of the earthly one (again based on the sense that this new body is different from the deceased one).[42]

Phillips also contends that when theologians refer to a transformation of the self in heaven, or a development of a deeper self, he does not know what this "deeper being" means but insists "it is not a human being."[43] He writes: "[W]hat can be said of human lives, from the perspective of eternity, cannot bypass the particularity of those lives."[44] He can, therefore, find no logical argument (he cites McCord Adams's position, in particular) to explain how individuals who have been crushed by life will be healed.[45] He also cannot comprehend what our postmortem development would entail or how the language of compensation would make any sense in some type of postmortem existence. In the latter example, he argues that just as we recognize that some losses, like the death of a child, cannot be compensated for in this world, the same judgment would apply if we altered the scene to a heavenly one.[46]

Writing about the part of a Holocaust survivor's self that seemed to die in the concentration camps, Lawrence Langer has argued similarly: "The quest for a rebirth of that part of the self is as futile as would be any effort to transform Hannah F.'s pile of corpses [murdered in the camps] into a sacred community of the dead. This may be a dark view, but there is overwhelming evidence from Holocaust narratives that it is a realistic one, from which we have much to learn."[47] Here Phillips and Langer are clear that seeking meaning, hope, or any grounds for

41. Ibid., 85.
42. Ibid., 89.
43. Ibid., 88.
44. Ibid., 272.
45. Ibid., 271.
46. Ibid., 86.
47. Langer, *Using and Abusing the Holocaust*, 4–5.

redemption when reflecting on atrocities like the Holocaust is to ignore the evidence. Such "proof" should obviously impact the possibility for a viable theodicy. And yet, while Langer speaks of "overwhelming evidence," we (and he) still need to grapple further with survivors who testify to opposite "evidence," what Langer above calls "a genuine form of chiaroscuro."[48] Olga Lengyl, for example, writes: "The Nazis succeeded in degrading [the inmates] physically, but they could not debase them morally. Because of these few, I have not entirely lost my faith in mankind,"[49] while Soon Ok Lee, who endured malicious torture at the hands of Korean Communist officials, still could claim: "Even now as I look back, I see where God led me and the miracles he did on my behalf."[50] Such positions do not expunge the reality of that pile of naked corpses in the winter snow that Hannah F. witnessed, but in trying to highlight the "overwhelming evidence" that many of us may not want to hear, we cannot then be too quick to dismiss or ignore the "evidence" that many of us want to hear: that redemption is possible, that God has not abandoned God's people, that the murder and mutilation inflicted or permitted by many does not thereby sully any possibility to speak of inherent goodness or a purpose and meaning within this life. Such positive possibilities should also impact the question of redemption in an afterlife context.

Phillips, however, also argues that theodicists have failed to articulate how redemption occurs or what development means in a postmortem context if the relationships we have in this world by which our character and moral life are framed do not transfer into the next life.[51] This issue of postmortem identities surviving the death of our bodies is clearly the lynchpin of his arguments against afterlife conceptions.

Most importantly, Phillips is right to want to know more about this "changed" being in heaven, an issue I will discuss in depth in chapter 11 when I analyze universal salvation. However, if one acknowledges individual epiphanies in this world, some of which can be quite radical (think of Ishmael Beah as a normal child, a child soldier, and then a rehabilitated activist and student), it is not illogical to imagine

48. Langer, *Holocaust Testimonies*, 36.

49. Lengyl, *Five Chimneys*, 229.

50. Lee, *Eyes of the Tailless Animals*, 9.

51. Phillips, *Problem of Evil*, 88.

a similar change without sacrificing one's core identity in the afterlife. If our distinctive relationships with some individuals are no longer operable and individual quirks and personalities are all made identical in heaven, then Phillips's reservation may be correct. However, based on acknowledging a God who has created such diversity in this life, it seems unlikely that the afterlife will be a ceaseless drone of homogeneity and monotony. Christians of course also point to the resurrected Christ to overcome many of these issues. The resurrected Christ still bore his wounds. While changed, he could still be recognized in the breaking of the bread.[52]

Moreover, if God created the world and gives us the grace to accept this life as a gift, what, according to Phillips, is God's relationship to the totality of our lives after we no longer exist? In addition, why describe a creator God who grants us this grace to view life with compassion, but is unable to raise us from the dead? Atheism seems to be a more reasonable option than this halfway position.

ASSESSMENT: A LISTENING GOD

"Nearer than anyone," Philips writes in regard to the lived sufferings of human beings and their cries, "God listens."[53] Phillips says no more of what God does. He writes: "Those who are crushed by life's afflictions are not going to enter a state where all this is to be put to right. That is to seek an outcome rather than the judgment of eternity. In that judgment, their story, which cannot be taken from them, is exalted, raised on high for all eternity, even if it is a story they cannot tell themselves."[54]

While this may be a consolation for the stoical few in this life, with the annihilation of the self one may also ask whether this remembering or listening matters. The God Phillips leaves us with is rendered into a divine memorial for the dead that no one ever visits to learn what was commemorated. This may prove everything was for God, but then one is still left wondering exactly what type of gift life is, especially for victims of atrocities and horrific sufferings in this life, as seen with Benja being tortured and executed in *The Little School*. Based on the events of this world, Phillips can only posit a loving God

---

52. John 21:13.

53. Phillips, *Problem of Evil*, 273.

54. Ibid., 273.

seemingly helpless to redeem or heal evils, whose power of love creates life and bequeaths the gift to view life as a gift, but little more. Why one must be grateful to such a God is never adequately developed. Nor is it entirely clear what is involved in one's story being "exalted, raised on high" in the judgment of eternity.

Phillips refers to "raising" in terms of Christ's resurrection and Kierkegaard's assertion that "eternity" is a spiritual category—that "raising up" is not referring to a spatial category.[55] But Jesus rose bodily into heaven. While the spatial direction of that rising is metaphorical, the bodily resurrection for Christians cannot be limited to a spiritual phenomenon. Likewise, spiritually raising up one's narrative without the individuals who embody those stories is an incomplete (if not empty) gesture of Phillips's God. While some individuals could die peacefully knowing that they served God and lived their lives as appreciation for the gift of life, there is little such comfort for the forsaken of this world, nor sufficient reason that one can believe in God but not in the possibility for healing and redemption in an afterlife context.

Because Phillips discounts the possibility of a heavenly realm of justice and redemption, though, one can see why he refuses to engage in theodicy. In fact, for Phillips, even the death of Jesus on the cross should not be justified or instrumentalized, even "*in order to* show us what love of God is. Once this is allowed, compassion for human life becomes the horror story I have objected to throughout this book."[56] Fighting instrumentalism is valid, but destroying any hope for healing seems asphyxiating. While Phillips's argument against an afterlife certainly has philosophical and scientific support, if life ends without any reunion of the body and soul in the presence of God, then based on atrocities in this world, to speak about (let alone worship) God is basically meaningless. If there is no possibility for the lives crushed and wrecked by suffering to be redeemed, then who cares if God listens and remembers?[57] Why believe in God at all?

Phillips's position ultimately supports the worldview of Partnoy and Nomberg-Przytyk. Faith is madness. God has no involvement in our lives. We must produce our own daily bread. However, how does

55. Ibid., 272.
56. Ibid., 273.
57. Ibid., 273.

one interpret stories (like Lee's) which claim that God was present among their afflictions and thus provided the "bread" they needed to survive? Moreover, Phillips leaves open the possibility that God gives us the grace to see life as a gift, but how grace "works" in the context of Phillips's purifying atheism remains ambiguous. Grace is defined in the *Catechism of the Catholic Church*, for example, as *"favor, the free and undeserved help* that God gives us to respond to his call to become children of God, adoptive sons, partakers of the divine nature and to eternal life."[58] While some sources may distinguish types of grace, all definitions point to a relationship with God and God acting outside the contingencies and limitations of this world. If so, then because of Phillips's support of grace, the purifying atheism that he espouses seems to falter, and we are back with a personal God who cares about our well-being and intervenes and is present in this world; a God who does not simply create this world and then abandon it, but who heals and strengthens those created.

Let us return to a fundamental question: if God created this world as a gift, why cannot God also raise us from the dead and heal and redeem our sufferings? The gift implies kindness and goodness. If life should be a gift, why would God not seek to heal or correct those cases where the "gift" is a torture and a bane? Why is God credited with the creation of galaxies and neurons, dinosaurs and wasps but unable to raise human beings from the dead and maintain their unique identities? If human beings are able to help heal others in this life, then it would only seem reasonable that if God is the healer, as John Paul II and Marilyn McCord Adams argue in the next two chapters, even the worst sufferers could be healed.[59]

Furthermore, Phillips's attempt to develop what he calls a "purifying atheism" has numerous spiritual, theological, and philosophical problems. Again, not all philosophical theodicists or theologians begin at his starting point nor are they weighed down by the problems of language, as Phillips tries to convince. In addition, his proposed path is too tenuous, linking two strands of thought by such a flimsy thread that it is more realistic to argue that one can arrive at some of Phillips's conclusions—on the dying of self or the aim for an ethical

58. *Catechism,* 538 (1996).

59. For my assessment of key soteriological and eschatological features in relation to victims of mass atrocity, see ch. 11.

life—without Christianity, or through the traditional access of an Augustine or Aquinas and so maintain a personal God who will judge and redeem humanity.

More problematically, *The Problem of Evil and the Problem of God* has been stripped of so many elements of the Christian tradition that if it is Christian, it is a skeletal Christianity. The God depicted by Phillips is not one many would want to worship, and so by implication, no worship means no relationship with God. It is certainly a position that offers little hope to Partnoy's husband or the murdered babies of Auschwitz. Without a teleology or exposition of a soteriological dimension, without the possibility of a deeply personal God, without probing further into the purpose of creation and the meaning of Christ's life, death, and resurrection, one is ultimately left with more questions and gaps when such questions have been "answered" in Christianity and such gaps have been "filled" within Christianity's developing, dynamic tradition. Phillips wants to maintain Christ in his arguments, but I am still left wondering why.

There also is a dearth of accentuating the beauty and majesty of creation so that self-love is a proper component of this "denial." In what I would call a "healthy" Christian practice of self-denial, one still loves oneself, but any renouncing is an expression of the love of God and the love of self. One denies oneself in part based on the belief that one's calling and true expression of self is embodied in service to God and others while also ensuring one's own soul is also nourished to fortify the integrity of such a commitment. This denial of self means often sacrificing one's wants (as opposed to basic needs) and one's tendency to focus inordinately on the self. It is a call to give of one's self to the Other—both stranger and friend. This type of clarification is not sufficiently developed by Phillips.[60]

Phillips's work is useful for the provocative issues he raises, his careful deliberations on God-talk, his moral reasons for denying theodicy, and his commitment to turn to the lives and words of those suffering in extremis. His bridging of a parsing philosophical mind linked with a profoundly mystical religious orientation is precisely the type of fertile imagination needed to construct a response to evil. His emphasis on a disinterested faith stance, furthermore, cuts across

---

60. Phillips, *Problem of Evil*, 183.

many mystical religious texts, from the poems of Rumi[61] or Lao-Tzu[62] to works like *The Bhagavad-Gita*,[63] *The Dhammapada*,[64] and writings from the Jewish Kabbalist tradition.[65] Such traditions also, of course, borrow from one another. Although believing in heaven, Augustine commends this detachment in *The City of God*: "There is a further reason for the infliction of temporal suffering on the good, as is seen in the case of Job . . . that he may learn for himself what is the degree of disinterested devotion that he offers to God."[66]

God may give us the gift of grace according to Phillips, but for many, life seems more of a curse than a gift if no healing or redemption is possible. One denies oneself to further the good in the world and to establish God's reign on earth with the fervid belief that one is called to the joy and bliss of the beatific vision. Now it can be argued from a Freudian or Marxist standpoint that one should not need such grounding, but Phillips deems his account a religious one. One may meaningfully choose to be a secular humanist like Dr. Rieux in *The Plague* and help others because one feels that is the only worthwhile response.[67] But within the resources of Christianity, there are existential and teleological reasons for choosing one path over another, intertwined with one's creation in goodness in the image and likeness of God that sets forth one's purpose, existence, and end, by and through

61. "Be melting snow. / Wash yourself of yourself . . . Try and be a sheet of paper with nothing on it. / Be a spot of the ground where nothing is growing, where something might be planted, / A seed, possibly, from the Absolute" (Rumi, *Essential Rumi*, 13, 15). See also Khalidi, *Muslim Jesus*, 141.

62. "I do my utmost to obtain emptiness; / I hold firmly to stillness" (*Tao Te Ching*, 20).

63. "But if one performs prescribed action / because it must be done, / relinquishing attachment and the fruit, his relinquishment is a lucid act" (*Bhagavad-Gita*, 144).

64. "He who has no craving desires, either for this world or for another world, who free from desires is in infinite freedom—him I call a Brahmin" (*Dhammapada*, 410 [91]).

65. "Think of yourself as Ayin [nothingness] and forget yourself totally . . . If you think of yourself as something, then God cannot clothe himself in you, for God is infinite. No vessel can contain God, unless you think of yourself as Ayin" (*Kabbalah*, 71). See also Unterman, *Kabbalistic Tradition*, 158–59.

66. Augustine, *City of God*, 17. Augustine also writes: "that the spirit of man may be tested"—which would not be pertinent for Phillips.

67. "No, Father. I've a very different idea of love. And until my dying day I shall refuse to love a scheme of things in which children are put to torture" (Camus, *Plague*, 218).

a God that is Love. The God that Phillips allows to remain is a scant reflection of divinity. Phillips is aware of this.[68] However, such reflection hardly gives a reason to sustain any theological sense and purpose to one's life. If such a God seems so unattached to my well-being while I am alive, it is hardly a comfort to know that the story of my life is dependent on this being's ability of recollection. A God who raises up one's broken, battered "story" but not one's broken, battered body and soul expresses a love that seems neither pure nor perfect, but mysteriously limited and characterized more by abandoning us than in creating us. While antitheodicists may be dissatisfied with the traditional concepts of God and so seek to minimize God's power or accentuate a passible God, against such (re)innovations, it is worth considering that such tested traditional beliefs still persist because they are the most plausible and meaningful if one wants to remain a theist.

In chapter 4, John Paul II will speak of suffering as redemptive mystery, while in chapter 5, Marilyn McCord Adams will argue why every person's life can be rendered meaningful—even the individual who has endured atrocious suffering or committed outrageous evil. While Phillips proposes a God who listens and remembers, John Paul II and McCord Adams assert a God who will redeem and save. Discerning which is the more useful and realistic path in the context of mass atrocity will thus be a key aim of the next few chapters.

---

68. "It is difficult for theodicists to accept the God who emerges from all these deliberations" (Phillips, *Problem of Evil*, 126).

4

John Paul II's *Salvifici Doloris*

Or like Donathille: She was raped and then sexually mutilated. "He said, 'Do you know what a Tutsi looks like between her legs?'" she recounted. "Then he took a scissors from his pocket. He cut me between my legs. I bled so much. He said he wanted to take a piece of me and put it where everyone could see."[1]

In chapter 3, D. Z. Phillips denied any afterlife and argued that theodicies try to justify the unjustifiable. He also claimed that the language of redemption makes little sense for a victim of horrific suffering because what has happened cannot be undone. Against Phillips's contentions, John Paul II argues in the encyclical *Salvifici Doloris* that belief in redemption and healing is possible because of Christ's life, death, and resurrection. In this chapter, I will address the following key questions:

1. How applicable is this encyclical to individuals like Donathille, the Tutsi survivor of genocide and rape referred to above; or the witness testimonies I examined in chapter 2?

2. Is all suffering meant to be redemptive as John Paul II seems to advocate?

3. Is the tradition of *privatio boni* (which John Paul II invokes) still useful when analyzing mass atrocity?

1. Neuffer, *Key to My Neighbor's House*, 264.

4. How does John Paul II maintain that Christ's solidarity heals and holds the key to the mystery of suffering?

5. Against Phillips's antimetaphysical (but "theistic") stance, does John Paul II's belief in the afterlife and the possibility for redemptive healing provide a more sustainable framework, language, and hope for the victims of mass atrocity? Does such a focus trivialize or detract from the need to protest suffering in this world?

6. When John Paul II writes that Christ "blots out the dominion of sin," how do we relate this sense of "blotting" out to Irving Greenberg's contention that "we now have to speak of moments when Redeemer and vision of redemption are present, interspersed with times when the flames and smoke of the burning children blot out faith—though it flickers again"?[2] Would John Paul II deny such a blotting out? And if so, what are the repercussions for a viable faith that ignores the need for skepticism and doubt?

7. How does John Paul II connect sin and suffering?

SHARING IN THE REDEMPTION OF SUFFERING

One of John Paul II's main intentions in this encyclical is to accentuate "the power of salvific suffering" through highlighting a gospel of suffering grounded in the possibility of eternal salvation.[3] Evil is not purposive and on no account is sent from God. However, the reality or memory of such evil could propel one to seek repentance or compel one to combat injustice.

The key term throughout this encyclical is *sharing.* As he writes: "Every man has his share in the Redemption. Each one is also called to share in that suffering through which the Redemption was accomplished."[4] This calling is supported by the Pauline contention that "in my flesh I complete what is lacking in Christ's afflictions for the sake of his body, that is, the Church."[5] Such realization—that

---

2. Greenberg, "Cloud of Smoke," 509.

3. John Paul II, *Salvifici Doloris*, Par. 26.

4. Ibid., Par. 15.

5. Ibid., Par. 1.

one's suffering can have a purpose—ends in "a final discovery, which is accompanied by joy." Here there seems to be no potential "useless suffering" in Levinasian terms.[6] Connecting suffering with eternal life because of Christ, John Paul II argues that without Christ willingly embracing the cross, redemption would not have been complete.[7] He strikingly adds: "Christ *did not* conceal from his listeners *the need for suffering.*"[8] Key concerns become how such remarks bear upon atrocity and senseless suffering and how John Paul II tries to integrate suffering in relation to the human condition.

SUFFERING AND THE HUMAN CONDITION

In highlighting the Pauline quotation above, John Paul II wants to stress that "what we express by the word 'suffering' seems to be particularly *essential to the nature of man.* It is as deep as man himself . . . Suffering seems to belong to man's transcendence: it is one of those points in which man is in a certain sense 'destined' to go beyond himself, and he is called to this in a mysterious way."[9]

I want to unpack a few of the ideas espoused here to clarify the theodicy being offered. The text carefully notes that suffering seems to be essential, as human beings are called "in a mysterious way" to go beyond themselves. However, he does not clarify or distinguish between the differing kinds and levels of suffering, though this "essential" suffering is a springboard in the text to discuss how humankind can and must reach ever higher for meaning, if the word "destiny" is taken in its full use and import. That millions of people endure oppression and extreme poverty makes such a reality true and scandalous, but not essential for life or meaning or the expression of one's faith, as Gustavo Gutiérrez and other liberation theologians would correctly argue. How then is suffering essential? And what is man's capacity for transcendence? For D. Z. Phillips, humankind is called to transcend egotism and selfishness. Does John Paul II also have in mind the need to transcend the meaning-destroying capacity of suffering

---

6. See Levinas, "Useless Suffering," 371–80. As John Paul II, however, writes in *Memory and Identity*: "There is no suffering which [God] cannot transform into a path leading to him" (189).

7. John Paul II, *Salvifici*, Par. 3.

8. Ibid., Par. 25.

9. Ibid., Par. 2.

or our own sinfulness? To begin to address some of these questions, I want to qualify John Paul II's support of the *privatio boni* tradition and how that tradition interprets the nature of the human person as both victim and perpetrator of suffering. To do so, I will turn to Didier Pollefeyt's reinterpretation of *privatio boni* and the inclusion of his additional term *perversio boni* to examine the relevance of the theory of *privatio boni* in the context of mass atrocity.[10]

A SEARCH FOR MEANING WITHIN SUFFERING

When John Paul II uses the phrase "mystery of suffering," he is not describing evil's origin but accentuating the good that can arise in response to it. The encyclical does, however, refer to Satan and original sin, which need to be contextualized and adequately explained. Monika Hellwig helpfully clarifies that original sin should not be a specified moment in some mythological or historical past "which somehow queered the pitch for all that followed in human history. Rather we are concerned with the cumulative effect of choices and actions which were less than worthy of human freedom and community. Each action has consequences that tend in greater or lesser degree to make it more difficult for others afterwards to act justly, truthfully, compassionately, constructively."[11] While John Paul II tends to view original sin as a specific moment, Hellwig's interpretation seems more credible and spiritually useful.

Evil as Privation

For John Paul II, moreover, such redemptive good and the existence of evil are discerned in part through the tradition of *privatio boni*. As he writes: "Man suffers on account of evil, which is a certain lack, limitation or distortion of good."[12] Especially in light of mass atrocities, the tradition of *privatio boni* is not without its detractors, who stress that evil is not merely an absence, as evinced in the massive destruction and suffering present in this world, or who argue that this tradition "fails to deal adequately with the virulent and aggressive forms evil

---

10. See also my "Destructive, Concrete Evil as Absence," 41–51.

11. Domning and Hellwig, *Original Selfishness*, 15. For a work examining the changing historical and biblical conceptions of sin, see Anderson, *Sin*.

12. John Paul II, *Salvifici*, Par. 7.

can take."[13] In applying such a term, one must also acknowledge that the theory of *privatio boni* has a contextualized meaning within the "traditional Western cosmology" of an Augustine or an Aquinas, which is not scientifically applicable today. As Peter Haas writes: "In this cosmology, the distance between the absolute perfect periphery and the earthly center was the space in which there was a *privatio boni*."[14]

As I interpret the *privatio boni* theory and apply it within my context, it is denying the possibility to judge that a human being is undeniably beyond redemption in this world.[15] Positively, it is stressing that all human beings are fundamentally good because God created them. As Didier Pollefeyt writes, *privatio boni* "does not deny the reality of evil at all, but only points out that evil is always parasitical. It always depends on a preceding, greater or more fundamental reality which is good."[16] However, because of the gift of free will, some human beings may commit deplorable actions, which can sully and corrupt their character.[17] This corruption contributes to why additional evil may then occur. The suffering (or consequences of these evil acts) as experienced by the victim—and the perpetrator—are real and often devastating.

Is such a term applicable to the case of perpetrators of mass atrocity? John Paul II does not analyze this issue, but Pollefeyt has offered what a "reinterpretation of *privatio boni* . . . could mean in wrestling with the evil of the Holocaust."[18] For Pollefeyt, such a reinterpretation entails recognizing that evil is often committed through self-deception or because of a fragmented self (in a process that Robert J. Lifton has called "doubling") by those whom I would describe as otherwise "morally mature or responsible" human beings.[19] As an example of

13. Lee, "Theodicy and Eschatology in John," 44. See also Hick, *Evil and the God of Love*, 52–4.

14. Haas, "Response to Pollefeyt," 235.

15. Aquinas asserts that "evil cannot wholly consume the good. . . [because] the aforesaid aptitude of the soul is not wholly taken away for [the good] belongs to its very nature" (*Summa Theologica*, 268 [Q.XLVIII.3]).

16. Pollefeyt, "Ethics, Forgiveness and the Unforgivable After Auschwitz," 144.

17. For a discussion of whether such corruption is ever final, see my analysis of McCord Adams' support for universal salvation in chs. 5 and 11.

18. Pollefeyt, "Horror Vacui," 220.

19. I use these terms to distinguish what Pollefeyt refers to as "psychopaths

doubling, think of a doctor in the concentration camps who could send people to the crematoria but be a (supposedly) loving husband at home. In the process of self-deception (which Pollefeyt connects with his term *perversio boni*[20]), he writes: "When evil is done, the good is not only absent but also manipulated, deceived, and perverted."[21] The theory of *privatio/perversio boni*, therefore, is a means not only to maintain the humanity of the perpetrator and to keep open the possibility for repentance and remorse, but "for the perpetrator to be made morally responsible (and punishable) for his or her evil acts."[22] According to Pollefeyt, to claim that an evil act was chosen for its own sake is to make such people "incomprehensible, even 'unpunishable.'"[23]

Of course, context is essential in coming to evaluate and interpret individual cases. Varnado Simpson, an American perpetrator of the My Lai massacre, who has confessed to murdering twenty-five people, acknowledges: "But like I say, after I killed the child, my whole mind just went. And once you start, it's very easy to keep on . . . Because I had no feelings or no emotions or no nothing. No direction. I just killed. It can happen to anyone."[24]

In this case, the "decision" or responsibility in committing such outrages has its "reasons" in a host of explanations and factors—the brutal context of the Vietnam war, the loss of fellow US soldiers, and the indoctrination process that named the Vietnamese as "gooks" or "enemy"—that do not exculpate Simpson, but prevent demonizing him as inhuman and so unable to be tried before the law.

"It could happen to anyone," Simpson remarks. Non-perpetrators resist such claims (often, perhaps, with good reason), but Pollefeyt is right in stressing why refusing to deny the humanity of the perpetrator is essential for justice, ethics, and faith after Auschwitz. Note, too, that Simpson said that he acted without feeling or reason. He is still

---

whose cognitive, affective, and moral capabilities are damaged severely" ("Response to Frede-Wenger and Haas," 239). Other exceptions can also be mentioned. As noted in chapter 1, though, the harm inflicted (regardless of intention or moral maturity or capability) is still applicable to challenge any theodic position.

20. Ibid., 239.

21. Pollefeyt, "*Horror Vacui*," 226–27. Notice that his description is similar to John Paul II's above.

22. Pollefeyt, "Response to Frede-Wenger and Haas," 242.

23. Pollefeyt, *Horror Vacui*, 221.

24. Quoted in Glover, *Moral History*, 62.

responsible but a lack of thinking or reasoning is what contributed to his crimes. Likewise, he admits how killing became easier after the first time. For others, it is not the first actual killing that is memorable, but something specific or unique in a subsequent one. Adalbert, a Hutu convicted of genocide, does not remember the precise details of his first killing, but he recalls the exact date in 1994, April 17th, when he shot and killed two children: "For me it was strange to see the children drop without a sound. It was almost pleasantly easy . . . Now, too often, I am seized by the memory of those children, shot straight out, like a joke."[25]

Pio, another Hutu convicted of genocide, admits: "I had killed chickens but never an animal the stoutness of a man, like a goat or a cow. The first person, I finished him off in a rush, not thinking anything of it, even though he was a neighbor, quite close on my hill. In truth, it came to me only afterward: I had taken the life of a neighbor."[26] What does one say, then, of a perpetrator who continues to participate in the murder of human beings? Does there not reach a point where such killings contaminate a person's character, dehumanizing him, as it were? What Pollefeyt calls this "fundamental reality which is good" is rightly tested by certain accounts of mass atrocity in which victims depict gulag or concentration guards or genocidal perpetrators who have abused and tortured them. In describing the liquidation of the family camp at Auschwitz, Filip Müller writes: "One could see that most of the SS men had a bad conscience. They hadn't shown any scruples about annihilating Jews . . . yet they clearly found it unpleasant and distressing to help exterminate people with whom they had been on quite good terms up to now."[27]

Müller is careful to distinguish between the sadistic guard who seems to brutalize others for his own pleasure, as seen in his depiction of *Hauptscharführer* (Sergeant Major) Moll, and the guard who feigned aggressiveness in front of his superiors or was "badly upset by the ghoulish spectacle."[28] Someone like Moll, however, does seem

---

25. Adalbert, interviewed by Hatzfeld, *Machete Season*, 25.

26. Pio, interviewed by Hatzfeld, *Machete Season*, 23–24.

27. Müller, *Eyewitness Auschwitz*, 151. Hatzfeld writes of one Hutu perpetrator of genocide: "Bitero was not born evil and did not grow up in an atmosphere of hatred. Quite the contrary: Like many great killers of history, at one point in his life he was cultured, friendly, a good father and good colleague" (*Strategy of Antelopes*, 92).

28. Müller, *Eyewitness Auschwitz*, 138.

to challenge what Pollefeyt refers to (and critiques) as the paradigm of "diabolicization," in which the perpetrator is deemed an immoral monster.[29] To some witnesses, there were individuals who (even if inherently good or meant to be good) became undeniably—and, perhaps, irrevocably—evil, regardless of how they treated their family at home.[30] Thirteen years after his role in the Rwandan genocide, Pio tells Jean Hatzfeld: "that killer, he was indeed me as to the wrong committed and the bloodshed, but he is a stranger to me in his ferocity . . . I am the same man as before, I am even a better person."[31] Who knows if these claims are true in this case, but in theory it is possible for a killer to repent.

The child soldier Ishmael Beah, moreover, writes of the point where such killings became automatic. Full of rage, high on drugs, and manipulated by his surroundings, he must have seemed a demon— to his victims, at least. As noted in the introduction to this volume, however, he is now rehabilitated. As Pollefeyt astutely remarks: "For a good post-Holocaust anthropology, the distinction between evil and evildoer is crucial."[32] Without such a distinction, we commit an injustice against the perpetrator and God by declaring that such a being is beyond redemption or justice, or by potentially ignoring those who were more responsible.

I remain skeptical of Pollefeyt's claim that "the theory of *privatio/ perversio boni* [can] sustain a 'religion without theodicy (Levinas)'"[33]— as I cannot envision a viable faith or religion that claims that the existence of evil "overcomes" the possibility to defend or justify belief in God despite such evil.[34] However, when linked with the gift of free

---

29. Pollefeyt, "Kafkaesque World," 219–39.

30. See Holocaust survivor Sidney Shachnow's response in Wiesenthal, *Sunflower*, 241–43. See also the reflection about General Vincent Otti and the atrocities he committed in Uganda in Dunson, *Child, Victim, Soldier*, 56–61.

31. Hatzfeld, *Strategy of Antelopes*, 223–24.

32. Pollefeyt, "Ethics, Forgiveness, and the Unforgivable," 154.

33. Pollefeyt, "Response to Frede-Wenger and Haas," 240.

34. See also ibid., 238–41. The *privatio boni* tradition can still be relevant for cases of so-called "natural" evil, but only to the degree that human beings' negligence or action is deemed to cause or exacerbate detruction and suffering in those specific cases. With knowledge that we live in a world of devastating tsunamis, birth defects, and disease, a theodicist (and, again, therefore a theist) is left to acknowledge the chasms, fissures, and caesuras between the God of mercy, love, and justice whom one wants to affirm, and the reality of the horrific and tragic deaths of millions upon

will, the theory of *privatio/perversio boni* is crucial for any theodicy to uphold the belief that even the worst of perpetrators were created and meant for good. In Christian theological terms, refusing to acknowledge the possibility for repentance and conversion tries to limit the potential for God's gift of grace and the power of the Holy Spirit to work even through the most depraved perpetrators. As Pollefeyt argues, however, some victims may view their perpetrators purely as evil, as the loss and pain suffered is too destructive and depersonalizing to begin the process of understanding and forgiveness.[35] In the context of Paul's Epistle to the Romans, Ched Myers highlights "the moral *authority* of the victim" and warns that victims must be prepared and "ready" before entering into the process of forgiveness. They certainly cannot be forced. He opines: "Rightly handled, the process of victim initiative is inherently empowering because she is prosecuting her own case on her own terms, not for purposes of retribution, but of restoration."[36]

Similar to Maimonides' continual emphasis on the need for forgiveness in his *Laws of Repentance*, Pollefeyt adds: "By not being able to forgive the perpetrator the victim gives evil the final word and he allows the memory of it to dominate his whole life in a negative way."[37] Charles Griswold, moreover, notes: "The offender does not have the right to forgiveness; and there are no rules for forgiveness comparable to those used by a court of law to decide conflicts. It is not unjust for a victim to fail to forgive the offender, though it may be blamable."[38]

While we will return to the question of whether forgiveness is always demanded or is always the most moral response, Pollefeyt's reinterpretation of *privatio boni* helps minimize many of the standard criticisms against the theory while providing reasons to validate

---

millions of human lives who are lost in spite of—and not because of—humanity's hopes and aims.

35. Pollefeyt, "Ethics, Forgiveness, and the Unforgivable," 158. For a victim of apartheid's encounter and subsequent meetings with the infamous Eugene de Kock, commanding officer of state-sanctioned death squads under apartheid, see Gobodo-Madikizela, *A Human Being Died That Night*. For a critical assessment of Gobodo-Madikizela's work, see Langer, *Using and Abusing the Holocaust*, 82–96.

36. Myers and Enns, *Ambassadors of Reconciliation*, 1:66.

37. Pollefeyt, "Ethics, Forgiveness, and the Unforgivable," 158. For his argument that "the basic structure of ethics after Auschwitz should be openness to the vulnerability of the other," see his "Kafkaesque World," 239. For a further discussion of the requirement of forgiveness within theodic language, see ch. 11.

38. Griswold, *Forgiveness*, 68.

the pervasive goodness of the world and giving grounds to hope that perpetrators of evil can be tried and, possibly, redeemed.[39] This hope (and testament) also supports the belief that suffering calls upon all of us to give freely to the other in need and so is a fundamental calling "to unleash" the love within us, as John Paul II writes.[40] All are summoned to transcend any selfishness (or sinfulness) and reach out both to victims and perpetrators, even, perhaps, if this entails additional hardship.

"Blaspheme God and Die"[41]

Helpfully, John Paul II acknowledges the sometimes desperate need to find the reason for some suffering: "Man can put this question to God with all the emotion of his heart and with his mind full of dismay and anxiety; and God expects the question and listens to it."[42] This is probably the most pastorally relevant section of the encyclical. The notion that it is morally permissible to raise these questions with God, and more importantly, that God knows human beings at their deepest core and expects to be questioned, could be a comforting hope and solace for many.

Putting questions to God (and questioning God) has a rich tradition in the Bible. Like other commentators, John Paul II turns to the book of Job, in which the question of innocent suffering is at the forefront. Although he notes that Job "does not yet give the solution to the problem,"[43] he agrees with the book's stance against the erroneous assertion that all punishments were deserved based on a "previous fault."[44] He also adds that the "Old Testament" often refers to suffering having an educational and redemptive value: "Suffering must serve for conversion, that is, for the rebuilding of goodness in the subject, who

---

39. The conversions of the Roman centurion, Zacchaeus (as a chief tax collector), the Apostle Matthew (tax collector), and Saul (a persecutor of Christians) are classic gospel examples. The Tanak, particularly the book of Judges, is one long story of a people faithful to God, then unfaithful, and then faithful again. In our contemporary times, the story of child soldier Ishmael Beah, as detailed in the introduction, also testifies to this phenomenon.

40. John Paul II, *Salvifici*, Par. 29.

41. Job 2:9.

42. John Paul II, *Salvifici*, Par. 10.

43. Ibid., Par. 12.

44. Ibid., Par. 11.

can recognize this divine mercy in his call for repentance."[45] While analyzing Palden Gyatso's testimony, I stressed how there are truths one does not need to experience to know. It is "useless knowledge," as Charlotte Delbo writes.[46] John Paul II's failure to clarify this need for conversion can have negative consequences, especially for an abused child or Donathille. In such cases, a focus on conversion could connote sinfulness or inadvertently provide the impetus to blame the victims. Although Echeverria reminds us that John Paul II provides multiple explanations for suffering dependent on context, greater nuancing and awareness of the powerlessness of some victims was needed here.[47]

The Antiworld of Suffering

While there may be solace in God expecting questions from us and in the hopeful theory of *privatio boni,* the extent of human suffering and evil can seem insurmountable.[48] Despite the isolation of many victims, John Paul II contends that they share hope in solidarity because of their mutual suffering, a hope embodied in the witnesses who strive to end such suffering everywhere. As Soon Ok Lee testifies after escaping from the North Korean gulags: "I wanted to gather the lamentations of thousands and millions of prisoners who live under conditions humans cannot bear . . . I wanted to proclaim on their behalf, 'We're human beings too. We have a right to speak!'"[49]

While not referring to any concrete cases, John Paul II writes: "In itself human suffering constitutes as it were a specific 'world' which exists together with man, which appears in him and passes, and sometimes does not pass, but which consolidates itself and becomes deeply rooted in him."[50] As Holocaust survivor Philip K. remarks: "I often say to people who pretend or seem to be marvelling at the fact that I seem so normal, so unperturbed and so capable of functioning—they seem

---

45. Ibid., Par. 12.

46. Delbo, *Auschwitz and After,* 115–231.

47. Echeverria, "Gospel of Redemptive Suffering," 119.

48. See John Paul II, *Memory and Identity,* 21–22. He writes: "To those who are subjected to systematic evil, there remains only Christ and his cross as a source of spiritual self-defense, as a promise of victory."

49. Lee, *Eyes of the Tailless Animals,* 9.

50. John Paul II, *Salvifici,* Par. 8.

to think the Holocaust passed over and it's done with: *It's my* skin . . . *You can't take it off. And it's there, and it will be there until I die . . .*"[51] Nomberg-Przytyk, for example, noted her disjointed reaction after being liberated from the camps and taking a civilian train—as opposed to the cattle cars that rumbled to the death camps while carrying many corpses, interspersed with the still living.[52] The worlds seemed utterly separate, though as Langer reminds us: "Auschwitz is often described (with a certain melodramatic flair) as an 'antiworld,' a separate planet, though in fact the camp was in Poland in Europe on planet earth, run by men and women like the rest of us . . . With the exception of a handful of sadists, they did their work of destruction routinely and with detached satisfaction."[53] Such a world exists within the "greater" world, but is especially concentrated for fellow victims on the side of justice and morality.[54] It possesses its own solidarity. For John Paul II, Jesus of Nazareth was also a victim who had to endure such a world as a fellow sufferer, but who as God Incarnate embodies the means to sacralize what otherwise seems degrading and painful.

THE MEANING FOUND?

Love amidst Suffering

John Paul II's main assertion is that through the suffering of Christ, God is united with all who suffer, thus redeeming all suffering and enabling everyone to share in this redemption through imitating Christ. It is through suffering that human existence becomes "particularly concentrated" with the potential to work for good. Because God suffered in the person of Jesus of Nazareth who also overcame the power of sin and death through his resurrection, Jesus, as a fellow human sufferer, is in solidarity with all those who endure affliction and offers hope for resurrection.[55] Only Christ, therefore, provides a meaning

---

51. Langer, *Holocaust Testimonies*, 205.

52. Nomberg-Przytyk, *Auschwitz*, 158.

53. Langer, *Admitting the Holocaust*, 6.

54. Whether a survivor of genocide in Rwanda or of torture and detention in Iraq, Zimbabwe, or China—one often encounters a common language and experience that transcends country, ethnicity, or cause. See Moorehead, *Human Cargo*, 277.

55. John Paul II, *Salvifici*, Par. 15.

for all suffering and a way to access God's love.[56] Death is proclaimed defeated. Contra Phillips, there will be resurrection.[57]

However, while some victims can participate and find meaning in this gospel of suffering that John Paul II highlights, some suffering is destructive and degrading. There are conditions that could very likely turn any of us into one of the *Muselmänner*, as Primo Levi and others witnessed in the camps.[58] Another question, then, is how this truth will redeem what had been lost.

Blotting Out "the Dominion of Sin"

While the magnitude of affliction still needs explanation, some suffering, according to John Paul II, must be endured for the greater good. He therefore quotes Jesus's chastisement of Peter, who rebuked Christ for predicting what was to happen to the Son of Man.[59] According to John Paul II, Christ's death was needed to redeem humanity from eternal punishment on account of original sin and to "blot out . . . the dominion of sin."[60] Although hopeful, this interpretation does not adequately address the suffering of an individual like Donathille or a child abused. To imply that the little child is also tainted with original sin—and so Christ's death is also a cause of joy for that child—seems neither pastorally nor spiritually effective. Thus, blotting out sin may not be the most important "accomplishment" when encountering a victim of horrendous evil and suffering, even as one acknowledges that victims are not immune from the need for forgiveness, as their "victimhood" is not (or should not be) their only identity marker. Another issue is how the necessity of Christ's suffering compares with other testimonial accounts from chapter 2 and whether such a focus minimizes Christ's solidarity with them. I want to focus now, however, on the issue of the meaning of suffering and who or what adjudicates what seems to depend

56. Ibid., Par. 13.

57. Ibid., Par. 14. For an excellent essay that challenges the dominant Anselmian theory of vicarious atonement, see Rohr, "Franciscan Option," 206–12. See also my "Healing the Distorted Face," 302–17, and Myers and Enns, *Ambassadors of Reconciliation*, 1:11.

58. On the issue of the "memory of Jesus' unjust suffering" and the reality of many women in oppressive situations, see Gebara, *Out of the Depths*, 85–90.

59. John Paul II, *Salvifici*, Par. 17.

60. Ibid., Par. 15.

upon a subjective and amorphous interpretive framework. John Paul II says that the love of Christ on the cross is the key, but how exactly does this love reflect upon and interpret another's suffering?

The Subjective Meaning of Suffering

While some suffering can be deemed meaningful, disentangling mere subjectivity within such claims remains problematic. For the paramilitary forces in El Salvador, Oscar Romero's murder was an accomplished goal, not a spiritually meaningful one. From the above reading, it is easier to apply John Paul II's interpretation of suffering to a Catholic victim like Leisner, who identified his suffering with Christ's, than to an atheist and social activist like Partnoy. The martyrdom of Leisner also supports why John Paul II can use the Pauline quote that present pains are "not worth comparing with the glory that is revealed in us"—but would need great clarification if he had included non-Christian sufferers more consistently in his reflections.

Because my aim is to keep such victims in mind, consider first that trying to quantify time—implying that in the context of eternal life, this life is a mere blip—can be morally dangerous. Perhaps in the context of the beatific vision, as McCord Adams will note in the next chapter, even the worst of the torture that many have undergone will lose its destructive and dominant force. But any experience of brutal torture and starvation, whether thirty years or thirty hours, will seem like an eternity in the context of our finite life on earth, and for all intents and purposes, are an eternity. As Charlotte Delbo writes: "O you who know / Did you know that a day is longer than a year / a minute longer than a lifetime?"[61] Rwandan genocide survivor Médiatrice similarly testifies: "Even if you count one by one each evening we stayed alive, those days in Kayumba count more than years, as much as an eternity."[62]

Secondly, such suffering also leaves a traumatic residue that persists long after the physical torture has ceased. It shatters many people's hope and trust in this world. Améry writes: "Twenty-two years later I am still dangling over the ground by dislocated arms, panting, and accusing myself."[63] Existentially, some pain may be so

---

61. Delbo, *Auschwitz and After*, 11.
62. Hatzfeld, *Strategy of Antelopes*, 60–61.
63. Améry, *Mind's Limits*, 36.

debilitating and destructive that even articulating the language of the beatific vision demands care and humility. Olga Lengyl, still tortured by how she inadvertently sent her parents and young sons to immediate death during a selection at Auschwitz, opens her testimony, *Five Chimneys*, with the words, "*Mea culpa*, my fault, *mea maxima culpa!* I cannot acquit myself of the charge that I am, in part, responsible for the destruction of my own parents and my two young sons. The world understands that I could not have known, but in my heart the terrible feeling persists that I could have, I might have, saved them."[64]

It remains unclear how the memory of those pains will be precisely overcome or how connecting them with Christ's love on the cross provides meaning for them. Moreover, as Phillips has argued, how will such pain be surmounted simply by altering the context to a heavenly one? While John Paul II does not treat these issues in depth here, he does stress that Christ's solidarity with the poor and oppressed through his own tribulations does give unto suffering a salvific character: it is through Christ's suffering and crucifixion that all were saved according to Christian dogma, and Jesus as God Incarnate sheds light as an example of a life lived according to the love of God and love of neighbor.[65] All are called to participate in Jesus's salvific mission by healing those who suffer, seeking to spread the reign of God on earth despite any suffering that may accrue, or by serving as inspiration for others in responding with faith and hope to one's own suffering. "In bringing about the Redemption through suffering," John Paul writes, "Christ has also raised human suffering to the level of Redemption. Thus each man, in his suffering, can also become a sharer in the redemptive suffering of Christ."[66]

Despite tribulations and affliction, through solidarity with Christ and so "suffering for the kingdom," all are meant to be inspired, comforted, and healed.[67] Recall, however, that Partnoy was imprisoned because she sought social justice in Argentina. As such an aim resonates with some interpretations of the life and mission of Jesus, one can say she shared in the redemption of the world. However, social justice is by no means the exclusive domain of Christians. Moreover, what

64. Lengyl, *Five Chimneys*, 11.

65. John Paul II, *Salvifici*, Par. 30.

66. Ibid., Par. 15.

67. Ibid., Par. 20. See also Par. 21.

about senseless suffering or a woman abused by her partner? How can such "useless suffering" be said to participate in the reign of God without promoting passivity in the face of evil or implying that such evil has meaning in itself? In addition, how can we apply John Paul II's claim that suffering can be a means of rejoicing because it is linked to a greater, meaningful end?

Rejoicing in Suffering?

According to John Paul II, "the final stage of the spiritual journey in relation to suffering [is] embodied in the statement: 'Now I rejoice in my sufferings for your sake, and in my flesh, I complete what is lacking in Christ's afflictions for the sake of his body, that is, the Church.'"[68] In this Pauline quote, there is no essential lack in Christ's Redemption which implies the Redemption is not complete. For John Paul II, "*It only means* that the Redemption, accomplished through satisfactory love, *remains always open to all love* expressed in *human suffering* . . . [It is] constantly being 'accomplished.'"[69] In addition, the Church plays a fundamental role in helping aid and support this accomplishing by "draw[ing] on the infinite resources of the Redemption, introducing it into the life of humanity, which is the dimension in which the redemptive suffering of Christ can be constantly completed by the suffering of man."[70]

As I interpret these somewhat mystifying claims, John Paul II wants to leave room for human participation in the saving work of Christ without implying that human actions (without the grace of God) are equally able to participate in the redemption of suffering or are completing Christ's mission. The Church, especially understood as the mystical body of Christ, plays an integral role in facilitating humanity's potential to share in this redemption and invitation. Ultimately, "credit" still belongs to Christ.

As John Paul II writes in *Memory and Identity*: "All human suffering, all pain, all infirmity contains within itself a promise of salvation, a promise of joy . . . all this evil is present in our world partly so as to awaken our love, our self-gift in generous and disinterested service

68. Ibid., Par. 24.
69. Ibid., Par. 24.
70. Ibid., Par. 6.

to those visited by suffering."[71] One rejoices because of this hope and promise and not because of the actual suffering. Humanity is called to give of themselves in self-love to others by following the example and witness of Christ. Thus, while also returning us to his description of suffering as essential, I still need to address what he means by "accomplishing" in the context of suffering.

As noted above, some suffering is simply loss, annihilation, human degradation—it is "excremental assault," to borrow Terrence de Pres's term.[72] All such loss of life remains a tragedy and a failure, regardless of any good that accrues. Rejoicing for a reward outside this life saves the problem and the solution for another time; it is to look elsewhere to condition meaning here. Eschatological hope, however, cannot expunge this world's concrete and devastating disasters from our theological and spiritual horizons. Approaches that imply automatic healing and forgiveness or call to forget or justify suffering because of an afterlife fail to deal adequately with the trauma and affliction experienced in this world. At the same time, Christ's beatitudes can provide great solace for the afflicted and those persecuted for holiness' sake, provided that justice and ongoing praxis are included in the agenda.

John Paul II's stress on the transcendence of self-giving love and the example of the Good Samaritan complements this praxic approach. Ultimately, while a Karl Leisner was theologically attuned to see his life as one of self-giving love to others and God, what of those who were not capable or aware of such an option? Calling rejoicing in suffering the "final step" also implies that everyone should reach that plateau, when the most ethical responses to some suffering may not be to rejoice, but to grieve and protest and funnel that energy into aiding others in a similar plight. There also remains the question of how this "rejoicing" is applicable to non-Christian victims of horrific suffering.

Christ's Solidarity with Other Victims of Atrocity

John Paul II reaches out to non-Christians at one key point in the encyclical, claiming: "*the glory that is hidden in the very sufferings of Christ . . .* must be acknowledged not only in the martyrs for the faith but in many others also who, at times, even without knowing Christ, suffer

71. John Paul II, *Memory and Identity,* 190.

72. De Pres, *Survivor,* 51–72.

and give their lives for the truth and for a just cause. In the sufferings of all these people the great dignity of man is strikingly confirmed."[73]

John Paul II therefore proposes that another potential redemptive element of suffering is "to manifest the moral greatness of man" or to reveal one's spiritual maturation. This last point is linked with suffering, giving us the opportunity to attain and practice the virtue of perseverance[74] and not to let suffering dominate our theological and spiritual faith. In partaking in God's love, John Paul II writes, "man rediscovers himself more and more fully in suffering: he rediscovers the 'soul' which he thought he had 'lost' because of suffering."[75]

These are also beautiful words, but are they applicable to Donathille or to a victim of child abuse? For the Jewish theologian Emil Fackenheim, "to find redemption in the suffering of these babies [burned alive in the camps], or of those cursed to hear their screams, is a human impossibility and—so one hopes—a divine one as well."[76] For Fackenheim, the gulf between Christ and these victims is not on account of the claimed divinity of the former. It is because these Jewish victims had no choice: "Hadrian created Jewish martyrs. Hitler murdered not only Jews but also Jewish martyrdom."[77] While there are some individual exceptions,[78] I agree with Fackenheim. To repeat: the dominant focus should address how these victims are not to blame, how God wants to heal them, that their anger is justified, and that the issue of a soul being lost is irrelevant.

---

73. John Paul II, *Salvifici*, Par. 22. Note also that the encyclical addresses the bishops, priests, religious families, and the "faithful" of the Catholic Church. Based on the salutation, this letter is not addressed to the Partnoys of the world, an omission that limits the value and interpretation of John Paul II's exegesis of the meaning of suffering.

74. In quoting Kierkegaard, D. Z. Philips also speaks of patience; see *Problem of Evil*, 212.

75. John Paul II, *Salvifici*, Par. 23.

76. Fackenheim, *Mend the World*, xivi.

77. Ibid., xlii.

78. Joseph Bau's wife, Rebecca, removed her own name from "Schindler's List" and replaced it with her husband's so that he would be taken to work in Schindler's factory. She instead was transferred to Auschwitz but survived. See Bau, *Dear God*, 158.

Jesus, Uncertainty, and Agitation

While the encyclical provides ample material stressing Jesus as redeemer, a greater emphasis on Jesus's humanity would provide a clearer sense of how human beings can also share in Christ's redemption. Such a focus would also clarify what suffering "accomplishes" according to John Paul II. He writes that Jesus heads towards "his Passion and death with full awareness of the mission he has to fulfill precisely in this way [through suffering]."[79] While John's Gospel may support this interpretation, turning to Mark's Gospel here would seem more pastorally effective when examining the possibility to participate in redemptive suffering. As David Neville writes: "Because Mark refused to soften the stark reality of Jesus' suffering, his crucifixion narrative is more likely to provide insight into the realities of evil and suffering as well as resources for grappling with these overwhelming forces."[80] Mark's Gospel better enables one to emphasize how Christ gradually comprehends the full extent of his mission, does not know every detail of what will occur, who himself suffers and is agitated at times, but courageously chooses to remain faithful to what he perceives to be the truth despite the likelihood of death.

For example, Jesus in Mark's Gospel is "distressed and agitated" in Gethsemane,[81] and his cry from the cross could be interpreted as a sense of abandonment (he does not quote the hopeful end of Psalm 22). This contrasts with a more self-assured Jesus in John and the absence of any such cry from the cross in Luke or John. At one point, Jesus also seems to think the second coming will be soon, though this also depends on how one interprets "the kingdom of God."[82] His assertion for the need for watchfulness because no one knows the time or day also needs to be considered.[83] Regardless, not every detail seemed foreknown but was a gradual unfolding. This space of uncertainty is extremely important to adhere to if one wants to link Christ's experience with the suffering of other human beings.[84]

---

79. John Paul II, *Salvifici*, Par. 16.

80. Neville, "God's Presence and Power," 21.

81. Mark 14:33; see also O'Collins, *Christology*, 67–81.

82. Mark 9:1.

83. Mark 13:32.

84. In *Christ and Horrors*, McCord Adams writes: "Overall, the scholastics painted a portrait of Christ's human nature as highly advantaged in comparison

Such a depiction would have prevented the possibility of inadvertently distancing Jesus of Nazareth from the majority of sufferers for whom affliction comes with a knock on the door in the middle of the night, as Aleksandr Solzhenitsyn reminds us.[85] Evil and suffering are most heinous when they are utterly unexpected, not chosen, and degrading (especially if they incorporate the suffering of loved ones). Plenty of individuals have had a fairly accurate anticipation of what would happen to them if they committed a certain act. We know of martyrs like Ignatius of Antioch who even pleaded with his fellow believers to let him be "a meal for the beasts, for it is they who can provide my way to God."[86] Like Rabbi Akiba, he knew torture and death would follow his refusal to worship the Roman gods.[87]

At stake here is whether Christ, if ceded this full awareness of his mission and purpose, remains the best model for those who suffer, who either have no idea why they are being tortured or murdered or know the reason is trivial or a mistake. As Phillips writes: "One misses something essential if one treats them [the Suffering Servant and the Passion of Christ] simply as marvellous examples of voluntary self-sacrifice. This leaves out the bitterness in the fact that they are *broken*. That cannot be accepted as a voluntary acceptance by the will."[88]

The language of brokenness needs further qualifiers, especially for Christians who believe Jesus persevered (and through the resurrection, triumphed). However, descriptions that stress Jesus's vulnerability better align his ordeal with those depicted in other testimonies of (mass) atrocity. Simone Weil succinctly touches upon what I have been concerned with above, namely, the need to clarify Levinas' sense of useless suffering with what can be deemed John Paul II's potentially "meaningful" suffering and the need to highlight what I would call the

---

with ours" (59); see also O'Collins, *Christology*, 266–9.

85. Solzhenitsyn, *Gulag Archipelago*, 3–4. See also Ginzburg, *Journey into the Whirlwind*, 3–5.

86. Ignatius of Antioch, "Epistle to the Romans," 86.

87. Harboring Hutus during Rwanda's most recent genocide, or speaking out against Mao or Stalin was also a guaranteed death sentence.

88. Phillips, *Problem of Evil*, 272. This interpretation of Jesus's suffering does not address a child abused, or those persecuted who do not belong to a cause or group. In fact, Jean Améry notes that unlike the isolated intellectuals, those who were Catholic, Communist, or Jehovah's Witness had a greater chance of survival because they were not facing their ordeals alone and had an ideology to combat the Nazi policy of dehumanization (*Mind's Limits*, 13).

humanization of Christ's bodily and earthly suffering. She writes: "The martyrs who came into the arena singing as they faced the wild beasts were not afflicted. Christ was afflicted. He did not die like a martyr. He died like a common criminal, in the same class as thieves, only a little more ridiculous. For affliction is ridiculous."[89] Weil's interpretation clashes with John Paul II's above. While also needing clarification—especially in the need to link Jesus's "criminality" with his living and dying in solidarity with the poor and the oppressed—her words encourage a greater connection for an intimate and possible *imitatio Christi*. If, indeed, the mission of Jesus is to establish the reign of God on earth through a life focused on liberating the poor and oppressed and challenging injustice in our world, then such participation is clear and possible to emulate, but seems otherworldly if Jesus simply looks upon such suffering as necessary and meant to be fulfilled.[90] Ignacio Ellacuría neatly encapsulates the above statements: "it cannot be forgotten that the historic Jesus sought for himself neither death nor resurrection but the proclamation of the Reign of God to the point of death, and that brought resurrection."[91]

ASSESSMENT: UNADDRESSED VICTIMS

John Paul II's highlighting of the possibility for a suffering victim to share in Christ's redeeming mission can be a great pastoral gift to many individuals because it connects that suffering to a greater good (the self-giving in love to others, thus sharing in the ongoing redemption wrought by Christ); gives hope that such suffering will not have the final word; and provides an example of how to respond to the suffering of others and one's own afflictions.

Nevertheless, gaps still remain in this encyclical's relevance to all types of suffering and in the need for greater clarification with some of its terms.[92] As evidenced above, applying the testimonies

89. Weil, *Simone Weil Reader*, 445. Weil writes that "affliction is an uprooting of life, a more or less attenuated equivalent of death, made irresistibly present to the soul by the attack or immediate apprehension of physical pain" (440).

90. Note that such a focus need not be opposed to interpretations of Christ as the new "Adam" and overcoming sin and death in sacrificial terms or his overcoming "original" sin. Nor is it antithetical to eschatological interpretation, as I will investigate more closely in the liberation theology chapters.

91. Ellacuría, "Crucified People," 589.

92. Biggar, *Aiming to Kill*, 51.

of a Partnoy or Gyatso to John Paul II's encyclical often produces disappointing results.

The encyclical's important point, though, is to restore the possibility for some suffering to be a conduit for inspiration, faith, and grace and the opportunity for the sufferer—in what seems a meaningless, horrific plight—to find purpose and dignity. We saw this process exemplified in the Catholic martyr Karl Leisner in the death camps. But I am less certain to apply these points to cases of child abuse or every instance of horrific suffering as exemplified by Donathille's ordeal. While such participation and redemption is possible for such victims, I would hesitate to apply most of John Paul II's language on suffering to every individual who had to undergo senseless, horrific torture or abuse.

In short, I am sympathetic to John Paul II's claim that Christ can be presented as the ultimate answer to the problem of evil. I also concur with his aim to show how we are called to respond to our own suffering and to the suffering of others as a means to share in healing and redemption. However, at stake is whether the hope and optimism of the encyclical's language can be applied to cases that seem beyond redemption. John Paul II's *Salvifici Doloris* does not explicitly treat these cases in great detail, but the following text does.

5

McCord Adams: Horror—but Redemption for All

Imagination decides everything . . .[1]

In *Human Cargo: A Journey among Refugees*, Caroline Moorehead identifies some of the key concerns of Helen Bamber's Medical Foundation for the Care of Victims of Torture: "How do you coax back to a bearable existence people whose bodies have been attacked, whose brains and memories have been weakened by blows to the head, whose privacy and pride have been invaded by rape and sexual assault, who have seen their families destroyed, and have lost everything that once mattered to them, though they have done nothing wrong?"[2]

Such questions are at the heart of Marilyn McCord Adams's *Horrendous Evils and the Goodness of God*, which focuses on how meaningful redemption can still be possible for everyone, especially because of our postmortem encounter with a personal, omnipotent, and imaginative God.[3] Thus, I will examine whether McCord Adams's project succeeds where Phillips claims it fails.[4] I will also examine whether her denial of a "morally-good God" and her support for a return of the language of aesthetics weakens or contributes to a

1. Pascal, *Penseés*, 41.
2. Moorehead, *Human Cargo*, 270–71.
3. McCord Adams, *Horrendous*, 82.
4. Phillips, *Problem of Evil*, 271.

theodicy. Lastly, I will test whether her theological attempts help to answer some of Helen Bamber's concerns above, which have great affinity with my own investigations.

SKEPTICAL OF THEODICY

While Adams and Phillips differ on the possibility of redemption and healing in an afterlife context, Adams would seem to agree with the gist of Phillips's argument against theodicies for trying to justify the unjustifiable. Though recalling Anselm's reminder that "the mystery of Divine Goodness is permanently inexhaustible to us,"[5] Adams, like Phillips, cannot accept any so-called reasons that supervene the value of an individual human life.[6] As she also notes in *Christ and Horrors*, "talk of theodicy—of *justifying* the ways of God to humankind—is misleading, because God has no obligations to creatures and hence no need to *justify* Divine actions to us. Personal though God is, the metaphysical size-gap is too big for God to be drawn down into the network of rights and obligations that bind together merely human beings."[7] She will instead steer a middle course between justifying and explaining.[8]

I do not find such a distinction useful in a theodic (and so theological) context because most explanations, especially within a "theodicy," are rarely value-free assertions, bereft of desires, motivations, and faith-beliefs. These qualities are embedded within most theodicies, and so share similar characteristics with the traditional practice of seeking justificatory reasons in a theodicy. Strictly speaking, to justify entails the additional step of claiming why a proposition is right, proper, or necessary. However, of more concern for me is the possible negative repercussion that may result from denying God's lack of obligation to us without sufficient clarification, an issue I will take up further below.

---

5. McCord Adams, *Horrendous*, 54.

6. McCord Adams, "Afterword," 196.

7. McCord Adams, *Christ and Horrors*, 43.

8. Ibid., 43.

THE HORRENDOUS

Adams accentuates the "horrendous" because the word connotes the worst of all objective evils for victims, perpetrators, and bystanders.[9] They constitute *"prima facie* reason" for an individual to doubt whether life has been valuable and good on the whole.[10] At stake is whether some types of suffering refute any assertion of a God of love and redemption and nullify any meaning and value of an individual life (and so life *in toto*). Like Job's complaint—"[W]hy was I not like a buried stillbirth, / Like babies who never saw the light?"[11]—for some individuals nonexistence or death seems more appealing than life. A viable theodicy, therefore, is denied.

For redemption to be possible for both victim and perpetrator, McCord Adams specifies her criteria: "I assume that for an individual's life to be a great good *to him/her* on the whole, it is not enough for good to balance off or defeat evil *objectively speaking.* The individual involved must him/herself also recognize and appropriate at least some of those positive meanings."[12] One issue is whether some individuals have never experienced or identified any act of meaningful goodness towards them. While McCord Adams will underscore how God can heal anyone, Holocaust survivors like Alexander Donat state that they will never forgive, forget, or understand the inexplicable horror they had to undergo: "The maddening and humbling feeling of the absence of the Divine accompanied us constantly. The experience is eternal, unforgettable."[13]

Theologians like Reeve Brenner, moreover, maintain that they will refuse to forget or understand God's inactions on account of victims like Donat.[14] Wiesel has noted that he will go on praying to God, but thinks he will never be satisfied by God's answers,[15] while Roy and Alice Eckhardt contend: "the only penitential act we know for God is his expression of genuine sorrow for his place in the unparalleled

---

9. McCord Adams, *Horrendous,* 26.

10. Ibid., 26.

11. Job 3:16.

12. McCord Adams, *Horrendous,* 82.

13. Donat, "Voice from the Ashes," 276.

14. Brenner, *Faith and Doubt,* 224.

15. Wiesel, *All Rivers Run to the Sea,* 103–5.

agony of his people."[16] These views, at the least, show that the process of God "convincing" some people may not be an automatic result, notwithstanding what Adams calls God's "superlative imagination," as will be detailed further below.[17] Keeping this tension of God's "convincing" us in mind, I now want to address why McCord Adams wants to minimize one's use of moral categories when examining horrendous evils.

RECLAIMING THE LANGUAGE OF PURITY AND HONOR

For McCord Adams, moral categories are deficient in addressing horrendous evils. In *Christ and Horrors*, she refers to the "lameness of moral categories"[18] while in *Horrendous Evils* she writes that "horror perpetration is no simple function of moral wrongdoing,"[19] as we often unknowingly and unintentionally produce horrors. Adding that "neither the Bible nor the major medieval and reformation theologians assert that God is *morally* good,"[20] she looks for an alternative "system of interpersonal evaluation" and takes from social anthropology that there are competing claims that could be useful in a theodic context, particularly the categories of purity and defilement and honor and shame.[21] For Adams the purity and defilement category is better suited than moral categories because it forces us to see our defilement compared to God's purity. It thus minimizes the dangers of overemphasizing "agent competence, indeed, to overestimate the capacity to subdue, with discipline, one's lower nature and to shoulder the responsibility to decide one's own destiny." She also claims that "[T]he lens of purity and defilement . . . replace[s] a priori idealized models with a more empirical psychology"[22] and that such a focus "is a good translation of Biblical and traditional declarations that God is holy while creatures are unclean."[23]

16. Eckhardt and Eckhardt, *Long Night's Journey*, 69.

17. McCord Adams, *Horrendous*, 82.

18. McCord Adams, *Christ and Horrors*, 36.

19. McCord Adams, *Horrendous*, 60–61.

20. Ibid., 61.

21. Ibid., 61.

22. Ibid., 103.

23. Ibid., 86. Issues of purity and impurity, of course, dominate certain biblical texts (Leviticus and Deuteronomy) and the sociohistorical context of the Christian

The category of honor and shame for Adams also underscores what persons are and not what they do.[24] It includes symbolic language which recognizes how horrendous evils have the power to "degrade" personal meaning.[25] To counteract this degradation, Adams stresses God as the ultimate meaning maker, fully "equipped" with Divine Imagination. She also contends that the honor code is "ideally suited to plumb the depths of what's wrong with horrors: namely their power to degrade by symbolizing that one is subhuman or worthless."[26] Other reasons include the code's highlighting of the "limits and source of human dignity," its denial of divine obligations (such a denial prevents one from claiming that God failed certain tests and so must not exist), the fact honor "can still be exchanged even when concrete needs are still lacking" or "fully supplied," and also because "the honor code *allows universalists to explain how in the Judgment, we will recognize how ascriptive honor is the cure.*"[27]

Before I proceed to critique these alternative means to conceptualize the problem of evil, I need to address McCord Adams's hesitation to call God "morally good," as this will bear on whether her alternative conceptions are more valid than moral categories.

IS GOD THEN IMMORAL?

As noted in chapter 3, Phillips highlights the problems of rendering God as a "fellow" member of our moral community, though his aim is to show the failure of theodic propositions. Adams will disavow theodicy and a morally good God, but still aim to prove how God can defeat horrendous evils.[28] Morality, as Adams conceives it, is a human-devised system that often seeks to judge God on human moral terms, as if there is no metaphysical size-gap between God and humanity. McCord Adams wants instead to advocate that God is not enslaved by our "lame" moral categories.

---

gospels, as seen with Christ's healing of lepers or the woman with the hemorrhage. The cross is also considered the ultimate act of restoring purity to what had been defiled (98).

24. Ibid., 107.

25. Ibid., 124.

26. Ibid., 124.

27. Ibid., 126–27.

28. Ibid., 192.

In support of Adams's position, Brian Davies contends that arguments based on God's moral goodness (that God is "well behaved"[29]) falsely claim to be traditional and biblically based.[30] Insisting that theists must also emphasize that God is "radically incomprehensible,"[31] Davies links existence with goodness and God as the only means for existence.[32] For Peter van Inwagen, on the other hand, "that God is morally perfect is a 'non-negotiable' element of theism."[33] I am particularly interested in assessing what gets lost in translation when Adams, Davies, and others deny the claim that God is moral in our contemporary situation of genocide, ecological crises, and endemic poverty.

What is implied if morality is simply a human affair? For Adams, is Christian morality not founded upon God's ongoing revelation in the Bible and in the life and witness of Christ? While diverse interpretations (some of which are clearly rooted in cultural constructs) outline the severity and conditions of moral and immoral acts, is it not standard Christian hope that the Holy Spirit—an "agency-enabler," in Adams's language[34]—works through individuals ("the Church" for John Paul II) to bring humanity to a closer relationship with God through right actions and right knowledge? In *Gaudium et Spes*, we read: "In a wonderful manner conscience reveals that law which is fulfilled by love of God and neighbor."[35] That Christianity decries slavery in any form today and deems it immoral is not merely a cultural, human-devised decree. For Christians, it is rooted in a greater understanding of revelation and a more mature following of Christ. In a world of mass atrocity, jettisoning a connection between God and morality would only seem to muddle how a theist is able to identify and find a ground for censuring immoral actions.

For Adams, though, not calling God moral also overcomes talk of God's obligation to us based on these faulty or lame moral categories.

29. Davies, *Reality of God*, 86. While the term "well behaved" is certainly provocative and tongue-in-cheek, it is also ethically inappropriate in the context of mass suffering, horrific evil, and an investigation of the viability of theistic faith.

30. Ibid., 87.

31. Ibid., 92.

32. Ibid., 193.

33. Van Inwagen, "Argument from Evil," 59.

34. McCord Adams, *Horrendous*, 104.

35. "Church in the Modern World," par. 16 (213).

In fact, Adams supports the language of honor and shame over morality when dealing with the problem of evil in part because "according to the honor code, God has no obligation either to take on God's clients or to service them once acquired."[36] According to the honor code, through covenantal relationships between God (the patron-king) and God's people (vassals), God's honor (as the patron or master) becomes invested in what happens to the people (patrons), and so what happens to them will reflect on God.[37] God does not act because God owes the people something. She similarly asserts that covenants in the Bible do not involve God "taking on obligations to created individuals or nations . . . Rather, God accommodates Himself to the human conditions to assure us of Divine good will."[38]

To illustrate Adams's contention, recall the story of Moses's intervention for the Israelites when they doubted whether they could conquer the Holy Land.[39] Moses does not argue on the basis of morality, but on God's honor. In fact, from God's command to the Israelites to commit genocide on foreign tribes[40] to calling Abraham to sacrifice Isaac,[41] biblical texts that attribute to God questionable moral acts or designs are not wanting. Nevertheless, one can turn to various schools of literary criticism or historical-biblical criticism to argue how best to read or interpret a biblical text without having to renounce that God is morally good. Contradictions are rife in the Bible, and some interpretive choices have to be made; however, on the whole, incidents of an amoral God are relatively rare when interspersed with dominant biblical tropes and themes. Our failure to reach and comprehend the "ultimate norms of morality" that *Gaudium et Spes* proclaims should not give us reason to undercut the value of moral categories. For Christians, moreover, striving to improve and clarify such norms is a fundamental calling, and so is a prerequisite for a theodicy.

36. McCord Adams, *Horrendous*, 112.

37. A similar rationale will be seen in the law court pattern of prayer in my discussion of theological protest in the Jewish tradition in ch. 8. However, in that tradition, God has clear obligations to God's people.

38. McCord Adams, *Horrendous*, 96.

39. Num 14:13–16. Like a wily lawyer, Moses often pleads to God in the hope of persuading God.

40. Josh 8:2; 8:24–26.

41. Gen 22:2.

At the same time, belief in moral progress has certainly been undermined because of catastrophic events like the mass killings in the Congo,[42] but such events also mobilize a greater calling to decry and denounce whatever degrades and dehumanizes the value of life. They are brutal reminders that failure to label and rebuke such crimes has dire consequences for everyone. While there are limits to the Nietzschean revaluing of all values, moral language must be constantly challenged and clarified.

Clearly, McCord Adams would have major problems ascribing immoral acts to God. However, what meaning does honor or shame and purity or defilement have for speaking about God and the problem of evil if God is not deemed morally good? Using the language of honor and shame is simply another way to frame and articulate the moral argument in which categories like purity and impurity mask or perform the traditional role of morality and immorality. If these other categories are ultimately to have any meaning, they are subsumed and defined by moral codes (and for a Christian like Adams, such moral codes are underwritten by the Christian Bible and tradition). Honor can be a good, but it is only a corollary of it; its meaning depends upon the good, not vice versa. These alternative models, therefore, seem best as supplementary ones to moral categories.

CONTRASTING ANTHROPOLOGICAL STARTING POINTS

Although McCord Adams claims that she affirms human responsibility, a dominant strand within her work is spent minimizing the profound connections between human identity and actions.[43] This has profound negative consequences for the dominant themes and language of her reflection on evil. While Adams believes her alternative categories are useful because they stress what human beings are and not what they do, it is difficult to separate this dichotomy so smoothly. A balance must be struck between upholding moral responsibility (and so not conflating the child burned in the pits with the Nazis who implemented, ordered, and enacted the policy) while recognizing that human freedom is always constrained in some way and one's intentions are never fully reflected in the consequences of one's actions.

42. Glover, *Humanity*, 2.

43. McCord Adams, *Horrendous*, 86.

This position in no way minimizes our moral responsibility for ignorance or carelessness, as Aristotle correctly notes.[44] Likewise, external factors (education, family upbringing, and societal and religious norms) may play a dominant role in forming and articulating one's moral horizon and language.

To illustrate some of the consequences of McCord Adams's contentions that God is holy while human beings are "unclean," I want to return to Didier Pollefeyt, whose position resonates with much of the writing of John Paul II, but is particularly applicable for my project because it is written in the context of mass atrocity, yet avoids pessimism or naïveté.[45] We cannot inhabit either extreme, but must accept our place within Levi's "gray zone." While identifying the presupposition to his approach to post-Holocaust ethics, Pollefeyt writes:

> Every human being, in being *human*, is structurally capable of developing an openness in himself or herself toward the vulnerability of the other. Consequently, I begin with an optimistic (theological) anthropology: every human being is capable of experiencing good and evil, or even stronger, each person discovers himself or herself as ethical, as connected with the good, even before he or she has consciously chosen good or evil.[46]

Pollefeyt also recognizes that one's capacity for the good can be constrained by exterior factors, but one is never beyond redemption. Such a position posits the goodness of humanity from an outside (theological) source while advocating a Levinasian-like calling to be "open to the vulnerability of the other."[47] Pollefeyt here strikes a proper balance between stressing individual choice and constrained freedom along with advocating responsibility for one's actions with the possibility to repent of wrongdoing.

To summarize these last few sections: Adams's tendency to separate and inflate one's being from one's actions and her refusal to proclaim a moral God[48] exposes some major flaws in her system and undermines

44. Aristotle, *Nicomachean Ethics*, III. 5 (358).

45. Pollefeyt, "Religious and Ethical Teaching," 181.

46. Pollefeyt, "Kafkaesque World: Response," 275–76.

47. Pollefeyt, "Kafkaesque World," 239.

48. In *Christ and Horrors*, Adams writes: "Thus, the Gospels give us a Jesus who was not only a victim, but also an occasioner and a perpetrator of horrors . . . [for] He joined every other subject in collective complicity in the horrors wrought by

the crucial roles of freedom, responsibility, integrity, and conscience. While adamant that "she does not deny great moral responsibility or culpability for deeds thus inadequately conceived by their agents,"[49] she diminishes these elements too drastically. The human person that emerges seems a faded shadow of our potential and essence.

THE RETURN OF AESTHETICS IN THEODICY

In addition to advocating alternative conceptual models and language for the problem of evil, Adams also wants to return the category of aesthetics back into a discussion of theodicy, but here boldly placed in relation to horrendous evils. She states that the "horrendous" is itself an aesthetic category and that "aesthetic goodness can play a significant role in Divine defeat of evils."[50] To make this aesthetic claim she will accentuate the creative imagination and goodness of God to defeat this evil.

One can imagine the difficulty of returning the language of aesthetics in a theodicy today.[51] Recall Little Eleanora, for example. Anticipating potential criticism, McCord Adams seeks aestheticism's renewal by emphasizing God's aesthetic powers of superlative imagination to defeat these evils.[52] For Roth, Adams's optimism does not adequately address those malicious evils that are beyond justification or redemption.[53]

While Adams agrees with Phillips and Roth that God cannot just expunge the slate postmortem—that such an act will not defeat the evils[54]—her answer is that "Divine *goodness* to creatures would not only balance off but *defeat* horrendous evil, and defeat it not simply

---

Rome" (71). As an example, she gives the case of his supposed advocating of paying taxes to Caesar. The example may not be apt, as Ched Myers convincingly argues. Jesus, who does not have any money, asks to see a coin that has the inscription that labels Augustus a God, sacrilege for a Jew and so a clear case of blasphemy. Giving unto Caesar does not mean Christ advocated taxes to Caesar (and so is an unwitting perpetrator of horrors). Instead, he was challenging his interlocutors' allegiances. See Myers, *Binding the Strong Man*, 310–14.

49. McCord Adams, *Horrendous*, 38.

50. Ibid., 61.

51. See Hick, *Evil and the God of Love*, 189.

52. McCord Adams, *Horrendous*, 147.

53. Roth, "Theodicy of Protest," 1, 3.

54. McCord Adams, *Horrendous*, 48.

within the context of the world as a whole but within the frame of the individual's own existence."[55] This is possible because God would have the power, imagination, creativity, and goodness to defeat those evils.[56] "God must *beautify* the person," she notes.[57] If God is perfect love and goodness, then there is great promise and hope in believing McCord Adams's claim that those who do not acknowledge God's love are like autistic children who are not aware of parental love. In the end, she exclaims: "Cognitive and emotional scales will fall and everyone will recognize the omnipresent tender loving care of God!"[58] For Adams, such hope is grounded in Christ.

CHRISTOLOGICAL UNDERPINNINGS

Similar to John Paul II's convictions, for McCord Adams, the life, death, and resurrection of Christ are crucial for additional scales to fall from the eyes. Christ is the keystone to all her thought.[59] Adams is not only stressing a personal God but advocating the Christian God who in the hypostatic union is both fully God and fully human. Similar to my claims in chapter 2, Adams stresses that through the human body, emotions, and experiences, Jesus endured suffering and so can particularly identify, commiserate, and be present in solidarity with all those who suffer in this life. She presents a God whose goodness, imagination, and creativity are enough to defeat all these horrors while having a unique bond with fellow sufferers in solidarity through Jesus's own ordeal and tribulations in this life.

The role of the beatific vision—and eschatology in general, therefore—is of crucial importance for McCord Adams's "theodicy." She contends that "God preserves created persons alive after their death in wholesome environments, that their relationships with God resolve into beatific intimacy so that the 'sufferings of the present life' are concretely balanced off."[60] According to Adams, God will convince everyone to accept the call to repent. All will be saved. She does not

---

55. Ibid., 53.

56. McCord Adams, "Afterword," 195.

57. McCord Adams, *Horrendous*, 149.

58. Ibid., 105.

59. McCord Adams, *Christ and Horrors*, 1.

60. McCord Adams, *Horrendous*, 162. I will return to this sense of "preserving" further below.

speculate here on how this encounter will play out. Perhaps, then, we are all Job-like, conjuring up fantastic arguments to and against God in the realm of our private thoughts, but fall silent when God finally speaks "out of the tempest."[61] I will return to her support of universal salvation in chapter 11, but I want to conclude this chapter by looking at a few other problematic assertions within McCord Adams's text (some of which are related to her support of universalism) that bear on the aims of my work and that limit the effectiveness of her position.

QUESTIONABLE ASSERTIONS

Wishing Suffering Away

To seek this redemption for all, Adams turns to the crucifixion as a means to state God's solidarity with all who suffer to transform what was disgraceful into the ultimate good. She agrees with Moltmann that Jesus knew what it was to be abandoned by God and so God must share our suffering.[62] She also agrees that Christ is a "symbol of transformation"[63] and so suffering can now have a positive moral meaning because of Jesus's suffering and murder.[64]

Problematically, though, she writes: "Retrospectively, I believe, from the vantage point of heavenly beatitude, human victims of horrors will recognize those experiences as points of identification with the crucified God, and not wish them away from their life histories."[65] This is a claim so broad and compelling that I need to spend a few moments to test its effectiveness.[66] In *The Gulag Archipelago*,

61. Job 38:1.

62. McCord Adams, *Horrendous*, 176.

63. Ibid., 177.

64. Ibid., 167.

65. Ibid., 167; *Christ and Horrors*, 40.

66. In her support of universalism, McCord Adams writes: "Still more amazing, God will be seen to have honored even the perpetrators of horrors by identifying with their condition, becoming ritually cursed through His death on a tree, taking His stand with the cursed to cancel the power of the curse forever!" (*Horrendous*, 127). It is worth questioning how Jesus's experience as a victim gives him the means to identify with all perpetrators (barring, of course, any reference to "hostage identification syndrome"). If the perpetrators were also victims, then the identification is meaningful. But it is a morally ambiguous and dangerous idea to make a claim that could imply that a victim of rape or abuse is therefore able to understand and empathize with the perpetrator's intent, moral framework, and human condition. I would argue that the opposite is more likely the case or one goes into therapy to

Solzhenitsyn—like Dostoyevsky prior to him[67]—encounters and reaffirms his faith in God through prison: "Bless you, prison, for having been in my life!"[68] Irina Ratushinskaya, Gilbert Tuhabonye, and Immaculée Ilibagiza make similar claims.[69] But these voices are relatively rare. The blank stares and animal-like groans of the *Muselmänner* are more than competing responses.[70] However, if God cannot redeem all evil—if, for example, the persons who have been crushed by affliction, forced to witness and participate in evils that led to their ultimate demise, cannot be in some way healed of these memories—then heaven as traditionally understood is closer to hell.[71] McCord Adams wants to maintain the integrity of all one's memory, but can one live and remember such life-destroying events and still participate fully in the beatific joy? As argued in the previous chapter, not all suffering can be or is meant as a means to identify with Christ. This claim is especially morally problematic for those forced to witness the torture and agony of a loved one.[72]

Suffering that torments, belittles, and dehumanizes—that ultimately leads to nothing but shame or, finally, one's murder—should not be so easily morphed into a means to identify with Christ. Palden Gyatso maintained his humanity and example of love despite the torture—not because of it. To say that God cannot find some way to heal this wound—especially as there are people among us today who have survived such trauma and find what can be called a "meaningful

---

overcome identifying with the perpetrator.

67. Dostoyevsky, *House of the Dead*, 340.

68. Solzhenitsyn, *Gulag Archipelago*, 313.

69. Ratushinskaya, *Grey Is the Color of Hope*, 148. Tuhabonye is a Tutsi from Burundi who was the only survivor of a mass atrocity committed against the Tutsis. He writes: "I kept asking Jesus to forgive me. In the fire, I saw that I had drifted . . . In his infinite mercy, God had forgiven me and let me live" (*This Voice in My Heart*, 201). Ilibagiza contends: "In the midst of genocide, I'd found my salvation . . . I'd been born again in the bathroom and was now the loving daughter of God, my Father" (*Left to Tell*, 107). A Tutsi survivor of the Rwandan genocide, Ilibagiza was forced to hide for three months with other Tutsis in a cramped bathroom. Most of her family was murdered.

70. For a reflection on the *Muselmann*, see Agamben, *Remnants of Auschwitz*, 41–63, and especially his inclusion of testimonies from those identified as "former" Muselmänner, 166–71.

71. See Volf, *End of Memory*.

72. Gyatso, *Fire*, Prologue.

life"—would be to speak presumptuously of God. But the moral and conceptual problems remain in how Adams articulates this redemption. Why would the horror victim not wish the suffering away? Is God's embrace "greater" because of this experienced evil, and would the effect not be the same without it? If horrific suffering for some individuals is the only meaningful way to identify with God, then it will take a lot of "convincing" on God's part to prove to every individual why life was good or valuable on the whole, especially if the suffering seems meaningless and was unwarranted.

Denying God's Obligation

The hope of Adams's universalism may also be tarnished by her disavowal of God's obligation to us.[73] While Aquinas contends that "God owes nothing to anyone other than himself," he clarifies: "So that when you speak of his not being able to do except what he ought to do you only mean that he cannot do other than what for him is fitting and fair."[74] In Adams's second volume of *William of Ockham*, she presents Ockham's more radical claim that "God is a debtor to no one unless He has so ordained it. With respect to His absolute power, He can punish a creature without any demerit and reward a creature without merit, without any injury to the person."[75] While Ockham notes the example of Christ who was sinless and yet was crucified, Adams explains Ockham's logic in part by showing how "arbitrary action on God's part is not necessarily foolish."[76]

It should be clear that the Supreme Being can have no obligation in the sense that I am obligated as a father to love my children. An obligation as decreed from an exterior source cannot of course apply to God. If God is the Good, then God could never simply allow evils to go unpunished and the suffering unredeemed. This is not, strictly speaking, an obligation. As Aquinas hints at above, it is a matter both of being God and God's being. In this limited but important sense, God is "obligated" (even if the obligation stems from God's Self). Furthermore, claiming that God is obligated to creatures because God chose to create this world—or, in biblical language, accentuating

---

73. McCord Adams, *Horrendous*, 158.

74. Aquinas, "Why Think of God as Omnipotent?" 421.

75. McCord Adams, *William of Ockham*, 2:1264.

76. Ibid., 1265.

God's covenant with humanity and the Israelites in particular—does not detract from the transcendence, ineluctability, and ineffability of God. But if God is a personal agent, as McCord Adams wants to stress, then the language of obligation, though needing clarification, is still apt. To redeem evil, God does owe the victims of the bubonic plague or Auschwitz or the tsunami of 2004 some means of redemption because God is obligated to be God. To redeem unjustified evils is a good, which is precisely why God would do so. Instead of trying to work out divine obligation with our human finite sense, it is more helpful to accentuate that God only does what is just and merciful or we are not speaking about God.[77]

Trying to Liberate Liberation Theology

Feminist-informed and postcolonial critiques of some aspects of liberation theology have been particularly useful in maintaining or restoring the relevance of liberation theology.[78] McCord Adams's critiques, however, only perpetuate the old, tired misreading of the movement. While one would think McCord Adams's aims would find substantial agreements with liberation theology because of her focus on horror participants, she instead distances herself from that theology. As John D'Arcy May writes: "Far from being crypto-Marxists and advocates of revolutionary violence, the liberation theologians, by and large, were motivated from the beginning of their movement by spirituality, learned from the oppressed people themselves in 'base Christian communities,' which integrate contemplation and praxis."[79] Unfortunately, McCord Adams either does not highlight these common tendencies of liberation theology in her arguments or misinterprets them. While partnering with the key tenets of liberation theology would have strengthened many of her arguments, her criticism of them instead points to some weaknesses within her own position. I will not highlight every instance of her misreading of liberation theology, but only what is pertinent to my focus. This section will also serve as a link to

---

77. Note that I use the word *endeavor* to maintain some sense of individual freedom, responsibility, and choice. In other words, some individuals may reject God's act of redemption and healing. I will return to this issue in ch. 11.

78. See the essays in Rieger, *Opting for the Margins*.

79. May, *After Pluralism*, 128.

the next two chapters, which include my evaluation of theodic texts from Jon Sobrino and Gustavo Gutiérrez.[80]

Instead of the preferential option for the poor, McCord Adams wants to assert "multisite solidarity,"[81] claiming it will guarantee a focus on God being equally good to everyone. She believes that the preferential option for the poor is too partial to be applied to the ultimate aim of God's goodness to everyone. It appears that she has misunderstood the term.[82] As Stephen Pope writes: "The preferential option, properly understood, appeals to an *expansion* rather than contraction of love and wisdom."[83]

Biblically what has to be stressed is the justice of God, a justice that aims to be fair to everyone: "You shall not render an unjust judgment; you shall not be partial to the poor or defer to the great; with justice you shall judge your neighbor."[84] The Jewish theologian Eliezer Berkovits notes some of the tensions of a God who is impartial and yet seeks to protect the poor and oppressed, as in the biblical passage of Deut 10:18, which speaks of a God "who regards no person" while adding: "He does execute justice for the fatherless and widow, and loves the stranger, in giving him food and raiment." Thus, "to seek justice is to relieve the oppressed."[85] At the same time, because judging is so closely linked with ethics, impartiality under the law remained the key rule.[86]

80. Other misconceptions include an outdated critique of some liberation theologian's use of Marxism (McCord Adams, *Horrendous*, 197), and her claim that liberation theologians idolize the poor (200). For clear rebuttals, see Petrella, *Latin American Liberation Theology*, xiv; and Gutiérrez, *On Job*, 94.

81. McCord Adams, *Horrendous*, 201.

82. For a critique of liberation theology somewhat parallel to Adams's argument, though from a liberation theologian, see Althaus-Reid, "From Liberation Theology to Indecent Theology," 20–38. Althaus-Reid argues that the original thrust of liberation theology did not address discrimination based on race, gender, or sexual orientation: "Liberation theology had built a concept of the poor within parameters taken totally from a strictly defined site of authority" (31).

83. Pope, "Proper and Improper Partiality," 242. See also Solomon, "Economics and Liberation," 130–31.

84. Lev 19:15; see also Exod 23:3.

85. Berkovits, *Essential Essays*, 133.

86. See also: Amos 8:4, 7; Ps 82:3–4; and especially the letter of James. At the very least, the Bible never advocates the option for the rich, and Christ's response that in performing acts like clothing the naked and feeding the hungry, one clothes and feeds Him (Matt 25:31–46) should settle the matter for most Christians.

In one sense, Pope agrees with McCord Adams by noting how there may be multiple "privileged locations" where aspects of God's goodness, mercy, and justice can be acknowledged and experienced. Poverty, or another form of marginalization, is not the only "privileged" location.[87] However, stating the notion of "preference" in the context of God's love can still maintain God's love for everyone—but in our world, choices have to be made. A God who is on the side of justice and love will—again, broadly speaking—be on the side of the poor and oppressed. This is in part because such people are voiceless and powerless for basic human rights and are hindered from the potential to develop even basic capabilities.

To try to poke holes in the argument by bringing up an example of a virtuous rich person versus a dishonest poor one is to miss the point. More useful is the inclusion of subaltern studies and the postmodern and feminist-informed critiques of identity, which expand our cognizance of the many kinds of marginalized and oppressed individuals and groups. As Joerg Rieger writes: "Thus the preferential option for the poor becomes much broader than before, a move which requires not only greater awareness of who is sucked into the position of the other in today's world, but also a whole new set of encounters with people beyond one's own horizon of class, gender, race, and social location."[88]

While Adams is aware of the criticism that her focus may seem to diminish our accountability and purpose in this world, she also unduly censures liberation theologians for what she believes is an inordinate focus on liberation from material misery in this world.[89] This position is linked with her tendency to minimize our responsibility for our moral choices, in part, to account for why universal salvation is a more just option for everyone.

A balance has to be struck here. Because of the extent and depravity of evil in this world and the limits of human justice, if suffering can be "overcome," the onus is mostly on God. Sadly, too much blood has been spilled; too many people have others' blood on their hands (remember, one call kill with an immoral law or embargo as easily as

---

87. Sobrino *No Salvation outside the Poor*, 22.

88. Rieger, "Theology and the Power of the Margins," 184.

89. For a similar critique of Benedict XVI on this idea, see Corkery, "Joseph Ratzinger," 191.

with a bomb or machete). Nevertheless, overreliance upon God need not be a negative faith practice if it also incorporates human responsibility and human effort to end gratuitous suffering in this life. McCord Adams instead seems to rebuke liberation theology's overemphasis on the goal to promote the reign of God here and now and to work for that justice because she seems to think their aims are constructed solely in the context of human intentions and effort.[90]

In this regard she is right to note our abysmal effort in making this world a utopia for all. But liberation theologians always see social justice through the biblical lens of the gospels: the life, death, and resurrection of Christ, and God's saving action in history, as depicted in Exodus and in other works from the Tanak. It is never purely a human affair.[91] Catholic liberation theologians, like most Christians, are straddling both this world and the next, and asserting that the saving presence of God is endowed in both worlds. Nothing radical there. As José Comblin writes: "God's grace enters human history . . . [it] is the force that awakens, animates, and maintains the struggle of the oppressed, who are victims of injustice and evil."[92] There is no separation, no dichotomy between establishing the reign of God on earth while also anticipating the transcendent redemption and flowering of that reign at the final judgment.[93] Again, rarely indeed would a liberation theologian call for justice without the concomitant plea for God's saving grace and intervention. The two paths are complementary, not contradictory.[94]

Contra Adams's interpretations, liberation theology is also not opposed to her focus on the individual.[95] Liberation theologians would applaud it, especially as she is referring to victims of oppression and violence who are often voiceless. Most liberation theologians are attacking systemic problems caused and perpetrated by individuals against individuals, and the focus on the suffering of individual

---

90. McCord Adams, *Horrendous*, 198.

91. Ellacuría, "Utopia and Prophecy," 304.

92. Comblin, "Grace," 530.

93. Phan, "Prophecy and Contemplation," 187.

94. See Limón, "Suffering, Death, Cross, and Martyrdom," 708.

95. McCord Adams, *Christ and Horrors*, 206. A better understanding of the option for the poor would prevent such a misunderstanding.

victims leads to a condemnation of the structures that promote that suffering. It is not a matter of either/or.[96]

Theological Language amidst Burning Children

In addition to demonstrating how Adams has misread liberation theology, I need to clarify her interpretation of Greenberg's "working principle." In chapter 1, I introduced the principle as a means to evaluate theodicies, though I left the question open whether it is the best litmus test for all theodic statements or whether it needs to be clarified or altered in some way. In this section, using McCord Adams's critique, I will further chart my own stance on this principle and how it connects to my aims in this work.

One of McCord Adams's worthwhile goals is to "chart a *via media* that rejects any dichotomizing of philosophical reflections on horrors, on the one hand, and praxis that copes with them, on the other."[97] She rightly questions whether the theoretical and practical approaches conflict or are separate. While there may be disagreement on whether theory or praxis is more important, they should have a symbiotic relationship.[98] Without theoretical probing, reflection, and articulation of moral language, the meaning and efficacy of a moral act could be diminished or misinterpreted. The theory ideally should nourish, challenge, and inspire such praxis; and where action is wanting or misapplied, theoretical language can be a means to redirect and channel one's energies to a more effective and moral end.

Advocating the role that theoretical and philosophical theology can play, therefore, particularly for horror participants, McCord Adams argues that "many (though, to be sure not all) participants in horrors, sooner or later, not at every stage but eventually, over and over, raise questions of meaning: of why God allowed it, of whether and how God could redeem it, etc."[99] The tentativeness and disclaimers of the sentence are duly noted. McCord Adams then boldly challenges Irving Greenberg's principle, writing: "Put otherwise more bluntly, it remains appropriate for philosophers to say things it would be inappropriate to voice in the presence of the burning children

---

96. Phan, "Prophecy and Contemplation," 186.
97. McCord Adams, *Horrendous*, 186.
98. Pope, "Proper and Improper," 271.
99. McCord Adams, *Horrendous*, 188.

because participants in horrors are themselves not always in the presence of burning children. Survivors have to deal with their experiences afterward."[100] This claim rests upon the notion that the actual moment of extreme suffering differs from what follows. It agrees with Greenberg's contention that one must reach into the pit while children are actually burning, but argues that at some point following the dreadful event, some truths not appropriate then need to be said after.

In chapter 1 we saw how traumatic memories can make the victim relive the trauma that remains with them forever.[101] For many victims, the issue of time is not relevant. In fact, Greenberg's point is that because we are more aware of these atrocities, saying anything becomes circumspect from now on. The memories or the witnesses—or the deceased of these ordeals—will not let us do otherwise. Thus, we are always in the presence of burning children. As we speak, somebody, somewhere, is being tortured and mutilated, or is suffering in agonizing pain. With the proliferation of mass media and the instantaneous transmission of news, one can be in the presence of a suffering human being through access to television or the Internet. When in the physical presence of such a victim (and, of course, distinctions like a victim's age, religion, and rational capacity are key factors), the paramount issue is that a victim may not want to hear these theodic arguments because the pain is too acute, and this could be during the ordeal or decades after. It should also be remembered that some individuals have engaged in theodicy amidst affliction and suffering, as Donat's quotation argues above, though he, unlike some rabbis, lost faith.[102] As a rabbi and author, Greenberg does not advocate total silence, but is urging that we take great care with what we say because of these horrendous truths.[103]

In Greenberg's subsequent essays he addresses his working principle, often clarifying its meanings and calling for humanity to take up greater responsibility in an ongoing, but voluntary covenant. He writes that the Talmud reveals that God respects human free will and

100. Ibid., 188.

101. Améry, *Mind's Limits,* 36.

102. The struggles of the young protagonist in Elie Wiesel's *Night* reflect some of these concerns. For this discussion, along with more analysis of Greenberg, see ch. 9.

103. Geddes, "Religious Rhetoric in Responses to Atrocity," 30. See also Steele, *Christianity, Tragedy, and Holocaust Literature,* 29

so does not intervene in our world but still supports life despite our failures. He writes: "This revelation summons humankind to secularity, to create and rehabilitate the divine image in a human community. This is the ultimate testimony—perhaps the only credible one—that can speak of God in a world of burning children."[104]

Thus, any act that seeks to mend the world can be a sign of that testimony. As a theist, Greenberg also knows there is a value and purpose to theoretical language.[105] Depending on context, one cannot necessarily say what was inappropriate during someone's ordeal as opposed to after it.[106] Finally, one needs to recall that McCord Adams often writes from a pastoral perspective based on her personal life. Her *Wrestling for Blessing* contains her sermons to members of her congregation who were often in great pain and misery from dying of AIDS, or who were sexually abused, or suffering other horrific ills.[107] This praxis is certainly praiseworthy, but such pastoral sensitivity, unfortunately, is not fully reflected in her challenge of Greenberg's "working principle."

On God-Tantrums

Another problematic component is McCord Adams's stress on a passible God. She states: "God the Son suffers in *both* natures—in the Divine nature (not only feeling our feelings but also 'God-sized' distress) . . . and in the human nature (participation in horrors within the framework of a finite consciousness)."[108] Basing her view predominantly on the Bible, she claims that "God could feel torn with anger and grief" or "exasperated"[109] while remaining stable compared to the frenetic alterations of our emotional frame of mind. This suffering and

---

104. Greenberg, *For the Sake of Heaven and Earth*, 137.

105. Ibid., 86.

106. While a student in Elie Wiesel's class some fifty-years after the Holocaust, I would never have voiced any Christological statement deemed potentially inappropriate to him, like emphasizing how Christ had been there to comfort him at Auschwitz.

107. McCord Adams, *Wrestling for Blessing*, 8.

108. McCord Adams, *Horrendous*, 174. For a rich account that turns to the writings of Arthur Peacocke to accentuate an "evolutionary theology of the creative suffering of the Triune God as a means to speak rightly about the mystery of God in the midst of a suffering world," see Schaab, *Creative Suffering of the Triune God*, 193.

109. McCord Adams, *Horrendous*, 173.

emotive God, then, never stoops to our level because God is "too vast and stable," but God's acute identification with our affliction puts God in a better position to redeem all horror participants.

It is a valid aim, but not ultimately convincing. While the utterly apathetic human person does not express the rich depth of humanity, a lack of stability and equanimity can influence our actions to be unjust or improper. Think of rage, for example. Aristotle writes: "Now *hot-tempered* people get angry quickly and with the wrong persons and at the wrong things and more than is right, but their anger ceases quickly—which is the best point about them."[110] Unless, of course, such a hot-tempered "fellow" is God, as the "literary" character of some of the stories in the Bible reveals.[111]

In an analysis of God's anger, particularly in the Hebrew Bible, Thomas Weinandy shows that for Novatian, "God's anger is not an indication of God's mutability or passibility, but an expression of his immutable perfection and passionate goodness."[112] Maimonides makes a similar claim in *The Guide for the Perplexed*, arguing that emotions attributed to God like "jealousy, desire for retribution, revenge, or anger . . . are in accordance with the guilt of those who are to be punished, and not the result of any emotion; for He is above all defect."[113] Contra Adams, a passible God may be emotionally appealing but is not therefore in a better position to redeem humanity. Weinandy continues: "If the whole ontological system, which includes God, is impaired by evil, then there is no one, including God, who can repair it and make it right . . . The consequences of a suffering God are dire indeed."[114]

---

110. Aristotle, *Nicomachean Ethics*, IV. 5 (390).

111. Gen 6:5–7; Exod 4:14; Exod 4:24–26; and Exod 33. Harold Bloom writes: "Mischievous, inquisitive, jealous, and turbulent, Yahweh is as personal as a God can be" (*Jesus and Yahweh*, 138). Also see Novatian above for an example of a patristic theologian not reading such passages literally. Finally, see Sweeney, *Reading the Hebrew Bible after the Shoah*, 25.

112. Weinandy, *Does God Suffer?* 106.

113. Maimonides, *Guide for the Perplexed*, 76. Interestingly, against McCord Adams's use of God's imagination, Maimonides claims that because of a defect in imagination, which is subject to change, "Imagination (*ra'ayon*), therefore, was never employed as a figure in speaking of God, while thought and reason are figuratively ascribed to Him" (64).

114. Weinandy, *Does God Suffer?* 157.

I agree with Weinandy that an impassible God is in a better position to guarantee truth, justice, and goodness to everyone.[115] To stress "God's compassion and mercy is seen most fully in its effect"[116] is to remember the promises revealed through a religion in which God champions the rights of the poor and the oppressed. Such a loving, merciful God is also a God of justice, and therefore those who have murdered and raped and mutilated and refuse to turn to God in repentance will reap what they sow.

Part of the current sympathy with arguing for a passible God is based both on a misunderstanding of the tradition and awareness of the magnitude of evil in our world. Weinandy critiques the common mistake made by advocates of God's passibility who equate impassibility with apathy and a lack of love. He writes: "Rather, to say that God is impassible . . . is to deny of God all those characteristics and properties of the created order which render him less than perfectly good, loving, and merciful."[117]

I support McCord Adams's aim to present a God worthy of belief and capable of healing the many wounds of this world. We just do not need a passible God to do that.

CONCLUSION

Recall Helen Bamber's concerns for how to treat people who have been tortured. McCord Adams's focus on horrendous evils while seeking a way for God to redeem all horror participants is noteworthy and commendable and could be a great hope for many sufferers. However, the use of testimonies of mass atrocity would have clarified some of the above problematic assertions and aided her aim. So, too, would a starting point that accentuates the goodness of humanity, as Pollefeyt aptly argues.

Nevertheless, if one acknowledges the God of creation and accentuates the beauty, creativity, and diversity of life and a God of superlative imagination, as McCord maintains, then belief in life after death, which is dependent on that God of creation, does not seem as impossible or absurd as Phillips implies.

115. Ibid., 160.
116. Ibid., 229.
117. Ibid., 94.

Assessment of Section 1

Before turning to liberation theology texts, I want to highlight features in section 1 that would be useful in developing a viable theodicy.

Though needing further refinements, Phillips's advocacy of a disinterested faith rightly touches upon a useful framework to view suffering in this world. However, from his analysis, I do not see the tenability of theism without theodicy or a theism that denies the afterlife and dismantles traditional conceptions of God. Theism needs theodicy and a theodicy needs an eschatological context.

John Paul II's *Salvifici Doloris* points to the possibility for meaning and healing of one's suffering through participation in the redemptive work of Christ and committing oneself to follow in Jesus's footsteps. While I remain skeptical that such a potentially empowering message is open to all types of suffering, the message brims with so much hope and optimism that it reopens the possibility to speak of meaningful agency for individuals (especially those in mass atrocity) who are often restricted and limited by their "victimhood."

McCord Adams's work is particularly helpful for her focus on the impact of horrific evils on the victims and perpetrators of horrendous suffering. While I was not convinced of the value of a return to aesthetics or a movement away from moral categories when examining a theodicy, her work is also valuable for accentuating that if a theodicy fails one person, it fails everyone.

It is surprising that McCord Adams distances herself from liberation theology. Such a theology's emphasis on the voiceless and the underprivileged demands that a theodicy focus on the most vulnerable so that all will be included. Just as I turn to witnesses of mass atrocity to ensure their voice and arguments are heard and reflected upon, liberation theologians do their theology from the underside of history, which necessarily colors and defines their theological concepts in a similar fashion. I will examine this key element more fully in the next two chapters.

Section 2

Liberation Theology: Doing Theology "While Ayacucho Lasts"[1]

In Scripture, the oppression of the poor in everyday life appears much more often than their repression in massacres. For that reason we shall refer more to everyday oppression.[2]

The next two chapters will analyze theodic texts from the Catholic Latin American liberation theologians Jon Sobrino and Gustavo Gutiérrez. With its focus on the preferential option for the poor, praxis, and structural injustice, liberation theology provides crucial theological tools and vocabulary for theodicists. While these texts will address issues of mass atrocity, their main focus, as the epigraph above acknowledges, is the mass exploitation and oppression of the poor on a daily basis. At the least, mass poverty and oppression are truths which certainly undermine arguments about the beauty and goodness of this world and so raise questions about God's active role or presence. One issue, then, is whether focusing on mass atrocity excludes or addresses such types of suffering or poverty. And more importantly, how does one talk about a loving God in the midst of such suffering and mass death?

1. Gutiérrez, *Job*, 102.
2. Sobrino, *Where Is God?* 80n11.

6

Sobrino's Praxic Theodicy

Half the newborn children in Cité Soleil will die before they reach the age of five.[1]

This chapter focuses on Jon Sobrino's *Where Is God? Earthquake, Terrorism, Barbarity, and Hope* for his assessment of the value of theodicy from the vantage point of the poor and oppressed. This aim is akin to my own use of testimonies of mass atrocity to gauge a theodicy's relevance to such victims. This chapter will be divided into two main headings: the first will highlight key features of his text that are helpful for any theodicy while the second part will examine his evaluation of theodicy in the context of the impoverished and the exploited of Latin America.

KEY FEATURES OF THE TEXT

(Un)natural Evil

Writing after the earthquakes of January and February 2001 in El Salvador, in *Where Is God?*, Sobrino grapples with natural and moral evil and usefully argues why instances of so-called natural evil often entail acts of moral evil.[2] For example, he highlights humanity's reluc-

1. Straub, *Hidden in the Rubble*, 5. See also Meredith, *Fate of Africa*, 682; McClelland, "Aftershocks."

2. For my examination of "natural" evil, see my "Dirt, Collapse, and Eco-responsibility."

135

tance to share resources and technology, which makes the poor more likely to die in certain catastrophes. One could also add the prohibitive cost of vaccinations to third-world countries. Thus, human negligence or greed often results in mass death. In El Salvador, a confluence of acts of moral evil coupled with natural disasters have led to avoidable disasters. Its victims, Sobrino writes, "are not only excluded but non-existent."[3] They are voiceless. Sobrino notes how to live in El Salvador is especially burdensome for the poor, particularly during an earthquake, which "is not just a tragedy, it is an X-ray of the country."[4] In a natural disaster, economic disparity is almost always exposed. The wealthy have insurance or live on higher ground or have buildings of more durable quality. The destitute do not. Sallie McFague, for example, links the fate of the impoverished to how nature is abused and exploited on a daily basis. McFague sees this exploitation encapsulated in a "poor third world woman of color who lives at the junction of human poverty and nature's poverty, often reduced to gathering the few remaining sticks of wood to cook her family's meal."[5]

Interestingly, a number of recent scientific and anthropological accounts have shown how human impact on the biosphere and ecology has often caused what are later determined to be natural evils. As geomorphologist David Montgomery writes in *Dirt: The Erosion of Civilizations*: "Although usually portrayed as natural disasters, crop failures and famines often owe as much to land abuse as to natural calamities."[6] Such a reality, which does not exculpate God as the creator of such a world, underlies how humanity is complicit in perpetrating and exacerbating events that inflict revolting torment and death.

Theodicy and Anthropodicy

To face these evils openly and honestly, Sobrino, as fellow Jesuit Georges de Schrijver writes, "refuses to separate the question of the justification of God (theodicy) from that of the justification of the human being (anthropodicy)."[7] This union of anthropodicy and theodicy maintains a layered perspective on the reality of evil. The

3. Sobrino, *Where Is God?* xxxiii.
4. Ibid., 3. See also Straub, *Hidden in the Rubble*, xxi, 102–3.
5. McFague, "Ecological Christology," 40. See also Meredith, *Fate of Africa*.
6. Montgomery, *Dirt*, 144. See also Diamond, *Collapse*, 230.
7. Schrijver, *Recent Theological Debates in Europe*, 285.

important issue, Sobrino argues, is to seek the whereabouts of both God and humanity: "Where are they today in the African Great Lakes, Haiti, Bangladesh, countries that live, as we do, side by side with the scandalous profligacy of the North?"[8]

Sobrino contends that if one cites the appearance of evil to prove that God does not exist, then any attempt at anthropodicy will also fail because "fifty million human beings die every year from hunger or hunger-related illnesses," and yet despite the access we have to resources, we do not halt this travesty. Therefore, "Fifty million human beings do not just die: they are killed. By the critical logic of theodicy, it may be that 'the human species' exists—but not 'humanity,' not 'the human family.'"[9]

Before we blame God, we need to take a longer look at our own actions and negligence. Nor should such suffering be blamed on fate, circumstance, or simply deemed a "tragedy" when the cause is human greed and carelessness. In the quote above, it is also relevant that Sobrino includes the devastating suffering that is present through both war and endemic poverty. Recall the OED's definition of "atrocity" in chapter 1. Sobrino and other liberation theologians argue that the suffering of millions in this world is an atrocity perpetrated by systemic structures that are planned, developed, and supported by individuals in various governments and companies, along with a majority of those in the "first world" or "Global North" who are often complicit in allowing such conditions or who benefit from them without reflection. For Ivone Gebara, we blind ourselves to "the hidden evil. The evil without fanfare, the evil that never enters into the annals of a country."[10] According to Thomas Pogge, moreover, "The annual death toll from poverty-related causes is around 18 million, or one-third of all human deaths, which adds up to approximately 360 million deaths since the end of the Cold War."[11]

Just as Partnoy opened her testimony with the Argentine government's denial of torture centers, similar equivocation is present whenever someone claims that the deaths of millions of children from malnutrition or preventable disease is not a mass atrocity. If

8. Sobrino, *Where Is God?* 27.

9. Ibid., 26.

10. Gebara, *Out of the Depths*, 22.

11. Pogge, "World Poverty," 307.

such suffering does not fit such descriptions, how do we describe the magnitude of so many premature deaths (see this chapter's epigraph)? In fact, because a theodicy seeks to uphold the beauty and value of creation and a healing and redemptive God of love and justice, Sobrino's text is invaluable for ensuring that such extensive suffering is included in any theodic discussion that also examines horrors like the Holocaust or Rwandan genocide.

Primordial Holiness

In chapter 2, we heard victims allege that God was absent while others maintained God's presence. Sobrino finds that "even in the midst of catastrophe and daily hardship, the poor and the victims—especially the women, and their children—put into practice and fulfill with distinction God's call to life, and to give life to others."[12] Such a practice he deems "primordial holiness." While such suffering is normally evidence against theodicy, Sobrino states that these struggles point to why one can begin to answer the question of how God is present in the midst of tragedy.[13]

Crucial to such an assertion is the option for the poor.[14] Because God is on the side of the poor and the oppressed, the poor often reveal the presence of God working within them, even if only in their responding to the call to live and to aid others to live.[15] While one rarely seeks to imitate such lives, the poor "inspire humanizing feelings of veneration, wherever there are people of good heart."[16] They are "sacraments," and thus signs of God's presence. Sobrino provocatively writes: "From the theological dynamic of 'from among the poor,' there developed also a rethinking of the locus from which salvation comes. In this way we arrived at the formula *extra pauperes nulla salus* (outside the poor there is no salvation)."[17]

I have already advocated my support of the preferential option (though siding with Stephen Pope's clarifications), and I am willing to support the formula above, especially if by "the poor" we mean those

---

12. Sobrino, *Where Is God?* 73.

13. Ibid., 150.

14. Ibid., 81.

15. Ibid., 73–74.

16. Ibid., 73.

17. Sobrino, *No Salvation outside the Poor*, 71.

who are oppressed and marginalized or lacking basic human needs. To perpetrate injustice against the poor and marginalized, whether through intent or indifference, is antithetical to seeking to spread the reign of God on earth. Such a formula, at the least, is more concrete and inclusive than the outdated one which claimed there was no salvation outside the church. Nevertheless, I still have questions concerning Sobrino's interpretations here: How, in fact, is God's presence made manifest in the dying poor, especially those who perish, abandoned and forgotten, or who commit injustice? What can be revealed of God (and humanity) with the deaths of millions of children from disease and starvation? If one rejects the liberation theologians' reading of the biblical stories, what becomes the basis for an option for the poor?

Sobrino believes that seeing the poor under the rubric of primordial holiness or saintliness will lead us to see goodness and God's presence where we often only see misery. This seeing will insist that we change our lives for the benefit of others in need: "It would be ironic if we focused on the exceptional saints and ignored the victimized majorities, because what the saints ask of us is precisely to stand at the cross with the victims . . ."[18] Such solidarity for Sobrino is present through the crucifixion and the resurrection, as both events testify to God's great love that gives hope for "the possibility of resurgent life."[19]

Sobrino's description of the lives of victims of poverty and oppression as "primordial holiness" or "saintliness" attempts to render as sanctified and meaningful what only seems to be loss and victimization.[20] Stressing that the poor's holiness does not "romanticize the poor"[21] nor deny that they can also be "holy sinners,"[22] Sobrino reflects upon child soldiers and writes: "no concepts can express the reality of these child-soldiers, these poor people and victims." The causes must be condemned, but he includes these children under the rubric of primordial holiness "from the standpoint of a world indifferent to, and co-responsible for, such a tragedy."[23] He is urging the world,

18. Ibid., 80.

19. Ibid., 150. See also Sobrino, *Where Is God?* 145; Sobrino, "Systematic Christology," 440–61.

20. Sobrino, *No Salvation outside the Poor*, 19–20.

21. See Gutiérrez, *On Job*, 94.

22. Sobrino, *Where Is God?* 74.

23. Ibid., 75.

complicit in its indifference to their plight, to see these children as they are: scarred, broken, and corrupted, but still children who are loved by God and in desperate need of conversion. He makes these hopeful claims about these victims while excoriating the complicit world because "Christ proclaim[ed] and inaugurat[ed] the Reign of God in behalf of the poor and outcast."[24] Such statements, as exemplified in the option for the poor and in Christ's solidarity with lepers and prostitutes, highlight how God is present in those who seek to spread the reign of God—even amidst tragedy.

Primal Solidarity

For Sobrino, as with Greenberg in his working principle, one must strive principally to heal victims and prevent the reoccurrence of such anguish. In addition to his term "primordial holiness," Sobrino speaks of a "primal solidarity" among the poor, who do not expect sufficient outside help and so band together to restore, heal, and save what they can.[25]

While the poor respond with primal solidarity, Sobrino advocates that outsiders in the first world should "let ourselves be affected by this tragedy, not to turn away or soften it." He believes this is not a type of masochism but an "initial moment of honesty toward reality."[26] To be open to this initial moment, however, is not a guaranteed state. In order to see, one has to know what to look for and be open to what one sees, which is why for Sobrino "there is also a salvific aspect to truly letting ourselves be affected by tragedy."[27] Sobrino's use of the term "salvific" in this context is particularly apt, as it reveals a person now oriented to see reality while acknowledging the struggles one must face. Such a reality is not exempt from theological questioning.

Theological Protest

While the presence of God for Sobrino is seen in the lives of the struggling poor and in individuals like Oscar Romero, he writes that faith in God often demands protest and questioning "the God they believe

---

24. Sobrino, "Systematic Christology," 453.

25. Sobrino, *Where Is God?* 6.

26. Ibid., 7.

27. Ibid.

in, who apparently cannot or will not prevent the catastrophes."[28] Note the balance trying to be struck here, not only between theodicy and antitheodicy but in the role of questioning and faith. As will be seen in my discussion of many Jewish theologians and Talmudic rabbis in chapters 8 and 9, theological protest and questioning can play an essential role in one's candid and authentic faith position and probing. While voices rejecting theological protest are prominent in Christian tradition,[29] Sobrino advocates such protest because it flows from "ultimate respect and unconditional love for the poor and the victims." It demands to know why such lives, valued and loved by God, have been suddenly cut off and forgotten. Such protest is especially linked with the need for justice.[30]

Uniting theodicy and anthropodicy is an important means to attempt to ask the right questions at the proper time to the deserving party. It maintains responsibility for human acts and the role of individual will and choice while also acknowledging God as the ultimate creator. Issues of responsibility will often be muddled. Ultimately, neither humanity nor God can be a scapegoat for the Other. Theists should never hesitate in blaming humanity for most of the ills in this world (the evidence is insurmountable), but—as Jewish protest theology will remind us—failure to question or challenge (or indict) God for earthly horrors and atrocities could be a failure of responsibility to that Other and to one's relationship with God. Thus, if one may speak of a fractured theodicy, one must always speak of a fractured anthropodicy. Or to put it this way: a fractured theodicy is spoken of with fear and trembling; a fractured anthropodicy is uttered without hesitation and any smidgeon of doubt.

Theological Memory

While theological protest is one response to suffering in our world, how and what one remembers (or forgets) plays a key role in forming a picture of our world and determining where injustice thrives. Just as the victors often write history, Sobrino argues that the powerful control and manipulate the tools and mechanisms of communal and "authorized" memory. Devastations within less powerful countries

---

28. Ibid., 26.

29. Augustine, *City of God*, 477.

30. Sobrino, *Where Is God?* 144.

or towards any marginalized people are often forgotten or silenced. Sobrino, therefore, calls for a more active and theological memory to ensure that the suffering of the forsaken is addressed and retold.[31] While forgetting such travesties seems to make defending a theodicy easier, remembering them complicates but also purifies the task, as a theodicy strives for more transparency, honesty, and humility. For Sobrino, such remembering demands that one's theological language and arguments are not removed from the realities of this world.

The question remains, however, whether this now clear and honest viewing of reality still allows for the possibility of a viable theodicy.

EVALUATING THEODICY

Theodicy amidst Suffering

How the poor and oppressed view their suffering is of fundamental importance to my aims and is a concern of Sobrino's as well. He states that few poor people doubted God's love and justice after the earthquakes, but instead feared that it was a punishment, or rejoiced because they survived.[32] In this vein, Sobrino rarely heard the poor in El Salvador during the earthquakes render the question of suffering in the traditional language of the theodicist[33]—asking how a good God could allow this to happen to them.

While he advocates a "praxic theodicy," Sobrino remarks: "We should say, at least in a footnote, that the religiosity of the simple people can perhaps benefit from a small dose of theodicy in order to avoid trivializing the reality of God, making that reality ahistorical, unverifiable from any viewpoint."[34] The language here is certainly measured. He adds: "What we call popular piety has nothing to lose by asking seriously about God in the earthquake; indeed it will gain if it at least stops its present slide toward infantilizing religiosity . . . and can help recover the old sense of 'popular conscientization,' at least under the rubric of anthropodicy."[35] While such a quote opposes those who dismiss theodicy, theodicy's apparent lack of deep relevance here

31. Ibid., xxiii.

32. Ibid., xxxviii.

33. Sobrino does note that the question of doubt did arise during El Salvador's civil war (ibid., 140).

34. Ibid., 143, 26n17.

35. Ibid., 27.

is noteworthy. Theodicy is thus implied as ineffectual or irrelevant to meeting the spiritual and theological needs of the poor and oppressed. He does not invalidate all of its potential worth, however. In the suffering present on the cross, the poor and oppressed can see that in Jesus of Nazareth the love of God reaches its apex in the Incarnation when God entered into history on the side of the oppressed, living in solidarity with all those seeking to walk in God's ways. Such a choice, sadly, entails suffering because "in history there is no such thing as love without solidarity and there is no solidarity without incarnation."[36]

Similar to John Paul's analysis, such solidarity also provides the context for suffering to be meaningful and shows why any theodicy must acknowledge that striving to follow Christ may entail suffering. As noted in chapter 4, such an emphasis could be comforting for the Benjas[37] of the world, even while unjustly dunked upside down into the well, but not for suffering that is random, inexplicable, and cannot be linked with any greater meaning or purpose. I return, then, to the limits of solidarity and the question of what value divine suffering confers to a victim who is not healed or redeemed in this world.

To answer this theological impasse, Sobrino turns to the poor, who want a God who can empathize, redeem, and save. Here the language of the beatitudes paints the scene: those who weep now, will be consoled; the poor will inherit the earth. Hope and justice are alive and dynamic.[38]

Option for Reality

This hopeful and utopian vision strives to confront and end injustice.[39] Likewise, the earthquake and all the uncomfortable faith-questions it invokes must be faced by Christians. Sobrino warns against "cheap faith, like the cheap grace that Bonhoeffer denounced." He adds: "Christian faith does not allow us to trivialize the victims' suffering, even by invoking God." Thus, he writes that the God we see in the earthquake does nothing to eliminate the negativity of natural reality. Christian faith does not magically cause the problematic truth of the earthquake, or the problematic truth of God,

---

36. Sobrino, *Jesus the Liberator*, 245.

37. See ch. 2.

38. Sobrino, *Jesus the Liberator*, 244.

39. Sobrino, *No Salvation outside the Poor*, 81.

to disappear. At first, rather, it can lead to confusion, questioning, and even protest. In short, the Christian faith "doesn't make things easy for God (the perennial problem of theodicy)."[40] This faith instead leads a believer to look to God without receiving any logically satisfactory response—or any response at all: "But in a mysterious way, that same God is bearing the burden of the earthquake. The earthquake expresses the reality of God, no longer as power but—scandalously—as solidarity, love, and hope."[41]

While Sobrino has linked the presence of God in part to the mystery of the primordial holiness of the poor and oppressed, one problem is whether a God of creation (and so a God who "create[s] an earth whose tectonic plates shift so destructively"[42]) can now be present as solidarity, hope, and love amidst the suffering caused from the earthquake. Sobrino rightly posits this occurrence as a "mystery," though this remains intellectually and spiritually unsatisfying.

Sobrino is aware of the paradox and the gaps touched on above. Shrewdly, he argues that looking at the problem of evil in this way serves a purpose. His dominant message is that solidarity with the poor and the oppressed is at the root and core of the Christian faith embodied in Christ's witness to the downtrodden and marginalized in the Bible. Ironically, therefore, such a faith "does a great service to our world by not minimizing the problem of God. The benefit is that the victim can and must demand an accounting. And those responsible—whoever they are—must render accounts."[43] In other words, the gaps that remain are not hidden, but demand a meaningful response, though this "accounting" may very likely lead to pronouncing the limitations, if not the failure, of theoretical theodicy.

The Failure of Theodicy

In one moving section of the work, Sobrino includes the thought of a European priest in El Salvador who was amazed at how the people could sustain their faith despite tragedy during the civil war. They told him: "God is acting, father . . . God is with us, father, because if not it would have been even worse." But then, the Massacre at El Mozote was

40. Sobrino, *Where Is God?* 24.
41. Ibid., 25. Note the affinity here with Phillips.
42. Ibid., 27n18.
43. Ibid., 25.

perpetrated. The priest could not believe that such an injustice, such evil, could have occurred: "'How could it be that here of all places, where I have come so many times to say that God is close to us and loves us, that God is not indifferent to sorrow, how could such a dreadful massacre happen precisely here?'"

Sobrino adds that the "peasants" were repeating the same question: "How many times have we said that God acts in our history? But father, if he does act, when will this end? Why so many years of war and so many thousands dead? What's wrong with God?"[44]

There are many haunting quotes in relation to suffering and evil, and geographic location should play no emotional role in accentuating the travesty, but for a massacre to happen among the poor and oppressed where the priest proclaims how God loves them and cares for them, seems to render all prayers, all hope and belief in God to be ultimately worthless. While Augustine felt that he could boast of God's providence because Christians were mostly protected in churches during the sack of Rome,[45] we know that Tutsis huddled in chapels or churches were easy prey for the killers "swinging their blades." Florence, a survivor of such an attack, remarks: "We had no weapons, no way to defend ourselves . . . There was some screaming and begging, but most of us just sat there waiting for our turn to be slaughtered." Florence was chopped between the eyes and was later stuck with spears and thrown over the cliff along with those who were actually dead, but she somehow managed to survive.[46]

Keeping in mind such horrific truth and the lives of these victims, Sobrino writes: "The attempt to justify God rationally in the presence of evil and suffering, has failed . . . Our only choice, I believe, is to live with a theodicy unresolved in theory, and with a practice that goes on opening a pathway—with God walking it beside us—through the

44. Ibid., 140–41.

45. Augustine, *City of God*, 12–13.

46. Florence told this story to fellow survivor Immaculée Ilibagiza at a refugee camp in Rwanda, and Ilibagiza retold it in her memoir, *Left to Tell*, 160–61. Florence was healed by a kind Hutu family, though their son (who lived with them) participated in killings every day until there were no other Tutsis in their town. If only such accounts depicting impenetrable humanity were not as rare as one would think. See also the inclusion of the role of religion for Confederate soldiers in the American Civil War in Faust, *This Republic of Suffering*, 189, 193. For the prayers of an eighteenth-century slave ship captain, see Rediker, *Slave Ship*, 157–86.

history of suffering."[47] Sobrino, therefore, seems to deny the possibility for a viable theodicy while still advocating a God of love and justice. He claims that there is little theoretical basis to give rational arguments for why evil and suffering occur in this world. Speaking from the vantage point of the poor and oppressed of Latin America, he does not renounce faith, but advocates a practical response, performed in solidarity with God, who walks with humanity in this struggle. While Sobrino grants that a small dose of theodicy may be valuable to the poor of Latin America, he is very clear that no theoretical theodicy can ever hope to be completely successful.

Sobrino reaches this conclusion because he situates his theological thought from the vantage point of the underside of history. Acutely aware of the affliction of the poor, he struggles to find any theoretical theodicy that satisfies the questions and concerns that arise because of this suffering. In this vein, he would be sympathetic with Greenberg's working principle. The aim of my use of testimonies of mass atrocity is to situate myself in a similar context, although I remain skeptical of his comment that the poor could only benefit from a "little dose" of theodicy. At the same time, nurtured by his own Catholic faith and the faith of the poor that he encounters, Sobrino does not assert that our failure to construct a perfect theoretical theodicy entails renouncing faith in God. Gaps remain, which must be acknowledged, but these gaps do not have the ultimate word.

As I noted in the introduction to this work, how a theology identifies, deliberates upon, and incorporates these gaps within any discussion of the problem of evil is of the utmost importance for there to be any possibility for a viable theodicy. Without such gaps and unresolved theories, faith would be a misnomer. Faith needs to acknowledge and grapple with such gaps in order to clarify what one holds with certitude and what one holds by faith. It is a major presupposition of this investigation that Christian theological faith in our contemporary age is a humbled faith, rife with nearly as many questions as answers. Such a faith, to borrow a term from post-Shoah Jewish thinkers, is "wounded" (or "fractured," in my terminology). But this does not imply that it cannot be viable or dynamic. As noted with the resurrected Christ who still bore his wounds, hope and life can thrive amidst affliction or gaps.

47. Sobrino, *Where Is God?* 142.

Suggestions for Theodicy

To make theodicy more reasonable on account of its failures, especially in the context of the poor and oppressed, Sobrino offers a few suggestions. As noted above, facing reality and the issues "soberly and humbly" is fundamental. Additional suggestions are not to "trivialize the problem God represents, not to approach it abstractly but in the presence of the poor and the victims, out of love for them . . . [and] not to trivialize the answer to the problem by invoking arguments of the necessity of free will, or creating good from evil."[48] Because he is unconvinced about theoretical theodicy, he focuses on the concrete and the particular lived situation of this world's victims and poor. Similar to McCord Adams's complaints that theodicy should not be carried on at too high a level of abstraction, he undermines the value of using abstract language in the context of theodicy. While he is right in stressing the need for a specific context, I would contend that abstract language is useful if it enables one to momentarily step away from a concrete situation to seek a wider and general perspective that one can then apply and test in a particular case. I have also argued (contra Sobrino) why the *privatio boni* tradition remains relevant.

Sobrino also proposes a praxic theodicy, which includes "*indignation* in response to human suffering . . . acknowledging there is something irremediable about suffering . . . [and] a utopian moment of *hope*, that God—whether or not God has the power to overcome suffering—does have the power to nurture human hope . . . In simple words, the decision to *practice* justice and kindness, and to *walk* humbly with God through history, in the darkness, protesting as we go, but always going."[49]

As we will see with Rabbi Anson Laytner in chapter 8, such protest can be linked with faith: "The engine of theodicy might be resentment against God," Sobrino admits, "but for us it is love." This love is a response to the call of the suffering.[50] Few would discount the importance of living out one's love and faith, but I need to reflect on the praxis that Sobrino highlights.

Sobrino advocates theological protest within this praxic response. It is a questioning love that stems from respect of God and

48. Ibid., 142–43.
49. Ibid., 143.
50. Ibid., 145.

respect of the poor and victims. It is a protest that says human beings should not be treated this way and God is outraged at such injustice and can redeem it. Indignation and hope can be strange partners, but then theological protest has a difficult line to tread as well, maintaining faith but sometimes sharing more in common with an atheist than a theist.

However, just as I critiqued McCord Adams for comments about God that made her theodicy less spiritually attractive or pastorally effective, I need to address Sobrino's statement "whether or not God has the power to overcome suffering." He does not deny the power and has pointed out that the poor want a transcendent God who can overcome evil and suffering, but here he doubts God's redemptive power. In my criticism of McCord Adams and John Paul II, I hesitated to claim that all suffering could be a participation in Christ's suffering and mission, or successfully wished away. As Levinas argues and Sobrino notes above, some suffering is useless or irremediable.[51] It serves no ultimate purpose, but can crush another human being's life and dignity, undermining the aim and mission of God for this world. It is linked with the anti-reign, to use Sobrino's language.[52] I would argue, similar lyto McCord Adams, that God could redeem the meaning and value of one's life in spite of the horrific suffering one endured, but not actually redeem some losses in the original context. In Job's case, the children who were murdered were not brought back to life in this world. Job was not compensated for the loss of his children simply by getting new ones. The new children no doubt help to assuage the pain and loss, but to say they fulfill the void completely is an insult to the life and dignity of his murdered children. To maintain the integrity of legitimate loss and questioning from that ordeal and the memory of that trauma, it would seem space would have to be left for absence, sorrow, and grief. It may not be a matter of redeeming that loss so much as living with it peacefully and without rancor. If God can help in that possibility, then one can say healing has occurred, if not redemption.

---

51. Levinas writes, "Thus, the least one can say about suffering is that in its own phenomenality, intrinsically, it is useless, for 'nothing'" ("Useless Suffering," 373).

52. See Sobrino, "Reign of God," 350–88.

ASSESSMENT

Of all the works examined so far, I share the most sympathies with Sobrino's efforts and his tentative "theodicy" language. I agree with his recognition of theodicy's limitations and his insistence on continuing to probe for answers. I agree that one should approach the problem of evil from a theodic and anthropodic perspective, recognizing the limitations in each approach. Such a perspective does not satisfactorily answer why there is evil in the world in the first place, but shows how human beings are often complicit in the suffering that is sometimes described as "natural" evil.

I also appreciate how Sobrino soberly looks at a devastating example of natural evil, one that pummels an already traumatized and poverty-stricken people, and yet still speaks a message of hope and solidarity, especially in viewing the poor under the rubric of primordial holiness. While such a term must also call for renouncing passivity and the scandal of such a condition, I appreciate Sobrino's aim in seeing the poor as sacraments of God, especially in his example of a child soldier forced to commit horrific acts. While the issue of how God is present with such a victim/perpetrator needs further analysis, my inclusion of witness testimony within this work means this position is not wishful thinking on the part of a theologian: some (though, of course, not all) victims assert that belief in God is still meaningful despite (or even because of) their ordeals. The issue though is why other individuals deny such a claim, and what the presence of God means in this world when atrocities and suffering seem to proliferate and many die seemingly broken and abandoned.

Another issue is Sobrino's dismissal of the general arguments in philosophical theodicies which often employ abstract language or the use of "trivial" arguments like free will or *privatio boni*. There is a danger when one jettisons such beliefs which provide a flawed, but still valuable framework for how to view this world. At the very least, one must continue challenging the limitations of these theories to search for what is still meaningful and useful about them.

Lastly, I share Sobrino's focus on Christ crucified and resurrected as a profound meaning to the mystery of suffering and the challenges and truths that the option for the poor brings in an analysis of suffering and victimization. His turning to the poor to ask if they want a suffering God and his calling to ask for their interpretation of the "holy" is also important,[53] as is his testifying to how the poor rarely thought in theodic terms in the midst of the earthquakes (though their questions were more critical in the context of mass atrocities[54]). Still, if theodicy is only of minimal worth for the poor and oppressed, according to Sobrino, its overall value is also questionable. I have included victims of mass atrocity because I have argued that their voices and interpretations need to be taken into account when developing a theodic position. Moreover, for a viable faith, I would argue that you need a viable theodicy. Sobrino seems to be challenging that claim. I also still need to grapple further with how testimonies from non-Christians like Gyatso and Partnoy challenge any "exclusively" Christian reading of the problem of evil that says Christ is the answer to the problem of suffering. Some crucial questions still gnaw at me: does the assertion that Christ is the answer to the mystery of suffering still make sense in light of those witnesses and interpretations of their suffering who deny Christ's relevance or presence in the midst of their ordeals? Does Christ become an (as opposed to *the*) answer to the problem of evil? If so, why, and if not, why not? Subsequent chapters must continue to examine these questions.

In the next chapter, Gustavo Gutiérrez turns to the book of Job to discuss credible God-talk from the dung heap. It is another relevant text for my purposes and one that also shares an aim with Greenberg's working principle.

53. Sobrino, *Where Is God?* 80. Elsewhere, Sobrino includes the words of a "poor woman, who possessed almost nothing and whose sons had been vilely murdered: 'A life after death, without sufferings? How splendid!'" (*No Salvation outside the Poor*, 103).

54. Of the Rwandan genocide, liberation theologian Mario Aguilar writes: "now is the time to start asking theological questions about the denial of God in the southern hemisphere from the perspective of Rwanda" (*Theology, Liberation and Genocide*, 10).

7

Gutiérrez's Job: God-Talk from the Dung Heap

Once, [Camp Kommandant Amon Goeth] caught a boy who was suffering from diarrhea and was unable to contain himself. He forced the boy to eat all of the excrement before killing him.[1]

In the work, *On Job: God-Talk and the Suffering of the Innocent*, Gustavo Gutiérrez uses the story of Job to articulate what it means to speak both of God and to God in the midst of affliction. The quote above, taken from Joseph Bau's *Dear God, Have You Ever Gone Hungry?*, presents another concrete case, not only of the "excremental assault" that De Pres writes about, but a story so brutal and graphic that it can stand as both reality and metaphor for the difficult task Gutiérrez takes upon himself, for how can one possibly speak of God while being forced to eat one's excrement? I refer both to the literal constraints that make speaking anything impossible and the condition that assaults the possibility for spiritual or theological language through the collapse of any discernible meaning and value to one's life. What could one possibly say in the presence of such a victim?

Bau, a survivor of the Plaszow concentration camp, tells of the boy's murder in the context of taking the reader through a "guided tour" of the camp, reconstructed from "the shards embedded in [Bau's] consciousness, to construct a verifiable model of this veritable

1. Bau, *Dear God*, 115.

hell on earth."[2] The task is all the more pressing because the camp was obliterated. He writes that he "owes it to the countless camp inmates, those who died there and those who will carry its imprint on their souls to the end of their existence."[3] The nameless child he depicts, then, is only told of in passing, but his is a case, like the babies burned in the pits, that differs greatly from Job's. First, of course, the child's dignity and possibility for speech are brutally violated. Job, despite all of his suffering, and unlike the babies and the boy, at least benefited from being able to reflect upon his suffering and the moral framework of his religious tradition. Second, God answered Job. For the boy, all language to and of God seems gagged and swallowed in his murder.

If the boy cannot speak of God, can others speak for him, and if so, how does one tread the line between speaking for the voiceless without violating their integrity and autonomy? More problematically for my purposes: do outsiders construct such language for their own comfort? Because the boy is presumably Jewish, a Christian theodicist must be particularly careful. If Jesus is the answer to the problem of evil, as John Paul II, Adams, Sobrino, and Gutiérrez argue, how can such a possible truth be spoken in the name of such a victim?

Amidst the scandalous destitution of Latin America (whose context can also apply to the murdered boy above), Gutiérrez asks: "How are we to acknowledge that God makes us a free gift of love and justice when we have before us the suffering of the innocent?"[4] Because of Job's own dramatic losses, Gutiérrez sees Job as a figure who undergoes a profound transformation in his relationship with, and beliefs in, God and in his new solidarity with the suffering victims of the world. Gutiérrez's Job becomes a figure one can follow and emulate, particularly in the context of the poor and suffering in Latin America.[5] The context of Gutiérrez's personal reading of the book of Job is essential to keep in mind. With such a well-known text, one expects a diversity of readings—and so some disagreement with Gutiérrez's methods or conclusions. I will highlight some cases below before presenting Gutiérrez's interpretation.

2. Ibid., 110–11.

3. Ibid., 111.

4. Gutiérrez, *Job*, xiv.

5. Ibid., xvii. See also Phan, "Prophecy and Contemplation," 186.

TEXTUAL ANALYSIS

The Book of Job: Theodicy or Antitheodicy?

While William Cenkner writes how Gutiérrez aims to "demonstrat[e] how the suffering figure of Job eventually realizes God's preferential love for the oppressed and disenfranchised,"[6] in *The Evils of Theodicy*, Terrence Tilley argues that "Gutiérrez simply reads divine love into a text where God's love is never mentioned . . . For Gutiérrez, the suffering of this innocent one was educative. But Job learned nothing."[7] Tilley questions Gutiérrez's optimistic reading of Job and his emphasis on God's love for all and accuses Gutiérrez of either silencing the victim of torture or promoting a soul-making theodicy.[8] Neither criticism, as I will show, is entirely valid, but then the context of Tilley's argument has to be stressed as well. He is critiquing the social situation of speech acts in theodic texts to prove how "engaging in the discourse of theodicy *creates* evil."[9] In justifying why evil occurs, one can come to accept the evils as normative, for example, or distribute censure to blameless victims. In Tilley's estimation, the book of Job is an anti-theodicy: "Job warns against the possibility of providing a theodicy . . . It is not a book of answers, but a text of warning, perhaps even a text of terror."[10]

Tilley's claims certainly have merit: for me the most damning evidence against a spiritualized reading of Job remains the wager God makes with the satan. If God had not distinguished Job to the satan, Job's individual torment likely would not have occurred. Maybe someone else would have been brutalized, but because God initiated the process, God is inevitably complicit in what then follows. The privileged knowledge of the reader adds irony to Job's faithful responses and hope for God's act of redemption. When Job's wife tells him to "blaspheme God and die!"[11] the cynical reader cannot but think, "If only you knew the full truth." God's response, moreover,

6. Cenkner, "Introduction," vii.

7. Tilley, *Evils of Theodicy*, 100. For other interesting accounts of Job, see Kugel, *How to Read the Bible*, 635–43; Sweeney, *Reading the Hebrew Bible*, 195–200; Burrell, *Deconstructing Theodicy.*

8. Gutiérrez, *Job*, 101.

9. Ibid., 3.

10. Ibid., 109.

11. Job 2:9.

as Alexander Donat similarly argues, "humiliates Job, degrades his value and honor, demonstrates his insignificance and unimportance, turns him into 'dust and ashes.'"[12] David Burrell, moreover, contends that "the book of Job effectively deconstructs sober efforts of philosophers to construct theories 'justifying the ways of God to men' (quite oblivious to the irony in that description of their task)."[13] According to Burrell, the tale of Job not only deconstructs theodicy, but illumines (and performs) the need of talking to and not merely about God.[14] The focus is on relationship with and presence of God, not an answer to why evil exists.

Amid these divergent opinions on Job, for Gutiérrez, "It is important that we be clear from the outset that the theme of the book of Job is not precisely suffering—that impenetrable human mystery—but rather how to speak of God in the midst of suffering."[15] He is therefore not engaging in an attempt to justify a "rational or definitive" explanation for suffering.[16] As with Sobrino's text, we seem to have neither a theodicy nor an anti-theodicy, though Gutiérrez's search for credible theological language in the face of evil shares great similarities with one of the main themes of Sobrino's work. The key word, of course, is "appropriate." Gutiérrez seeks a balance between respecting the dignity and anguish of individuals while maintaining a faith position that asserts that healing and redemption are still possible because of God's love and justice. For Gutiérrez, the relationship between gratuitousness and justice "is the key to the interpretation of the book of Job."[17] Finding an appropriate theodic language that can articulate these seemingly polar terms will be one reason why Job's own journey is so relevant. Like Sobrino's aim, this theodic language cannot flinch from reality.

Tilley's criticisms about Gutiérrez's optimistic reading, therefore, need further clarification. Gutiérrez (and most liberation theologians) are unrelenting in stressing the reality of random and often

12. Donat, "Voice from the Ashes," 283.

13. Burrell, *Deconstructing Theodicy*, 107.

14. Ibid., 19.

15. Gutiérrez, *Job*, 13.

16. Ibid., 93.

17. Ibid., 82.

undeserved suffering.[18] Gutiérrez is also cognizant that his call for others to work for peace and justice will likely lead to persecution. Such an emphasis makes the theology of liberation indispensable for any Christian theodicy because it is always looking to the worst cases (recall the plight of the suffering boy forced to eat his own excrement), yet strives to uphold faith in God's love and commitment.

For Gutiérrez, "Job shows us a way with his vigorous protest, his discovery of concrete commitment to the poor and all who suffer unjustly, his facing up to God, and his acknowledging of the gratuitousness that characterizes God's plan for human history."[19] Key questions are whether the book of Job gainsays any meaningful talk of God's gratuitous love, and what are the merits of this type of love? It is also legitimate to ask (along with Tilley) whether God permitted Job to undergo his torment to teach him a lesson. While Gutiérrez aims to examine Job's catharsis as a model for how one can speak of God and to God amidst affliction, I will also address how his depiction of God would bear on a theodicy.

Disinterested Religion and the Right of Protest

Like Sobrino, Gutiérrez acknowledges that the question "'My God, where are you?' . . . springs from the suffering of the innocent, but it also has its source in faith."[20] This questioning and protest—which never have the last word—are also uttered and prayed in the context of disinterested religion. Because a disinterested religious ethic has been a reoccurring motif in previous chapters, I will examine how Gutiérrez employs the term.

Because Phillips disavows the afterlife, one's love of God is always removed from any possibility of gain, and so such a love is never tainted by self-serving motivations for heaven or earthly benefits. John Paul II writes of the believer turning to God with "disinterested service," but soteriological and eschatological concerns and hopes remain essential aspects of his theology.

Despite these differences, for Gutiérrez, Job embodies the ideal of disinterested religion. Moving away from the satan's *quid pro quo*

18. Ibid., xv.

19. Ibid., 102.

20. Ibid., xv.

worldview,[21] Job sees that no promises of great lands or many de-
scendents should make one follow God.[22] Despite Job's ordeal, he
maintains his faith in God and, as importantly, comes to see in greater
depth the plight of the poor and afflicted. He becomes a human example for believers to follow—especially for those of us today in the
first world—as he learns to speak of God in the midst of affliction. He
is also an example to individuals in the third world who repeatedly
have to bear this undeserved suffering.

Such a religious response is disinterested to Gutiérrez but it is not
bereft of sincere questioning, challenging, and remonstrating God. A
primary question is whether a disinterested faith position can also
practice theological protest. While a wide range of viewpoints try to
locate and interpret the nature of Job's grumbling, Gutiérrez acknowledges Job's protests, but maintains that Job complains about God, but
never curses Him.[23] Thus, protest is kept within clear limits. According
to Gutiérrez, this "spiritual struggle with God" culminates in chapter
9 where Job even accuses God of injustice, saying that God "'laughs
at the plight of the innocent.'"[24] Gutiérrez calls these "bold words" but
notes the rich tradition in the Bible of theological protest against how
God has treated God's people or allowed others to mistreat them.[25] As
we will see in the next chapter, Job is a pivotal figure in this tradition.
Gutiérrez calls him a "*rebellious believer*. His rebellion is against the
suffering of the innocent, against a theology that justifies it, and even
against the depiction of God that such a theology contains."[26]

In this vein, Job is not simply protesting against God, but also
against the human interpretations of God embodied by Job's companions, who maintain that all suffering is deserved and that if God is
propitiated, good fortune will come. In rejecting this worldview, Job is
seeking a more authentic faith.[27]

21. Ibid., 89.
22. Ibid., 1.
23. Ibid., 8.
24. Ibid., 57.
25. Ibid., 57.
26. Ibid., 14.
27. Ibid., 10.

While elements of this protest will need to be renounced in light of God's response to Job,[28] Gutiérrez asserts that "this cry cannot be muted. Those who suffer unjustly have a right to complain and protest."[29] If one questions whether a Christian has this right, Gutiérrez is clear: "The Son of God teaches us that talk of God must be mediated by the experience of the cross."[30] Furthermore, because some of Jesus's last words can be discerned both as protest and faith, he adds: "in the Bible complaint does not exclude hope; in fact, they go together."[31]

Gutiérrez also reminds us that despite Job's complaints and emotional protests, which sometimes border on despair, God sanctions Job's language by later telling Job and his companions that he had spoken correctly of God, validating theological protest kept within certain limits.[32]

The Development of Theological Language through Praxis

Gutiérrez employs two types of theological language as valid means of speaking about God amidst affliction. Acknowledging the ineffability of God, he writes that "theological thought about God is *thought about a mystery*."[33] Using Job as his guide, though, Gutiérrez wants to trace Job's struggles to identify what I would term Job's God-language epiphany. Unfortunately, for Job such an epiphany entailed the loss of almost everything he held dear. According to Gutiérrez, contemplating and formulating sound discourse on God within such a mystery requires preparation and training. Job's experiences after his losses were part of this training: "God is first contemplated when we do God's will and allow God to reign; only after that do we think of God." Gutiérrez is not claiming that one simply acts, but for theological language "to be authentic and respectful" one must "first establish [oneself] on the terrain of spirituality and practice."[34] Job's sudden losses accelerate this "learning" process as his agonizing experiences alter everything he thought he knew about God.

28. Ibid., 87.
29. Ibid., 101.
30. Ibid., 97.
31. Ibid., 98.
32. Job 42:7–8. See also Gutiérrez, *Job*, 11.
33. Ibid., xi.
34. Ibid., xiii. See also Réjon, "Fundamental Moral Theory," 213.

According to Gutiérrez, through Job's afflictions, Job recognizes the plight of the poor and the oppressed, and this awakening changes his theological language and enables him to speak more truthfully about God. Gutiérrez writes that the language of contemplation and the language of prophecy (as evinced in the book of Job) offer the best approaches of how one should talk about God and to God amidst suffering.[35] He is careful, however, to stress that he is not trying to over-rationalize a deeply poetic text[36] and that these two types of languages are meant to "move apart and intermingle."[37] Thus, he tries to show how "[P]rophetic language supports and reinforces language inspired by contemplation of God."[38] The joining of these two types of languages, as William Cenkner adds, enables Gutiérrez to include "worship, prayer, and mysticism as integral to the struggle for justice."[39]

Prophetic Language amidst Affliction

To seek an appropriate language about God, Gutiérrez looks to the prophets of the Bible. They not only speak to God but also for God as well. They challenge unjust and sinful structures, decrees, and actions.[40] Job also speaks prophetically as his moral vision and theological views change, inspiring him to speak on behalf of the oppressed.[41]

Like Sobrino, Gutiérrez argues that "commitment to the poor provides firm ground for prophetic talk of God."[42] Because the poor are the "favorites of God," Job establishes a venue to find God when he tries to aid the poor and "wants justice."[43] In a seminal passage, Job describes and laments the exploitation of those in poverty by the wicked: "They drive away the orphan's donkey, as security they seize the widow's ox . . . From the towns come the groans of the dying / and

---

35. Gutiérrez stresses that these two languages are "two ways of drawing nearer to the mystery of God" (*Job*, 88). They are obviously not the only ones.

36. Ibid., 16.

37. Ibid., 16.

38. Ibid., 94.

39. Cenkner, "Introduction," vii.

40. Gutiérrez, *Job*, 97. See also Phan, "Prophecy and Contemplation," 190.

41. Gutiérrez, *Job*, 16.

42. Ibid., 33, and Sobrino, *Jesus the Liberator*, 245. The biblical passage is from Job 24.

43. Gutiérrez, *Job*, 48.

the gasp of the wounded crying for help. Yet God remains deaf to the prayer."[44] Such response to suffering is for Gutiérrez the embodiment of the language of prophecy.

Such prophetic language rebukes those individuals and structures that perpetuate injustice and misery but also announces to the poor that liberation is near. It calls people to move beyond their individual suffering and base their outlook on "the needs of others who cannot be ignored."[45] Job's initial focus was on his own misfortune. He wanted retribution and a hearing from God to right these undeserved wrongs. As the story progresses, he includes the misfortune of others in his arguments and questions where God was for them, too. His faith in God also prompts him to reject "the doctrine of retribution that his three friends expounded in a pompous and abstract manner."[46] He also finds deeper answers through the mystical language embodied in contemplation of God.[47]

Disinterested Religion and the Language of Contemplation

In addition to the language of prophecy, Gutiérrez also argues that the language of contemplation is another resource to aid one in speaking about God. It acknowledges that everything comes from God's unmerited love and reveals solid means to hope.[48] The point of faith and grace is to show the transcendence of God and the gratuitousness of God's love, which are not constrained by our failures in moral action or in formulating moral concepts.

I agree that our conceptions of justice are limited, which is why one needs to turn to a God who transcends such conceptions. Based upon my earlier clarification of God's moral obligations, I could also agree with Gutiérrez's remarks—"God does what God pleases to do. No love at all can be locked in."—as a response to why retribution in this world based on individual pleas for justice is problematic. But when I recall Camp Kommandant Goeth and the boy forced to swallow his own diarrhea, I stammer at the justification that God's gratuitousness entails letting such perpetrators have the opportunity to repent

44. Ibid., 33.
45. Ibid., 48.
46. Ibid., 47–48.
47. Ibid., 49.
48. Ibid., 89.

when no such opportunity is permitted for the boy to live his life as it was meant to be. As Rubenstein argues: "This has had the paradoxical consequence that while God shows forbearance with the wicked, He must turn a deaf ear to the anguished cries of the violated."[49] We saw Phillips raise similar objections.

In the works of Partnoy and Nomberg-Przytyk, moreover, we read how experiences of God were nonexistent in moments of torture and trauma. Cries to God were made, but responses were not forthcoming. Benja, a believing Christian, was not rescued by God. God did not liberate Auschwitz. And Stalin's Russians, who did liberate some of the Nazi concentration camps, still went on to murder a staggering number of people in the gulag system. Job, however, gets his day in court. God responds to his complaints, though in an unpredictable way—making no reference to concrete problems and therefore not responding to the distress and questions of Job.[50] Again, for Gutiérrez, this reality accentuates not retribution but disinterested religion[51]—"the free and gratuitous initiative taken by love."[52] Such a speech rejects anthropomorphism—we cannot judge only from our perspective.[53]

Gutiérrez also claims that "in [Job's] final reply what Job is expressing is not contrition but *a renunciation of his lamentation and dejected outlook.*"[54] He eventually sees that God is not a prisoner "of a particular way of understanding justice."[55] Because of his emphasis on Christ crucified and the "crucified people," Gutiérrez contends that we need to "understand God's gratuitousness in relation to God's justice—to situate justice within the framework of God's gratuitous love."[56] Rebutting a claim like Rubenstein's, Gutiérrez asserts: "Belief in God and God's gratuitous love leads to a preferential option for the poor and to solidarity with those who suffer wretched conditions, contempt, and oppression, those whom the social order ignores and

---

49. Rubenstein, *After Auschwitz*, 195.

50. Gutiérrez, *Job*, 68.

51. Ibid., 72.

52. Ibid., 71.

53. Ibid., 74.

54. Ibid., 87.

55. Ibid., 87.

56. Ibid., 88.

exploits."[57] There is, therefore, an ethical calling and obligation to heal the wounds of division and injustice, although it remains unclear how God is present in the life of those who live and die broken and despondent. Nor is it clear what happens when one applies this sense of "preference" (in the preferential option for the poor) to the boy and the commandant who mercilessly murdered him. What, for example, does God's love demand for the boy in light of this atrocity? Gutiérrez does not address issues of the afterlife here, in part because he is constrained by his focus on the book of Job, which was written in a period dominated by "vagueness about any life beyond the present."[58] While I will return to these issues in chapter 11, further reflection by Gutiérrez along these lines would have been helpful in his aim of developing God-talk in the context of the poor and oppressed in Latin America.

ASSESSMENT

Gutiérrez's aim in seeking to answer how one should talk about God and to God from the dung heap, amidst suffering, is essential for any theodicy. Like Phillips, Gutiérrez's emphasis on disinterested religion also encapsulates the believer's need to maintain faith in a world where no one is shielded from grief and agony. While Tilley's argument has great persuasive and textual force, Gutiérrez has presented an important midrashic reading of Job.[59] Because Job opens with God making a wager with the satan, it is a stretch to ascribe benevolence to that book's depiction of God. Even if one follows certain rabbinic readings that assert that Job's children deserved to die (based on the fact that Job offered sacrifices for them), God still appears culpable and complicit. To me, the deaths of Job's children are the most gratuitous acts in this book, if I take a different meaning of Gutiérrez's focus on the word "gratuitous."

57. Ibid., 94.

58. Ibid., 89. An anonymous reviewer reminded me of Job 14:13–15 and 19:25–27. The passages still seem enigmatic in terms of whether there is a notion of meaningful postmortem existence in Job, but they keep the issue open.

59. Here I take the definition of midrash from Norman J. Cohen as presented by Rabbi Laytner: "midrash was the means by which Rabbis filled in the 'spaces between the sacred words of Scripture,' extending 'the text as far as they could, detailing the characters' missing actions, thoughts, and feelings' in order to answer a multitude of questions and articulate a message of contemporary and often timeless value" (*Arguing with God*, 42).

Moreover, if the moral of Job is so pellucid, then the biblical text did not have to be so opaque. If it is "simply" a matter of acknowledging our need to help the poor and to identify the link of justice and God's gratuitousness, God's response could have been a little more explicit in this paramount matter when addressing Job. Instead, as Donat argues above, God seems to bury Job—and thus the supposed didactic moral—with questions and comments about all the great beings God created. Further grappling with a conception of God's justice in response to mass atrocity in an afterlife context would also have been helpful here, along with how God's "gratuitousness" responds to such a dilemma.

In addition, Gutiérrez's coining of the terms "language of prophecy" and "language of contemplation" in the context of Job is interesting, but is not the most sound interpretation of Job. I could even wonder if we are reading the same text based on his overall conclusions. A text with the magisterial lineage of Job, however, cannot be dismissed easily. In this regard, I could concede to Joel Burnet's positive evaluation of the book when he writes that it "answers the concern for divine absence in human suffering with a distinct theodicy of presence. The problem of evil is not solved, but behind this apparent divine absence lies the presence of a God who responds to Job's demands for a hearing."[60]

God is, indeed, present and aware of Job's afflictions. God does respond. I also grant that a reader could interpret Job's coming to understand the plight of the afflicted at a deeper level, but in this instance, what matters more is how God responds, not simply that there is a response. While I would not go so far as Terry Eagleton, who quips that God "more or less tells [Job] to go to hell," I remain unimpressed by any claim that stresses that at least God responded in some way to Job's complaints or that maintains that God is deeply involved in creation, even if an individual life seems unimportant.[61] The God of Job, to me, is on a power trip, wanting to prove the satan wrong. God treats Job (and especially Job's children) so indifferently that if such a text were all we had about God, I would not engage in any theological, let alone theodic, undertaking. Such a God would be linked with the one who urged total warfare and the annihilation of all the enemies

60. Burnett, *Where Is God?* 111.

61. Eagleton, *On Evil,* 142.

of Israel in other biblical passages that we have been burdened with.[62] Fortunately, a reader can enjoy the text of Job for its narrative and poetic flourishes and its philosophical probing, but (hopefully) turn to other works for a more realistic and soothing portrait of God.

Despite these reservations, Gutiérrez's text is a useful reflection on "'the evil of misfortune,' the evil suffered by the innocent."[63] His attempt to develop the models for how one can talk about God amidst that suffering—a suffering that is often meaningless, undeserved, dehumanizing, and fatal—is also pertinent for my context.

Ultimately, for Gutiérrez the struggle for justice and the search for language about God finds its source in Jesus on the cross, which reveals that there is solidarity amidst suffering and hope. While this Christological focus is developed in his other works,[64] he states that prophetic and contemplative languages reach a nexus in the language of the cross.[65] In speaking such a language, believers commit an act of remembrance as they seek to follow the life of Christ in their thoughts and actions. For Gutiérrez, "only within the following of Jesus is it possible to talk of God."[66] Palden Gyatso, Nomberg-Przytyk, and Partnoy would obviously differ with this idea. But in reading the book of Job through the lens of the poor and oppressed in Latin America, Gutiérrez provides a fruitful attempt to discuss how to talk to God and of God in the midst of loss and destruction. Whether such a language is applicable to the murdered boy of Plaszow and other victims of atrocity will be further assessed in the next section on post-Shoah Jewish theology.

So, too, will Job's dilemma. While God appears to Job in the Bible, Berkovits writes: "No such denouement to the drama of faith took place in the camps . . . Millions were looking for him, in vain. They had heard of him by the hearing of the ear, but what was granted to their eyes to behold was 'dust and ashes,' into which they and everything

---

62. Such passages make for interesting reading—or teaching—but not as spiritual guides. Still, see Berkovits's fascinating exploration of the rabbinic interpretation of the injunction in Deut 21:18 on how to treat the "stubborn and rebellious son" (*Essential Essays*, 72).

63. Gutiérrez, *Job*, xv.

64. See, for example, *Theology of Liberation*, 102–5, 112–16, 130–40.

65. Gutiérrez, *Job*, 101.

66. Ibid.

dear to them were turned."[67] These are sobering words that make the task of theodicy a precarious one, but one that the Jewish theologians I now turn to have faced candidly and credibly.

67. Berkovits, *Essential Essays*, 317.

Assessment of Section 2

Liberation theology, especially as interpreted by Sobrino and Gutiérrez, offers rich theological and spiritual insight for any theodicy. Its unrelenting focus on the downtrodden and subjugated prevents any theodicy from being too abstract or ignoring the "difficult cases." As Mario Aguilar writes: "liberation theology provides a praxis and a hermeneutics from the point of view of the poor and oppressed even after the atrocities committed during the Rwandan genocide. It argues that this praxis is meaningful even after a period in which for most Rwandans it seemed that God was silent, powerless and sometimes dead."[1]

Such a commitment also requires an honest theological memory that does not flinch at recalling the failures, sins, and tragedies of our world. A Christian theodicy, therefore, must straddle the reign of God on earth and in heaven. It looks to the eschaton for divine justice but also believes that through God's love, Jesus's example, and the guidance and inspiration of the Holy Spirit, human beings are not alone in their commitment to establish the reign of God on earth.

Sobrino's emphasis on primordial holiness helps accentuate the meaning and significance of the lives of the voiceless and exploited. His interlocking of theodicy and anthropodicy usefully orients theodicists to search for the motives and whereabouts of each during times of suffering and loss.

Gutiérrez's disinterested religion seems essential for a theodicy because it warns against having unrealistic expectations of God in this world and prepares one for that self-giving love that reaches out to

---

1. Aguilar, *Theology, Liberation and Genocide*, 13. Hatzfeld, however, claims that "in Africa, atheism seems incomprehensible . . . it's impossible to find a single person in the Nyamata area who admits out loud to becoming an atheist because of the genocide" (*Strategy of Antelopes*, 176).

others in need. The support of theological protest by both Gutiérrez and Sobrino ensures that injustice in this world is confronted and remembered so the need for healing is never lost. This theme in particular will be examined in more detail in the next two chapters.

Section 3

Post-Shoah Jewish Theology:
Faith in Spite of God

And [God] said, "Do not come closer. Remove your sandals from your feet, for the place on which you stand is holy ground."[1]

The aim of the next two chapters is threefold. One goal is to trace the role and history of theological protest within the Jewish tradition to test whether such theological—or believing—protest should be a crucial component of a theodicy. Secondly, I want to examine some of the writings about the Holocaust by key Jewish thinkers and whether their influential ideas and innovations should be incorporated into any Christian theodicy. Such an enterprise, of course, is worthy of a book in itself. And as Katz reminds us: "there is a pre-Holocaust and post-Holocaust Jewish reality that must be considered when dealing with the Nazi epoch."[2] While reaching such a position involves a lifelong process of study,[3] a modest aim of these chapters will be to argue how even a cursory glance at the depth and breadth of Jewish theodic sources provides an indispensable historical perspective and a rich tradition of theological argumentation for a Christian theodicist. Thirdly, I want to examine the need for and commitment to memory

---

1. Exod 3:5.
2. Katz, "Issue of Confirmation," 15. So, too, Edward Kessler writes in his informative *An Introduction to Jewish-Christian Relations*: "Yet although the Holocaust is of immense importance, it is misleading if it so dominates Christian-Jewish relations as to eclipse all other concerns" (137).
3. Katz, "Issue of Confirmation," 54n5.

within the Jewish tradition[4] and why such a focus is also crucial for a Christian theodicy. I have touched on this issue and its role in trauma in chapter 1, but here I want to establish further the links between memory, protest, and faithfulness and why such a memory both sustains one's belief in God and provides "evidence" to doubt God's love and care.

---

4. In *Zakhor*, Yerushalmi argues persuasively that throughout vast stretches of Jewish history there was a lack of interest in writing about and interpreting contemporary events (22 and 74).

8

The Jewish Tradition of Arguing
with God

His workmanship is perfect in regard to all creatures and no one has a right
to complain in any way.[1]

The rabbinic quote above unequivocally denies the right to question God. And yet, we have seen John Paul II, Sobrino, Gutiérrez,
and even God (as depicted in Job)[2] advocate some form of theological
protest. Though the tradition of questioning (or arguing with) God
has always been marginal within Judaism, as we will see below, its long
lineage offers an indispensable resource and guide for the Christian
theodicist. In this chapter, therefore, I will turn to Anson Laytner's
Arguing with God: A Jewish Tradition and examine how this practice
has developed in biblical, rabbinic, and Jewish liturgical sources.
Because of the cited gaps, limits, or failures of theoretical theodicy,
I want to probe further into the fruits and riches of the tradition of
arguing with God to conceptualize and flesh out why certain features
of it are necessary for a Christian theodicy. As Irving Greenberg has
commented, "To not argue with God, to not question, to not admit
that there are serious problems, is to be in denial."[3]

1. Hammer, *Classic Midrash*, 350. The sages are commenting on Deut 32:4—"His
deeds are perfect."

2. As noted in the last chapter, God sanctions how Job has spoken of God.

3. Quoted in Feinstein, *Jews and Judaism*, 136.

To help overcome this form of denial, this chapter will begin to address the following questions:

1. What, if any, are the limits to protest within the Jewish tradition, and are similar limits meaningful for any theodicy?

2. What is the point of such questioning and how can it be considered an act of faith?

3. Is such a position antithetical to disinterested faith as some of our authors interpret that practice?

4. What are the consequences for a theodicy that follows the rabbinic advice above and denies the right to protest?

5. Anson Laytner argues that contemporary Judaism's failure to incorporate meaningful opportunities to express doubt, anger, and fears within a spiritual and religious context has alienated some Jews from their tradition. How and in what way could I apply this argument to my project, which seeks to identify key features that a theodicy must identify with to be viable despite the reality of mass atrocity?

A TRADITION OF THEOLOGICAL PROTEST

Covenantal Theodicy

Like its Christian and Islamic counterparts, Jewish theodicy, according to Zachary Braiterman, has "created a profusion of theodicies meant to explain the presence of suffering in the world. They have included the denial of evil as a 'real' phenomenon; dualism; just deserts; deferred compensations; divine pedagogy; free will; vicarious atonement; [and] appeals to mystery."[4] In addition to working with the formula of justifying a loving, omnipotent God despite the reality of evil, Jewish theologians must also justify a covenantal God who has made promises of fidelity to Israel. Such a relationship encompasses the belief that while God is still able to redeem evil, a faithful response looks at reality honestly to identify injustice and evil and to name where both humanity and God fail to live up to the agreement of healing the world. As Eliezer Berkovits writes: "After the Holocaust,

---

4. Braiterman, *(God) After Auschwitz*, 21.

Israel's first religious responsibility is to 'reason' with God, and if need be, to wrestle with him."[5]

Arguing along similar lines, the Christian theologian Darrel Fasching highlights Judaism's "narrative tradition of audacity or *chutzpah*. This tradition of audacity exemplifies a capacity to desacralize the sacred in the name of the dignity of the stranger, expressed in a hospitality for—and audacity on behalf of—the stranger."[6] Such *chutzpah* is represented by Abraham's pleading to God to spare the inhabitants of Sodom and Job's calling of God to trial for his undeserved suffering. Like the notion of the covenant, this *chutzpah* is also at the heart of the tradition of arguing with God, as those deemed faithful to God's covenant call God to task to redeem the world and right certain wrongs. This process is often exemplified in the law-court pattern of prayer.

The Law-Court Pattern of Prayer

Taking the reader through significant biblical, rabbinic, and liturgical texts, Laytner's *Arguing With God* reveals how a faith-practice of "wrestling" with God has been sustained during periods of waxing and waning throughout Judaism's history. From such a perspective, one is reminded that as destructive as the Shoah was—as systematic the slaughter by the Nazis and their allies—rabbis and faithful Jews in ghettos and camps did not have a dearth of historical and biblical material from which to draw some previous historical parallel.[7] The destruction of the temple in 70 CE was a watershed event in this regard, but there were others as well. According to Laytner:

> The Jewish literary heritage is replete with laments and dirges, complaints and arguments, all protesting God's mistreatment of His people . . . This history of suffering has given rise to a unique literature of argument prayers . . . Argument with God—called the "law-court" pattern of prayer by scholars—is a particularly (and perhaps uniquely) Jewish response to the problem of theodicy . . . [that though] rooted in deep faith,

5. Berkovits, *Essential Essays*, 316.

6. Fasching, "Ethics after Auschwitz and Hiroshima," 17.

7. Laytner, *Arguing with God*, 131.

nevertheless calls God to task for his lapses of duty which result in suffering and injustice.[8]

This calling of God to task, embedded in the uniqueness of the Abrahamic covenant, makes it seem as "though God and the Jewish people grew up together and so treat each other with the familiarity of old friends or lovers."[9] Just as God is supposed to be patient with the Jewish people, so, too, must they be patient with God, trusting that God will maintain God's side of the covenant. And yet, the reserve of patience is not unlimited, and so in particularly troubling times, the rabbis plead for divine aid and redemption and remind God of God's promises. As Laytner elucidates, the Hebrew word for prayer, *tefillah*, comes from the verb root *palal*. In addition to being "originally associated with the concept of sacrifice" in the Bible, *palal* meant

> manifesting "a bargaining spirit" in a legal, or law-court, context . . . This second understanding of *palal* corresponds to the use of other legal terms to describe varied aspects of the divine-human relationship generally associated with the concept of "prayer." Chief among them was *riv*, a legal case or controversy, which was also applied to the divine-human relationship . . . In the Bible and rabbinic literature, this law-court pattern is used in three situations: in the human court, in the heavenly court, and in human-divine controversies . . . [T]he third usage depicts situations in which an individual (or Israel) brings a charge against God Himself. The appeal is thus both against God yet also to God, making Him, paradoxically, both judge and defendant.[10]

We will see how this process has developed after the Shoah and whether God can be blamed and accused, yet still relied upon and trusted for deliverance; considered unjust in one regard, but still the ultimate God of justice; hidden or silent in the face of mass atrocity, yet still the Supreme God of mercy. How these contradictions are maintained and formulated approaches the root of post-Shoah Jewish faith, and any theodicy.

8. Ibid., xv.
9. Ibid., xvi.
10. Ibid., xvii.

Because "Jewish conversation always begins from the Bible," as Sheldon Isenberg writes,[11] I will first assess how the tradition of arguing with God developed in the Tanak.

Biblical Examples of Protest

The Bible is replete with examples of protest, as Laytner reminds us.[12] One can turn, for example, to Abraham's pleading with God to spare the innocent before the destruction of Sodom and Gomorah[13] or to Moses's imploring of God not to destroy the Israelites on various occasions.[14] The latter example invokes a number of tropes in the tradition of arguing with God: recalling God's own words of promised fidelity, playing on God's honor—"God's own name will be besmirched"[15]—and arguing from merit, "linking his personal fate with the fate of the people."[16] Some other biblical examples include the prophet Elijah's challenge to God in front of the priests of Baal on Mount Carmel,[17] the "confessions" of Jeremiah,[18] and the Psalms of Petition and the book of Lamentations.[19]

Psalm 22 is a typical example of the law-court pattern of prayer. In Mark's Gospel, Jesus's words on the cross—"My God, my God, why have you abandoned me?"—are the lament and opening address, but if one reads the rest of the psalm, we get the lengthy presentation of facts—"All who see me mock me; / they curl their lips, / they shake their heads. / 'Let him commit himself to the Lord; let Him rescue him'"—and a concluding petition: "Deliver me from a lion's mouth; / from the horns of wild oxen rescue me. / Then will I proclaim Your fame to my brethren . . ."[20] Notice the use of the conditional—if you do this, then I will do that. Lastly, there is a "divine response to the petition." Here, the psalmist anticipates God's answer, so he can

---

11. Isenberg, "From Myth to Psyche," 17.

12. See also Laytner, *Arguing with God*, 252–53.

13. Gen 18:23–32.

14. Exod 32.

15. Laytner, *Arguing with God*, 11.

16. Ibid., 11.

17. 1 Kgs 18:36–37.

18. Jer 11:20; 20:12.

19. Laytner, *Arguing with God*, 16–17.

20. Ps 22:8–9 and Ps 22:22–23, respectively.

proclaim: "the Lord's fame shall be proclaimed to the generations to come; they shall tell of His beneficence to people yet to be born. For He has acted."[21] While the prophets also embody such faith and trust, they too are not without some acute questioning of God and moments of doubt.

According to Laytner, "The problem of theodicy lies at the heart of Jeremiah's complaints." While having faith in God, Jeremiah is still troubled by how long he is waiting for a just verdict. In this sense, Jeremiah joins other believers who cry, "Why does the way of the wicked prosper? Why are the workers of treachery at ease?"[22] In chapter 2, Alicia Partnoy expressed how she expected no such divine aid while tortured and imprisoned in Argentina.[23]

Unlike Partnoy, and despite the ambiguity in God's answer, Job is privileged to hear God in the whirlwind. Not surprisingly, Laytner places the story of Job firmly within the "law-court pattern and the arguing with God motif" and writes that the book's author "builds upon them with such intensity that he has been regarded as the apex of the law-court-form."[24] We encountered some of these arguments in the previous chapter. Laytner notes that part of the explanations in Job arises from the postexilic experience. He identifies three common themes in books like Job and Ezekiel: "First, against the threat of Persian dualistic theology, we find the assertion that the Lord is the sole author of all, both light and dark, good and evil . . . Second, Job (21:19–20) and Ezekiel (18; 33:10–19) propose a system wherein each individual, each generation, is rewarded or punished according to their deeds alone . . . Third, all these works hold out to Israel the hope of redemption."[25]

This hope of redemption and trust in the Lord, according to Laytner, "brings us to the very threshold of the rabbinic point of view, which *ultimately* resolves the problem of theodicy along the lines developed by the postexilic prophets and Psalm 73, that is, through the belief in the Messianic Redemption, retribution in the World to Come,

---

21. Ps 22:31–32.

22. Laytner, *Arguing with God*, 20. He is quoting Jer 12:1. See also Sweeney, *Reading the Hebrew Bible after the Shoah*, 104–27.

23. See Partnoy, *Little School*, 86.

24. Laytner, *Arguing with* God, 32.

25. Ibid., 36–37.

the resurrection of the dead to eternal life, and the acceptance of suffering as chastisements of divine love."[26] While this position becomes the dominant strand, it is not without some opposition—as elements of the tradition of arguing with God occupy their own place amidst the traditional practices.[27]

Rabbinic Use of Biblical Arguments with God

In *The Classic Midrash: Tannaitic Commentaries on the Bible,* Reuven Hammer notes the rabbis' interpretation of Exod 15:6 ("Your right hand, O Lord, magnificent in power, your right hand, O Lord, has shattered the enemy"): "Ingeniously the Sages inserted missing elements into Biblical stories, in this case the concept of repentance . . . It was inconceivable to them that God would not be willing to offer even the worst sinners an opportunity to repent and would destroy them, unless there was clearly no hope for their salvation."[28]

Such an attempt sought to justify cases of apparently innocent suffering that were wrongly interpreted to prove an unjust response of God. Of Deut 32:4—"His deeds are perfect"—we read in the commentaries: "His workmanship is perfect in regard to all creatures and no one has a right to complain in any way. No one can consider things and say, 'If only I had three eyes! If only I had three hands!' . . . The verse says YEA, ALL HIS WAYS ARE JUST (Deut 32:4). He judges all creatures and gives them what is appropriate for them."[29]

As Isenberg adds: "Rabbinic explanation of suffering or evil emphasizes that no suffering is undeserved and no sin ultimately remains unpunished."[30] Similarly, Laytner refers to "the triumph of Rabbi Akiba's submissive theology" in which suffering should be borne in hope and trust.[31] As Berkovits comments: "The classical example of Jewish martyrology is the manner of the death of R. Akiba. As they were tearing the flesh from his body with iron-pronged combs, 'he

---

26. Ibid., 37.

27. Ibid., 37.

28. Hammer, *Classic Midrash,* 112.

29. Quoted from ibid., 350.

30. Isenberg, "From Myth to Psyche," 22. See also Neusner, "Theodicy in Judaism," 685–729.

31. Laytner, *Arguing with God,* 62.

took upon himself the yoke of the kingdom of heaven."[32] Rabbi Akiba dies without protest or questioning but with the Shema on his lips.[33] His martyrdom was even more heroic because he faithfully fulfilled the requirements of the law until the end.[34]

While we will encounter rabbis who refuse to go to this extraordinary length—or do so and are still not satisfied—we need to remember that most mainstream Jewish thinkers prior to the Holocaust would profess traditional faith and trust in God and seek reasons for why suffering was deserved. We also need to keep in mind the historical context in which a rabbi resorted to a law-court prayer, often "to refute the attacks of gnosticism and Christianity while responding to the ultimate questions and doubts of the Jewish people."[35]

As Laytner notes, "the law-court prayer never acquired the stamp of legitimacy, nor gained the currency in normative Jewish practice that Akiba's teachings did, nor could it, for it was unsuited to the task of sustaining the people over an indefinite length of time such as the Exile represented."[36] D. Z. Phillips, in his comments on John Roth's protest theology, expresses his hesitation in supporting protest as a faith response, as he felt such a confrontation with God would eventually lead to the dissolution of the relationship.[37] Phillips seems to imply that because of the extent and magnitude of evil in the world, once one embarks on this path of protest, the accusations and the rebuke of God would seem constant, hardly the "ingredients" for a dynamic, right relationship. The same tendency is likely to occur with the law-court prayers if not used carefully and in moderation.

It is also important to remember that both the example of Rabbi Akiba and the questioning of God tradition are two poles within Jewish theodic responses rooted in faith in and love of God. As Braiterman stresses:

32. Berkovits, *Essential Essays*, 328.

33. Ibid., 329.

34. Ibid., 329. According to Sweeney, such justification of God often "charges the victims with responsibility for their own victimization" (*Reading the Hebrew Bible after the Shoah*, 236).

35. Laytner, *Arguing with God*, 129.

36. Ibid., 129.

37. Phillips, *Problem of Evil*, 118.

Despite the boldness of these texts, rabbinic authors do not complain against God lightly. Their challenges must meet proper conditions. Torah constitutes one crucial criterion. In the Lamentations Rabbah trial scene, Moses holds God to His own law . . . [and] God can only be tried before the law by those who champion it. The author of one midrash clearly makes his point when he asks: "Do you know who can protest against His decree and say to Him, 'Why do you do such a thing?' He who observes the commandments" . . . [O]nly authorized persons are entitled to complain—and only for the right reason.[38]

And yet, despite its traditional restriction to the religiously orthodox and devout, for Laytner, the arguing with God tradition can be effective as a personal and spiritual response for all Jews. Such protest could also be a spur towards a deeper faith that faces evil and suffering honestly while still articulating a convincing case for belief in God. Even to hear such stories or comments—recall Jeremiah's questioning above—and to suspend one's strictly metaphysical or philosophical notion of God, can be cathartic in a time of spiritual crisis. Phillips may be right in critiquing the practice of placing God as an agent among agents within the human moral community, but there is something endearing and spiritually satisfying in these rabbinic attempts to speak of God and to God amidst suffering.

In fact, midrash, Talmud, and *piyyutim* ("poetic embellishments [that] take the form of hymns to be sung prior to, or after, the standard prayers, and of poetic inserts in the standard prayers themselves"[39]) contain a number of insightful and provocative attempts to address the question of suffering and God in the context of prayer. Such attempts are often last resorts uttered only by those who are faithful to the covenant.

Laytner's focus on some humanizing and insightful rabbinic commentaries helps illustrate his overall thesis on the relevance of the arguing with God tradition for contemporary Jews. In one instance, the rabbis tried to add further reasons to Abraham's pleading on behalf of Sodom and Gomorrah: "Address: Master of the Universe! Argument/ Petition: You swore that You would not bring a flood upon the world [again] . . . [Isaiah 54:9]. A flood of water You won't bring, but a deluge of fire You would bring!? Would You with subtly evade Your [the]

---

38. Braiterman, *(God) After Auschwitz*, 53–54.

39. Laytner, *Arguing with God*, 127.

oath? . . . If You don't let up a bit, Your world cannot endure."[40] The idea of God being persuaded by this remark may be humorous, but the rabbis are also raising a legitimate protest: how can God allow and inflict such devastation without dire consequences? They are also following precedent. If such arguments worked for Moses or Abraham, why can they not work again?

In another common motif, the rabbis portray Cain rebuking God for not acting to stop the first murder: "This resembles the case of two who quarrelled and one is killed. But a third fellow was there who did nothing to intervene between them. Upon whom does the blame rest if not the third fellow? Thus it is written: [His blood] cries out to me [Ĕly]—it cries out against me [Aly]."[41] Calling God an immoral bystander is a stark religious step. If a human being is guilty who idly stands by while another is bludgeoned to death, what does such culpability mean if the "bystander" is God? In other instances, Cain laments the imperfection of human nature—the argument of humankind's evil inclination noted in Genesis—and prays for leniency in judgment. "The Rabbis recognized that even someone like Elijah made use of this argument when he said to God on Mount Carmel: 'You have turned their hearts backwards.'"[42] In this vein, the rabbis engage in anthropodicy and place a fair share of censure and responsibility on God. If God created human beings with an "evil inclination,"[43] it should not be surprising that they inevitably sin and thus need repentance.

The postexilic community, as Lamentations testifies, had to face abandonment and catastrophic loss. In a rabbinic countersuit from Lamentations Rabbah, the rabbis try to justify why the Jewish people are punished in the Babylonian exile (which also applies to the Roman destruction of the temple). In the text, as Laytner describes, "Jeremiah, at God's behest, rouses the Patriarchs and Moses from their graves to weep and lament over Israel's destruction for (and with) God. But the occasion for lamenting soon turns into a confrontation between Israel's ancestors and God in which the patriarchs and Moses accuse God of great injustice."[44]

40. Ibid., 46.

41. Ibid., 58–59.

42. Ibid., 62. The biblical quote is 1 Kgs 18:37.

43. Gen 8:21.

44. Laytner, *Arguing with God*, 76–77.

One by one, Abraham, Isaac, Jacob, and Moses describe the difficulties they had to endure while remaining faithful. Arguing on account of ancestral merit (*zekhut avot*), they plead their case in the hope of eliciting a response from God. God is silent. Finally, Rachel comes before God and poignantly depicts the ordeal she endured when she overheard that Jacob would be tricked into having Leah as his first wife but how she still showed compassion on her sister:

> Sovereign of the Universe . . . I gave my sister all the signs that I had given my husband, so that he might think that it was I. Not only that, I crept under the bed in which he lay with my sister and when he spoke with her, she was silent and I spoke for her so that he would not recognize my sister by her voice . . . Now if I, who am but flesh and blood, dust and ashes, was not jealous of my rival and did not put her to shame, why should You, O Eternal King, the loving and merciful one, be jealous of idols who have no reality in them, so that You have sent my children into Exile and let them be slain by the sword and suffered their enemies to do what they wished with them?[45]

Note the clever textual additions to the Genesis story, from Rachel initially overhearing the news of her father's plot and sharing signs with Jacob to thwart Laban, to then feeling pity for her sister and rival and so choosing to hide under the bed as the love of her life, Jacob, consummates his marriage to Leah. Rachel also highlights her perceived "degraded" state as a woman who still shows inspiring feats of kindness, patience, and empathy, while God seems to flounder in comparison.

Although God is silent after the pleadings of the patriarchs and Moses, Rachel's candid and sincere speech elicits a surprising reaction.[46] As Braiterman notes: "Here it is God who must withdraw his complaint against Israel and repent before Rachel!"[47] Christians would never expect Jesus to repent or seek forgiveness from another. It would be considered blasphemy and heresy. And yet there is something reassuring about the notion of God apologizing here, though such an apology also raises deeper, problematic assertions about God's transcendent nature and omnipotence. Braiterman continues:

45. Ibid., 79.

46. Ibid., 80.

47. Braiterman, *(God) After Auschwitz*, 52.

Authors of other aggadot [narratives] go further still and depict divine *malevolence*. Exodus Rabbah contains a remarkable story comparing Job to a drunken palace guard rashly cursing the Governor and His justice . . . In the midrash, Job begs for forgiveness upon witnessing God imprison Miriam, banish Moses, blind Isaac, sentence Abraham, and cripple Jacob. While rare, the motif of a violent God is not isolated to this retelling of Job. Inverting the kindly paternalism more common to classical Jewish sources, some rabbis depict God as a violent *pater familias*—a wife-beater, an abusive parent, and a child killer.[48]

In a well-known Hasidic story, we hear how the Rabbi of Berditchev asked a tailor to retell his argument with God from the day before. The tailor says: "I declared to God: 'You wish me to repent of my sins, but I have committed only minor offenses . . . But You, O Lord, have committed grievous sins . . . Let us be quits: may You forgive me, and I will forgive You." The Berditchever replied: "Why did you let God off so easily? You might have forced Him to redeem all of Israel!"[49] Here again, we see the affirmation that God must address and respond to the extent of evil in the world and that faith demands a response and answer, even while recognizing that the ways of God are a mystery. Such a faith response of questioning is also represented in Jewish liturgy.

Protest within Liturgy

The provocative tradition of *piyyutim* in the Jewish liturgy is for Laytner a long-lost resource. As noted above, these were poetic embellishments spoken or sung before or after a standard liturgical piece of liturgical praise. Of one example, Laytner writes that:

Sandwiched between . . . two pious assertions lies Issac bar Shalom's bitter protest. "There is no God besides You," says the liturgy.—"There is none like You among the dumb," cries out Issac bar Shalom . . . It is obvious that the tone of Issac bar Shalom's poem is wholly out of keeping with that of its adjacent prayers . . . In the prayer book, protest came to coexist

48. Ibid., 53.

49. Laytner, *Arguing with God*, 184.

with faith: the celebration of the redemptive past became co-
eval with the lamentation of the unredeemed present.[50]

One can imagine how provocative such an effect could be.
Latyner writes: "When these poems were incorporated into the worship service, a dialectic dialogue was created in which faith and love
of one generation were displayed alongside the doubts and anger of a
later generation . . . [B]oth sought to affirm the same beliefs and values: love of God, faithfulness to the Torah, trust in God's power . . ."[51]
While such a tradition has a long history in the Jewish faith (its origin
is considered between the second and sixth centuries CE),[52] according to Laytner, this tradition is tragically minimal, if not nonexistent,
within contemporary Judaism.[53] What he laments can also be said of
many Christian churches and believers: "Cut off from the tradition
of protest and argument that is the heritage of earlier times, ignorant
of the concept of prayer as protest, and deprived of the rich vocabulary of liturgical protest, modern Jews have no outlet to express their
darker thoughts to God—certainly not through conventional worship
services in a contemporary synagogue or temple!"[54] Expressing those
"dark thoughts" to God in a liturgical and religious context may be essential to face and accept such a reality and come to see how God can
still be present within such suffering. Repressing such thoughts could
also inhibit an honest spiritual struggle and relationship with God.

In this context, Laytner illustrates how the arguing with God
tradition has been reinvigorated and altered by contemporary Jewish
poets and authors. While the rabbi was the people's voice in the medieval period, the poet and author also assume that role today. Laytner
cites the work of Irving Howe and Eliezer Greenberg, who point out
that the heart of the post-Shoah Yiddish poet "was pledged neither to
the world nor to God, but the people who believed in God or had only
yesterday believed, or for whom the vision of God was inseparable
from the vision of peoplehood."[55] Such a representative voice could
be far removed from the faith-filled cries of Jeremiah. Salient ques-

50. Ibid., 135–39.

51. Ibid., 174–75.

52. Ibid., 127.

53. Ibid., 175.

54. Ibid., 176.

55. Quoted in ibid., 197.

tions are whether it is meaningful for anyone to protest God and when theological protest courts blasphemy.

CONCLUSION: THEOLOGICAL PROTEST AND BLASPHEMY

It is crucial to recall the traditional criteria for protest as one treads the line between hope and despair, faith and blasphemy. There may be something liberating and authentic about a no-holds-barred protest of God that is available to anyone, but such protests need to have some limitations to maintain a living connection to traditional faith and religious identity. While some theologians will call God abusive[56] to maintain faith, and others seem to advocate a complete severance from Jewish covenantal and biblical belief, change can become so radical that all continuity with one's faith tradition is lost, and with it, one's religious identity. The rabbis who protested did so because of the injustice they witnessed or experienced and the belief that God opposed such injustice and would heal or redeem it. Without that belief, the protest becomes an empty curse, adrift from any theodicy.

Consider the rabbinic commentary of Exod 15:11, "Who is like You, O Lord, among the celestials (*elim*)? Who is like You . . . among the silent (*ilmim*), O Lord. Who is like You—seeing the shame suffered by Your children and remaining silent . . ."[57] Playing on the Hebrew word *elim*, the rabbis question why God is silent (*ilmim*) or refer to a hidden God. It is a daring interpretation. Invoking Isa 42:14–15, however, the rabbis still affirm that God will intervene in the future: "*in the past* I kept still and restrained myself *but from now on* I will scream like a woman in labor, I will pant and I will gasp."[58] While God is accused of failing to fulfill present duties, additional words are added to Scripture to speak faithfully and audaciously for God and claim God will "scream like a woman in labor" from now on. A close line is walked, but the text still remains faithful to Jewish tradition and beliefs.

To a Christian theodicist, the arguing with God tradition in its biblical and formulaic outline is not completely viable today.[59] One

---

56. See the section on Rabbi David Blumenthal in ch 9.

57. Hammer, *Classic Midrash*, 117. The passage is from *Mekhilta Shirata* 8, II 60.

58. Ibid., 117. Italics added to highlight the words added by the sages to the biblical verse.

59. Laytner writes that the theme of arguing with God remains widespread, but

does not want to maintain that God can somehow be persuaded by mere human reasoning or must be reminded of the need to act. Such a stance implies that God is easily malleable or negligent. And yet, at its core, this tradition speaks of a personal, dialogic relationship between God and the individual (or community) that is sustained and guided by the love of God and belief in God's plan for this world. The individual denounces injustice and expects a God of mercy and justice to act. In the previous chapter, Gutiérrez stressed that awareness of God's gratuitousness demands a disinterested faith position. In the next chapter, I will highlight how Berkovits in particular expands these ideas. Also important here is the nature and context of prayer, an issue I will return to in chapters 10 and 11, particularly in asking how mass atrocities and evil subvert the role and value of prayer.

Finally, while doubt and questioning of God occurred before the Holocaust and will continue in this post-Shoah period, the one difference according to Laytner is that "other generations may have doubted, but only today has this doubt reached epidemic proportions."[60] While I advocate the need for a believer to have a venue to express what Laytner calls "dark thoughts" to God, can faith still survive amidst such grave doubts? "For many of us today," Laytner writes, "the argument is no longer rooted in faith: it is rooted in doubt."[61] When one's religious faith is grounded in such unstable roots, it is not surprising that traditional theodicy would be entirely rejected or altered to an almost unrecognizable state. At the same time, there is the compelling argument that such unstable roots provide the possibility for a more authentic, dynamic faith. I will examine this contentious assertion in the next chapter.

---

rarely depicted in the law-court pattern of prayer. He speculates this may be due to "the changing nature of Jewish education (and the knowledge of classical Jewish prayer formats), perhaps due to the full transformation of the theme from liturgy to folk culture" (*Arguing with God*, 197). See also Kugel, *How to Read the Bible*, 662–89. In the gospels, Jesus also speaks of the value of the persistence of prayer (Matt 7:7; Luke 18:1–8), an issue I will address in ch 10.

60. Laytner, *Arguing with God*, xxi.

61. Quoted in ibid., 236.

9

Jewish Post-Shoah Theodicy and Antitheodicy

The Israelites cried out to the Lord, and the Lord raised a champion for the Israelites to deliver them . . .[1]

In the previous chapter I examined the Jewish arguing with God tradition and sought to develop how Christian theodicists could benefit from incorporating various features of this tradition within their theodic positions. In this chapter I will highlight salient features supported by some post-Shoah Jewish thought, which offers invaluable insights or challenges to the Christian theodicist. Just as I turned to liberation theology because of that theology's focus on the voiceless and the forgotten of society, I turn to Jewish post-Shoah theodicy because of that tradition's grappling with whether and how faith in God can still be possible despite the Holocaust and other historical ruptures. If a Christian theodicy is to be viable in the face of mass atrocity—in Greenberg's terms: to speak in the presence of the burning children; and in my context: to incorporate and address the horrors witnessed within testimonies of mass atrocity—turning to Jewish post-Shoah thought seems a necessary step. I'll present my case below.

1. Judg 3:9.

"POST"-SHOAH JEWISH THEOLOGY[2]

Overview

In *(God) After Auschwitz: Tradition and Change in Post-Holocaust Jewish Thought*, Zachary Braiterman focuses on two generations of Jewish post-Holocaust thinkers and argues that the first group—Martin Buber, Abraham Joshua Heschel, Joseph Soloveitchik, and Mordecai Kaplan—only spoke of the Shoah obliquely, as the wounds were too raw.[3] Braiterman claims that within their works, traces of distress and despair mark their texts while they try to "affirm guardedly optimistic appraisals of God."[4] The next generation had the benefit of the widespread publication of Holocaust memoirs and more information and time—providing a "sufficiently developed discourse"—to try to assess the meaning of such a catastrophic event. One of Braiterman's main arguments is that after the Shoah, "Jewish thinkers make little to no use of theodicy—explicit or implicit."[5] Antitheodic strands dominate. This insight also comes as a warning to those who refuse to acknowledge this truth: "Indeed, sole recourse to theodicy may ultimately cripple contemporary religious discourse by forcing philosophers and theologians to defend the indefensible."[6] In addition to the questions raised in the previous chapter, I will also test and examine this claim below.

Affinity with Postmodernity

One of Braiterman's theses is to show how postmodern theories—despite different characteristics and aims—"help illuminate post-Holocaust thought on at least two counts: First, they provide analytical tools with which to identify and evaluate the play of difference that permeates tradition . . . Second, postmodernism has come to shape the very same thematic horizons occupied by post-Holocaust Jewish thinkers."[7]

2. "After? Did you say: after? Meaning what?" (Wiesel, *One Generation After*, 57).

3. Braiterman, *(God) After Auschwitz*, 7. For a different view, see Gershon Greenberg, "Introduction [to] Ultra-Orthodox Responses." Greenberg contends that there were earlier Jewish accounts dealing with the Holocaust but that "the sources were almost exclusively Orthodox (and in Hebrew and Yiddish), and they tended to be ignored by the non-Orthodox" (11).

4. Braiterman, *(God) After Auschwitz*, 7.

5. Ibid., 5.

6. Ibid., 32.

7. Ibid., 9. See also Ochs, "Renewal of Jewish Theology Today," 324–48.

From the works of Levinas, Foucault, Derrida, Lyotard, and other postmodern thinkers, Braiterman identifies four recurring themes crucial to analyzing and phrasing (or rephrasing) the questions raised in our post-Holocaust world: "[1] the unstable field that constitutes historical consciousness, [2] the experience, memory, and threat of catastrophe and rupture in the twentieth century, [3] the impotence of language and reason before the 'tremendum,' and [4] the potentially reorienting significance of the supplement, the trace, and the fragment."[8]

We saw many of these same issues at play within my analysis of testimonies of mass atrocity. The key strand is the theme of the probable, the sense of dissolution and instability, along with the proliferation of radical doubt into all the horizons of identity within humankind—their conscience, reason, memory, language, and history—which are normally relied upon to navigate one's way between truth and falsity, light and darkness, right and wrong. One of the key issues for Braiterman in discussing these contemporary Jewish thinkers is to examine how they revise tradition—seeking to forge new ground in Judaism—though with mixed success to continuity.

Postmodern thought and the historical caesuras like the Shoah that mark its boundaries and limitations have overturned and sown mass confusion into traditional categories and guides. It is thus inevitable that their effects would be felt in the realm of theology.[9] "As I see it," Braiterman argues, "post-modern and post-Holocaust thinkers inhabit different sectors of style, mood, and use within the same mental and cultural universe."[10] My use of texts from cultural studies and literary criticism in the first two chapters underwrites and develops this important insight. It also influences how one forms a theodicy, particularly in reading and interpreting the events, signs, and symbols of our contemporary world.

---

8. Braiterman, *(God) After Auschwitz*, 9.

9. For a helpful introductory essay to postmodern theology, see Ward, "Postmodern Theology," 322–38.

10. Braiterman, *(God) After Auschwitz*, 10. For his argument that "the writings of Rubenstein, Berkovits, and Fackenheim coalesce into what Michel Foucault called a common discursive formation," see ibid., 12–13, and the conclusion, "Discourse, Sign, Diptych."

The Rise of Post-Holocaust Discourse

According to Braiterman, in the aftermath of the Shoah, following the Eichmann trial and Arendt's prognosis of the banality of evil, and after Elie Wiesel's *Night*, a few key Jewish theologians and philosophers relentlessly investigated the truths and challenges inflicted by the Holocaust. What came to be called post-Holocaust theology was initiated and developed within a growing discourse throughout the 1960s and 1970s and developed in such fields as law, literature, cinema, theater, philosophy, sociology, history, and psychoanalysis. Richard Rubenstein's book *After Auschwitz* remains the fulcrum upon which many subsequent theologians turn.[11] Braiterman writes that its publication "marks a milestone distinguishing modern Jewish theology from contemporary Jewish thought."[12] He continues: "In the late 1960s and throughout the 1970s, Rubenstein, Berkovits, and Fackenheim began to rework received notions about God and covenant by rereading traditional Jewish texts. In the process (and despite fierce disagreement among themselves), they have articulated a uniquely post-Holocaust theological sensibility dominated by what we are about to call *antitheodicy*."[13]

Just as I challenged whether Phillips could advocate theism without theodicy, an issue here is whether antitheodicy is compatible with theism or whether theism needs elements of antitheodicy.

Between Theodicy and Antitheodicy

If one speaks of traditional Jewish thought—especially as embodied in ultra-Orthodox Jewish positions—the God of the Bible and of today is a God of both justice and mercy who during various times of history, inflicts punishment upon the Jewish people for their transgressions. For some, even the Holocaust fits into this paradigm or

---

11. Rubenstein and Roth, *Approaches to Auschwitz*, 335. Saul Friedländer highlights the pivotal role of the NBC miniseries *Holocaust* in 1978–79 ("Facing the Shoah," 3).

12. Braiterman, *(God) After Auschwitz*, 87.

13. Ibid., 4. In the "Problem of Evil" (1977), Swinburne writes that the antitheodicist "denies [the claim that it is 'not morally wrong for God to create or permit various evils'] by putting forward moral principles which have as consequences that a good God would not under any circumstances cause or permit the evils in question" ("Evil Does Not Show That There Is No God," 600).

becomes interpreted "as a sacrificial precondition for the coming of the Messiah, embodied further in the creation (resuscitation) of the State of Israel."[14]

However, according to Braiterman, "against the grain of rabbinic Judaism and modern Jewish thought, post-Holocaust thinkers turned to the drama of priestly cult, a morally absent deity, the protesting Job, the heresy of Elisha b. Abuye,[15] abandoned wives, a plaintive community. These once marginalized but now privileged antitheodic subjects acted as a warrant allowing post-Holocaust thinkers to voice their own doubts about God and suffering."[16]

For Braiterman, antitheodicy is the refusal to explain, justify, or give meaning to God's role amidst tragedy. "Antitheodicy mirrors theodicy in reverse . . . but it is not atheism . . . Rather than defend God or accept catastrophe, the authors of antitheodic statements justify human figures and reject suffering along with its rewards."[17] The term as employed by Braiterman and used by Roth and others takes a clear stance against traditional theodicy. According to Bernard Schweizer, however, antitheodicists are engaged in weak compromises and a failure to follow the full import and logic of their arguments, which is best represented by the term *misotheism.* Misotheism differs from atheism by acknowledging the existence of God, but "misotheists are genuine accusers of God, and they will hold him accountable for random evil and undeserved suffering."[18] While Schweizer argues that some of the Jewish thinkers below have misotheistic tendencies, he also acknowledges that wrestling with God is a rich part of Jewish tradition.[19]

One should always be careful when advocating paradox;[20] however, I want to develop why a theodicy needs to incorporate select antitheodic features. Such attributes include a pastoral focus on the

14. Rubenstein and Roth, *Approaches to Auschwitz,* 330.

15. Elisha b. Abuye was the arch-heretic of rabbinic times, who in the sight of suffering said, "There is neither judgment nor judge."

16. Braiterman, *(God) After Auschwitz,* 163.

17. Ibid., 37.

18. Schweizer, *Hating God,* 217.

19. Ibid., 151–52.

20. Katz, writing of Irving Greenberg, remarks: "Merely holding, or claiming to believe, two contradictory propositions simultaneously is not a fruitful theological procedure" ("Issue of Confirmation," 50).

individual sufferer, a sustained grappling with the magnitude of some affliction, and a deep skepticism of theoretical justifications in the context of horrific suffering. Such an "alliance" with antithodic tendencies will prevent religious believers from severing themselves from some of the valid tenets of traditional religious belief (as a misotheist would) without seeming detached from the reality of atrocity or succumbing to a hatred of God as in misotheism. Does a Christian, for example, want to claim that God is completely transcendent and so utterly unknowable or is not a God of love and redemption?[21] While maintaining key traditional beliefs, a stance sympathetic with elements of an antitheodicy may also ground and sharpen one's theological language by demanding the need for nuance and facing paralyzing evils (many theodic arguments will, therefore, simply fail). This approach ensures that God will not be completely removed in an argument so crucial to one's faith: how to believe in a loving God despite evil.

Moreover, if the focus turns to humanity, as Braiterman seems to do,[22] then this attempt does nothing to solve the problem of evil. It only further idolizes humanity—even if in the process humanity is degenerated as evil and culpable because they are at the center without stating why they deserve to be. Recall how Sobrino advocated a theodic and anthropodic approach. Because antitheodicy is not necessarily atheism, one cannot say that such evil exists because there is no God. Does humanity now have the intrinsic power to do anything? Braiterman is aware of these conflicts. Under the heading "Between Theodicy and Antitheodicy," he points out: "Theodicy and antitheodicy do not represent stable entities. Instead, they constitute interpretative boundaries between which religious discourse plays back and forth. To determine the actual theodic or antitheodic significance of a given statement requires semantic and temporal context."[23] In this instance, Braiterman offers caution to assign the label "antitheodicy" to any ancient text.[24] While this caution is certainly understandable, what I take from Braiterman is the point that one may find tendencies

---

21. For a fruitful work that examines the doctrine of God through the writings of Aquinas, Maimonides, and Ibn-Sina and (consequently) how such a study contributes to contemporary interfaith and intercultural conversation and exchange, see Burrell, *Knowing the Unknowable God*, 3.

22. Braiterman, *(God) After Auschwitz*, 37.

23. Ibid., 58.

24. Ibid., 59.

for both paths in a particular discourse on the problem of evil, which is evident in my approach as well.

SOME KEY JEWISH POST-SHOAH THINKERS

This section will briefly examine the thought of a select group of seven post-Holocaust Jewish thinkers whose theological probing and analysis raise fruitful challenges and approaches for any Christian theodicist. I will focus below on Richard Rubenstein, Eliezer Berkovits, Emil Fackenheim, Irving Greenberg, David Blumenthal, Elie Wiesel, and Melissa Raphael.

Richard Rubenstein and the Death of the Biblical God

Conservative Rabbi Richard Rubenstein was one of the first Jewish theologians to respond to Holocaust literature and virtually invented post-Holocaust theology with his publication of *After Auschwitz* in 1966.[25] It was Rubenstein who placed the Shoah as a central locus of investigation in his own theology, raising theological questions that remain unsolved. He writes: "After Auschwitz . . . events make a mockery of the construction of immanence as endowed with a meaning radiated by an affirmatively posited transcendence . . ."[26]

In the first edition of *After Auschwitz*, Rubenstein supports an "insightful paganism," a return to nature that is deemed a better grounding for one's faith and spiritual formation. In subsequent editions, though, he distances himself from the radical nature of this claim. What originally distinguished the book and caused a minor uproar was a Jewish rabbi declaring the "death of God" and any notion of a viable Jewish covenant. The potential for the Holocaust to be a part of God's plan is for Rubenstein an idea "simply too obscene" for him to accept.[27] Ignaz Maybaum, a careful and judicious post-Shoah thinker involed in dialogue among the Abrahamic faiths, gingerly tried to argue that the third *churban* entailed "progress," as it signified the end of the Jewish (and Christian) Middle Ages, and that the innocent martyred in the Holocaust served as a vicarious sacrifice of atonement for the sins of others. Maybaum was searching for answers

25. Ibid., 8.

26. Rubenstein, *After Auschwitz*, 158.

27. Rubenstein and Roth, *Approaches to Auschwitz*, 340.

based on prior biblical precedent and knew much was at stake to disavow that heritage.[28] For Rubenstein, either God has abandoned God's people or the Holocaust is a part of God's plan for them. Either way, the God that remains is not worth believing in and the covenant is no longer operable.[29] The notion of a personal or communal relationship with God as grounded in the Tanak seems dead and buried.

Despite the radical nature of this claim, Rubenstein does not consider himself an atheist. Regarding his infamous proclamation of the death of God, he clarifies that no one can prove or disprove God's existence, but maintains that "the thread uniting God and man, heaven and earth, has been broken. We stand in a cold, silent, unfeeling cosmos, unaided by any purposeful power beyond our own resources. After Auschwitz, what else can a Jew say about God?"[30]

While such a description of the world and God seems nihilistic, it does not explicitly say that God does not exist; Rubenstein clarifies that no human being would be able to prove that assertion. As I interpret this quote, if any faith in God remains, it is deist or one that must endure a powerless God.

Ultimately Rubenstein is saying there is no way of knowing God because there is no conclusive means to argue from the events of this world to a loving, involved God. The God of the Bible and history was silent at Auschwitz. For Rubenstein, this fact speaks volumes. I remain unconvinced, though, that Rubenstein's clarification above does not, at least, imply God's death, as the failure to believe or argue in a Jewish context for the existence of the traditional biblical (and so good and covenantal) God comes very close to stating God is dead. Possibly, Rubenstein is not saying that such a conclusion about God's goodness is definitively wrong, but asking how else a Jew can interpret these events without skepticism and doubt. As he writes in *The Cunning of History*: "We live in a world that is functionally godless."[31]

There is certainly reason to question whether Rubenstein weighs the evidence of counter-testimony to the Shoah as much as he cedes

28. See Maybaum, *Ignaz Maybaum*, 156, 165, 168, 173. For critiques, see Katz, *Post-Holocaust Dialogues*, 248–67; Raphael, *Female Face of God*, 33–34.

29. Katz, *Post-Holocaust Jewish Dialogues*, 147.

30. Quoted from Roth and Rubenstein, *Approaches to Auschwitz*, 343.

31. Quoted in Fasching, *Ethical Challenge of Auschwitz and Hiroshima*, 65.

Auschwitz with a defining negation of the biblical God and covenant.[32] Nevertheless, while Rubenstein's daring and blunt language strikes a chord and asks questions that still need answers, other Jewish theologians, while painfully grappling with the reality of the Shoah, do not believe such devastation has the final word on their faith in God and the covenant. One of those theologians is Eliezer Berkovits.

Eliezer Berkovits: Between Illuminating and Forsaken Faith

According to Braiterman, Orthodox Rabbi Eliezer Berkovits, while seeing some validity in Rubenstein's questions and challenges, rebukes Rubenstein for using terms like the "death of God" (as opposed to Berkovits's use of the motif of "God's Hiding Face"[33]) and for addressing the Holocaust out of historical context.[34] For some of these reasons, Braiterman places Berkovits in stark contrast to Rubenstein, arguing that Berkovits "denied that the Holocaust posed any unique theological challenge to traditional belief and Jewish texts."[35]

This is true to a point. For Berkovits, there is no doubting that Auschwitz for his generation "represents the supreme crisis of faith"[36] and is unique in history because of the systematic nature of the slaughter, but not for the theological questions that arise from it. Berkovits sympathizes with those who lost their faith in divine providence during the Holocaust because of what they suffered. He justifies their defiance and even calls it holy. However, in the nature of the faith crisis, he turns to a figure like Rabbi Akiba and what he had to endure—seeing vast similarities to his historical, theological crisis, especially after the failure of the Bar Kochba rebellion (132–35 CE). Berkovits therefore disagrees with Rubenstein, basically saying that if one can believe after the events of the destruction of the first temple in 586 BCE, why cannot one maintain elements of the traditional faith after Auschwitz?

While Berkovits is sympathetic to those who lost faith, he himself cannot accept their rebellion. As Braiterman writes, "To do so would mean that he must ignore those Jews whose faith survived intact. How dare he reject faith in providence when they did not?! And yet again

---

32. Katz, "Issue of Confirmation," 16.

33. Braiterman, *(God) After Auschwitz*, 126.

34. Ibid., 8.

35. Ibid., 8.

36. Berkovits, *Essential Essays*, 316.

how can he dare to believe in the face of those who refused?!"[37] In this light, Berkovits straddles a middle ground somewhere between theodicy and antitheodicy, although his faith, suffused at times with doubts, can also seem traditional in many of his writings.[38] However, in the midst of various pious statements is a faith battered by doubt and suffering, as we also hear: "One must approach the problem of faith presented in the crematoria in the agony of one's soul."[39] Such an approach gives no easy answers. According to Braiterman, "This intermediate position defines the theological reflections that appear throughout the remainder of [Berkovits's] *Faith after the Holocaust.*"[40] I would contend that this intermediate position correctly acknowledges that some gaps or indeterminate positions are essential for a theodicy to be viable in this post-Holocaust or postmodern (using Braiterman's term) world. Irving Greenberg will develop these ideas below.

Moreover, while Braiterman believes that "solidarity with the believers and the 'heretics' precludes theological coherence,"[41] Berkovits advocates that it is better to live at this threshold in the hope that from it a breakthrough can come.[42] It is a position similar to many of the liberation theologians who argue that one must look at reality openly and honestly even if such awareness can lead to legitimate and deep questions about God and humanity. From that difficult location, the hope remains that God will sustain an individual and will work to bring justice for all; that the reign of God is at hand and will continue to be implemented in our midst.[43] Remaining at this threshold, even while tempted by and sympathetic to radical doubt, still maintains hope for redemption from God. In imagining the rabbis at prayer, praising God for preserving the faithful in history, Berkovits writes: "Yes, all these attributes of God in history are true; for if they are not true now, they

---

37. Braiterman, *(God) After Auschwitz*, 117.

38. Berkovits, *Essential Essays*, 3.

39. Ibid., 316.

40. Braiterman, *(God) After Auschwitz*, 117.

41. Ibid.

42. Berkovits, *Essential Essays*, 331.

43. The Tanak is full of the happy, surprising ending or the unorthodox savior. In the book of Judith, for example, the Jewish people are saved at the last moment through an unlikely source, but they are saved nonetheless.

will yet be true."[44] Here there is no blindness to the present failing on God's part, but neither is there all-consuming despair.

Braiterman also argues that Berkovits succeeds in revising Jewish tradition—through his strong misreading of it—while Rubenstein lacked "strength," as Harold Bloom employs the term. "For Bloom a strong misreading of tradition is one in which a young poet succeeds in forcing his precursors to speak in his own voice. 'The mighty dead return,' Bloom writes, 'they return in our colors, and speaking in our voices.'"[45] Braiterman argues that what makes these post-Shoah Jewish theologians unique is how they attempt to revise tradition, seeking to forge new ground with mixed success. His argument is that the Holocaust raised questions that were similar to those that previous generations had grappled with, but never reached their extent and depth, and this new context has required a deft and dynamic approach.

More traditionally, according to Braiterman, a crucial component of Berkovits's hope is based on his advocacy of a free will theodicy with elements of soul-making. Steven Katz writes that for Berkovits, "God's hiddenness (the Biblical doctrine of *hester panim*) is required for man to be a moral creature."[46] In addition, many critics contend that Israel becomes for Berkovits a concrete testament and symbol for why it can be argued that despite Auschwitz, God is still active and involved with the Jewish people. For Braiterman, Berkovits's love of Israel equals or outweighs his love of God, and Israel becomes a "payment of the debt" owed to the Jews.[47] Steven Katz makes a similar assessment.[48] Berkovits does believe a moral Israel can be a sign and symbol that God's covenant remains viable, and he questions why Israel cannot be a sign of God's active love and involvement in history while Auschwitz is supposed to prove conclusively that God is no longer or never was involved in history. He also stresses that the only way fully to practice being Jewish is through living in a land that is immersed in the Jewish way of life. This is encapsulated for him in the rabbinic notion that

---

44. Braiterman, *(God) After Auschwitz*, 129.

45. Ibid., 132–33. For Bloom's development on this theme and his interpretation of Mark's Gospel, see *Jesus and Yahweh*, 64.

46. Katz, *Post-Holocaust Jewish Dialogues*, 270.

47. Braiterman, *(God) After Auschwitz*, 121.

48. Katz, *Post-Holocaust Jewish Dialogues*, 166–67.

"there is no Torah like the Torah of the Land of Israel."[49] Thus, the Torah cannot be fully implemented and followed while living under another people with their set of laws and traditions.

While Israel's role above needs nuancing, the context of why Israel matters for Berkovits should be noted: Israel is a means not an end. Faith in God is the ultimate concern.[50] For Berkovits, advocating questioning or "wrestling"[51] with God acknowledges that "what faith is searching for is, if not to understand fully, at least to gain a hint of the nature of God's involvement."[52] Because such understanding is inevitably limited—as all honest theodicists recognize their limitations—the search is for a meaningful faith despite the contradictions, doubt, and caesuras. Again, Braiterman criticizes such a position as "incoherent," but in order to remain within the context of the postmodern world that he also advocates, a world characterized by flux, uncertainty, and doubt, such a faith position may be the only meaningful and "coherent" one remaining—especially when the believer seeks to look directly at evil and injustice.

Two aphorisms of Berkovits summarize his overall position: "Faith, because it is trust in God, demands justice of God"; and "The man of faith questions God because of his faith."[53] The answers that result are always fragmentary, but because they remain immersed in faith, they are honest, authentic, and religiously orthodox. Drawing upon a wide range of philosophical, biblical, and rabbinic material, Berkovits also brings to these questions a refreshing historical and interdisciplinary focus.[54] We will see the same tendency with Emil Fackenheim.

Emil Fackenheim and the Search for Tikkun Olam

Rabbi Emil Fackenheim (1916–2003), a survivor of the Nazi camps,[55] was a religious thinker who, according to Braiterman, "stands at the midpoint of post-Holocaust Jewish theology having combined Richard

49. Berkovits, *Essential Essays,* 209.

50. Ibid., 332

51. Ibid., 316.

52. Ibid., 316.

53. Ibid., 316.

54. Katz, *Post-Holocaust Jewish Dialogues,* 95.

55. Fackenheim, *Mend the World,* 218.

Rubenstein's rhetoric of radicalism with Eliezer Berkovits's rhetoric of tradition."[56] Katz praises Fackenheim's philosophical Holocaust reflections as the "most intriguing and . . . [the] most influential."[57] Like Greenberg (see below), Fackenheim accentuates human acts of *tikkun* (mending, repair) to help "restore this broken Godhead to a state of primordial wholeness."[58]

In *To Mend the World: Foundations of Post-Holocaust Thought*, Fackenheim argues that "*the* Tikkun *which for the post-Holocaust Jew is a moral necessity is a possibility because during the Holocaust itself a Jewish* Tikkun *was already actual.* This simple but enormous, nay, world-historical truth is the rock on which rests any authentic Jewish future identity."[59] After bringing the reader to the utter depths of the Holocaust, which would seem to deny any possibility to combat this "*novum* of inexhaustible horror,"[60] Fackenheim locates the possibility for a Jewish future (whether secular or religious) because one can perceive this "ontological Ultimate—a *novum* of inexhaustible wonder" in individuals like survivor Pelagia Lewinska, who identified the core of the Nazi logic while in the camps and was able to avoid succumbing to its humanity-destroying ideology.[61] While Lewinska does not cite the source for this order to live, for Fackenheim this is a "pivotal moment" as counter-testimony to the horror of Auschwitz, a possibility Rubenstein minimizes or gainsays. It points to the possibility for healing, though never complete healing. Fackenheim comments: "[W]e must accept from the start that at most only a fragmentary *Tikkun* is possible. This is because we are situated in the post-Holocaust world. We must accept our situatedness. We must live with it."[62]

For Christians, the crucial phrase of the Our Father—"thy kingdom come, thy will be done on earth as it is in heaven"—identifies the heart of this dilemma. While John Paul II and McCord Adams stress

56. Braiterman, *(God) After Auschwitz*, 134.

57. Katz, *Post-Holocaust Jewish Dialogues*, 205.

58. Braiterman, *(God) After Auschwitz*, 144–45.

59. Fackenheim, *Mend the World*, 300. While Fackenheim believes that the Holocaust was unique (xiv–xv), he is referring to the *Tikkun* as a world-historical truth because it provides for all people an example of individuals who were able to fight and not "indiscriminately fall prey to the logic of Nazi destruction" (303).

60. Ibid., 301.

61. Quoted in ibid., 217.

62. Ibid., 256.

how Christ's life and resurrection provide complete redemption (or in Fackenheim's term, *Tikkun*), at issue is what it means to be "situated" in this post-Holocaust world but go beyond advocating a fragmentary *Tikkun*. Also of import is whether acknowledging only fragmentary healing may be a more meaningful and spiritually satisfying claim than a "complete" one in light of the extent of atrocities in our world. One may also claim that a fragmentary *Tikkun* is possible in this world, but a complete one is only plausible in the afterlife. For Fackenheim, though, "we must *stay with* our singled-out, this-worldly anguish, and cannot escape from it."[63] Fackenheim's focus on this world is not a uniquely Jewish position, though a rich afterlife theology is also present within Judaism.

As George Robinson remarks: "Jewish thought generally emphasizes our actions in this world, *olam ha-zeh*, and not in the next, *olam ha-bah*. The one certain form of life after death is the deeds we do while we are here."[64] However, as Robinson also adds: "Contrary to popular misconceptions, Jewish thought does not reject the idea of life after death."[65] As I have noted, denying or minimizing any afterlife redemption, whether in Phillips, Job, or Fackenheim, accentuates the tragedy and suffering of this world, which may be why the worldview presented by Rubenstein, above, or Blumenthal, below, may seem so bleak for the religious believer. While Fackenheim does not refute the relevance of making a commitment to transcendence,[66] he tries to elucidate how the Holocaust has altered one's hopes and perspectives: "Yom Kippur *after* Auschwitz cannot be what *at* Auschwitz it still was."[67] He refers to the martyrology *Ele Ezkera* in which ten rabbis defied the decree of Hadrian that forbade the practice of Judaism. For this rebellion, the Roman soldiers tortured the rabbis to death. "Then the angels in heaven cried out, 'Is this the Torah, and this the reward?' And a voice from heaven replied, 'If I hear another word, I will turn

---

63. Ibid., 330.

64. Robinson, *Essential Judaism*, 193. See also Telushkin, *Hillel*, 186–89.

65. Robinson, *Essential Judaism*, 192. For a concise historical account, see Gillman, "Judaic Doctrines of Death and Afterlife," 593.

66. Fackenheim, *Mend the World*, 322.

67. Ibid., 322.

the world to water.' The voice went on: 'This is my decree: accept it, all you who love the Torah!'"[68]

Fackenheim marvels how such words can be cited during the Yom Kippur Mussaf liturgy today, as the prospect of martyrdom for the likes of Rabbi Akiba were not possible for many of the victims of the Holocaust: "For the children, the mothers, the *Muselmänner* had not chosen to be martyrs: and that God needs *that* death is unacceptable. Hence, even the most devout Jew at prayer today must ask, on the holiest day of Judaism: why is the world today not water? He must ask the question but he cannot answer it."[69] It is interesting that Fackenheim raises the question of why there is still something but not nothing and yet decrees that one should not answer the question. Is it because to justify the world would be to justify some of the horrors, or that in light of such horrors, only a world of water is just?

Fackenheim shares with Jon Sobrino a mixture of an honest assessment of reality, a commitment to praxis, and hope for the future, though one focused solely on this world. In *To Mend the World*, Fackenheim, like Berkovits, admits that one is pulled by one's fidelity to those victims like the *Muselmänner*, which seems to preclude the possibility for a *Tikkun*, while also refusing to forget those who were able to resist, which obligates "our *Tikkun*." Thus, post-Holocaust thought "must dwell, however painful and precariously, between the extremes, and seek a *Tikkun* as it endures the tension."[70] One means to inhabit this tension is through theological protest.

For Fackenheim, such theological protest is an important and expected theological response in the face of such affliction and is emblematic of the Jewish faith. He writes: "There is a kind of faith which will accept all things and renounce every protest. There is also a kind of protest that has despaired of faith. In Judaism there has always been protest which stays *within* the spheres of faith."[71] After citing various biblical precedents, he adds, "in modern times, the Hasidic Rabbi Levi Yitzhak of Berdiczev . . . once interrupted the sacred Yom Kippur service in order to protest that, whereas kings of flesh and blood protected their peoples, Israel was left unprotected by her King in heaven.

---

68. Ibid., 329.
69. Ibid., 329.
70. Ibid., 310. See also Katz, *Post-Holocaust Jewish Dialogues*, 150.
71. Quoted from Fasching, "Ethics after Auschwitz and Hiroshima," 17.

Yet having made his protest he recited the Kaddish, which begins with these words: "Extolled and hallowed be the name of God throughout the world . . ."[72]

Fackenheim, according to Katz, "is adamant in his refusal to allow any theological *explanation* of the Holocaust . . . Yet, despite the implications, despite the absolute failure of theodicy, despite the seeming absurdity, Fackenheim urges men to believe."[73]

This stance is most evident in his famous 614th commandment, formulated in 1967, in which the Jewish people must believe so as not to give Hitler posthumous victories. Rubenstein and Roth, while noting the religious and existential problems of the commandment, refer to it as "a cry of the heart transmuted into the language of the sacred."[74] Like Pascal's wager, it has an emotive energy that begins to fizzle when examined more closely. Despite its flaws, however, it remains rhetorically potent and effective.

The first criterion of the commandment is that "Jews are bidden to survive, even if unable to believe in a 'higher' purpose." Reflecting on these points some thirty years later, Fackenheim acknowledges the criticism that so-called mere survival may not seem enough to constitute Judaism, but asserts: "*In a world that often seems on the verge of despair, is not this Jewish testimony, more perhaps than any mitzvah that Jews are bidden to perform, what makes them a light unto the nations?*"[75] Jews testify within their tradition to their God intervening to save God's people, and yet they now live in the site of "the most radical attack ever on the divine image in humanity. [At the least,] Jews are called to rebuild the belief that humanity—every member of it—is created in the Divine image."[76] Legitimate issues remain about the lack of dynamism and growth in such an anemic faith, but through acts of healing and mending, one may very likely encounter the presence of God through restoring the brokenness of our world.

There has been much debate about the naming of the "614th Commandment" if no one actually heard God's voice. As Steven Katz also reminds us, "the God of Biblical faith is *both* a commanding and

72. Quoted in ibid., 17.

73. Katz, *Post-Holocaust Jewish Dialogues*, 151.

74. Rubenstein and Roth, *Approaches to Auschwitz*, 350.

75. Fackenheim, "614th Commandment Reconsidered," 193–94.

76. Ibid., 194.

a saving God . . . Fackenheim has made much of the commanding presence of Auschwitz, but where is the saving God of the Exodus?"[77]

Painfully aware of these two facets, Fackenheim has accentuated the role of Israel as part of that saving presence of God: "I confess that all this would be for me humanly impossible were it not for the reality that is Israel—the state, the land, the language, the people."[78] Rubenstein and Roth understand why Fackenheim would give such moral significance to Israel, but opine that he "may have overloaded" Israel's significance.[79] Braiterman believes that Fackenheim "has failed to describe the State of Israel and Jewish identity with the same measured ambiguity, the same rhetoric of rupture and fragmentation, with which he meets God and Torah."[80] They also note how God becomes a nominal figure in Fackenheim's later discussion of evil and suffering.[81]

Fackenheim, however, asserts that the 614th commandment was often misunderstood, or even distorted.[82] Looking at the tragedies of 70 CE and 1492 CE, he acknowledges how sufficient time had to elapse before the full truth of those events could be faced. Believing the Holocaust "is a far more devastating catastrophe than these other two," he acknowledges that waiting is not a possibility. In the second preface to *To Mend the World*, he quotes Rabbi Tarfon: "It is not incumbent upon you to complete the work. But you are not free to avoid it."[83] Just as Katz praises Fackenheim for his "ability to incorporate radical negativity into overarching religious commitments," so too are his reflections, particularly on the 614th commandment, a valuable means to approach some of the key problems raised in response to the Holocaust. They are not, of course, the final word, nor are they meant to be. Despite its flaws, Fackenheim "remains with the 614th

---

77. Katz, "Issue of Confirmation," 23. See also Sacks, *Future Tense*, 59; Raphael, *Female Face of God*, 30–31.

78. Fackenheim, *Mend the World*, ix.

79. Rubenstein and Roth, *Approaches to Auschwitz*, 351. Fackenheim does write: "On their part, others may wish to raise 'Israel' to the same preworldly, post-worldly universality the Jewish tradition already ascribes to 'God' and 'Torah.' But heir to the *kedoshim*, to the 'holy ones,' the flesh-and-blood Israel cannot rise, or wish to rise, above a heritage that is itself holy" (*Mend the World*, 330).

80. Braiterman, *(God) After Auschwitz*, 160.

81. Ibid., 156.

82. Fackenheim, *Mend the World*, xix.

83. Ibid., 30.

commandment" some thirty years later, as it is still an important impetus for dialogue and analysis.[84] Our next thinker, like Fackenheim, also knows the problem of the Holocaust cannot be avoided, but the faith he espouses, though "broken" in some ways, still aims to be more dynamic and living.

Irving Greenberg: Seeking "Credible" Theological Statements

Orthodox Rabbi Irving Greenberg, whose approach closely resembles the focus on praxis among liberation theologians, argues that especially after Auschwitz, one must perform "acts of love and life giving" that reaffirm "meaningfulness, worth, and life."[85] As Katz writes: "Greenberg's reconstruction of Jewish theology after the Holocaust . . . presents a fascinating, creative reaction to the unprecedented evil manifest in the death camps."[86]

I have already noted how Greenberg's working principle[87] is often invoked and alluded to in many texts dealing with the Holocaust.[88] In chapter 5, I also clarified McCord Adams's critique of it.[89] While Katz has correctly pointed out some of the problems of the creed—particularly with the word "credible," as what is credible is so subjective[90]—it still retains rhetorical and moral force, though further clarifications are needed by looking at the principle in its original context and at some of Greenberg's subsequent works.

In his essay "Cloud of Smoke, Pillar of Fire: Judaism, Christianity and Modernity after the Holocaust," Greenberg seems to focus on the moment of suffering when he refers to this principle, although, as noted, I interpret it as a reminder that all theological (or any type of) statements are made in the presence of victims of horrendous slaughter and suffering, no matter where a particular theologian (or individual) is actually situated. It is also stressing that to say anything is secondary; first, one must reach into the pit and pull the children out.

---

84. Ibid., xx.
85. Greenberg, "Cloud of Smoke," 514.
86. Katz, "Introduction [to Part 3]," 363.
87. Greenberg, "Cloud of Smoke," 506.
88. See ch. 1.
89. See ch. 5.
90. Katz, "Issue of Confirmation," 51–52.

Though the burning babies are the intended "audience" in the "working principle," the example Greenberg uses after introducing it in the text is that of Sarah, a young girl Wiesel describes in *Night*. According to Wiesel, Sarah is forced into prostitution to save herself during the Holocaust and later offers herself for free to a young, Jewish survivor of the camps. Here, traditional moral concepts and normative religious claims conflict with (or are in a dialectic relationship with) these "new revelatory events."[91] In other words, what once was outright wrong is not clearly so in this context. Amidst a world that formed and sought completely to adulterate her, Sarah survives and "retains enough feeling to offer herself to a shy, survivor boy."[92] The old language deems it "adultery" and "sin," and yet such an act from such a person in such a world also reveals goodness and healing and reaching out to the Other.[93] It may also highlight the girl's further exploitation, though now in times of peace.[94]

To recognize the development of this "working principle," recall that for Greenberg, after Auschwitz we can only speak of "moment faiths," instances when a vision of redemption is present, interspersed with the "flames and the smoke of burning children." He remarks that "you *can't* talk about God. You can only recreate the image of God."[95] Thus, meaningful actions are still possible, and in many ways are extended to a wide variety of mundane and heroic acts: whatever aims to reflect the goodness and love of God. Here Greenberg's focus shares many similarities with Sobrino's primordial holiness, acts that respond to God's calling to give and foster life.

Also note that the emphasis on human responsibility does not mean that God is absent; and yet, understandable doubts and questions persist, as God's role in our daily lives seems drastically devalued. This precarious position between faith and doubt and hope and despair may be the best lens through which to form any theodicy, though such a dialectic produces a faith that is no longer whole. "After Auschwitz," Greenberg writes, "there is no faith so whole as a faith

---

91. Greenberg, "Cloud of Smoke," 506.

92. Ibid., 506.

93. See a similar comment in Gebara, *Out of the Depths*, 41–42.

94. See Lederach and Lederach, "When Mothers Speak," 155–59.

95. Greenberg, *For the Sake of Heaven and Earth*, 52.

shattered—and re-fused—in the ovens."[96] The imagery and rhetoric with Greenberg is always striking but he is expressing how faith can still be possible amidst such horrific instances of suffering, though it is unclear to me how faith can still be viable after being "placed" in the ovens. Of this hellish process, Filip Müller writes: "Once the pits had been emptied and the ash taken to the ash depot, they were piled up in man-high heaps. However, in these heaps there were many limbs and other parts of bodies not completely burnt."[97] These body parts were "fished out" and then burnt in a separate fire. Müller continues: "The rest of the ashes were then pulverized on the concrete slab . . . by first being pounded and then passed through different-meshed sieves." He then adds that in the early stages of this system, pits had to be dug for the ashes though they were later removed in trucks. Nothing remains of the original human person. Applying his metaphor, what is left of one's faith? One could refer to the smoke which rose from the crematoria, but how far does one want to extend the jarring conceit?

Ultimately, Greenberg's focus is a pragmatic response to evil, though he adds, "moral necessity requires the search for religious experience rather than surrender to the immediate logic of nonbelief."[98] This search culminates in acts of *chesed*, "loving kindness that seeks to create an object of its love, that sees that life and love can overcome the present reality."[99] He claims "human testimony" is the one "fundamental testimony that can still be given"[100] which is linked to an act that "recreate[s] the image of God." There remains, however, a tension or paradox that needs further clarification.

At various points Greenberg contends that "words are useless," or in one of his often-quoted passages: "to talk of love and of a God who cares in the presence of burning children is obscene and incredible; to leap in and pull a child out of the pit . . . is to make . . . the only statement that counts."[101] I examined the core of this issue with McCord Adams's argument that contra Greenberg, there are some statements that victims may need to hear after their ordeals that would not be

96. Greenberg, "Cloud of Smoke," 507.

97. Müller, *Eyewitness Auschwitz*, 139.

98. Greenberg, "Cloud of Smoke," 511.

99. Ibid., 515.

100. Ibid., 514.

101. Ibid.

permissible in the presence of the burning children.[102] Is Greenberg saying that all words at all times are useless, or only in the presence of burning children? Again, I see this principle as one that theodicists need to face, though bearing in mind the specific audience and context they are working within. Babies cannot understand a theodicy, but a theodicist may need to speak for the most vulnerable, the voiceless who are unable to speak for themselves. Babies burnt to death are a classic case of this reality. Theodicists must also be aware of the Sarahs of our world, whose moral framework and conceptions are formed in utter opposition to a "traditional" theodicist. I have also pointed out that theodic discussion has also occurred in the midst of atrocities.[103] In Greenberg's defense, he calls his formulation a "working principle," which implies that it must be adjusted depending on circumstance. It is not applicable to all victims in all situations. As I have noted in chapter 5, some victims look back on their horrific experiences and are grateful for their religious conversions. They bless their horrors with words.

When Greenberg refers to "religious experience," words will be needed to clarify what is good or religious and why certain actions need to be performed or condemned. Bereft of a context or meaning, any action becomes difficult to differentiate and evaluate. Such a process is what enables Greenberg to cite the prostitute Sarah's actions as one of "suffering sainthood."[104] Not all words are obscene in the presence of "burning babies." Also recall that Greenberg has continued to write essays and books after stating this "working principle," particularly highlighting the increasing responsibility of humanity[105] within an evolving covenant with God.[106] Greenberg thus finds a way to maintain continuity with the core beliefs of the Jewish faith tradition while forging a dynamic, organic theology that strives to address our contemporary situation.[107] His working principle is only one small facet of his reflections on suffering and evil.

---

102. McCord Adams, *Horrendous*, 88.

103. Fasching, *Narrative Theology*, 57.

104. Greenberg, "Cloud of Smoke," 506.

105. Greenberg, *For the Sake of Heaven and Earth*, 159.

106. Ibid., 159.

107. For a contrasting interpretation, see Katz, "Introduction [to Part 3]," 361.

To repeat: theodicies are fashioned through reflection, prayer, and praxis. Babies are not yet capable of this, though their suffering must be carefully considered when formulating theodic statements. And burning babies are being murdered. If one chooses to talk while one could save a human being, then talking is "obscene and incredible." But our cognizance of such atrocities should test, clarify, and purify our theodic concepts and language. Where appropriate, the goal is to listen to victims and not wound them with inappropriate words or silences. This is a necessary reminder, but words can also mend. They can provide hope, solace, and healing. A theodicy, at its best, has these intentions. If silence is all that is ever heard, then the goodness that is practiced and witnessed—even in acts like Sarah's, which can be morally impenetrable for some—remains smothered, and distinctions of what is moral and immoral or which act restores or sullies the image of God are lost. Lastly, not all theodic responses are morally equivalent. Some responses, like the tradition of *privatio boni*, with clarifications, can still be held, while the mantra "For our sins we are punished" generally cannot. Silence in this context negates everything with equal uselessness or obscenity. To maintain some sense of one's religious continuity and tradition, all of these theodic responses cannot simply be discarded without major ramifications.

Our next theologian, unlike Greenberg but similar to Rubenstein, seems to break with that tradition of continuity, although his overall aim is to leave open the possibility for a relationship with God despite the pervasive loss and destruction of the Holocaust.

David Blumenthal's Abusive God

David Blumenthal in many ways takes the main points found in Laytner and Braiterman and carries them as far as his mind and faith permit. He is an "agonistic misotheist," according to Schweizer.[108] I turn to Blumenthal because his thoughts are provocative, and because I am using them to support my argument that one cannot be a theodic-agnostic (but must weigh in and decide on this issue for a viable faith).

In *Facing the Abusing God: A Theology of Protest*, Blumenthal investigates victims of child abuse and victims of the Holocaust, and he draws "from the book of Job and Elie Wiesel to suggest that a theology

---

108. Schweizer, *Hating God*, 169–70. Blumenthal still urges belief in God, unlike an "absolute misotheist" (223–24).

of protest and suspicion, coupled with the religious affections of distrust and challenge, is the proper post-holocaust, abuse-sensitive theological stance."[109] Blumenthal sees God as an abusive parent who can still be loved only after the victim accepts his justifiable anger, hurt, and disappointment with God. No longer can believers blindly accept God's actions and decrees. No longer is God beyond our doubt and questioning. Death of God theology takes up these stances to suggest, as Richard Rubenstein writes, that such positions "face more openly than any other contemporary theological movement the truth of the divine-human encounter in our times."[110]

In seeking a Jewish response to the Holocaust, Blumenthal notes that "the idea that God is an abuser is new in terminology but it is an old idea."[111] He asks:

> If one is religious, if "God" means something to you, who is to blame? If one has lived a life in which God's presence has been felt, if religious ritual has been an important part of your spiritual life, who is to blame? . . . Most religious folk, and most religious thinkers . . . do not want to ask this question . . . They do not want to contemplate, not even to think about, how God might be responsible for the shoah.[112]

He calls for praxis and not theology and mentions how atheists and heretics grapple with this same question but still strive to make the world better. He argues that we must take a clear stance "if God is integral to who [we] are."[113] This stance is rooted in the Bible, as he turns to stories like Abraham protesting God's intended destruction of Sodom and Gomorrah. Blumenthal continues: "In the end, Abraham loses the argument, but his reaction is the correct one: not to deny God, not to deny God's power or right to act, but to protest God's *judgment*."[114]

Blumenthal's strong biblical foundation and direct approach are rhetorically effective. In a similarly provocative vein, Simone Weil has written: "If God had not been humiliated, in the person of Christ, he

---

109. Blumenthal, "Despair and Hope," 177.

110. Rubenstein, *After Auschwitz*, 250.

111. Blumenthal, "Auschwitz and Hiroshima," 252.

112. Blumenthal, "Despair and Hope," 177.

113. Ibid., 178.

114. Blumenthal, "Cross-Disciplinary Notes," 165.

would be inferior to us."[115] From a religiously orthodox standpoint, both Weil's comment and Blumenthal's position should be rebuked. And yet, in the context of mass atrocity—and according to Christians like McCord Adams, John Paul II, Sobrino, and Gutiérrez—Christ is said to be the key and answer to the problem of evil. On the one hand, a Christian, ultimately, needs to examine theodicy from a Trinitarian standpoint, accentuating the relationship of the three persons of the Trinity and the relational (and outpouring) love that is antithetical to the reality of evil.[116] And yet, there is something rhetorically and theologically comforting in the notion that God, as incarnate in Jesus of Nazareth, had to endure—and succumbed to (at least initially)— violence and injustice in this world. It can be reassuring to examine the life of Christ in the gospels (which reflects, in so many ways, the calling for mercy and justice in the Tanak), and so be in a position to claim that God has incontrovertibly intervened, has chosen, has entered intimately into solidarity with the marginalized, the poor, and the voiceless. And yet, Weil's comment overstates her case.

Blumenthal makes a similar but no less faith-filled error. While Blumenthal's advocating of protest has been recommended throughout this work, his contention that it is the only viable response is debatable, and from a faith standpoint, problematic. One protests because of faith and hope, as Berkovits has argued. Protest is senseless wailing if God is abusive because the hope is so contingent upon God's state when the protest or prayer is uttered. Such a God may help or may make matters worse. Protest seems fruitless with such a view of God because at some point the logical issue is to refrain from protesting since it serves no purpose, and so all connection with this fickle, abusive God fizzles altogether. It is understandable to fear that redemption and healing are not possible or are false projections of our desires; and if so, then perhaps one can claim God is abusive. But

---

115. Weil, *Simone Weil Reader*, 436. See also Levinas, *In the Time of Nations*, 145–50.

116. Roger Haight writes: "[A]n account of Christian salvation is unaccountable without trinitarian language. For Christian salvation is a narrative of God's saving action in history, and the story cannot be told without reference to God creator, Jesus Christ savior, and God as Spirit at work in the church and in the world" (*Future of Christology*, 53). For Michael Kogan's critique of an exclusivist Trinitarian conception in the document "A Theological Understanding of the Relationship Between Christians and Jews," promulgated by the Presbyterian Church (USA), see *Opening the Covenant*, 216–18.

without knowing what will happen beyond this world, no final verdict is possible.

Blumenthal laments that more people do not join him in his stand, though he feels it is the only one he can make to face God and do his duty.[117] He notes that anger causes theological despair in response to fundamentalist orthodox positions that blame the Shoah on our sins. Many hear this and have little response except to say that there is no more covenant.[118] Echoing Rubenstein, he believes Jewish assimilation is a result of this theological despair, for how could a Jewish person still maintain belief in the God of the covenant and the Bible?[119] And he too feels this state of theological despair—"a doubting of the One Who lends meaning to that history." One could say that this sign of doubt is more radical than his stand to accuse God of being abusive because an abusive God may be good and loving, whereas an utterly absent one cannot. In the end he believes that the only answer is theological protest as a "first step." His faith position is a tenuous one, but persistence is his focus: "I am not sure I hope, but I persist in the face of despair."[120] As noted with the law-court pattern of prayer, after accusation, one ends with a petition of trust and hope. Blumenthal is still awaiting an answer, though he perseveres. But what if, as McCord Adams and others argue, God is under no obligation to redeem evil and injustice? Would God be abusive if there were no afterlife for healing and redemption? I will address this issue in chapter 11, but Blumenthal's radical statement—like Weil's—cannot be dismissed too easily.

Moreover, from the perspective of Nomberg-Przytyk or Partnoy, Blumenthal's position may be the most honest and revealing. For a traditional believer, however, the idea that God could be both loving and abusive would seem too remote from traditional religious conceptions. For Christians, it would seem infinitesimally removed from the God whom Jesus calls "Abba." But again, Blumenthal's questions, while being radical, are challenging and, paradoxically, faithful. It would seem easier for Blumenthal to reach this point and renounce God. But he perseveres.

---

117. Blumenthal, "Auschwitz and Hiroshima," 178.

118. Ibid., 180.

119. Ibid., 181.

120. Ibid., 183.

A similar perseverance is embodied by my next Jewish thinker, whom many see as an inspiration and guide for how to maintain faith in God despite horrific atrocity.

Elie Wiesel: Unending Sea[121]

Anson Latyner writes that "Wiesel's experience of theodicy during the Holocaust is exactly the problem that perplexes so many post-Holocaust Jews still . . . For Wiesel, the centuries of suffering, culminating in the Holocaust, present an overwhelming obstacle of faith in the traditional sense . . . the smoke of Auschwitz has obscured the view of Sinai. [While] Sinai remains, so too does the cloud that envelops it."[122] This conflict is brimming throughout Wiesel's works of nonfiction and fiction, a few of which I will touch upon here.[123]

In Wiesel's *Night*, we have a poignant display of rebellion by a believer who loves God passionately, and for whom to love God is to live. When Moishe the Beadle questions why the young Wiesel cries when he prays, he can only think: "Why did I pray? Strange question. Why did I live? Why did I breathe?"[124] He learns early on from Moishe a valuable lesson: "Man comes closer to God through the questions he asks Him . . . therein lies true dialogue. Man asks and God replies. But we don't understand His replies. We cannot understand them. Because they dwell in the depths of our souls and remain there until we die. The real answers, Eliezer, you will find only within yourself."[125]

While the language is mystical and raises more questions than answers, it may also cut to the heart of a theodicy. Nevertheless, these thoughts plague Wiesel during the Holocaust and beyond. Throughout

---

121. I had the pleasure of taking a course of Elie Wiesel's at Boston University while I was a graduate theology student at Boston College. I sat for those two hours every week writing down almost everything he said. I was amazed that this kind, soft-spoken man was one and the same with the figure who had seen—actually seen and heard and smelled—the children of Auschwitz burning, and yet, as he writes, somehow remained sane, let alone a theist. I could not begin to reflect that what I read with horror, he lived amidst horror. My experience with Wiesel will inevitably sway and prejudice everything I have to say—and not say—about theodicy.

122. Laytner, *Arguing with God*, 216.

123. For Schweizer's argument that Elie Wiesel upholds many tendencies of an agnostic misotheist, especially in his early fiction, see *Hating God*, 149–71.

124. Wiesel, *Night*, 5.

125. Ibid., 5.

Night, the endless question of the whereabouts of God echoes within Eliezer and the thoughts and hearts of the other prisoners. "It's over," Akiba Drumer tells Wiesel. "God is no longer with us." Then regretting his words, Akiba tries to mention humanity's insignificance, but he remains angry: "Where's God? How can I believe, how can anyone believe in this God of Mercy?"[126]

After a prisoner is hung, Wiesel again hears the question, like a refrain: "For God's sake, where is God?" He writes: "And from within me, I heard a voice answer: 'Where is He? This is where—hanging here from this gallows . . .' That night the soup tasted of corpses."[127] Sadly, the same "taste" seems to dominate most theodic attempts, as the sheer magnitude of murder and torture seems to overwhelm all one's senses and faith. Amidst all the putrefaction and decay of humanity, how could Wiesel not begin to feel that God was curling through the chimney as well? He asks: "'What are You, my God?' I thought angrily. 'How do You compare to this stricken mass gathered to affirm to You their faith, their anger, their defiance? What does Your grandeur mean, Master of the Universe, in the face of all this cowardice, this decay, and this misery? Why do you go on troubling these poor people's wounded minds, their ailing bodies?'"[128]

The faith of the stricken mass, still striving to care about God, seems more honorable than God. Here, poignantly, it is not just the thought of God's demise that torments people, but the constantly reoccurring voice of doubt and hope in God, as if the human mind is never completely willing to extricate God for once and forever. Yet, as Wiesel comments, the torment is too cruel. During a service in which the liturgical verses praise God, Wiesel cannot help protesting and questioning: "Why, but why should I bless him? Every fiber in me rebelled. Because He caused thousands of children to burn in His mass graves? Because He kept six crematoria working day and night, including Sabbath and the Holy Days? Because in His great might, He had created Auschwitz, Birkenau, Buna . . . ?"[129]

This rebellion had a price for Wiesel. "I was the accuser, God the accused. My eyes had opened and I was alone, terribly alone in

126. Ibid., 76–77.
127. Ibid., 65.
128. Ibid., 66.
129. Ibid., 67.

a world without God, without man. Without love or mercy."[130] This "great void"[131] seemed to be finalized in Wiesel's last explicit comment about God in *Night*: "And in spite of myself, a prayer formed inside me, a prayer to this God in whom I no longer believed."[132]

While God is absent from the rest of the text, the death of his father also seems to imply the death of God. In the "Preface to the New Translation," Wiesel includes the harrowing scene of how his dying father was calling out his name, pleading for Wiesel to hear his last words, while the SS guards were pummelling his father to death: "Instead of sacrificing my miserable life and rushing to his side, taking his hand, reassuring him, showing him that he was not abandoned, that I was near him, that I felt his sorrow, instead of all that, I remained flat on my back, asking God to make my father stop calling my name, to make him stop crying. So afraid was I to incur the SS wrath."[133]

Wiesel still blames himself for not comforting his father during his last moments: "His last word had been my name. A summons. And I had not responded."[134] And yet, one can say, all his life has since been one long response to his father's call.

Throughout his life, Wiesel has been a preeminent example of an individual who still believes in God after Auschwitz. In *All Rivers Run to the Sea*, Wiesel testifies that "if Nietzsche could cry out to the old man in the forest that God is dead, the Jew in me cannot."[135] It is a stubborn faith that clings to him in spite of himself, a shadow that is a part of him and cannot be sundered. Still, his faith—his struggle with God—has never ceased. He states that he will never understand God's role amidst Auschwitz[136] and questions whether contemplating God's sadness "helps us bear our grief, or simply augments the weight."[137] He adds: "Perhaps God shed more tears in the time of Treblinka,

130. Ibid., 68.
131. Ibid., 69.
132. Ibid., 91.
133. Ibid., xi.
134. Ibid., xii.
135. Wiesel, *All Rivers Run to the Sea*, 84.
136. Ibid., 105.
137. Ibid., 104.

Majdanek, and Auschwitz, and one may therefore invoke His name not only with indignation but also with sadness and compassion."[138]

According to Laytner, "Wiesel's God remains a caring God. Yet Wiesel's vision—his re-creation and revival of the anthropopathetic God—is tempered by the reality of the Holocaust."[139] Like Berkovits, Wiesel finds himself straddling two different and often contradictory realms. While McCord Adams believes that God will be able to convince every individual of God's overall goodness and the value of each person's life, Wiesel notes: "Perhaps some day someone will explain how, on the level of man, Auschwitz was possible, but on the level of God, it will forever remain the most disturbing of mysteries."[140] Here, it seems, no matter how creative or imaginative God's answer, it will not be sufficient.

While Wiesel still shows remarkable compassion for a God who loves us so much although we commit so much evil, Berish, one of the characters in Elie Wiesel's play *The Trial of God*, remarks: "If I am given the choice of feeling sorry for Him or for human beings, I choose the latter anytime. He is big enough, strong enough to take care of Himself; man is not."[141] As Laytner adds, "Over and over again, Wiesel advocates faithful defiance as the post-Holocaust expression of a Jew's relationship with God."[142]

We can see this tendency in his often retold conversation with Rebbe Menaham Mendel Schneersohn: "'Rebbe,' [Wiesel] asked, 'how can you believe in God after Auschwitz?' He looked at [Wiesel] in silence for a long moment, his hands resting on the table. Then he replied in a soft, barely audible voice: 'How can you not believe in God after Auschwitz?'"[143] Ultimately, Wiesel's message resonates with hope and faith amidst the (necessary) accusations and rebellion, a tension he lives with and can find no other path to avoid. This struggle culminates in an extant but wounded faith. As Irving Greenberg adds: "If faith be wounded in the process, let it be recognized that, after the

---

138. Ibid., 85.
139. Laytner, *Arguing with God*, 217.
140. Wiesel, *Legends of Our Time*, 6.
141. Wiesel, *Trial of God*, 133.
142. Laytner, *Arguing with God*, 222.
143. Wiesel, *All Rivers Run to the Sea*, 405.

Holocaust, no faith is so whole as a broken faith."[144] Despite the fissures, the doubts, and the moments of recrimination, Wiesel similarly remarks:

> I would be within my rights to give it up. I could invoke six million reasons to justify my decision, but I don't. I am incapable of straying from the path chartered by my ancestors. Without this faith in God, the faith of my fathers and forefathers, my faith in Israel and in humanity would be diminished. And so I choose to preserve the faith of my childhood. I never gave up my faith in God even *over there.* I went on praying. Yes, my faith was wounded and still is today . . . but it is because I still believe in God that I argue with him.[145]

Fackenheim looks to Lewinska as counter-testimony while Sobrino looks to Romero and the lives of the poor. I often look to Wiesel. The point is that despite the gaps and the fissures that evil and suffering unleash, despite a faith that is wounded or fractured, one need not automatically cede to these horrific events the final word; nor can a believer in God allow such atrocities to monopolize all testimony that questions the goodness of others and of God's presence. But a choice must be made: theodic-agnosticism or positing the "end of theodicy" is not ultimately viable if one wants to speak of a relationship with God. Wiesel and others struggle—doubt is never too far removed from belief—but their stance is clear.

What should also be clear above, however, is that all the post-Shoah thinkers focused upon so far are male—an issue that cannot be overlooked—which is why I want to close this chapter by turning to Melissa Raphael's *The Female Face of God in Auschwitz* (2003).

Melissa Raphael: Jewish Women in the Camps—Embodying (and Restoring) Shekhinah

In Melissa Raphael's *The Female Face of God in Auschwitz*, she argues that post-Holocaust theology has been dominated and undermined by a patriarchal monopoly that mistakenly privileges the question of

---

144. Greenberg, "Foreword," 11.

145. Wiesel, *And the Sea Is Never Full*, 70. Schweizer cites passages like these to note that "Wiesel's religiosity, his blaspheming against God, and his doubts about divine treachery and malevolence gradually weakened as he grew older" (*Hating God*, 165).

where was God—and not who was God—in Auschwitz.[146] Arguing that Shekhinah—"the traditionally female image of the indwelling presence of God"[147]—has been forgotten, buried, and overlooked within the majority of (patriarchal) Jewish tradition, she contends that interpreters claiming that the evils of the Holocaust disprove an omnipotent God succeed only because that construction of God never really existed.[148] Such a God was "morally flawed from the outset."[149] Raphael also maintains that women's experiences of the divine, especially in traditional orthodox interpretations, were never suited to a kingly, omnipotent God expected to intervene and overcome evil forcefully. It is through daily acts of welcoming, kindness, and presence towards the other that the face of God is made manifest.[150] Raphael contends that in the camps, despite the degradation and mass death, the presence of God, as Shekhinah, was embodied through the acts of bodily cleaning and healing that women often exhibited towards one another and themselves.[151] Thus, the women testify to their own sacred, fragile, but still potent means of expression and presence of God.[152] Such a presence was often not seen (especially by men and male outside interpreters) because they were not looking for—or aware of the need to look for—Shekhinah who remained among her people.[153] She argues that "in Auschwitz, in discharging the covenantal obligation to be holy as God is holy, women took themselves and the world they represented up into the drama of divine being and becoming. The redemption of God among women in Auschwitz was to return and reconcile God to the world by the restoration (*tikkun*) of her divine image in women."[154]

Interestingly, *The Female Face of God in Auschwitz* does not include the word *theodicy* in its index, though Raphael's work is a finely crafted attempt at one. I am sympathetic to many of her arguments,

146. Raphael, *Female Face of God*, 28 and 54.
147. Ibid., 5. See also Hammer, "To Her We Shall Return," 22–34.
148. Raphael, *Female Face of God*, 52.
149. Ibid., 37.
150. Ibid., 41.
151. Ibid., 13 and 54.
152. Ibid., 81.
153. Ibid., 54.
154. Ibid., 133.

and especially her similarly demanding use of witness testimonies. Indeed, the work persuasively argues for recognizing the female face of God as Shekhinah in the acts of goodness and welcome among women in the camps.[155] The kenotic role ceded to Shekhinah, moreover, shares much in common with the portrayal of Christ in my work, especially as presented in solidarity with the poor and oppressed. Raphael understandably does not make such a connection, but, interestingly, she writes: "Because classical theology generally postulates an omnipotent God who subjects history to the mysterious purpose of his will, Holocaust theology to date does not (and perhaps *cannot* in the counter-evidential light of bottomless human suffering) take the love of God as its determining theme."[156] Christians are, at least, unburdened with this tragic dilemma.[157]

In addition to challenging many of the prominent views of the theologians above, Raphael also claims that afterlife redemption, free will, and theological protest are rooted in patriarchal misconceptions of God, and, thus, she also contests some of my main positions.[158] She writes, for example, "God is not a supernatural arsenal. Rather, it should be asked how we could and can protect God's presence as it is this which makes it possible to know God in the other and for God to know God-self in creation."[159] There is a cost, however: God seems to be rendered into a passive, dependent "presence." Problematically, Raphael insufficiently recognizes that to be a God of love entails more than creating or welcoming. God must be a healing, sustaining presence that balances a kenotic outpouring with a divine embrace of responsibility. If this resembles the role of a parent, it should; but unlike us, God (in order to be God) can mend and redeem beyond this world. In short, a God of creation bereft of such responsibility cannot be deemed a God of presence and love. Like the God of Phillips, who is powerless to redeem or restore, Raphael's God seems to care little or to have no interest in what happens when that creation mirrors dis-creation. Sadly, accompanying one's people in *galut* (exile) or even within the crematoria is insufficient—when speaking of God. Raphael

155. Ibid., 125.
156. Ibid., 121.
157. 1 John 4:8.
158. Raphael, *Female Face of God*, 28, 35, and 174n47.
159. Ibid., 156.

labels free will and afterlife justice as patriarchal, when responsibility for what one creates is the more life-giving imperative. Raphael's work is too important to ignore and should always be mentioned in the same standing as the more recognized voices in this chapter, but always with the aim to integrate the Shekhinah she advocates with many of the ("patriarchal") images of God that remain viable.

Assessment of Section 3

Because Jewish post-Shoah thought is written within a rich tradition of thousands of years amidst the specter of the Shoah, many of its authors inevitably present ideas and dogma both imposing and spiritually sensitive. Through Anson Laytner's work, we have seen how theological protest is not only possible within a faith tradition, but is essential for a religious tradition to confront the evils of this world and those within its own specific history.

Zachary Braiterman's text is useful for his argument on the similarities and shared conceptual space between postmodernity and post-Holocaust Jewish thought. For my context, the theodicist is confronted with historical caesuras, theoretical gaps and fissures, and a radical doubt in some circles that challenge any stable sense of truth, identity, morality, or the good. I also agree that antitheodic elements must be included in any theodic attempt. My calling for all theodicists to integrate comprehensively the testimonies of mass atrocity within their theological and theodic discourse is a means to prevent a theodicy from "defending the indefensible," as Braiterman and others fear.[1]

I concur with Eliezer Berkovits that a theodicist needs to be faithful both to those who maintained their beliefs while in the camps and those who could no longer believe. I also agree that one questions God because of one's faith in God. Theological protest would not be "theological" if there is no relationship with God.

Emil Fackenheim's 614th commandment is also applicable for my context because it provides an outlook or perspective to challenge the desire to renounce one's faith. It causes one to rethink one's position, which may encourage further reflection and, perhaps, a commitment to God, or the search for God. Here the consequences of one's

---

1. Braiterman, *(God) After Auschwitz*, 32.

choice to remain committed to one's faith is not isolated and unconnected to other human beings. Moreover, while I would not limit the possibility for *Tikkun* to this world, I agree with Fackenheim that there is counter-testimony to the aims of the Holocaust. Such a truth can provide hope to believe in God and God's presence in this world as human beings made in the image of God reflect (no matter how limited) the goodness and holiness of God.

Irving Greenberg's working principle has caused many theologians to stop and ponder, perplexed as to what can be said in the presence of the burning children and what, if anything, can be said after the occurrence of such suffering. I addressed my concerns with the principle in chapter 9, but I believe the principle is important because it demands a careful response to some fundamental questions on the purpose, audience, limits, and value of a theodicy.

I do not agree with David Blumenthal's conclusions, but (as with Rubenstein) his challenges cannot be cursorily dismissed. He is forcing believers to make a stand on the problem of theodicy and demanding reasons for that position to be given.[2] In this light, like theological protest, Blumenthal's stance should be taken to a point, but to cross the Rubicon which he does, is ill-advised for a theodicist—and so any believer's—stance.

Melissa Raphael's work points to the future and ongoing relevance of post-Holocaust Jewish studies, especially from gender-informed and feminist theologians. In a roundtable discussion of *The Female Face of God in Auschwitz*—which was the focus of a 2010 issue of *Holocaust Studies*—Raphael wrote that her book "should be read as a theology of visual revelation where survivor testimony to the endurance of women's relationships in Auschwitz is also situated within the theodrama of redemption history as narrated by traditional

---

2. As with the story of the Exodus read in the context of the Holocaust, here, too, theological memory has been tainted by historical and political awareness of atrocity. If such a biblical quote comforts some, its imagery may also lead others to remember tragic events, further muddying the sense of hope in divine justice. One may recall shackled African slaves who were injured or pregnant and so jumped, fell, or were thrown overboard amidst that murderous ocean journey; or the victims who were blindfolded and dropped alive into the sea amidst the horrors perpetrated in El Salvador, Argentina, and Guatemala. In *The Gospel in Solentiname*, Laureano comments: "I remember what happened in Chile . . . many people were taken up in airplanes and thrown out into the sea" (in Cardenal, *Gospel in Solentiname*, 40).

and modern Jewish accounts of God's appearance in history."[3] While additional Jewish feminist voices on the Holocaust are still needed, Raphael has provided an influential and groundbreaking work.

To close Part 2, we return, not surprisingly, to Elie Wiesel, who writes: "Sometimes we must accept the pain of faith so as not to lose it. And if that makes the tragedy of the believer more devastating than that of the nonbeliever, then so be it."[4] Such a faith is no doubt wounded, or broken, as Greenberg would argue. And such a faith maintains that no justification would ever fully satisfy why God could allow such senseless events to happen, but faith in God nevertheless remains essential for meaning in life. Recall the Shema: "Hear, O Israel! The Lord is our God, the Lord alone."[5] But then in the face of what seems divine negligence, what better way to express one's faith in a loving God of justice than through such a moral and spiritual response of questioning faith, even one that says we will continue to do Your will and follow Your laws even if You seem to be no longer watching and are deaf to our cries. As Levinas has written, "Loving the Torah even more than God means precisely having access to a personal God against Whom one may rebel—that is to say, for Whom one may die."[6] For perhaps, in the calling to confront and heal the other amidst that faithful rebelling and obdurate belief in God, one will eventually sense God's presence and encounter what one was determined to find all along. Perhaps it is only a matter of time. Perhaps, for those who have endured such travails, it, too, can be said: "God heard their moaning, and God remembered His covenant with Abraham and Isaac and Jacob. God looked upon the Israelites and God took notice of them."[7] I will examine such a possibility in the final part of this work.

3. Raphael, "Historiography to Theography," Abstract.

4. Wiesel, *All Rivers Run to the Sea*, 84.

5. Deut 6:4.

6. Levinas, *Difficult Freedom*, 145.

7. Exod 2:24.

PART 3
Seeking a Viable Theodicy despite Mass Atrocity

A lot of people got killed here. I myself killed some of the children ... We had eighty kids in the first year. There are twenty-five left. All the others, we killed them or they have run away.[1]

Christianity preaches a God who loves every individual: thus, the slain children and the Hutu murderers referred to in the epigraph above are all beloved of God. A Christian theodicist, therefore, must weigh the evidence of slaughter and brutality, and yet must not call for revenge but for justice that is fair to victim, perpetrator, and society. Theologically, how one interprets divine justice and how it is manifested within this world and in the world to come are crucial components for how and whether one can speak of the goodness of God and the beauty and value of creation.

To address the above issues, in Part 1 I analyzed testimonies of mass atrocity, focusing on how witnesses interpreted their experiences of unfathomable evil and suffering. I began with these testimonies because I argued that if theodicists are credibly to maintain that God and God's creation are good, they have to incorporate and work closely with the accounts of individuals mired in dehumanizing and destructive suffering.

---

1. Quoted from a Hutu teacher during the Rwandan genocide in Meredith, *Fate of Africa*, 515.

Part 2 turned to Christian philosophical theodicy, Catholic Latin American liberation theology, and Jewish post-Shoah thought to evaluate a theodicy's honesty towards reality, pastoral validity, and relevance in the face of mass atrocity and horrific suffering. Because the latter two fields focus on the voiceless and oppressed of Latin America and the six million murdered Jews of the Shoah, respectively, I expected some of their key thinkers to share an affinity with my aims and concerns, and indeed, much of their thought will resonate in the next two chapters.

In the third and final part of this work, I will examine the main issues posed by the testimonies from Part 1 to the theodicies in Part 2 and the responses and questions these theodic works could pose to those testimonies. This investigation or "dialogue" will be my focus in chapter 10. In the context of interreligious dialogue, John D'Arcy May has suggested that "the acknowledgement of failure, one's own and others', could be a fruitful medium of communication within the dialogue itself."[2] May's claim would also seem to be a reasonable starting point for the theodicist turning in dialogue to a witness of mass atrocity. As David Tracy adds, "For there is no genuine dialogue without the willingness to risk all one's present self-understanding in the presence of the other . . ."[3]

In chapter 11, I will return to the issue of justice and the afterlife by examining whether universal salvation aids or hinders a theodicist and how to address the role of memory, identity, and healing when reflecting upon victims of mass atrocity and the afterlife. Drawing upon the wide range of theological, philosophical, and literary texts examined over the course of this work, chapter 12 will identify and evaluate my five criteria for a Christian theodicy that seeks to develop a viable theodic stance despite—or perhaps, because of—mass atrocity and horrific suffering. In the epilogue, I will conclude by advocating the value of acknowledging a fractured faith buttressed upon a fractured theodicy.

2. May, *Transcendence and Violence*, 134. See also Tracy, *Dialogue with the Other*; O'Grady and Scherle, *Ecumenics from the Rim*, 197–341; O'Neill, *Mending a Torn World*; Cornille, *Im-possibility of Interreligious Dialogue*; my "Other as Oneself within Judaism," 113–24; and my "Interfaith Dialogue as Presence, Gift and Obligation," 6–9.

3. Tracy, *Dialogue with the Other*, 73.

10

Testimonies of Mass Atrocity and Theodicy: A Dialogue

During that twenty-year period . . . millions of Christian men professing the law of love of their fellows slew one another. What does it all mean? Why did it happen? What made those people burn those houses and slay their fellow men?[1]

The motivations for why we commit some acts and avoid others are complex and often conflicting, an issue that often muddles how justice should be enacted. Tolstoy's questions above underlie how precarious are the means to locate rational explanations for what we do. Ultimately, only God can judge an individual's motivations and intentions, which is why most theodicies must grapple with issues of soteriology and eschatology. As Christiaan Mostert writes, "Christian theodicy cannot be attempted without eschatology: not only in its reliance on an eschatological verification of its hopes but also in the substance of this hope. The world's evil and suffering cannot make theological sense in any other framework; neither can it be incontrovertibly demonstrated other than eschatologically."[2] Where there is no afterlife, or where healing and redemption make little sense in a heavenly context (as Phillips argues), the theodicy project fails. Denying the possibility for healing and compensation for children burned alive

1. Tolstoy, *War and Peace*, 1314.
2. Mostert, "Theodicy and Eschatology," 116.

along with the fair judgment of an unrepentant mass murderer who died peacefully from old age, makes the worship of God a tenuous and, I would argue, dumbfounding position. Put simply: to acknowledge a God who creates the universe but who does not have the means or desire to right wrongs in this world makes far less sense than not believing in God. As argued throughout this work, in order for one's theistic belief to be reasonable, one must develop a theodic position and response to mass atrocity and horrific suffering. As a productive means to work this out, this chapter aims to present and explore a "dialogue" between the testimonies of witnesses to mass atrocity from Part 1 and the theodic responses analyzed in Part 2.

In the course of doing so, I want to evaluate and answer the following questions:

1. What challenges have testimonies of mass atrocity raised for theodicies, and what, if any, answers or further challenges have these theodicies offered to these testimonies?

2. How should a theodicist envision God's encounter with a victim of mass atrocity? How does one articulate a continuity of identity while speaking of traumatic memories and heavenly bliss?

3. Does belief in universal salvation strengthen or undermine a theodicy?

4. Echoing Pilate's retort, "Truth, what is truth?" many of us admit that we live in an age in which seemingly everything is questioned and doubted (language, history, identity, religious texts and traditions, and so on). If so, how does recognizing discontinuities, absence, limitations, and fragments lead to a more authentic theodicy?

THE CHALLENGES TESTIMONIES OF MASS ATROCITY POSE TO THEODICISTS[3]

On the Magnitude of Evil and Suffering[4]

In *Christianity, Tragedy, and Holocaust Literature*, Michael Steele asks: "[D]oes individual suffering take on different values when portrayed and experienced in the context of tragedy as opposed to the context of atrocity and concentration camps?"[5] While Steele wants to examine why we need to revise literary theories of tragedy in light of the Holocaust, I have examined the experiences of victims of mass atrocity because these types of testimonies pose more severe challenges to a theodicist than other types of evil or suffering. Where some examples of affliction may be (grudgingly) deemed justifiable, or rather, still enable the possibility for a satisfactory theodicy,[6] mass atrocities and horrific suffering limit what theodicists can say. As repeated by a Phillips or a Braiterman, certain evils should prevent a theodicist from trying to "defend the indefensible."[7]

As my analysis in chapter 2 illustrates, some witness testimonies reveal examples of individual losses so concretely and brutally that even without the full knowledge of the genocidal forces that are at work beyond Nomberg-Przytyk's bunker or Gyatso's prison, the case of horrific evil and suffering have enough "evidence" and testimony on their own to counteract traditional claims of theodicy. What type of world produces doctors who order a mother and her newborn's death immediately after the birth, or trains guards to torture a Tibetan monk? When one tries to contemplate the extent of the evil or the number of people murdered in the greater historical context of those individual crimes, the reality is beyond human imagining. The scale and scope of the loss seems to render circumspect the language of

---

3. An earlier version of this section can be found in my "Testimonies of Mass Atrocity and the Search for a Viable Theodicy," 88–99.

4. For an etymological discussion of suffering-evil, doing-evil, and sin, see Paulson, *Sin and Evil*, 1–33. See also Pocock, "Unruly Evil," 42–56.

5. Steele, *Christianity, Tragedy, and Holocaust Literature*, 106.

6. See my discussion of magnitude in ch. 1. Magnitude can be a fairly subjective term, but common illnesses or allergies, the pain of a broken wrist, or more importantly, the fact of death for all of us (take the ideal example of a person living a long, fulfilled life before dying in her nineties), will no doubt cause some pain and suffering, but would not, in my estimation, challenge the meaning and value of this world.

7. Phillips, *Problem of Evil*, xi; Braiterman, *(God) After Auschwitz*, 32.

"good" creation, God's presence in the world, or the possibility for God to redeem or heal these evils. When a large part of our world seems mired in nihilism and savagery, arguing for inherent or pervasive goodness seems a hopeless task.

Questioning why God did not stop atrocities like Auschwitz is to say that God should not have allowed the little people to be cruelly experimented on and then sent to the gas chambers; and for Graciela, five months pregnant, not to be "tortured with electric shocks" and later removed from the Little School and never heard from again.[8] Thus within the issue of scale are the individual lives that, as Ivan Karamazov argues, are reasons enough to question the existence of a loving God. But with knowledge of the number of lives senselessly murdered and the civic and religious institutions that benefited or were silent about such atrocities, not to mention the larger world's inaction, it is difficult not to admit that such evils point to a world gone awry, a world made difficult to justify when so many of its inhabitants have been cruelly tortured, murdered, and abandoned by their fellow human beings. In such a world, God's presence seems obscured by the screams of victims, the machinations of perpetrators, and the silence of bystanders. Moreover, in turning to history for evidence or testimony of God's presence despite these obstacles, one is hard-pressed to find a lucid, overarching metanarrative that proves a meaningful *telos* or a God that remains firmly in control despite these atrocities, as the next challenge argues.

Historical Caesuras and the Presence of God

To locate (or speculate upon) God's active presence in the world, a theodicist may turn to history to try to identify the holy and spiritual within both the common and the dramatic events of our lives. Testimonies that witness these ruptures within history, however, challenge and undermine the issue of God's presence within our world or the belief in Christ's solidarity with victims of oppression. When a fellow Jewish prisoner of the *Sonderkommando* began to pray, Filip Müller, for example, writes: "To me it seemed sheer madness to pray in Auschwitz, and absurd to believe in God in this place." While Müller and the others participated in these prayers, he writes that it was "probably because we had nothing else left or because we felt strengthened by

---

8. Partnoy, *Little School*, 123–24.

his faith."[9] He does not speak of God's presence, though. While acts of ordinary goodness are depicted in some witness testimony, as seen in chapter 2 when Partnoy distracted the guard who was torturing Benja or when Gyatso prayed for the condemned woman,[10] the dominant message gleaned from the majority of witness testimonies is bleak and senseless. Children "displayed a frightening and incorrigibly vengeful cruelty, without restraint or responsibility";[11] prisoners were forced to pummel and torture one another;[12] and neighbor viciously attacked neighbor.[13] While perpetrators of mass atrocity often acknowledge, as one Hutu did, that "through killing well, eating well, looting well, we felt so puffed up and important, we didn't even care about the presence of God,"[14] other accounts speak of perpetrators invoking God amidst the slaying and mutilation. Another Hutu, for example, describes how Hutus and Tutsis participated together in choir rehearsal at church on the Saturday before the genocide began, and after Sunday mass (which only Hutus attended because Tutsis were hiding by then), the Hutus "left the Lord and our prayers inside to rush home. We changed from our Sunday best into our workday clothes, we grabbed clubs and machetes, we went straight off to killing."[15] Of some Nazis, Emil Fackenheim writes: "As early as 1936, Julius Streicher [whose crimes included publishing three anti-Semitic books for children for the Nazi regime] was quoted in print as follows: he 'who fights the Jew fights the devil! Who masters the devil conquers heaven!' Streicher no more than echoed the Führer himself who earlier still had written: 'In defending myself against the Jew, I fight for the work of God.'"[16]

While most theists would resolutely refute Streicher's and Hitler's words, the historical record becomes a difficult account or drama to posit conclusively God's role and presence.[17] These atrocities,

---

9. Muller, *Eyewitness Auschwitz*, 29.

10. For an examination of the "banality of goodness" and the question of ethical choice in the camps, see Pollefeyt, "Victims of Evil or Evil of Victims," 67–82.

11. Lev Razgon, quoted in Applebaum, *Gulag*, 332.

12. Gyatso, *Fire*, 132.

13. Neuffer, *Key to My Neighbor's House*, 185.

14. Léopold, interviewed by Hatzfeld, *Machete Season*, 147.

15. Adalbert, interviewed by Hatzfeld, *Machete Season*, 140.

16. Fackenheim, *Mend the World*, 188.

17. In his essay "Sacraments in General," Regis Duffy writes: "A sacrament, then, is a presence-filled event in which God gratuitously enables us to welcome the mes-

perpetrated by humans upon humans, were also, eventually, halted or momentarily controlled by humans; perhaps by a treaty, but almost always accompanied by a tank and army. If God's presence was amidst that conquering, it was often difficult to gauge, at least historically. The Soviets liberated some Nazi concentration camps, but the gulags continued to imprison millions of human beings at an alarming rate; reprisal killings and rapes meant liberating Soviet forces raped or abducted German women,[18] and some moderate or innocent Hutus were slain by the finally "liberated" Tutsis of Rwanda, whose government-backed army later (post-1998) looted the Eastern Congo and treated it as a "fiefdom" until a series of "tortuous negotiations" established the interim government led by Joseph Kabila in 2002.[19] We often are left with fractured justice, fractured innocence, and fractured language where "liberation" can mean slavery for so many. Seeking direction and identity by turning to one's history, we are instead often left with contradiction and concealment, a distortion that plays havoc with one's memory and sense of self. Testimonies that account for these evils and contradictions again challenge a theological belief of God involved within and beyond history, especially when an outsider is confronted by internal witnesses who experienced these evils and can testify to their horrors, and often, the failure of any theodicy to make sense of their predicament or to speak credibly of God's presence in the midst of their affliction. Seeking evidence for a theodic position is further complicated by the inevitable role that subjectivity and

---

sage of salvation more deeply in the paschal mystery, and to receive gratefully that transforming and healing power that gathers us as the community of God's Son so as to announce the reign of God in the power of the Spirit" (185). Speaking of God's sacramental presence has great potential to help one articulate God in the midst of atrocity, but again, some accounts of mass atrocity are very resistant to such a hopeful and promising reading, offering few, if any, signs of fellowship or love. On the whole, anti-signs of God's presence seem to dominate. Consider this harrowing scene from Tadeusz Borowski's *This Way for the Gas, Ladies and Gentlemen*: "Between two throw-ins in a soccer game, right behind my back, 3,000 people had been put to death" (84). We must also recall the ordination of Karl Leisner from ch. 2. Such an issue is worth pursuing in greater depth.

18. See Dempsey, "German Women Seized During World War II Seek Recognition."

19. Meredith, *Fate of Africa*, 543–44. See also Gettleman and Kron, "Report on Congo Massacres Draws Anger." The cited UN report alleges genocide committed by some Rwandan forces in the Congo from 1993 to 2003.

interpretation play in forming one's religious faith (or lack of faith), as these testimonies show.

Faith Mired in Subjective Interpretation

This distorted knowledge and fractured memory that result from a contested, multifaceted, and multilayered history inevitably can cause a faith crisis in interpreting the "truth" of any particular event and in trying to argue for the presence of God. Darrell Fasching, for example, writes: "the Holocaust has become the occasion for a hermeneutical rupture—a crisis in the interpretation of meaning."[20] This is especially the case if one's theological or ethical framework has been complicit or silent in the face of mass killing. Such a crisis implies that no stable, objective methodology or belief system can be unquestionably relied upon to interpret, judge, and promulgate a proper theological and ethical response because of the Holocaust and other mass atrocities. As Pollefeyt aptly writes: "Every person, every philosophy, and every political system after Auschwitz should be questioned ethically in this way: 'Is it open for alterity, for the vulnerability of the weakest, for growth, discussion, questioning, hesitation, falsification, new challenges, for transcendent experiences?'"[21]

To challenge and purify my theological grounding and identity as a Catholic theologian, I have turned to witnesses of mass atrocity and, in particular, to select Catholic Latin American liberation theologians who live among the poor and the oppressed, and post-Shoah Jewish theologians trying to persevere in their faith. My focus is a conscious decision to change the *social locus* of most theodicists, to borrow a phrase used by Azevedo in his essay "Basic Ecclesial Communities." He writes: "*Social locus* is the point from which people perceive, understand, and interpret their reality or from which they act upon it."[22] I have been arguing that one needs to develop a theodicy from the "underside of history," from the perspective of the marginalized and voiceless. The key issue, however, is whether my (Catholic Christian) theological grounding can still be relied upon in light of the existence of mass killing and suffering. When my faith tradition asserts a loving God in solidarity with the poor and oppressed, how do I interpret the

20. Fasching, *Narrative Theology*, 22.
21. Pollefeyt, "Critique" [of "Emmanuel Levinas and the Primacy of Ethics"], 31.
22. Azevedo, "Basic Ecclesial Communities," 648.

following claim by Pio, a Hutu convicted of genocide: "Many Tutsis . . . stopped hoping, they knew they had no chance for mercy and went off without a single prayer. They knew they were abandoned by everything, even God. They no longer spoke to Him at all"?[23] And yet, this is a perpetrator's interpretation of his victims. To cede him authority on his victims' last moments seems to be a further desecration of their lives and memories. He could not know what they were thinking; and yet, one of his fellow killers, Élie, admits that their gang, which includes Pio, mocked another group of Tutsis who had prayed before being murdered: "We made fun of them, we laughed at their *Amens*, we taunted them about the kindness of the Lord, we joked about the paradise awaiting them. That fired us up even more."[24] Pio interpreted as despair the other Tutsis' silence mentioned above. Perhaps he was wrong and they did not feel abandoned by God, but if he is right, how does this reflect upon theodic arguments and positions that want to assert otherwise?

It is important to grant that all interpretation, whether of a text or a historical event, at some point involves faith: faith in an author's or witness's intentions; faith in the sources one consults; faith in the ideological or social location one inhabits to view this history (often misleadingly deemed an "objective" vantage point); faith in the general consensus of a community one trusts; and faith in the methodologies of analysis and interpretation one has been taught to employ or has come to believe are more valid and useful. How one processes and articulates this "faith" inevitably colors and determines one's narratives and judgments, the selection of facts, and the focus or lens one uses to promote the seminal figures or events one chooses to describe. As Fasching contends, the Holocaust and similar historical ruptures have challenged any certitude in the objectivity and superiority of one's interpretative moral framework and methodology.

However, while it is specious of Christian theodicists to avoid identifying their own limitations, biases, and potential blindspots, there still needs to be some criteria that one can employ to try to judge which viewpoint or method may be more likely to come closer to an approximation of the truth, properly called, and reach a reasonable and credible position. But based on what (or whose) criteria? In light

---

23. Pio, interviewed by Hatzfeld, *Machete Season*, 143.

24. Élie, interviewed by Hatzfeld, *Machete Season*, 143.

of those who are skeptical of the possibility for reaching a rational consensus on what is true, right, just, and good, John Roth refers to Michael Berenbaum's description of the Holocaust as a "negative absolute." However, Roth adds that such a phrase does not "reinstate confidence in moral absolutes" because Berenbaum's term also refers to ethics itself, which was not "immune from failure and, at times, complicity in the pathological conditions and characteristics that nearly destroyed Jewish life and left the world morally scarred forever."[25]

One can already see some of the challenges raised by many postmodern thinkers, as Braiterman argued in the previous chapter. Identity, truth, meaning, history, morality, objectivity—all are rendered potentially suspect by the Holocaust and other mass atrocities. When such basic identity markers are challenged, asserting any truth, let alone the presence of God, becomes contestable and subjective. Turning to testimonies of mass atrocity illustrates how core moral and religious beliefs are denied or manipulated: giving birth to a child means automatic death for mother and child,[26] crimes of genocide are denied and concealed as they are perpetuated,[27] and children are taught how to cut and slice a human being, as Clémentine, a Hutu woman admits: "I saw papas teaching their boys how to cut. They made them imitate the machete blows. They displayed their skill on dead people, or on living people they had captured during the day. The boys usually tried it out on children, because of their similar size. But most people did not want to involve the children directly in these bloody doings, except for watching of course."[28] Particularly troubling for me is Clémentine's last sentence. Just as she mentions some parents not wanting their children to participate in the killing—and I anticipated her saying how some parents opposed the killings—she adds matter-of-factly that all children watched the murders, "of course." Because it was "as if there was a kind of collective insanity,"[29] these occurrences challenge any sense of moral stability, or more prosaically, a means or methodology of interpretation and judgment that one can

25. Roth, *Ethics during and after the Holocaust*, 26.

26. See Lengyl, *Five Chimneys*, 113–16.

27. Müller, *Eyewitness Auschwitz*, 25–26.

28. Hatzfeld, *Machete Season*, 40.

29. Quoted in Neuffer, *Key to My Neighbor's House*, 259.

rely upon to navigate the complexities and contradictions rife within a world seemingly gone awry.

And yet, we also know there were exceptions to this "collective insanity." Can these exceptions be a ground to maintain a position of stability and objectivity that can still morally evaluate, judge, interpret, and analyze these events, as Fackenheim hoped in chapter 9? In order to (re)establish some sense of a stable theoretical framework and methodology, one needs to (re)develop and test a firm but flexible hermeneutical practice that

1. values questions as much as answers;

2. is characterized by an open, reflective, sobering mind;

3. employs diverse "textual" analysis, interpretations, and viewpoints;

4. seeks to isolate and determine the sources, influences, and themes within specific "passages" in addition to the overriding meaning(s); and

5. can recognize congruities (along with incongruities) in other contexts to argue for a basic (or potentially comprehensive) meaning, structure, narrative, or argument.

Have any metanarratives, for example, survived our postmodern, postsecular, and post-Auschwitz world? Perhaps, but any such method will never be free of potential distortion, error, or misjudgement. If any metanarrative survives, it will be critiqued and hounded with questions. These acknowledgements mean that proving a universally valid principle of organization or meaning in regards to truth claims likely remains out of reach. John D'Arcy May, writing about the possibility to state "universal" principles as the basis of morality, argues: "The human sciences have not yet reached the stage of objectivity where their findings can be regarded as devoid of all prejudice or distortion, and they now build this subjectivity and contextuality of viewpoint into their own methodologies."[30] The interpreter, ultimately, must at some level trust and have faith in the honesty and integrity of an actor or author and in the mode and method of his or her inquiry. While subjective, isolated interpretation will never be as fruitful as one that engages in dialogue with a larger community or group, in a

---

30. May, "Whose Universality?" 201.

world turned upside down, when children are taught how to kill other children, and society at large sanctions it or is indifferent, how does one claim and maintain a reliable (if not "objective") status and refute the assertion that one's faith is not merely personal and subjective? If one cannot refute such a claim, then trying to argue for God's active presence in this world is simply based on opinion or, less charitably, mere projection.

Sadly, it seems there will never be unanimity in stating the exact truth of a certain event, or whether God's presence was or was not felt at a certain moment. For every voice that sings and praises the saving work and grace of God, there will be others who deny the possibility or remain unsure or undecided on the matter. Such varied and conflicting assertions indelibly mean one must choose and decide which view is likely true. While a believer in God may feel tempted to discount, or momentarily evade, or minimize the significance of some opposing arguments, sooner or later one must acknowledge the moral obligation to seek the truth. And in doing so, truth claims often clash, as Eliezer Berkovits emphasized in chapter 9 and the next section develops further.

When the Languages of Levi and Wiesel Collide

Theodicists attuned to the witnesses of atrocities are forced to confront a variety of conflicting views and testimonies, some of which they will highly prize and admire even though such witnesses may assert the opposite picture of a God of love and involvement in our world (the writings of Primo Levi, for me, for example). Such testimonies reveal that no discernible divine presence accompanied many people during and after their torture and mutilation. They paint human beings metamorphosed to *Muselmänner*, dehumanized and broken.[31] They depict children and babies annihilated before their lives had a chance to blossom.[32] They narrate individuals coerced to commit horrendous acts upon those they love and care for.[33] They testify to a God whose people feel abandoned.[34]

31. Levi, *Survival in Auschwitz*, 90.

32. Chang, *Rape of Nanking*, 91. See also Di Giovanni, *Place at the End of the World*, 341–59.

33. Beah, *Long Way Gone*, 37.

34. Bau, *Dear God*, 74.

At the least, these texts deny any meaningful connection between God and this world. Or if a tenuous connection exists, the picture is of a God who saves a few and abandons the majority based on unknown criteria or who is impotent to do otherwise. The evil is rarely purposive, rarely cathartic. It often crushes and eradicates, as I emphasized in chapter 4 with my analysis of *Salvifici Doloris*. And yet, this world is also replete with cathartic and sublime moments of beauty and union. To elucidate this last point, I have also included stories that accentuate the goodness of humanity in horrific conditions or those individuals who maintained—or even discovered—faith in God during their trauma and torture. Grace Akallo, for example, abducted and coerced to be a child soldier in Uganda, still begins her memoir: "First, I dedicate this book to God, who gave me the gift of life, protected me and gave me his love."[35]

Thus, one is at an impasse. Reading the gulag accounts of a Harry Wu or Irina Ratushinskaya[36] may mean that one can still hope and have faith in God and humanity's goodness, but this realization in no way annuls or subsumes its polar opposite tales. We are left with paradox and conflicting accounts. One person may cling to the Christ-filled life of Karl Leisner, and someone else to Alicia Partnoy's heroic but pragmatic atheism, and each would have sources and evidence.

The reason that we need to account for these contrary assertions is to seek to do justice to the stories of all victims. The fact that some individuals aver that God did not abandon them means, at the least, that God has not been totally extricated from God's people. While a survivor's testimony about feeling God's presence cannot be scientifically proved, neither can all such assertions be scientifically disproved. One could argue that God is arbitrarily selective in comforting or appearing to certain individuals and not to others, or one could contend that the fault lies not with God but with the individual who did not seek God or was unable (or unwilling) to intuit God's presence. The latter position would argue that Partnoy's goodness and heroism were never totally removed from God's presence. Despite her denial of this contention, it may not be duplicitous to speak of the Holy Spirit accompanying her (or that she was filled with the Spirit when she tried to help Benja as he was being tortured before he was later shot and

---

35. McDonnell and Akallo, *Girl Soldier*, "Dedication" page.

36. See Wu, *Bitter Winds*; Ratushinskaya, *Grey Is the Color of Hope.*

murdered[37]). And yet, this assertion blames a sufferer who already has endured enough and limits human responsibility and goodness, while the first assertion would not reflect a magnanimous, loving God to all in this life. The conflict, then, as Berkovits and others have highlighted, is whether and how one can honor both the faithful and the despairing with equal respect while still advocating a theodicy. These testimonies make such a commitment a precarious and paradoxical exercise.

Why Some Evil Resists Transformation

Though one's response to another's suffering is essential, as discussed throughout this work, certain acts of evil are senseless and meaningless in themselves. One cannot justify them by claiming that such acts teach lessons or are conducive to soul-making. As Langer writes: "There is nothing to be learned from a baby torn in two or a woman burned alive."[38]

In short, some of the suffering and deaths in these testimonials resist any interpretation that seeks to justify their occurrence. It refutes any who argue that suffering is meaningful because it is a way to identify with Christ (McCord Adams), or is a means to participate in Christ's redemption (John Paul II), or helps one join in solidarity with the plight of the poor and oppressed and so can be transformative (Gutiérrez). Phillips, therefore, is right to resist such justificatory or causal language, which implies that any evil transpired for some greater benefit. The depiction and interpretation of such evils within these texts problematizes any attempt to maintain that all suffering is necessary, redemptive, or part of God's plan. Moreover, such texts also scrutinize and deflate the power of prayer, which is often deemed a potential link to God and proof of God's active presence. I will examine such claims below.

The Testimonials' Impact on Prayer

Recall the tragic story from chapter 1 of Little Eleanora, victim of the Soviet gulag despite all her mother's prayers and effort. Such cases challenge belief in the "power of prayer" as a means to serve as an

---

37. Partnoy, *Little School*, 125.
38. Quoted in Roth, *Ethics during and after the Holocaust*, 34.

intimate contact between God and the believer. Wiesel writes: "I don't know *how* I survived . . . a miracle? Certainly not. If heaven could or would perform a miracle for me, why not for others more deserving than myself? It was nothing more than chance. However, having survived, I needed to give some meaning to my survival."[39] Such a response seems the most rational, humble, and sobering, especially as Wiesel still asserts that he has an additional moral responsibility because he survived. On the other hand, a different type of belief in God's continuing presence in this world and in the power and healing of prayer may seek to make grand, but still potentially true, claims.

In the *Massacre of El Mozote*, Mark Danner revisits the scene in El Salvador from 1981 where the Atcatl Battalion massacred every man, woman, and child in the village save two who managed to escape. One was Rufina Amaya. The soldiers entered the village, separated the men from the women, and then proceeded to slaughter the men and then rape and murder the women. Amaya recalls: "I was crying and miserable, and begging God to help me." The killing continued. "I promised to God that if He helped me, I would tell the world what happened here." As she describes how the soldiers began to kill the children, she adds: "There were animals there, cows and a dog, and they saw me, and I was afraid they would make a noise, but God made them stay quiet as I crawled among them."[40]

Similar remarks are made by Immaculée Ilibagiza, who depicts numerous incidents where she was surrounded by Hutu killers and yet managed to live. In one instance, three *Interahamwe*[41] followed her:

> "I know this cockroach," [one of them] said. "This is Leonard's daughter—we've been looking for her for months! I can't believe she's still alive . . . we killed the rest of them, but this little cockroach gave us the slip!" [Clutching her father's rosary, Ilibagiza prayed fervently]: "Only You can save me. You promised to take care of me, God—well, I really need taking care of right now. There are devils and vultures at my back, Lord . . .

---

39. Wiesel, *Night*, vii–viii.

40. Danner, *Massacre at El Mozote*, 74–75.

41. Meaning "those who work together," the term *Interahamwe* morphed from referring to youth groups called to rebuild Rwanda in the 1970s to Hutu paramilitary groups seeking to establish and maintain a Hutu government in Rwanda. They also participated in the genocide of 1994 among other mass killings. See Emmanuel Viret, "Interahamwe."

please protect me. Take the evil from the hearts of these men,
and blind their hatred with Your holy love . . . If they kill me,
God, I ask You to forgive them."[42]

The group disbanded. She lived. Other calamities have similar instances of unexpected survivors or witnesses. One is almost
tempted to believe that such survivors are granted life as witnesses
so that the world would discover the truth, but there have been some
massacres without survivors. Moreover, if God chose to save this or
that individual, the conclusion one could draw is almost worse. In
this case God specifically saved certain people or listened to certain
prayers (if indeed the prayer played any role in the selection) but
not similarly "worthy" individuals who were then raped, abused, or
tortured to death.

Of course, biblical history is steeped in the drama of God select-
ing certain people to lead or guide others amidst adversity and persecution. As noted in chapter 8, rabbis employed theological protest
in part to claim that the present circumstances may be bleak but God
will save and redeem. The hope hangs on the precipice of the present
calamity supported by past deeds. And yet it is very difficult to sustain
this hope without rendering the losses that have already happened as
somehow forgivable if God acts "now."

In an often-cited passage of *Survival in Auschwitz*, Levi describes
a situation after a routine selection had decided the fate of numerous
prisoners. One man, Kahn, prayed and thanked God for surviving a
selection despite knowing that there were individuals in bunks next to
him who had been condemned for the ovens. Levi writes: "Does Kahn
not understand that it is an abomination which no propitiatory prayer,
no pardon, no expiation of the guilty by the guilty, which nothing in
the power of man can ever clear again?" Thus, because of these atrocities, some prayers or prayer practices ironically become unethical and
inappropriate. Or, without saving everyone, any prayer becomes an
abomination, as God then seems carelessly to select some to die and
some to live. As Levi has remarked: "Barring [being in good health
and knowing German], luck dominated. I have seen the survival of
shrewd people and silly people, the brave and the cowardly, 'thinkers' and madmen."[43] Rwandan genocide survivor Eugénie Kayierre

---

42. Ilibagiza, *Left to Tell*, 173.

43. Quoted in Roth, "Conversation with Primo Levi," 180.

concurs: "Anyway, the most important thing wasn't your legs or wind or even your morale: it was really luck."[44]

However, prayer broadly understood prevents the assertion that all prayer is inappropriate or meaningless. Bernard McGinn writes: "One customary division of prayer (based on 1 Tim 2:1) speaks of four forms: praise, thanksgiving, penance, and petition."[45] The divisions are flexible enough to admit a wide spectrum of actions and practices. In this vein, these texts do not obliterate the power or purpose of one's prayer life—especially in the sense of one's life as a potentially continual contact and private communion with God. As Origen writes: "He 'prays without ceasing' who joins prayer to works that are of obligation, and good works to his prayer."[46] Similarly, Dean Brackley adds: "When we serve God habitually, everything we do becomes a kind of prayer. Thomas Aquinas applied the word 'prayer' in this broad sense: 'As long as one is acting in one's heart, speech, or work in such a way as to tend towards God, one is praying. One who is directing one's whole life towards God is praying always.'"[47]

Recall also Metz's famous comment: "We can pray *after* Auschwitz because people prayed *in* Auschwitz."[48] Former child soldier Grace Akallo, for example, narrates how she suggested to her companions that they pray while they were on the run from their captors. "The girls looked at me strangely but obeyed silently."[49] Amidst unspeakable torment, some people prayed in both the traditional sense and in the broader notion of doing good deeds for others.

These testimonies do, however, clearly raise questions against the standard interpretation of prayer as "knock, and the door will be opened unto you."[50] At the same time, miracles, mystery, and murkiness pervade not only the Christian religion, but the reality of our world. This is not to deny that one can also argue for a sense of order, rhythm, and law in the universe, but mystery and the unknown

44. Hatzfeld, *Strategy of Antelopes*, 44.

45. McGinn, *Christian Mysticism*, 79.

46. Origen, "Prayer," 84.

47. Brackley, *Call to Discernment*, 246.

48. Metz, *Emergent Church*, 19. Fackenheim raised a similar rationale, as noted in ch. 9.

49. McDonnell and Akallo, *Girl Soldier*, 160.

50. Matt 7:7.

remain a palpable and formidable presence. Because some individuals have sensed and assertively claim the power of prayer (and so the presence of God) while others have denied this possibility, does not automatically prove that the latter are more correct or trustworthy. Perhaps one is again staring at two conflicting truths. A faith-position or faith-searcher who relentlessly plumbs the depths to which some individuals have suffered agony and torment ironically can come to acknowledge the greater need for belief in a God of justice and mercy.[51] This does not mean that faith in God becomes an opiate or psychological neurosis, but is recognized as a genuine calling and *telos* that reveals the type of moral life that is best suited to the essence of becoming fully human—the path that helps answer our deepest mystical and ontological searches for our purpose and destiny. Confronting the truths of such evil and suffering points to a need to look beyond ourselves and this world with a concomitant calling to transform our way of life even more deeply in order to decry similar injustice. While questions of the origin of this evil remain empirically illusive, the options before us, amidst the conflicting views and evidence, offer a few stark choices, all of which leave some inevitable trace of doubt and uncertainty. All the choices will rest on what can only be deemed "faith." The key question is in where that faith resides.

Uniqueness and Meaning of Christianity

For Christians, these testimonies can brutally challenge the belief in the uniqueness of Christ as the answer to the problem of evil. They particularly gnaw at the relevance of Christ's presence amidst such despondency and torture and the purpose and tangible accomplishments of Jesus's life, crucifixion, and resurrection. This important but complex issue must at least be raised here again because it in many ways cuts to the heart of the uniqueness of a Christian theodicy. In truth, however, it is a topic too controversial and intricate to treat here without slipping into superficiality. A few general remarks, however, for future direction may be of interest.

While responding to a passage of John Paul II's *Crossing the Threshold of Hope*, in which John Paul writes that "Christ is absolutely original and absolutely unique," Thich Nhat Hanh comments: "Of course Christ is unique. The idea behind the statement, however, is

---

51. Müller, *Eyewitness Auschwitz*, 66.

the notion that Christianity provides the only way of salvation and all other religious traditions are of no use. This attitude excludes dialogue and fosters religious intolerance and discrimination."[52]

Recognizing that the concept of uniqueness may vary in different cultures, Hans Waldenfals points out: "Western people, also Western Christian thinkers, cannot and simply should not presuppose that Asian people easily understand the important role which individuality, singularity, and uniqueness play in Occidental thought and life."[53] Theodicists who turn to the words of survivor testimony—especially of those outside their faith tradition—must remain open to the possibility that they will not only learn from the Other but that the Other's face, words, and experience may challenge them to change or clarify aspects of their own theological and moral position.[54]

A fundamental problem is how I can argue for a Christian theodicy when voices and perspectives that I respect (Partnoy and Levi) point to their wounds and scars and argue against the relevance of a Christian theodicy for their ordeals. Without disparaging Jesus of Nazareth's crucifixion, they may also question why Christians interpret the meaning of Christ's life as the highest ideal of facing and enduring suffering and as the ultimate act of God's love for all. As Charlotte Delbo writes: "You who have wept two thousand years / for one who agonized for three days and three nights // what tears will you have left / . . . for those who agonized through so many agonies

---

52. Quoted in Hanh, *Living Buddha, Living Christ*, xx–xxi.

53. Waldenfals, "Ecclesia in Asia," 201.

54. There are a number of insightful and engaging works that examine the uniqueness of Christianity, often in the context of interreligious dialogue or a discussion of religious pluralism, and that are relevant to a Christian theodicist. Here is a sample: Hick and Knitter, eds., *The Myth of Christian Uniqueness*; Gillis, *Pluralism*; D'Costa, ed., *Christian Uniqueness Reconsidered*; Knitter, ed., *Myth of Religious Superiority*, 133–207; Pope and Hefling, eds., *Sic et Non*; Phan, *Being Religious Interreligiously*, 85–101, 137–46; Haight, *Future of Christology*, 115–20, 156–64, 186–95; Hanh, *Living Buddha, Living Christ*, Introduction and 34–60; Pawlikowski, *Christ in the Light of the Christian-Jewish Dialogue*, 108–35; May, *Transcendence and Violence*, 137–41; May, "Catholic Fundamentalism?" 112–23; de Schrijver, *Recent Theological Debates in Europe*, 230–61; Kendall and O'Collins, eds., *In Many and Diverse Ways*, 33–100, 194–208; Song, *Third-Eye Theology*, 119–41; Meyer and Hughes, eds., *Jesus Then and Now*, 143–69; O'Grady and Scherle, eds., *Ecumenics from the Rim*, 197–341; Pieris, *Fire and Water*, 69–78, 143–69; and my "All lost! To prayers, to prayers! All lost," 79–98.

/ and they were countless // They did not believe in resurrection to eternal life / and knew you would not weep."[55]

Non-Christians who have experienced horrific evils, moreover, would doubt that Jesus's death and resurrection provided the means for complete redemption of the world.[56] They may also credit their own traditions and beliefs for how they survived their ordeals. Beri Laga, a Tibetan prisoner of the Communist Chinese, amazed "even the Chinese guards by her tenacity. 'They found it incredible that I was still alive,' she told [Mary Craig], 'and even more incredible when I said it was because of my religious faith. I had prayed night and day to the Three Jewels to come through the ordeal; and my faith kept me going.'"[57] Clearly, one treads a fine line when making christological statements to victims who are either atheists or believers of a non-Christian religion. If one attempts to use words, they must be chosen carefully.

Impact on Evangelizing and Apologetics

Although it is rarely noted, these texts of mass atrocity also challenge the place and role of evangelizing, and so an underlying task of theodicy.[58] In fact, because theodicy seeks to justify traditional belief in God and so shares affinity with evangelization and apologetics, these testimonies challenge how one defends and seeks to spread one's beliefs. Because they undermine the presuppositions and rationale of some theodic arguments, they challenge the foundation of one's faith.

As argued above, the more one exposes oneself to divergent voices, the more difficult it can be to assert theological statements without qualifiers. This does not imply that theists must be silent. We reach a choice or belief on an essential matter after much deliberation, questioning, testing (and for many, praying). The fact that we could be theoretically wrong does not necessarily dampen our fervor and commitment to what we ultimately assented to or decided. Moreover, theodicies benefit from exposure to individuals or groups who do not

---

55. Delbo, *Auschwitz and After*, 10.

56. Langer's comment that "neither Job nor Jesus illuminate the Holocaust" would be echoed by many survivors of atrocity (*Admitting the Holocaust*, 27).

57. Craig, *Tears of Blood*, 206.

58. Take Greenberg's working principle. How would one evangelize Christ to any surviving parents or siblings of those burned Jewish babies?

share a theodicist's specific religious foundation because they demand (and deserve) a careful, nuanced articulation of sometimes obtuse and unclear beliefs.

Christological statements, theoretically, have their place in the context of dialoguing with non-Christian sufferers and victims, and may be words that some individuals desperately need to hear, as I touched upon in discussing Greenberg's working principle.[59] Despite its challenges, maintaining Christ's uniqueness can remain a spiritually and rationally rich claim, particularly if one emphasizes the scandal of the cross as a link to fellow sufferers and argues why such solidarity matters. While seeking to heal the person's wounds or simply listening to the traumatic story may be the more proper representation of the love and life of Christ than traditional evangelizing or apologetics, these have their rightful place as well, especially if such a dialogue is characterized by listening, openness, honesty, and humility.[60] And yet, for a Christian, respecting the integrity of the non-Christian Other and one's Christian beliefs is to inhabit a theological terrain of constraint, disagreement, awkwardness, and vulnerability.

Before I address some of the responses of theodicists to these challenges, I want to return to another area these testimonies challenge: the issue of God's omnipotence.

The Limitations of Omnipotence 2

The unceasing cries of victims, the manifestation of atrocious acts by perpetrators, and the overwhelming sense of loss and isolation that haunts many victims and perpetrators demand a clarification or reformulation of what it means to speak of God's omnipotence while maintaining the notion of a God of perfect love. The prominent issue is how one can promote a kenotic, Self-denying God who relinquishes power and dominion so that life can be free and flourish even as this freedom entails suffering and atrocity towards life.

Aware of Raphael's critique, I must return to the issue of God's relationship with this world and what it means to speak of an intervening and omnipotent God. On the one hand, Brian Davies writes: "Talk about God as intervening has to presuppose that there is commonly

59. See chs. 1, 5, and 9.

60. Moreno, "Evangelization," 573. See also my "Mission in Remission" and my "Overcoming 'Mere Oblivion.'"

a serious absence of God from created things."[61] Contra Davies, one may instead speak of the presence of God as being made more manifest within certain moments, people, or natural events. Biblical history can surely be read this way. From a Christian standpoint, as Ignacio Ellacuría writes: "[Jesus's] unique way of intervening in history, of making God historically present among human beings, is of course proclaiming the Kingdom of God, making it present in himself and setting it in motion."[62] In a similar vein, José Comblin writes: "God delivers the people by means of the forces and energies that God places within the people, by means of the enlightenment and prophetic charisma of mighty leaders, by means of the union and solidarity of living communities, and by means of the enthusiasm of the multitudes these communities and prophets succeed in arousing."[63]

From the exploitation and extermination of the native peoples of the Americas to the attempted genocides committed against the Armenians, Jews, Roma, [64] Tutsis, and others; in light of the millions upon millions of people who are murdered from starvation and curable diseases, not to mention victims of natural disasters, one is almost forced to reconsider and refashion the traditional concept of God's omnipotence along the lines of Comblin above.

A Christian also has to face the issue of the redemption of the world and the coming of Christ (a fundamental issue of difference between Christians and Jews). As Pollefeyt notes: "Christians must agree with Jews that the world is not yet redeemed."[65] On the one hand, I want to maintain God's omnipotence in order for transcendence and redemption to be possible for the lost, broken lives of this world. Remove that possibility, and life for so many is extinguished of all meaning. Theism is tarnished irrevocably. Christians, however, turning to the gospels and gazing upon Jesus on the cross, see a power that eschews the sword but becomes a victim and martyr. Jesus' subsequent resurrection and His bringing the Reign of God into sacred fruition do not cease the groans and cries of many victims. So many

61. Davies, *Reality of God*, 75.

62. Ellacuría, "Historicity of Christian Salvation," 282.

63. Comblin, "Holy Spirit," 463–64.

64. An indispensable text about the lives and history of the Roma remains Fonseca, *Bury Me Standing*.

65. Pollefeyt, "Church and the Jews," 142.

souls continue to thirst and crave for redemption and healing in this world, often futilely.

To repeat: theists need a God who will heal and save in a post-mortem context: this is the only hope to maintain a viable theodicy and so a viable theism. At its most basic and clear level: why a loving, supposedly omnipotent God could "allow" such misery and abuse is the ultimate question that exemplifies why any theodicy (and so theism) is fractured and fragmented. One can cobble together a theodicy with free will elements, the theory of *perversio/privatio boni*, along with a general soul-making telos, but these promising features ultimately fail in the face of atrocity from human and nonhuman sources. If one needs an adjective before the term "omnipotence of God," then consider: fragmented, inconsistent, mysterious, kenotic, vulnerable, or fragile. From an earthly perspective, there is a lot of reason to doubt the "omni" in omnipotence, but theists must cling to it all the same.

For Christians, speaking of Jesus's kenotic (self-emptying) life of love (that does not culminate on the cross but continues with the gift of the Spirit) testifies to a power far removed from the might of military empires. Such a self-giving or renouncing love is not passive, as Walter Wink has argued by highlighting Jesus's acts of nonviolent resistance.[66] Such power testifies to the "violence of love," as Oscar Romero remarked.[67] The power therefore is not denied, but it is a power rooted in the scandal of the cross. Note also that Comblin and Ellacuría share much in common with Irving Greenberg's notion that the covenant has evolved so that one speaks today of humanity having more responsibility in establishing and evoking the presence of God among us. Similarly, the gospels also accentuate the role of the healed in receiving a cure at Jesus's touch or word. It is their faith that saves.[68] Without this faith, few miracles happen, as at Nazareth.[69] Because no clear "saving" occurs for many in this life, I will reexamine the problem of postmortem redemption and God's omnipotence in the next chapter.

---

66. Wink, "Jesus' Third Way," 98–111. For a discussion of *kenosis* and the Buddhist term *sunyata* (emptiness), see May, *Transcendence and Violence*, 16. See also Cobb and Ives, *Emptying God*.

67. Romero, *Violence of Love*, 12.

68. Mark 2:5; Mark 5:34.

69. Mark 6:5.

In continuing this attempt at dialogue, I will now, however, evaluate how the theodicies from Part 2 "answered" or challenged some of the above assertions and how these testimonies may interpret such responses.

THE RESPONSES OF THEODIC WORKS TO WITNESSES OF EVIL

Preliminary One: Encroaching Upon Holy Ground

This section is fraught with potential misinterpretation and the possibility of falling into insensitivity and religious hubris. Recall John D'Arcy May's remark that the "acknowledgement of failure" may be a sound basis for dialogue,[70] especially as I would contend, for the theodicist. Individuals who have suffered inordinately and witnessed the malicious actions of human beings with no clear response from God cannot be refuted as in a law court or investigative inquiry. With awareness of the historical record, we must take their impressions and accounts as authentic and honest. The goal of a Christian theodicist is to draw upon the life and mission of Christ (and carefully select relevant resources within Christian tradition) to begin to work out a careful, faithful language that can remain resonant despite this world's evil. The aim is to provide a framework to begin to give meaning to each life as a whole and to instill a means to cope with suffering and trauma. Because Jesus of Nazareth for Christians is also the God of Mercy and Justice, Christians have unlimited resources to plumb the depths of meaning that Christ can be the source for redemption and for personal connection. Obviously these statements or challenges are posed in fear and trembling as much as they are sustained and enriched by one's faith.

Preliminary Two: What Theodicists Cannot Offer

As we saw in chapter 2, Alicia Partnoy can only look to herself and her fellow prisoners for "bread" and rescuing. For Nomberg-Przytyk, faith is madness in the concentration camps. Theoretical theodicy can offer little tangible means of bread or liberation, though a theodicy must not simply try to justify why belief in God is still reasonable without also advocating and illustrating how that faith is made manifest

70. May, *Transcendence and Violence*, 134.

in acts of love and mercy. Theodicists seek to argue why belief in a loving God despite evil is still reasonable and necessary. A theodicist should not, therefore, delve too deeply into the sordid business of justifying specific concrete events as part of God's plan or as a sign of divine punishment. Theodicies have their limits, and one needs to be cognizant of them. Resonating with Greenberg's working principle, or liberation theology, theodicies should empower their readers and listeners to commit themselves to a praxis that seeks to heal the victim. Such a moral and philosophical outlook could give a survivor the means, support, and vocabulary to persevere through the trauma and affliction, provide a way to combat the ideology of the perpetrators, and come to see the goodness and meaning of this world. The fact that there are individuals who have been aided by such an outlook and connection with others through their faith provides some tangible "proof." As I will repeat below, a nonbeliever in God can also point to theists who were corrupted or who disavowed their faith. Ignace, a Hutu convicted of genocide, remarks: "The white priests took off at the first skirmishes. The black priests joined the killers or the killed. God kept silent, and the churches stank from abandoned bodies . . . For a little while, we were no longer ordinary Christians, we had to forget our duties learned in catechism class."[71] A theodicy can only be fruitful if it accepts its limits, failures, and fragility.

The Value of a Humble, Dynamic Faith

While humility is an essential component of any religious position, a dynamic faith is able to adapt in some way to changing times or contexts and to co-opt what is attractive in other fields but often neglected in one's own. A dynamic and humble faith listens to the assertions and claims of these witnesses and begins the process of self-examination to seek forgiveness. It also aims to maintain or clarify the integrity of one's faith while searching for more consistent moral approaches when facing new and dangerous threats or challenges.

We saw this process examined in Zachary Braiterman's interpretation of Jewish post-Shoah theologians, as he asserts how they subtly, and sometimes radically, encroached upon unfamiliar or less-travelled territory in Judaism, or spotlighted traditionally marginal figures or textual passages to accentuate such meaning and "answers"

---

71. Ignace, interviewed by Hatzfeld, *Machete Season*, 142.

in a post-Shoah, Jewish context. Irving Greenberg, for example, accentuated the role of an evolving covenant between God and the Jewish people. While the onus of responsibility had once been heavily upon God, Greenberg contends it is now more and more humanity's concern and obligation. As noted in chapter 9, Melissa Raphael advocates for the presence of Shekhinah (and so the female face of God) through the ethical acts of caring and bodily cleaning among women in the camps. Echoing Greenberg, she writes: "Humanity was redeemed in God's redemption by humanity."[72] More radically, David Blumenthal seems to say to a Partnoy or Nomberg-Przytyk that what they suffered is an injustice and God should be held accountable, but if they can see beyond this legitimate pain and isolation, God can be found amidst and beyond their affliction. Not every adaptation will have sufficient continuity with its core tradition, but those that do will subsequently be in a better position to respond authentically to contemporary problems.

The Flexibility of Theological Protest

Just as a humble, dynamic religion can meet some of the challenges posed by nonbelievers, a similar means of connection or dialogue between these theologians and our witnesses to radical evil is possible through the tradition of theological protest. In chapter 8, I traced the role of theological protest in the Jewish tradition through Anson Laytner's study. We have also seen protest given similarly qualified support and credibility by John Paul II and the liberation theologians. This type of protest resonates with many of Partnoy's and Nomberg-Przytyk's statements that such conditions are absurd and can in no way be a punishment by God or an intended part of some divine plan. With Partnoy and Nomberg-Przytyk, theodicists decry the scandal of these horrors and urge the need to work for change. The difference between a Partnoy and a Berkovits, of course, is that Berkovits protests to God as a type of prayer with the hope and faith that God will, in some way, respond. This theological protest is rooted in love of God and God's calling to love and respect the stranger and the neighbor.[73] Such a stance is one way for theodicists to respond meaningfully to

---

72. Raphael, *Female Face of God*, 84.

73. Fasching, *Narrative Theology*, 75.

the cries and accusations of some victims and not fall prey to being complicit in injustice.

The Call for Praxis and Change

In addition to the candid acknowledgement of the scandal of horrific suffering and the questions and protests that can be spoken by both believer and nonbeliever, is the call for tangible action to work for change and justice. Such a praxic focus and aim contributes to how one views the goodness and beauty of this world, a crucial task of any theodicy, as seen from the emphasis of Greenberg's working principle; Fackenheim's *Tikkun Olam*; John Paul II's calling to share in the redemption of the world completed by Christ through our attitude to our own suffering and the suffering of others; and the option for the poor and the commitment to work for individual and structural change in liberation theology. It is no surprise that Partnoy, for example, refers to fellow friends and workers for justice who were sustained and led by their religious faith. Néstor Junquera and María Eugenia González de Junquera shared many of Partnoy's same goals and visions for a better Argentina. As Partnoy writes of Néstor: "He, Christian to the marrow of his bones, found the tools to fight injustice in the Theology of Liberation."[74] Part of Partnoy wishes she could share the same conviction in those tools, or the Jewish faith of her ancestors, but as noted in chapter 2, she is unable to do so, in part because she also sees how high members of the church supported the military junta in Argentina. Nevertheless, the example of Néstor and María stays with her.

One of the best testaments to the vitality and integrity of a religion is its believers working on the side of justice and sharing the fate of the destitute and being ostracized while bulwarked and sustained by their faith. Néstor and María embodied this ideal, although, like many, they greatly suffered for it. According to Partnoy, they "were taken away in the middle of December 1976. Nothing more is known of them, though a writ of habeas corpus was filed."[75] While such stories are tragic, the lives and martyrdoms of Rabbi Akiba, Karl Leisner, Maximillian Kolbe, Ignacio Ellacuría, and the "primordial holiness" that Sobrino elevates, clearly position those religious believers on the

74. Partnoy, *Little School*, 62.
75. Ibid., 129.

side of the subjugated and testify and give credibility to their theological beliefs in following and worshipping a God of love and justice.

A Disinterested, Other-Centered Faith

While not unique to the Christian faith, a theodicist may also point to an outlook of faith that acknowledges that being a theist does not shield one from this life's miseries, but in certain situations, makes one more susceptible to the threat and reality of evil. For a Christian, this insight is linked with the concomitant belief that some suffering (the martyrdom of Oscar Romero, for example) could be a means to participate in furthering the goals of Christ's mission. Such a stance could also help provide the spiritual and theological resources to sustain one's sense of identity (and sanity). It also could, in theory, be another tool to help individuals whose faith has been shattered because of this world's injustice. I have argued (contra Phillips) that to make this disinterested faith (or other-centered faith) effective, a Christian would need to connect it with Christ's life and example and the meaning ascribed to his crucifixion and resurrection. Such a connection testifies to the saving grace and mercy of God. It points the way to our purpose and essence and reveals the extent to which a personal God will go to combat the degradation committed by human beings and so calls for a love of self that expresses one's theological and moral identity primarily through loving and serving others. Its hope and aim point to the possibility for the salvation of all, so that one's disinterested faith still brims with hope in God's promise of the beatific vision while striving to keep one's faith despite setbacks, and even monstrocities, in this world. Partnoy, of course, could not accept this type of faith in her friends, but their memory and commitment caused her to reflect favorably on them years later.

Emphasizing Christ as Healer

The most important resource a Christian theodicist can give a sufferer is the witness of Christ in the gospels. For a Christian, the story of Christ as a fellow sufferer who is God Incarnate can endow one's life with meaning and purpose. It can provide inspiration and strength, particularly if a person sees that Christ was persecuted and murdered for his choice to side with the poor and outcast and his challenge of those who oppressed others. *Gaudium Et Spes* proclaims: "Christ entered this world to give witness to the truth, to rescue, and not to sit in judgment, to serve and not be served."[76]

In chapter 2, I presented the life and testimony of Christ as a fellow sufferer for other victims of trauma and persecution to identify with. In addition, Jesus's moral message would clearly resonate in principle with Partnoy, Nomberg-Przytyk, and Gyatso, who all sought justice and aimed for a conversion of our world. That a Christian thinker like Bonhoeffer claims that the Holy Spirit's presence ensures that one is not alone, and that, potentially, such suffering can be a means to participate in Christ's redemption, could also bring comfort and peace to many.[77] It can also attest to why this world has meaning and value and how God is calling all of us to participate in Jesus's redemptive work. In particular, the Christology of the liberation theologians, which sees in Jesus someone who embodies the prophetic calling of the option for the poor in the Tanak, sanctifies the marginalized and voiceless of this world and calls on everyone, radically, to deny themselves, take up their cross, and serve God and others in discipleship with Jesus. Such following is best glimpsed in the inclusive sayings of the beatitudes and in this well-known verse: "Truly I tell you, just as you did it to the least of these members of my family, you did it to me."[78] Such a faith can at least provide a moral philosophy to help thwart total despair. As

---

76. *Gaudium et Spes,* 3(201).

77. Bonhoeffer, *Letters and Papers from Prison,* 11.

78. Matt 26:40. For relevant works on post-Holocaust Christologies examining the issues of the Jewishness of Jesus; the question of a single, double, or alternative covenant model; the moral errors of supersessionist theology (also known as the theology of substitution); the important and clear distinctions between "Christologies of Discontinuity" as opposed to "Christologies of Continuity," the "end of christological salvation triumphalism," (Pollefeyt, "Christology after Auschwitz," 233); the moral, historical, and theological errors (and repercussion) of the deicide charge against the Jewish people, the expectations and fulfillment of the Messiah, and the "newness" and uniqueness of Christ in light of the ongoing Jewish covenant, see Pawlikowski, "Search for a New Paradigm for the Christian-Jewish Relationship," 25–48; Pawlikowski, *Jesus and the Theology of Israel*; Pawlikowski, *Christ in the Light of the Christian-Jewish Dialogue*; Pollefeyt, "The Church and the Jews," 131–44; Pollefeyt, "Christology after Auschwitz," 229–48; Pollefeyt, ed., *Jews and Christians*; Bruteau, ed., *Jesus through Jewish Eyes*; Foley, "Heir or Orphan," 308–39; Haas, "Judaism in Protestant Encounters with the Shoah," 59–83; Kogan, *Opening the Covenant*; Cunningham et al., eds., *Catholic Church and the Jewish People*; Berger and Patterson, eds., *Jewish-Christian Dialogue,* 74–81 and 184–245; Moyaert and Pollefeyt, eds., *Never Revoked*; and Levine and Brettler, eds., *Jewish Annotated New Testament.*

such it could be useful to certain atheists or agnostics, though perhaps less so in the case of Gyatso, who turns to his own rich resources and cultural traditions that were the cause of his own persecution.

The Beauty of This World and Creation

Lastly, a theodicy that speaks of the innate goodness and dignity of all human beings through God's creation resonates with hope. It testifies to the purpose of every human being. It also highlights how far astray some individuals have fallen from their inherent dignity, while keeping open the possibility for redemption and transformation.

There must then be a way to reject those acts that aim to destroy the beauty and integrity of creation while still siding with the narrator's comment in Genesis that "God saw all that [God] had made, and found it very good."[79] Some people may argue that the world has lost all meaning and value or never had meaning because of Auschwitz or the actions of a rapist or the sudden death of a loved one. However, as Fackenheim's 614th commandment similarly argues, such a position inadvertently yields inordinate power or "victory" to those individuals who aimed—but ultimately failed—to sully all the goodness of this world and to imprint the world in their distorted image. While Fackenheim is speaking specifically in the context of Jewish belief and identity, such a "commandment" can be extended to all theists.

Moreover, atrocities must not be given the symbolic potency to impugn every person who has been—and will be—created. As Elie Wiesel writes: "To say that every one of them could have become a killer is to indict the whole world. It is to compare the privileged kapos with the moribund *Muselmänner* . . . It is to punish the innocents who have been punished enough."[80]

Making a case for the overall goodness of the world need not diminish the value and witness of those lives ended prematurely or savagely. Such lives highlight further what should have been the type of life and death all deserve. Remembering such lives also helps restore the shock and reality that human beings have played a definitive role in preventing this possibility for so many. However, some evil definitely raises questions of the value of this world for certain individuals crushed and abandoned as a result of their trials. The existence of such

79. Gen 1:31.
80. Wiesel, *And the Sea Is Never Full*, 347.

evil is where a religious believer must admit defeat based solely on the recourse of limited justice and reparation in this world. Because earthly justice is fractured, Christians revisit the tradition of God's creation of the world and God's response to suffering and evil. Based especially on the life, death, and resurrection of Christ, Christians hold firmly to the promises of the beatitudes: "Blest are those who mourn, for they will be comforted . . . Blessed are you when people revile you and persecute you and utter all kinds of evil against you falsely on my account. Rejoice and be glad, for your reward is great in heaven."[81]

Such a world is fostered by and focused on the reign of God within and beyond our midst. And so, while never tiring in the commitment to establish the reign of God on earth, a theist must also look to the afterlife and the individual's encounter with God for true redemption and transformation. Phillips denied such a possibility. McCord Adams accentuated this encounter with God and the size gap and qualities of God that make it plausible to believe God could heal and redeem the pernicious concrete and symbolic effects of such life-defeating evils. She does not speculate in detail on what the encounter will be like, though a Christian could turn to the Scriptures and tradition for hints of which direction to take. Again, for a Christian, the answer and key is both the Christ of Mercy, comfort to the sinner—"Father, forgive them; for they do not know what they are doing"[82]—and the Christ of Justice, companion to the oppressed and suffering of this world, who tells some perpetrators: "it would be better for you if a great millstone were fastened around your neck and you were drowned in the depth of the sea."[83] How to address these seemingly conflictive titles will be one of the issues addressed in the next chapter.

81. Matt 5:4, 11.

82. Luke 23:34.

83. Matt 18:6. For prescient commentary on this verse, see Myers and Enns, *Ambassadors of Reconciliation*, 1:59–61.

11

Afterlife Dilemmas: Identity, Atrocity, and Divine Embrace

If Becker had escaped German justice, I felt that at least he could be given his appropriate place in historians' hell.[1]

A TEST CASE FOR UNIVERSAL SALVATION

In an account of Sudan's devastating civil war, one of the lost boys of Sudan, Alepho Deng, recalls an encounter with a five-and-a-half-year-old girl who had "hobbled up to [him] like a weak and wounded gazelle." Curious about her condition, he asked a relative, Angong, about her. Because Alepho was then six-and-a-half years old and so "nearly a man and this is a time of war," Angong told him the girl's story. During a raid on their village, an attacker tried to take the girl with him while she "clung to a small bush screaming in terror so it was difficult for him to remove her hands."

---

1. Browning, *Remembering Survival*, 2. According to Browning, Becker played a key role in the "liquidation of the Jewish ghetto in Wierzbnik on October 27, 1942—an action in which 4,000 Jews were sent to their deaths in the gas chambers of Treblinka, some sixty to eighty Jews were murdered on the spot, and about 1,600 Jews were sent to three slave-labor camps..." (1). Becker escaped postwar justice, despite extensive witness testimony at his trial, dismissed on various technicalities under a presiding judge, Wolf-Dietrich Ehrhardt, with deep Nazi sympathies (289–90).

"You a stupid little girl," the man shouted. "I will give you the medicine you will never forget." He stooped over her and pulled out his penis. We screamed but there was nothing her mother or I could do. They had us tied lying on our stomachs and held us back with guns. The man tried to dig his penis into the girl, but he couldn't get it in while he was holding her down too. He got up and tied her hands to that small bush. He pushed it in and pushed and pushed on her with his full weight. At first she struggled and screamed, but a few minutes later the loud cries stopped. The little girl had passed out.[2]

Without mitigating the need for justice in this world and the calling to heal victims like that little girl, I want to examine two opposing afterlife claims within Christianity while keeping in mind such victims of atrocity.[3] It is my contention that theodicy (and so credible theism) needs to retain the possibility for "hell," though I do not pretend to have any definitive explanation of what "hell" is or how it "operates." I also agree with Pollefeyt's assertion that "after Auschwitz, the theological task is to avoid both *apokatastasis* and Manicheanism [characterized by a clear division of "us" (as holy) and "them" (as evil) with no possibility for forgiveness]; it is to keep God's justice and mercy in tension, to experience and think about them together."[4] What follows, therefore, in the next few sections is an attempt to maintain this tension while focusing on a victim of atrocity's postmortem encounter with God. My main concern is examining the context for articulating how the suffering and crushed of this world could be healed while grappling with the issues of identity, memory, forgiveness, and justice. To do so, I also want to examine how and whether universal salvation (*apokatastasis*) in particular solves or exacerbates the theodicy problem.

I am clearly trespassing on highly suspect ground and ultimately agree with the contention of Ched Myers and Elaine Enns: "In the end, our theological speculations on the shape of God's eschatological judgment should be modest, even perhaps agnostic. This is terrain

---

2. Deng, Deng, and Ajak, *They Poured Fire on Us*, 97–98.

3. For a concise examination of soteriology and the world religions in the context of religious pluralism, see Gillis, *Pluralism*, 101–32. See also Hick, *Death and Eternal Life*.

4. Pollefeyt, "In Response to Haas and Manemann," 78–79.

beyond the metaphors, and we should tread there meekly."[5] Milton hoped his "plant eyes" could be "irradiate[d]" by the Spirit to "see and tell / Of things invisible to mortal sight."[6] I, of course, claim no such inspiration. And yet, silence, or even dogged trust, does not seem to be a sufficient moral response in light of what Mario Aguilar calls "a hermeneutic of bones at the periphery." Such a hermeneutical approach turns to the unburied bones of the victims of the Rwandan genocide, for example, to seek answers, perhaps even to decipher "divine interpretation."[7] Just as bones have much to tell a forensic psychologist, so, too, may they reveal much for the theistic searcher. The evidence, however, is rarely comforting. When confronting the extent of suffering and evil in this world, a theist must acknowledge that the viability of faith is grounded in the *hows* and *whys* of postmortem Divine responses. These responses, of course, remain inscrutable to those of us still in this world. And yet, it is not amiss to articulate what one hopes those responses will be as reflected in the sacred texts and traditions inscribed in one's religious faith.

Without downplaying the "power of God's love,"[8] moreover, I also want to examine the claim that if our unique identities carry over into the next life, then it is likely there will be individuals who reject God, who choose sin, and who imprison themselves in extreme egotistical, narcissistic hatred of all that is good and all that has the potential to heal. While not necessarily Dante's Inferno, hell is everything one creates and chooses for oneself against God's will. It is a distorted mirror of one's distorted desires. Or as Ronald Paulson writes: "Hell is the interface of suffering-evil and doing-evil."[9]

Bear in mind that reflecting upon the postmortem encounter with God is of preeminent importance in the context of atrocity and theodicy. Remove the possibility for this encounter, as Phillips wants to contend, and every theodicy collapses. As I have argued, there can be no meaningful theism without striving to develop a viable theodicy.

5. Myers and Enns, *Ambassadors of Reconciliation*, 1:100.

6. Milton, *Paradise Lost*, II.52–55 (1520).

7. Aguilar, *Theology, Liberation and Genocide*, 11.

8. Pollefeyt, "Forgiveness after the Holocaust," 70.

9. Paulson, *Sin and Evil*, 48.

TOGETHER AT LAST IN HEAVEN: HITLER, THE DEVIL, AND THE BLESSED MOTHER

Advocates of *apokatastasis panton* (the restoration of all things) point to a few scriptural passages that may speak of God redeeming all evil. Origen is usually cited as a main early proponent of universalism,[10] while some contemporary advocates include Thomas Talbott, Marilyn McCord Adams,[11] and Jürgen Moltmann. Not surprisingly, the Bible is cited by proponents and skeptics of universal salvation.

While Moltmann, for example, notes that the term *apokatastasis panton* only appears in Acts 3:21[12] but does not clearly refer to universal salvation, he contends that he finds other scriptural passages that seem to refute the notion of "a judgment with a double outcome." He cites passages like Eph 1:10: "to unite all things in Christ, things in heaven and things on earth"; Col 1:20: "to reconcile to himself all things, whether on earth or in heaven, making peace by the blood of his cross"; and Phil 2:10–11: "that at the name of Jesus every knee should bow, in heaven and on earth and under the earth, and every tongue confess that Jesus Christ is Lord, to the glory of God the Father."[13] Others like Talbott focus on Paul's Epistle to the Romans.[14]

One could respond that from Paul's Letter to the Colossians, Paul does admit that Christ enables us to "be holy and blameless and irreproachable before him." However, there is an important stipulation: "provided that [we] continue securely established and steadfast in the faith."[15] This additional clause is imperative: one must maintain holiness; otherwise, one cannot be presented as holy and blameless. Similarly, while the quote above from Ephesians could be used for universal salvation, the same letter more clearly proclaims: "Be sure of this, that no fornicator or impure person, or one who is greedy (that

10. See Bettenson, ed., *Early Christian Fathers*, 257.

11. McCord Adams, *Horrendous*, 127.

12. Moltmann rightly notes that Peter's use in Acts of the phrase "the restoration of all things" cannot be cited as biblical support for universal salvation. While the passage seems to imply that such a claim originated with the prophets, Peter adds: "Moses said . . . 'And it will be that everyone who does not listen to that prophet will be utterly rooted out of the people'" (Acts 3:23) (Moltmann, *Coming of God*, 240).

13. Moltmann, *Coming of God*, 240–41.

14. See, in particular, the three essays of Thomas Talbott in *Universal Salvation*, 1–52.

15. Col 1:23.

is, an idolater) has any inheritance in the kingdom of God."[16] Lastly, the Epistle to the Philippians also notes: "For many live as the enemies of the cross of Christ; I have often told you of them, and now I tell you even with tears. Their end is destruction."[17] The vagueness in the language "of all things" that Moltmann cites, therefore, is given more concrete sentencing elsewhere in the epistles.

Of the passages Moltmann quotes, the one from Phil 2:10 is the most interesting. I cannot envisage someone confessing that "Jesus Christ is Lord" in any meaningful sense without then embarking on the path to salvation. In this light, one would have to make sense of what Paul refers to by "confession" above.[18] In Mark's Gospel, the demons and evil spirits name Christ,[19] but they certainly do not love and worship him. At his command, their "knees" may bend, but not their "hearts" and "minds." In light of the other Pauline passages, however, it seems that the act of confessing Jesus's divine status does not guarantee salvation.

If there is a cohesive and sustained message of universal salvation in the Bible, I remain skeptical.[20] Someone may want to desire universal salvation, but the Bible is not exactly one's best advocate and support. However, universalists raise important philosophical and moral issues which attest to their position's appeal and are ones theodicists must address.

WHY UNIVERSALISM REMAINS RHETORICALLY POWERFUL

The Bible's ambiguous support of universalism does not completely disprove a universalist's provocative challenges. Talbott, for example,

---

16. Eph 5:5.

17. Phil 3:18–19.

18. Thomas Talbott cites J. B. Lightfoot to contend that the Greek verb that Paul uses for confessing also connotes praise and thanksgiving when used throughout the Septuagint ("Christ Victorious," 23).

19. Mark 1:24; 5:7.

20. To his credit, Moltmann also cites various passages from the gospels and the Pauline Letters that "address a double outcome" like the story of the rich man and Abraham in Luke 16:23 or the notion of an "everlasting fire that is not quenched" in Mark 9:48. However, he concludes that "universal salvation *and* a double outcome of judgment are therefore both well attested biblically." I am less convinced of this claim.

asks how people can be condemned to hell if they remain held captive by some disordered desire or ignorance. He contends that if one is not fully informed and capable of accepting or rejecting God, then any punishment would be unjust and irrational. "Do you really believe that the difference between you and the world's worst criminals, lies in the superior character of your own free choices?"[21] It is a "dreadful" question, like Solzhenitsyn's, who writes: "And just so we don't go around flaunting too proudly the white mantle of the just, let everyone ask himself: If my life had turned out differently, might I not have become just such an executioner?"[22]

While these are humbling questions, a theodicist must support the notion of our fundamental autonomy and responsibility in order to avoid tainting everyone as equally culpable. Of what value and goodness is creation if everyone can be a murderer and willing participant in genocide? How can one speak of the Holy Spirit as an "agency-enabler," as Adams writes, if forces of darkness will always overcome our divine calling to be loving and self-giving? As the atheist Primo Levi, echoing the theist Wiesel above, remarks: "I do know that I was a guiltless victim and I was not a murderer. I know that the murderers existed, not only in Germany, and still exist, retired or on active duty, and that to confuse them with their victims is a moral disease or an aesthetic affectation or a sinister sign of complicity . . ."[23]

Against Talbott, reaching a state of full knowledge about God and the capacity to choose God, still involves a desire and choice. One needs to be open to receiving and accepting such grace, which may be permanent, universal, and gratuitous,[24] but is not coercing and self-annihilating. While the conflict between God's desire that we accept such transformative knowledge and the reality of our free will may be disproportionate, one should not underestimate the human will in whose power the fact of the crematoria of Auschwitz mingles along with the moral strivings of St. Francis or Rabbi Akiba. As Monika Hellwig writes: "The encounter with the living God refines, purifies, and transforms those who are open to conversion, but destroys those

---

21. Talbott, "Reply to My Critics," 260.

22. Solzhenitsyn, *Gulag Archipelago*, 75.

23. Levi, *Drowned and Saved*, 48–49.

24. See Galvin, "Sin and Grace," 137.

who persist in asserting the self as independent of God and of God's reign in the world of creatures."[25]

Furthermore, according to Parry and Partridge, Talbott and other universalists argue that it is "awkward to imagine that God would send people to a hell that has the effect of hardening its occupants against him when he could . . . have a hell that would educate them and draw them towards him."[26] Phrasing the issue in this way, however, is misleading. First, while one should never underestimate the enduring love of God and the possibility that the most morally depraved individual may repent and seek forgiveness, to remove the possibility for hell not only desecrates the meaning and purpose of God's created world but undermines any theodic attempt that aims to remain faithful to the traumatized cries of victims of atrocity. Without any ultimate consequences, without the divine judgment of those individuals who have committed brazen acts "free" of remorse, the cries of victims from atrocities like the Armenian genocide are doubly ignored and doubly violated. Thus, the connections among autonomy, responsibility, and consequences are severed.

Secondly, who is to say that hell is not self-punishment instituted by one's deluded rejection of God? The onus here should not be on God but the individuals who have made themselves impervious to God's embrace. Such a response, however, calls us to compassion, and to try to understand why certain people commit atrocious acts. We may employ various psychoanalytic and psychological approaches and bear in mind that our genetic makeup (as some evolutionary psychologists may claim) and our social and familial environment often play a crucial role in how we mold our character.[27] Although spoken in a political context, Rousseau's famous remark—"Man was born free, and he is everywhere in chains"[28]—remains fairly accurate today from a theological, psychological, economic, and political standpoint. Nevertheless, the majority of us are blessed (and burdened) with enough capacity for choice to exercise our free will through delibera-

25. Hellwig, "Eschatology," 368.

26. Parry and Partridge, *Universal Salvation*, xxviii.

27. For an overview of perspectives on the causes and nature of evil from some of the prominent figures in evolutionary psychology, evolutionary biology, psychoanalysis, social theory, feminist theory, liberation theology, and other sources, see Cooper, *Dimensions of Evil*.

28. Rousseau, *Social Contract*, 49.

tion, intention, and action so as to be (in some way) responsible for what we do to others and ourselves.

Moreover, even if hell were conceived as a means of educating victims, this would still not determine that all victims would choose to accept and integrate such values, especially if continuity of identity is maintained.

ON EARTH AS IT IS NOT IN HEAVEN?

In chapter 5, McCord Adams argued how God's imagination and boundless love "will convince us"[29] of the overall value and goodness of our lives. If anyone, God could persuade us to change our ways and thoughts, but questions remain about the context, approach, and meaning of such "convincing." One of the key issues here is what would make individuals desire in heaven what they may not have desired on earth if such persons are recognizably the same people, and God does not coerce conversion. In response to the Sadducees' convoluted and deceitful question about the woman who had been married to seven brothers through the practice of levirate marriage, Jesus tells them that the "worthy"[30] will be like angels in heaven, and so there will be no marrying.[31]

This passage implies we will be qualitatively different beings (at least in some aspects) in heaven. However, as Phillips[32] also noted: if we are like angels, are we therefore no longer like us? And if we are no longer like us, then what or who are we? The postmortem encounter, it seems, becomes even more opaque and impossible to speculate about. Moreover, if our premortem identities and relationships are seemingly distinct from our postmortem ones, then the value of this world is again brought into question. This world formed who we are. If this identity is so radically changed, what was the purpose of enduring this world's tragedies?

---

29. McCord Adams, *Horrendous*, 127.

30. Matt 21:34.

31. Mark 12:25. The happily married among us tend not to take this passage literally. The context of a levirate marriage and the Sadducees' denial of an afterlife must also be remembered. On the issue of Jesus and divorce, see Swidler, *Jesus Was a Feminist*, 28.

32. Phillips, *Problem of Evil*, 88–90.

Perhaps, the dissolution of marriage (and thus a part of some individuals' identities, as Phillips maintained) cuts to the root of the universalist argument: everyone is created in the image of God, everyone is loved by God, and everyone is called to God and is redeemed by the blood of the cross. Distinctions fade away. In this sense, the language of "saint" and "innocent" may seem problematic and irrelevant, an issue I will address below.

RETAINING THE "INNOCENT" AND THE "SAINT"

Saints are not always perfect, and even those involved in massacring Jews and concealing Nazi crimes of atrocity are in need of "spiritual care," as Colonel Montua of the Police Regiment Center wrote to battalion and company commanders in regards to their officers.[33] Moreover, recall Sobrino and Gutiérrez's honest assessment of the poor: they, too, are often sinners.[34] And as Pollefeyt writes: "[Post-Holocaust ethics] should deal with the complex genesis of good and evil, and the daily steps that eventually lead to demonic or heroic acts, steps that ultimately bring each of us to be moral or immoral human beings."[35] As my qualified support of the *privatio boni* tradition shows, I believe in the inherent dignity of every human person made in the image of God, which calls for the hope and belief that even the most depraved human being can repent. Such a hope also admits that some perpetrators, for example, have been mentally ill, or have been victims themselves, as former child soldier Ishmael Beah testified in front of the UN Economic and Social Council: "I have been rehabilitated now, so don't be afraid of me. I am not a soldier anymore; I am a child."[36]

In Irmtraud Heike's article on female concentration camp guards, numerous reasons are given for German women who chose to be guards, and the job path was often quite ordinary. Heike writes: "Advertisements for employment as a guard were typically placed in newspapers, and advisers in employment offices drew attention to vacancies in concentration camps. On applying for a post as a female guard in Ravensbrück a woman would receive an information sheet

---

33. Browning, *Ordinary Men*, 14.
34. Sobrino, *Where Is God?* 74.
35. Pollefeyt, "Response," 279.
36. Beah, *Long Way Gone*, 199.

in which the duties were extolled as 'light physical work.'"[37] Other advertisements emphasized Ravensbrück "as a new place of work within easy traveling distance."[38] Monetary pressures and nationalistic pride were other major reasons that happened to coincide with a deep dislike of the non-German, and often, a hatred of Jews in particular. When one is reminded of the bureaucratization and the seeming ordinariness in the path to becoming a concentration camp guard, one is struck by the familiarity of that job process. The perpetrator begins to be humanized again.

Although we need to overcome the temptation to demonize an individual (avoiding what Pollefeyt calls Manichaenism above, and elsewhere diabolization[39]), I believe there are examples of genuine innocence and goodness and sufficient responsibility and autonomy to hold most of us accountable for what we do.[40] I cannot know what I would do in a situation like the Rwandan genocide, but I know there have been those who have acted morally, if not heroically and nobly. Because of them, we must especially question those who concocted, organized, and unleashed the terror. Those caught up in the whirlwind may be a different matter.

In Miroslav Volf's *Exclusion and Embrace*, he asks: "How will we disentangle those who are innocent from those who are blameworthy in the knotted histories of individuals, let alone the narratives of whole cultures and nations? The longer the conflict continues, the more both parties find themselves sucked into the vortex of mutually reinforcing victimization, in which the lone party appears more virtuous only because, being weaker, it has less opportunity to be cruel."[41] While Volf's specific context in this quote is the theology of forgiveness amidst the Balkan wars, I am interested in how Volf speaks of innocence within such conflicts for the purpose of my discussion of the afterlife. For Volf, the dichotomy of victim/victimizer is problematic, as a "blameless victim" is only one who may not have the opportunity

---

37. Heike, "Female Concentration Camp Guards," 125.

38. Ibid., 126.

39. Pollefeyt, "Kafkaesque World," 213. For Pollefeyt's use of these terms in the context of the Israeli-Palestinian conflict, see his essay "Between a Dangerous Memory," 135–46.

40. For a brief clarification to this remark, see Svendsen, *Philosophy of Evil*, 196.

41. Volf, *Exclusion and Embrace*, 103.

to be cruel. "No one is exempt,"[42] as he writes, for "no one is exempt of sin." In Volf's theology, admitting our solidarity in sin becomes a further means of recognizing our need for others and God. There is no presumed goodness, "no escape from noninnocence, either for victim or perpetrator or for a 'third party.'"[43] He also distinguishes between equality and solidarity in sin,[44] denying the polarity of good and evil by stressing that no one should be excluded. He writes: "The answer I hope would be that at the core of the Christian faith lies the persuasion that the 'others' need not be perceived as innocent in order to be loved, but ought to be embraced even when they are perceived as wrongdoers."[45]

These are moving and powerful assertions. And in a conflict, especially a civil war, where atrocities are committed on all sides, such an outlook would seem to be the most helpful and practical towards achieving some type of stability, peace, and tentative embrace. What I object to is his unequivocal placement of all of us as sinners without more clarification or nuance. As Solzhenitsyn challenges, I may become such a perpetrator under certain conditions, and that is a powerful and humbling notion, but there have been individuals, tested by such fires, who, miraculously or doggedly, have stepped out (basically) unscathed.[46] To assert the great moral force of their lives we need to highlight the role of freedom and responsibility. And once we do that, we then must deal with those who have willingly committed heinous acts without remorse.

Recall Himmler's speech on October 4, 1943, to his subordinates: "Most of you know what it means to see a hundred corpses lie side by side, or five hundred, or a thousand. To have endured this—and excepting cases of human weakness—to have remained decent, that is what has made us hard. In our history, this is an unwritten and never-to-be-written page of glory."[47] One could dissect and analyze such a speech ad infinitum. And perhaps, Himmler has since acknowledged his sins before God. But as Wiesel notes: "In truth we have not left the

42. Ibid., 81.
43. Ibid., 84.
44. Ibid., 82.
45. Ibid., 85.
46. See, for example, Malham, *By Fire into Light*.
47. Quoted in Fackenheim, *Mend the World*, 186.

kingdom of the night. Or rather: It refuses to let us go. It is inside us. They wait for us. They help us by forcing us to appreciate things and sensations at their just value. They are judging us."[48] If the dead victims are judging us, they are no doubt judging the likes of Himmler, too. Jesus did not say anything to the other criminal who rebuked him. Maybe there was a conversion in the afterlife; maybe for Himmler, too. But without a Saul-like conversion, if Himmler is still to be Himmler, his salvation, which may be a hope for some, is no guarantee, as the universalists would claim. Moreover, if victims, who are often nameless and voiceless (like the little girl encountered at the opening of this chapter), are to be healed, some tangible, conciliatory act of God is necessary to right such wrongs. Such a concrete response may lead to profound transformation for both victim and perpetrator, but it may also mean that there will be "weeping and gnashing of teeth."[49] Either way, such justice will not be enough. For everyone, but especially for the victims and those perpetrators of atrocities who seek forgiveness, there is the desperate need for divine embrace.

GOD'S EMBRACE

In this section, I will not speculate on God's encounter with a Mao or Hitler, though these remarks could pertain to a perpetrator of atrocity who has expressed remorse for his or her deeds and seeks forgiveness. As Fulgence, a Catholic "deacon" convicted of genocide in Rwanda, remarks: "I know that only God can understand what we did. He alone has looked at every detail. He alone knows who drenched his arms and who did not. And regarding those last, it will not take Him long to count them up."[50] But especially for the innocent victim, such an encounter must be a loving embrace of transformation and healing, a space for the individual to grieve and question as much as to be solaced and receive "answers."

Some, for example, may contend that the encounter itself with God would heal. Meister Eckhart proclaims: "Yet I declare that if ever there were a single person who in intellectual vision and in truth should glimpse for a moment the bliss and joy therein, all his sufferings and all God intended that he should suffer would be a trifle,

---

48. Wiesel, *And the Sea Is Never Full*, 254.

49. Luke 13:28.

50. Fulgence, interviewed by Hatzfeld, *Machete Season*, 142.

a mere nothing to him—in fact I declare it would be pure joy and comfort to him."[51] But that is the believer speaking. The despairing and the broken deserve "more" than the rest of us, especially if they are still dominated by such sensations during that postmortem encounter. Such an encounter may not be a magical erasure of all that was unpleasant, or even horrific, but it should heal and redeem.

Perhaps God reassures victims that they were loved throughout their ordeals, as Adams argues, but because the victims felt abandoned in their earthly afflictions, will any words or action in heaven completely fill that void for everyone? Recall Donat's convictions from chapter 5. In a pastoral context, especially when addressing the most vulnerable in our world, the aim could be reaching a middle ground that lauds God's love and power to redeem, in addition to maintaining the possibility that some experiences and memories of loss and suffering cannot be fully compensated, justified, or explained away. Such a perspective for some individuals may be spiritually and personally needed to recall and give meaning to that loss and fissure. Other individuals may instead pray for such memories to be cleansed and "forgotten." There have been some experiences so brutal and dehumanizing that the best healing could be the gift to "forget" them completely. After his rehabilitation from being a child soldier, Ishmael Beah writes of going dancing at a pub but suddenly being overwhelmed by violent memories from his past: "I didn't want to talk anymore. A memory of a town we had attacked during a school dance had been triggered. I could hear the terrified cries of teachers and students, could see the blood over the dance floor. Allie tapped me on the shoulder and brought me back to the present." [52] From the standpoint of those murdered teachers and students, such a "final" memory without healing could also be a dominant and demoralizing identity marker that overshadows any good in their lives and their ability to be healed.

In this context Miroslav Volf has written: "If our memory is made and remade of gathered fragments, the non-remembrance of suffered wrongs will not violate our sense of identity."[53] Like McCord Adams, Volf's aim is to show how healing is possible for perpetrators

---

51. Meister Eckhart, "Sermon 2," 38–39.

52. Beah, *Long Way Gone*, 184.

53. Volf, *End of Memory*, 198.

and victims of atrocious suffering. While his claim that memories of wrongs will "not come to mind" in heaven[54] may be one way to articulate such a possibility, I would argue that it is also important to stress that one's memories are not isolated, unconnected nodes of perception so that one can simply recreate or "forget" certain memories without repercussions to present and future identity and without severing continuity with the reality of previous memories. Some of my recollections and how I interpret them may change or be forgotten, but our identities are formed through the interpretation and retention of certain key, fundamental memories, sometimes at a conscious or unconscious level. Remove too many of these strands and nodes, and identity becomes fractured and dissolved. For postmortem embrace to be meaningful, a person's identity must embody honesty and integrity to one's entire life, whether as healer or sinner, victim or perpetrator, or more realistically, some medley of each.

Regardless, if the human person's identity and autonomy are to be fully respected, God must come to a victimized person more in the guise of the "soft murmuring sound" heard by Elijah, or the calling of Samuel, than "out of the tempest" in Job or "in a blazing fire out of a bush."[55] The role of the Incarnation and the life of Christ provide a dizzying array of possibilities to speculate about and imagine this encounter. Christians, therefore, hope that the same God (in the human person of Jesus of Nazareth) who insisted that Zacchaeus "hurry and come down" from the sycamore tree; who wanted the little girl to eat after he raised her from the dead; who wept after Lazarus's death; who restored the Syrophoenician's daughter on account of her mother's words after his initially curt reply; who agonized in Gethsemane; and who groaned in torturous pain on the cross, can apply the right tone, approach, and response to each individual's need.[56]

It is this Godhead who suffers—and has tasted loss, agony, and brokenness—who, according to Christians, offers a means both to unite in intimacy and solidarity with fellow victims and provides the means and access to lead to healing and transformation. It is this belief, which again resides in a speculation anchored to Scripture

---

54. Ibid., 145. In the context of the beatific vision and heaven such memories will no longer come to one's mind.

55. 1 Kgs 19:12; 1 Sam 3:1–10; Job 38:1; Exod 3:2.

56. Luke 19:5; Mark 5:43; John 11:35; Mark 7:26–30; Matt 26:37; Mark 15:37.

and tradition, that illumines the greatest hope for Christians, the most promising image for how all individuals in need of such healing and embrace can find it. Forgiveness, of course, resides at the heart of this hope.

SHOULDN'T FORGIVENESS GET THE LAST WORD?

The question above is an important one, but consider Elie Wiesel's remarks at the commemoration of the fiftieth anniversary of the liberation of Auschwitz: "God of forgiveness, do not forgive those who created this place. God of mercy, have no mercy on those who killed Jewish children here. Do not forgive the murderers or their accomplices whose work was to kill . . . Remember the nocturnal processions of children, so many children . . . God of compassion, have no compassion for those who had none."[57]

These are chilling words. Wiesel was right to preface these remarks with his comment that they "will offend some Christians." John Roth speculates whether Wiesel's words would still hold for him if a perpetrator were repentant, but Roth also adds that if God were to forgive an unrepentant perpetrator, God would become "complicit with that perpetrator" and: "[E]ven if all Holocaust perpetrators were genuinely repentant and all Holocaust victims had shown mercy, God could still not rightly grant forgiveness for the entire Holocaust. God could forgive the wrong done to God, but the victims' prerogative to grant or to withhold forgiveness for what happened to them would still be theirs and not God's."[58]

I do not know if the line separating the wrong done to God and humanity is so easily divided. However, in the context of key differences in Jewish-Christian dialogue, Berger and Patterson have written: "[T]he Jewish tradition attests that there are two types of sin, each of which requires a different agent of forgiveness. There are sins committed by one human against another (*beyn adam l'adam*) and sins committed by humans against God (*beyn adam le makom*). Only the person sinned against can forgive the sinner, and only God can forgive the trespasses against the divine. Consequently the Jewish understanding of forgiveness requires a personal, one-to-one encounter."[59]

---

57. Wiesel, *And the Sea Is Never Full*, 194.

58. Roth, *Ethics during and after the Holocaust*, 134.

59. Berger and Patterson, *Jewish-Christian Dialogue*, 134–35. See also Verbin,

This one-to-one encounter may not always be possible, although, as Maimonides has classically written, there are various rituals or liturgical acts one can perform to show *teshuvah* (turning back to God; repentance) even if one does not know whom one offends or the victim is no longer alive. Of utmost importance is for the person guilty to show true repentance. "What is repentance?" Maimonides asks in *The Laws of Repentance*. "Repentance is when one who sinned now refrains from doing the sin, and he removes it from his thoughts and resolves never to commit it again."[60] One of the best testaments to true repentance is when a person finds himself or herself in the same situation but refuses to commit the wrongful deed.

However, as Peter Haas remarks: "There is no mechanism within Jewish law for extending forgiveness to perpetrators who did not, and cannot repent."[61] Thus, Wiesel was right to preface his remarks with the comment that they "will offend some Christians" who may immediately (and problematically) think of the theory of vicarious atonement. [62] At the very least, I agree with Wiesel that protest in the name of the victims is one of the ways to balance and join justice and forgiveness. In Jewish thought, a crime against an individual is a crime against God because humankind is made in the image of God. However, while Wiesel's position clearly would condemn universalism, Roth's question of the unrepentant Holocaust perpetrator is at the heart of my inquiry here, especially on the possibility of the unforgivable. As Charles Griswold writes: "The issue of 'unforgivability' arises with respect to levels of evil that elicit resentment so deep as to be accompanied by rage, indeed outrage."[63] Claudine Kayitesi, who survived the Rwandan genocide, tells Jean Hatzfeld: "I myself would have no trouble watching [the Hutus who murdered] be shot, one after the

---

"Forgiving God," 201–16.

60. Maimonides, *Laws of Repentance*. See also Haas, "Forgiveness, Reconciliation, and Jewish Memory after Auschwitz," 5–15.

61. Haas, "Forgiveness, Reconciliation, and Jewish Memory after Auschwitz," 14.

62. The theory of vicarious atonement is riddled with moral and theological holes. Turning to Dun Scotus' primacy of Christ, Ilia Delio writes: "Scotus maintains that God became human in Jesus out of love (rather than because of human sin) because God wanted to express God's self in a creature who would be a masterpiece and who would love God perfectly in return" (*Franciscan View of Creation*, 34).

63. See Griswold, *Forgiveness*, 91. Notice its link with Card's definition of atrocity, above. See also the challenging essays in Caputo et al., *Questioning God*.

other, in public. They cut hard enough to break their own arms, in broad daylight. Forgiving them means nothing human. That may be the will of God, but not ours."[64]

The arguments in the previous sections emphasized that the value and significance of God's plan for creation is not sullied or riddled with failure if some individuals are incapable and unwilling of turning to God and seeking mercy, forgiveness, and judgment. Biblically I tried to contend that few if any passages make a clear, unambiguous case for universal salvation and that passages that seem to argue against a double outcome are immediately convoluted with contradictory statements. I was also concerned with issues of personal identity and autonomy and the meaning of this world if God will simply convince all of us that life was good on the whole or prove that we must renounce our ways.

In *Evil and the Justice of God,* N. T. Wright interprets the book of Revelation to argue for hope in the creation of a new world, one similar to ours but without all the loss, suffering, and pain, thus overcoming any fears of total discontinuity. In such a world, we remain ourselves but are morally renewed and reinvigorated.[65] The possibility to be freed of one's inordinate resentment or loss or to be healed of one's inability to trust would indeed be heavenly for so many. Therefore, the issue is how to maintain an identity that may have been shaped by some potentially horrific or searing memories and yet be immersed in the love and mercy of God.

Justice in heaven and justice on earth will necessarily be of a qualitatively different character because of the presence of God. I have argued that a victim's identity is in part shaped by (or against) those horrific memories, and so effacing them (especially without addressing them) could distort any sense of the continuity of one's self-identity. At the same time, I have also acknowledged that some memories are so destructive and depersonalizing that "removing" them may be the greatest gift one can receive. As noted above, Miroslav Volf argues that "memories of suffered wrong will not come to the minds of the citizens of the world to come, for in it they will perfectly enjoy God and one another in God."[66] Such memories, he contends, do not shape but

64. Hatzfeld, *Strategy of Antelopes,* 16.

65. Wright, *Evil and the Justice of God,* 142.

66. Volf, *End of Memory,* 177.

simply erode or paralyze one's stable identity. Immersed in bitterness and regret, they may hinder that perfect enjoyment of God. Instead, the horror participants are eventually freed from the imprisonment of such memories because of the context of heaven.

While such memories must be faced, it is because some victims cannot forget these traumatic atrocities, that there must be a suitable means and safe environment for the victim to come to terms with those atrocities. In light of this, I have argued for the relevance of a God on the side of the victims of oppression and injustice. For Christians, Jesus of Nazareth embodies this divine solidarity as a fellow sufferer in this world, for whom Golgotha did not have the final word. Regardless, for all victims of mass atrocity and horrendous suffering, the postmortem encounter with God is envisioned as a sanctuary for healing, and through the moral renewal Wright discusses above, a means to become vindicated and graced with the capability to forgive.

As Staub and Pearlman write: "Forgiveness is essential for reconciliation to take place and both arise from and contribute to healing."[67] While heaven should be a site of reconciliation and moral renewal, some people may remain closed to accepting or seeking forgiveness, and so reconciliation may not always lead to an embrace of perpetrator and victim. Turning back to Wiesel, if the pain and anger (he was adamant that it was not hatred) is still vivid fifty years later, what will have to occur for reconciliation from the victims' perspective, even in a heavenly context? If a perpetrator is unrepentant, one can allege that this does not defeat the ultimate aim and good of creation, though one should still grieve for the lost and those who stray because their decision to turn away from God and life remains a tragedy. However, what if a victim refuses or is simply unable to forgive a repentant perpetrator, as Roth asks above?

After one has been embraced by God and gifted with moral renewal, perhaps one's attitude toward the perpetrator will no doubt be changed, and so, too, may be the issue of universal salvation. Once this moral renewal occurs, we again confront the issue of individuals unable or unwilling to partake of that heavenly bliss. It would seem to follow that once some individuals reached such a state of moral renewal, they would not rest until their perpetrators were healed. However,

---

67. Staub and Pearlman, "Healing, Reconciliation, and Forgiveness," 205.

even if we acknowledge that there is continuity in identity despite this moral renewal in heaven, thinking further along these lines is tantalizingly out of reach. After the renewal, in the midst of a new creation, there will also be a new language. We can only stutter and stumble through such a language here on earth, so these few words will have to suffice. Hopefully, such words can provide some solace for victims like the little girl referred to at the beginning of this chapter and for those like Wiesel who have had to live and reflect upon their losses for so many years. Hopefully, such a language and context can enable one to speak of such a girl being healed and embraced by God and for the anger and questions of a Wiesel to be justified and resolved.

WHY UNIVERSAL SALVATION SULLIES THE THEODIC PROJECT

After an injustice in this world, we can choose to re-violate a victim by remaining silent, exacerbate the suffering through some intentional act, or to quell such suffering through solidarity with others, what Oscar Romero calls "the violence of love."[68] This love—violent only in its passion for reconciliation and justice—becomes a response linked to knowing the past and then acting responsively and peacefully once the veil of ignorance is removed. It calls for accepting the fact that our destiny is inextricably linked with the destinies of those victims upon whose shoulders we stand tall. As James Baldwin eloquently writes: "The truth concerning the White North American experience is to be deciphered in the hieroglyphic lashed onto the Black man's back . . . and this truth cannot be overcome until it is confronted."[69] While Baldwin writes of a specific discrimination, such hieroglyphics are imprinted upon all victims entombed with a truth that may not be discovered on its own. No human form of reparation or apology will right such wrongs, but recognition frees the potential for authentic communication and growth. To proclaim that all individuals will experience heavenly bliss regardless of circumstance or desire seems to mock and conceal the injustice that has already caused so much damage.

One also runs into a problem when one turns this hope of universal salvation into a dogma despite the possibility that some individuals

68. Romero, *Violence of Love*, 12.

69. Baldwin, *Evidence of Things Not Seen*, 47.

could refuse forgiveness and God's embrace. When a person can rape a baby or slaughter children, no possibility is inconceivable. Regarding such an individual, Michael Stoeber writes in *Reclaiming Theodicy*: "[H]*e or she might choose to maintain such an orientation indefinitely,* eternally languishing in his/her own immersion in self-isolationism. That is the possibility of hell. It is important that this *possibility* be included in one's theological framework."[70]

In the end, it is the possibility of hell—and not universal salvation—that salvages theodicy and so theological faith. Thus, I am mystified by accounts of survivors like Immaculée Ilibagiza, who forgave the unrepentant perpetrators who gruesomely slaughtered her family during the Rwandan genocide.[71] I agree that releasing such hatred and anger through the process and decision of forgiveness could be cathartic and that taking one's pound of flesh will often not heal and will not restore what was taken. Moreover, unlike the young girl referred to above, I have had no personal reason to begrudge anyone's "right" to heaven, let alone desire that someone remain locked in some hell of their choosing, in perpetuity. I admit I am probably treading on thin moral ground.[72] I candidly acknowledge that these doubts do not embody the ideals of forgiveness. I also agree with Pollefeyt that one must condemn religious Manichaenism—which claims "we" are the saved and "they" are the depraved—and resist forever burying perpetrators with the impossibility for repentance while the (still living) "victim" is somehow forever incapable of committing any wrong. Even a cursory glance at the gospels and Jesus's table fellowship with prostitutes, tax collectors, and other "sinners" should dispel any sense that humans can unequivocally distinguish the sheep from the goats, the wheat from the chaff.[73] And yet, I believe the theodicy project, an attempt to argue for the overall value of this world while maintaining a belief in a God of perfect love and power, is weakened—not emboldened—when everyone must be saved for any value or purpose to be maintained.

One may say, "Who cares about some 'project'?" But I am interested in the integrity of God's justice, the meaning and purpose of

70. Stoeber, *Reclaiming Theodicy*, 98–99.

71. See Ilibagiza, *Left to Tell*; Tuhabonye, *This Voice in My Heart*, 204.

72. As a Catholic, of course, my stand on this issue is orthodox. See Hellwig, "Eschatology," 367–68.

73. Matt 25:32; Matt 3:12.

creation, and the finite lives smothered and annihilated in this world. Maybe I am overly concerned about a human conception of justice, and I need to renounce trying to find tangible connections between our lives and identities in this world and the one beyond. But if this world does not matter; if our lives here ultimately do not impact what happens to us postmortem (because eventually everyone must be saved)—if it really is true that I am a drastically changed being and identity in heaven—then why did God become incarnate in Jesus and endure all that frustration, loss, suffering, and failure? Why did that little girl from Sudan have to be raped and why does having this freedom and responsibility remain vital for our purpose? If there was no urgency, if in the long run, both Bartimaeus and Pilate are eventually saved, if the thieves on Jesus's right and left are both with him in paradise, then why the pleadings, the prophecies, the parables, the plight of the passion play?

Lastly, in tandem with a disinterested faith, a faith that believes without seeking earthly reward or compensation, "radical forgiveness" may be the most distinctive and essential element of a religious stance amidst the reality of suffering. As to what role radical forgiveness should play in the context of the afterlife, I cannot help recalling victims like that little girl from Sudan above. Perpetrators of genocide like Fulgence claim that only God "knows who drenched his arms and who did not." However, I question anyone who contends that the little girl's assailant must be in heaven, especially with the possibility that he remains unrepentant without some coerced or drastic "convincing."

CONCLUSION

In the last two chapters, I have sought to frame key questions that these testimonies of mass atrocity raise and how theodicists have tried to respond or rephrase those questions or challenges. In the end, neither the theodicist nor the witness to devastating evil and suffering has the ultimate word on God. No human being can be granted that power and burden. Nevertheless, theodicists must heed and incorporate the stories of the lost and abandoned of this world into their lives and theologies. Such a commitment should test and clarify theological language to orient a theological practice that contributes towards healing. With such a practice comes the hope that one's religious faith is not a delusion but nourishes a rich, transformative context for individual and collective redemption and meaning. Likewise, those who have suffered so horrendously, including believers in God who have since felt abandoned and forsaken, must at least listen to the stories and accounts of these theodicists and the other victims who testify to God's presence and love. To close that possibility permanently could prevent the real chance for a breakthrough or change (in Catholic theology, the infusion of grace). It also may eternally (albeit unwittingly) grant to those perverse and atrocious acts a victory over any substantial or fundamental meaning of our world, our lives, and of (belief in) God.

To counter this possibility, a Christian theodicist should accentuate the life and example of Christ, who reveals the tendency and bias of God to practice the core love of the stranger and oppressed, infused with a commitment to truth and compassion. For this, Jesus pays the ultimate price; though for Christians, ironically, this price provides the means and the direction to live, in ever-greater assurance, a God-infused life with the possibility for eternal life. Such a response will also look to the beginning and end of a creation suffused with the love of God in which all that is created is good, with human beings fashioned in the Divine image and likeness. This revelation marks humanity with a purpose and goal. Our world, however, does not often reflect these ideals, even (or especially) for Job or Jesus of Nazareth, who embody the highest notions of that destiny and moral calling on earth. Again, for many, especially because of the magnitude of mass atrocity and the existence of horrific suffering, the postmortem encounter with a God of mercy and justice will become the lynchpin upon which the whole theodic system will turn, determining whether God and creation are ultimately good. For others, the pummelling of lives and of moral frameworks by such evil precludes the possibility for any meaningful redemption.

How to develop a viable theodic position based on sound argumentation and well-tested features, then, becomes my final task. In the final chapter, I will present a guide and interpretive framework through which to construct the most viable approach to the problem of theodicy. The question—and key issue—is whether such criteria does the justice of the victims, the justice of believers, and the justice of God due service.

12

Five Criteria for a Viable Theodicy

As soon as Zyclon B crystals came into contact with air, the deadly gas began to develop, spreading first at floor level and then rising to the ceiling. It was for this reason that the bottom layer of corpses always consisted of children as well as the old and the weak . . .[1]

I did not know it at the time, but God was carrying me on His back when I thought I was walking by myself.[2]

The two epigraphs above build upon the back-and-forth nature of the dialogue throughout this work between and among testimonies of mass atrocity and theodic accounts, while also embodying the conflicted, contested space within which any theodicist must labor. The first quote is from Filip Müller, an eyewitness account to the gassings and the crematoria of Auschwitz. The image is as grotesque as the observation is clinical and scientific. Such an image and reality seem to make all God-talk circumspect. The other quote is from Grace Akallo, a former child soldier of Uganda, who amidst her sufferings and torture and while desperately seeking to flee her captors, reflects upon her experiences and proclaims that God was supporting her and was present in the midst of such degradation and despair. These are the two types of extreme, polar assertions a theodicist encounters, along

1. Müller, *Eyewitness Auschwitz*, 117.
2. McDonnell and Akallo, *Girl Soldier*, 141.

with the myriad and more ubiquitous "gray zones" that uncomfortably contain elements of each position.[3] Having outlined the consequences of working within these opposing assertions in previous chapters, (contra Langer and others), I will now argue below why turning to testimonies of mass atrocity supports the task of theodicy. Drawing upon the most promising features of the theodic texts I looked at in Part 2, I will also present my five criteria for a Christian theodicy and will argue why each criterion is needed to develop a viable theodic position. I am not asserting that such features solve the problem of evil nor justify the existence of all types of evil. Instead, I offer them as theological resources to support one's faith position to be more credible and reasonable in light of such atrocities. Such resources are intended to combat the assault on meaning that gruesome evils inflict and enable a believer in God to turn to tested and pastorally sensitive approaches to face such reality honestly and openly but still hope and believe in a loving God who can heal the broken lives of this world and the suffering that has crushed and humiliated so many.

WHY TESTIMONIES OF MASS ATROCITY SUPPORT THEODIC ATTEMPTS

The introduction to this work began with a quote from Rabbi Unsdorfer, who questioned what right human beings had to try to understand God's ways. In my context, such a quote questions the moral right and value to engage in theodicy and prudently stresses the severity and inevitable limitations of such a task. It also resonates with antitheodicists, who claim that theodicy is a failed theoretical enterprise complicit in, or culpable for, defending the existence of some evil that should only be condemned and combated. In "justifying" certain evil, a theodicist is said to aid and abet an evil's existence or desecrate the morale and integrity of victims who have already suffered enough. For antitheodicists who are theists, such a practice may also impair belief in God by implying that God is constrained by our moral paradigms or conceptions, thus not speaking of God rightly and justly.

While I share some of the convictions of antitheodicists and appreciate Rabbi Unsdorfer's caution above, if such a warning were ever possible to heed, it cannot be morally followed today because of our greater awareness of the horrors of Majdanek, the Khmer Rouge, or

---

3. See Levi, *Drowned and the Saved*, 36–69.

the endemic poverty and disease that crushes so many in our world. Instead, faith in God demands that one seek understanding, pray for understanding, and have the courage to place one's theological beliefs and arguments, which can never encapsulate the reality of God, at the mercy of the desolate cries from the gulags, concentration camps, and other sites of mass atrocity and torment. As noted in chapter 1, while such conflicting cries should not ultimately decide what can and cannot be said about God, one would expect that such a focus and demand would further muddy the already messy enterprise of theodicy. Moreover, because I argued in chapter 10 that theodicy also shares similar aims with evangelizing and apologetics, challenges and doubts inflicted upon theodic arguments also fester at the root of an individual's faith and so the ability to defend or preach it. How, then, can I argue that such texts also support the task and possibility of a viable theodicy?

In this work I have incorporated these testimonies to purge and cleanse one's theodic arguments and language. I focused on the most extreme forms of evil so that every voice is included and all types of suffering are acknowledged. I also examined mass atrocity to place all theodicies on trial and so give potential credence to positions of anti-theodicy. As a theist, I was seeking to test my contention that theism needs a viable theodicy. If a viable theodicy fails, a viable theism would seem to fail, also. I therefore studied various theodic approaches to gauge if they could still be considered viable with knowledge of such horrendous suffering or in the midst of such agony. In the course of this work, it became clear that any theodic approach that carelessly, or generally, blames the victim or implies such suffering was necessary, purposive, or didactic must be considered dubious. I am not denying that even some hideous suffering could be rationalized as necessary, or purposive, or didactic, but am insisting that its existence remains a scandal and horror: utter abjection. Christ's resurrection does not glorify the cold, calculated torment inflicted through the crucifixion. The agony of Jesus of Nazareth, the anguish of his followers and onlookers, the complicity of individuals who orchestrated his sentence and the abuse that he suffered, are never justifiable in themselves. I thus agree with Phillips that language of justification amidst dire suffering is morally reprehensible. It is a scandal and a shame that Jesus was crucified, though one can take comfort in Jesus's life and convictions, which offers us a way and a path despite (not because of) the affliction that may follow.

These testimonies describe and are witness to abomination and horror. They are the nadir of the extremities humanity can perpetrate or must endure. Charlotte Delbo writes:

> There she is in the hollow of the ditch with her hands scratch-ing the ground, her feet looking for support, straining to lift her heavy head. Her face is now turned towards us. Her promi-nent cheekbones are violet, her swollen mouth a black violet, her eye sockets filled with dark shadows. Her face reflects naked despair.[4]

As Clendinnen acknowledges in *Reading the Holocaust*: "Those books I discuss are those which proved their value by providing me with the system of ladders I needed to scramble out over the abyss."[5] Unfortunately, I read these testimonies with the expectation, if not the result, that I would not scramble over the abyss but sink further and further into it. What I hoped would provide the ladder, if not the exit, was a potent theodicy, or failing that, a biblical story of some mean-ing. It is as if, to counteract the evil one encounters, one needs to arm one's memory with an analogous good, a complementary mechanism of salvation or liberation, while painfully aware that some of these wit-ness testimonies—some of these once living people—stare out at me from a void that refuses such palliative soothing. Like Christ and his silence toward Dostoyevsky's "Grand Inquisitor," these witnesses "lis-ten" to a theodicist's appeals, hope, and protestations that such biblical stories can combat a sense of helplessness in the face of evil. But they, of course, can say nothing. And it is that silence, the silence of these victims, which always threatens to render any theological enterprise null and void.

As is evident in this work, many victims deny the tenability of faith in God and present human beings as broken, conquered, and corrupted by their perpetrators. Perhaps, worst of all, such accounts reveal individuals coerced or manipulated into committing acts of cruelty and injustice against their fellow victims or family members. Deeming such a world "good" or "holy" seems to mock that reality. At the same time, one must be careful giving these highly manipulated

---

4. Delbo, *Auschwitz and After*, 26.

5. Clendinnen, *Reading the Holocaust*, 4.

and morally depraved scenarios (planned, enacted, and continually "improved" upon by the perpetrators) too much emphasis as a means to judge the worth of all humanity or the value of creation. How one acts in a concentration camp, for example, is not a valid indicator of one's morality or humanity. One must recognize that "there is a bottommost limit to ethical life."[6] A Jobian "test" of terror and evil reveals little about the victim. In the book of Job, the wager revealed more about the satan and God.

While responsibility can still be spoken of for many victims, I prefer to speak of the responsibility of many of the perpetrators and organizers. But as Fackenheim notes with the "counter-testimony" of Lewinska, and as Berkovits describes those who still believe despite the utter decrepitude and hopelessness of their situations, some maintain their integrity or their belief in God's presence. Some pray; some are converted; some insist that God not only "walked" with them but "carried" them. These are truth claims that "collide" with their polar opposite tales, but their existence means that one's faith, which remains immersed in mystery and grace, is not without "evidence" and supportive testimony. Maybe such testimonies are minimized as the exceptions to the "overwhelming evidence," as Langer argues,[7] but we still have their testimonies, and they too are voices that we must listen to and heed. For some survivors, there are reasons to believe. If Grace Akallo, after being a child soldier, speaks of God; or Harry Wu while a prisoner in the Chinese gulag; or Immaculée Ilibagiza amidst the Rwandan genocide; if one reads of the martyrdoms of a Rabbi Akiba or Karl Leisner; such testimonies (in such diverse and extreme circumstances), which do not subsume and silence the opposite stories, still offer a means to hope and argue that faith in God remains a viable stance. While atheists can come to an opposite conclusion, these accounts also debar anyone from claiming that all victims deny God's presence in these horrors, rendering theistic belief to be groundless and counter to evidence. Atheists must also rely upon faith and interpretation.

I have stressed throughout this work that a theodic response is viable based on how it responds and incorporates the inevitable gaps, fragments, and caesuras within one's faith stance on account of the

---

6. Pollefeyt, "Victims of Evil or Evil of Victims?" 68.

7. Langer, *Using and Abusing the Holocaust*, 4–5.

magnitude and extent of suffering in this world. Grounds for skepticism and protest will influence and color one's faith, but it is precisely such doubt that calls for a humble, post-Holocaust, pastoral approach. In the next section I will develop key benefits of this approach and outline features that a Christian theodicy must include for one's faith stance to be viable and rational.

THE CRITERIA

To an antitheodicist, my demand that theodic arguments be scrutinized by turning to witnesses of mass atrocity would seem to prove the failure of all theodicy, though some antitheodicists would still claim to be theists. I have argued that such a stance is not meaningful or possible.

There can be no theodic-agnostics. The problem of evil must be addressed, and an approach must be offered to develop how one can still speak of a meaningful faith despite, or because of, these horrors. I cannot envision a meaningful faith in God that claims that this world and creation are not worth justifying or can never be justified, thus implying that this world is malevolent or that life in this world is meaningless. To repeat: How can one worship a God who is said to create such a world for such a meaningless or imponderable end? Hoping to find a theodicy that could prove antitheodicists wrong, I turned to key thinkers in three theodic fields whom I thought would be the most promising for my task. Individually, and as isolated groups, no one path was sufficiently successful. But if one highlights prominent strands or features that often overlapped among disparate thinkers, a path emerges to develop a viable theodic position.

The following, therefore, are the criteria that any Christian theodicy must include to be viable despite mass atrocity:

1. It should employ a pastoral approach informed by a post-Holocaust perspective.

2. It should testify to the pervasive goodness of creation and the need for a disinterested faith.

3. It should promote a prayerful commitment to remember the victims of atrocity.

4. It should orient and sustain a devoted praxis.

5. It should integrate theological protest and radical forgiveness.

Criterion One: Employs a Pastoral Approach Informed by a Post-Holocaust Perspective

Pastoral theology is concerned with the care of the soul, and a theodicy not similarly engaged may be a reckless and fruitless enterprise. Pastoral theology recognizes the struggles and conflicts within each individual and how the same good person remains prone to sin and self-centeredness, embodying the Pauline quote, "I do not understand my own actions. For I do not do what I want, but I do the very thing I hate."[8] A theodicy must reflect upon the ideal trajectory of the human soul and the disordered desires and choices that cloud and pervert one's judgment and decisions. Such an approach invokes reason and passion, deliberation and feeling, body and soul. It strives for totality and wholeness. Here, too, there is no discernible separation of a theoretical or practical approach to theodicy. Both approaches intertwine and mutually support one another.

Moreover, one's engagement with testimonies means one is immersed and informed by a post-Holocaust perspective that seems to challenge and undermine many traditional beliefs and hopes. In addition to utilizing the classic texts and practices within one's faith tradition, David Tracy contends that theologians need to employ "a hermeneutics of suspicion upon the possible errors, illusions, and distortions that may also be present in so long, so rich, so complex, and so ambiguous a tradition as that of Catholic Christianity."[9] This first criterion, therefore, calls for the need to see things honestly and openly—reality, raw, with all its disparate pieces and contradictions. Whether one nominates the Holocaust or another historical tragedy, such systemic evils have shed substantial doubt on belief in order, progress, morality, meaning,[10] and goodness.

In her lecture on "Collective Responsibility," Hannah Arendt, for example, asserts how facile it is for systems of morals to "collapse overnight"[11] and return to their original meaning as *mores*, customs.

---

8. Rom 7:15.

9. Tracy, "Religious Values after the Holocaust," 87–88.

10. "the Holocaust has become the occasion for a hermeneutical rupture—a crisis in the interpretation of meaning" (Fasching, *Narrative Theology*, 22).

11. Arendt, *Responsibility and Judgment*, 50.

Arendt's observation in the wake of World War II in many ways defines our contemporary era. In such a world, truth seems to fluctuate and change, where nearly all elements are protean—vehicles for morphing and changing at will or in violation of one's convictions otherwise. Identity is mired in displaced communal and family memories, where home, job, and national identities seem lost in a globalized, diasporic context. Language, meaning, and history seem subjective, and often, predatory on the weak and defenseless. Many religions, despite their protestations and attempts to act otherwise, are often an accessory to these developments or are pushed further and further to the margins, to inhabit a self-contained world within a specific sphere. In this globalized, pluralized world, one is also confronted with competing religions that challenge a believer to maintain why one's religion is unique and true against, or perhaps in solidarity with, other religious claims. Amidst a preponderance of doubt and choices, one knows that one can be wrong, and that one's Church or institution has condoned or been negligent in combating and admitting some sin within its history. One struggles, for example, to admit aspects of one's faith that cannot be compromised in interreligious dialogue.

As noted above, my demand that theodicists must turn to the words of the victims of mass atrocities is a concurrent call to become open to the possibility that one's theological doctrines, tradition, and grounding will be questioned and challenged, potentially calling for change and clarification. As Thich Nhat Hanh writes: "We have to appreciate that truth can be received from outside of—not only within—our own group. If we do not believe that, then entering into dialogue would be a waste of time."[12] This is especially the case when a Christian confronts non-Christian victims of atrocity whose own faith tradition has comforted them and provided a meaningful framework to face their affliction.

In this work I have argued that these testimonies must be given the authority to place all of one's theological doctrine, traditions, and beliefs into question. I am also, however, suspicious of Christian theologies that have radically altered traditional components of theological belief, especially in regards to God's moral goodness, God's power to redeem, God's mercy, God's connection with human suffering, and God's relation to this world and humanity. Without these aspects, I

12. Hanh, *Living Buddha*, 9.

cannot fathom a viable faith or theodicy, but I also acknowledge that even these core elements may not withstand a sustained turning to the victims of atrocities of our world.

It is within this complex, conflicting, and often paradoxical context that a theodicy has to operate. The role is made even more precarious and questionable after knowledge of mass killings like the Holocaust. With each new or ongoing disaster or atrocity, the evidence then is continually piling up, often lopsidedly. After every disaster, a theodicist is put on the defensive, and often succumbs to trying to defend the indefensible. It is, perhaps, because most suffering comes so unexpectedly and randomly that a theodicy also must highlight the (less-heralded) goodness of the world while also advocating a disinterested faith, as the next criterion elaborates.

Criterion Two: Testifies to the Pervasive Goodness of Creation and the Need for a Disinterested Faith

A theodicy defends the reasonableness of belief in God not simply by trying to justify the presence of evil but by elucidating how the biblical tradition that asserts God's purpose of creation is still relevant today. It thus highlights the goodness and beauty of this world and the dignity of the human person made in the image of God. Such an endeavor aims to unite more fruitfully ecological concerns with theodic ones.[13]

A theodic response should also stress the value of a disinterested faith to attune a person to be grateful for this life but to expect suffering in this world. A disinterested faith shares much in common with the Buddhist sense of *dukkha* as analyzed in chapter 2. Ultimately, this criterion promotes a language that does not denigrate God's creation nor unduly inflate the value of this world's transient goods. It accentuates a language of humility that properly assesses the value of this world in light of God's heavenly promise.

One way of accentuating this initial goodness in humanity despite the reality of sinfulness is the theory of *privatio boni*, whose continued relevance I argued for in chapter 4 while examining Didier Pollefeyt's useful reinterpretation of *privatio boni* and his additional term *perversio boni*.[14] This theory of *privatio boni* stresses how humanity, made in

---

13. Ruether, "Eco-Justice at the Center of the Church's Mission," 610. See also my "Dirt, Collapse, and Eco-responsibility."

14. See also my "Destructive, Concrete Evil as Absence," 41–51.

the image and likeness of God, is inherently good. Such a position not only claims that there are no inherently evil creatures, but that even the worst sinner is never beyond redemption in this world. It is therefore not only a foundational element of a Christian anthropodicy, but also of a Christian theodicy because it contains within it the doctrines of creation and redemption.

To depict only violence and meaninglessness, or focus only on "wretched" humanity, is to paint an incomplete picture of our world. Sobrino aptly encapsulates this idea with his term "primordial holiness."[15] Where many only see exploitation and misery, he points to life and hope. To deny such a position is to empower suffering and evil as normative and ignore the ubiquity of profound or commonplace acts of goodness and tenderness, along with a world that glitters with order and, at times, magisterial beauty. Because our world remains in need of healing, though, a disinterested faith stance is also essential.

A disinterested faith has been one of the main strands advocated by figures as diverse as Phillips, John Paul II, and Gutiérrez, although they all differ in their interpretation, especially as linked with the notion of an afterlife. As I have argued, faith in God (and the possibility for a viable theodicy) is only reasonable with the hope that the mercy and justice of God will heal and redeem in the afterlife. Without such a possibility, and because life for too many here has been one of horrendous suffering and affliction, theodicy and theism would both falter. Such a position is cogently summarized by Bernard of Clairvaux: "God is not loved without a reward, although he should be loved without regard for one."[16]

A disinterested faith does not mean one is passive or apathetic to one's struggles or the injustice committed against another. It does not desacralize one's life, nor does it imply that we are not meant to flourish. One must believe that God is concerned about our well-being but must not recklessly blame God when conditions are harrowing. In fact, it is belief in the goodness of God's creation and the concurrent cognizance of the devastation and misery of this world that further strengthen the need for a disinterested faith. We are called to avoid attachment to the ephemeral goods (honor, riches, and so on) of this world and not to expect to be given such excessive riches here because

15. Sobrino, *Where Is God?* 73.

16. Bernard of Clairvaux, "On Loving God," 434.

of our faith in God. Concurrently, we cannot accept conditions that are dehumanizing and degrading for ourselves and one another. It is a disinterested service in trying to live out the will of God, but it does not tolerate human-enacted conditions that cause injustice and suffering, as the call for protest (Criterion Five) and praxis (Criterion Four) make clear.

Such a self-giving call is lucid in the gospels: for the sake of Christ and to establish God's reign in our midst, one may encounter additional suffering and persecution. Just as a lack of celebrating the beauty of creation sullies God's intentions for this world, so, too, for a Christian, must one's following of Christ be realistic about suffering in this world to prevent unjust accusation and judging of God. While acknowledging the haphazard dispersion of good and evil makes it more cumbersome to argue for a God of love and justice, it can also provide a realistic moral framework through which to live and survive with one's religious faith intact. To ignore such a stance could render one's theodic language impotent and detached from the lived reality of so many.

A Christian theodicy without a need for faith has not and will never exist. They need each other to survive. Their survival is also embedded within the role of one's memory—in recalling the life, death, and resurrection of Christ and the promises of eternal life. However, the same process of theological memory focuses on Christ's message of repentance and calls for a commitment to heal the sufferings of others. This dual commitment necessarily leads to a mnemonic and ethical clash. Such is the focus of my next criterion.

Criterion Three: Promotes a Prayerful Commitment to Remember the Victims of Atrocity

"The danger of emphasizing memory and mourning," Gabriele Schwab warns, "lies in using trauma as the foundation of identity."[17] Like Leys in chapter 1, Schwab comments upon an oversaturated wound culture where everyone can claim to be a victim without distinction. The warning is valid, which is why a proper balance, a type of Aristotelian mean, is being sought here: an ethical call to remember loss and devastation along with joy and beauty (Criterion Two). For any theist, it often means living with and enduring gaps, holes, and a

17. Schwab, *Haunting Legacies*, 19.

spiritual emptiness. The nontheist may employ different phrases, but the mystery of goodness should seem as impenetrable as the mystery of evil. Either way, how and whether one remembers and what one remembers are integral in positioning oneself in relation to those gaps and trying to name and decipher them. Are we obligated to remember? Shoah survivor Helen "Zippi" Spitzer Tichauer has remarked that "people forget very quickly, but you cannot tell people 'you must remember' . . . you cannot force anybody to become aware of what happened."[18] As a survivor, her words bear moral weight, but why cannot people be obligated to remember such events? Moreover, what is the ethical relationship between forgetting and remembering?

Commitment to Remember

W. James Booth writes of a qualified "duty to forget, to heal ourselves, and to allow a rebirth or a strengthening of our civic ties."[19] In the previous chapter, the need for a delicate balance of memory and forgetting was touched upon in the context of justice and postmortem existence. The balance is even more haphazard and slippery in this life because "justice," as Claudine Kayitesi, Rwandan genocide survivor, remarks, "is not worrying about the feelings of survivors."[20] Or as fellow survivor Berthe Mwanankabandi adds: "Priority must be given to the fields, the harvests, the country, and so to the killers as well and to their families, who are many and strong. What would become of a nation lying fallow, without schools, or sturdy houses, eyed greedily by neighboring countries?"[21] Those who have survived the maelstrom and the outsiders who guiltily or curiously look within it may need to respond differently to the agonistic tension of remembrance and forgetting.[22]

Such a distinction no doubt further restricts what a theodicist (and so theist) may hope for and articulate. Often, pragmatic concerns trump seemingly pure theological ones; or one can say that theology

18. Quoted in Lower, "Distant Encounter," 117.

19. Booth, *Communities of Memory*, 145.

20. Hatzfeld, *Strategy of Antelopes*, 130.

21. Ibid., 130–31.

22. The Hindu scholar Wendy Doniger writes: "given the power of revenge, sometimes it pays to have a good forgettery" (*Hindus*, 689). Her use of Sandburg's term is humorous, but she employs it in her very serious discussion of violence and the abuse of history within and about India.

is cast further down to the earth. Nevertheless, a theodicy must address the need for a religious conversion and commitment to support further the grounds for justifying faith in God amidst evil. In the context of formulating a faith practice that subverts "the existing forms of political life," Johannes Baptist Metz, for example, writes: "At the midpoint of this [Christian] faith is a specific *memoria passionis* . . . [which] articulates itself as a memory that makes one free to suffer from the suffering of others, and to respect the prophetic witness of others' suffering, even though the negative view of suffering in our 'progressive' society makes it seem as something increasingly intolerant and even repugnant."[23]

Making a commitment to remember victims of suffering and atrocity is one potential way to develop and sustain such a conversion or purification of one's faith. While nagging questions remain of whether anyone is ever obligated to remember, or to what degree and duration depending on the specific case or link to one's identity and past as a familial, communal, or group member,[24] theological memory is a particular commitment grafted unto the skin and sinews of the Abrahamic faiths. In other words, the demand, obligation, and expectation, not only to remember, but to stave off the "attrition of memory"[25], is indelibly linked to what it means to be a Jew, a Muslim, or a Christian. Despite the need for clarification regarding some problematic biblical passages,[26] for example, I would claim that biblical stories are composed in part to address and accommodate the role that remembering and forgetting constitute for a people's religious and moral identity. As Yosef Hayyim Yerushalmi remarks: "Only in Israel and nowhere else is the injunction to remember felt as a religious imperative to an entire people . . . Memory [is] crucial to its faith and ultimately to its very existence."[27]

23. Metz, "Future in the Memory of Suffering," 10–11.

24. Blustein, *Moral Demands of Memory*, 291–93.

25. Ibid., 245

26. The call to blot out Amalek (Exod 17:14) is also an example of a biblical passage that one remembers now in a different light, namely by critiquing what is often considered "cultural genocide" that is advocated by the biblical God. Again, such mnemonic conflicts are inevitable. For an explanation of cultural genocide, see Kiernan, *Blood and Soil*, 13.

27. Yerushalmi, *Zakhor*, 9.

For Christians, Christ's message at the Last Supper—"Do this in remembrance of me"—becomes a liturgical, sacramental, and moral memory-act that is often deemed the heart of that faith.[28] For Metz, such a *memoria passionis* calls us to develop a "language of Holy Saturday."[29] In this world, Christians live amidst and after the throes of the suffering and death of the cross but still awaiting (with anxiety and anticipation) the final resurrection of the dead. In the theodic response I am trying to develop, a response that remains character-ized (but not solely defined) by its fragmentary and fractured state, such a memory and image is particularly pertinent, as troubling as it is hopeful. Christian theodic language today should resonate with the language of Holy Saturday. A burning question for me is whether such a commitment to remember in forming a theodicy—integrating such memories within one's faith tradition, rituals, prayer, and litur-gies—can also be a means to ensure that one combats new or ongoing evils (praxic-memory).

To aid in this combating, remembering victims of horrendous suffering points to how our identities are entangled with the lot of those forsaken. Writing in the context of the civil rights movement in the United States, James Baldwin cogently remarks: "Our dehu-manization of the Negro then is indivisible from our dehumanization of ourselves: the loss of our own identity is the price we pay for the annulment of his."[30] So, too, with the victims of trauma and atrocity. Manipulating or isolating their ordeals to protect one's own (naïve) faith will only dehumanize and betray one's beliefs and positions. "Memory-justice-truth," as Booth elucidates, "is the ingathering of the past in fulfillment of an obligation to the dead and for the sake of continuity of the community across time."[31] The search for justice and truth are also constitutive of any theological memory. Such a memory can indeed serve as a marker of healing, but it also wounds and com-plicates one's sense of self, history, and beliefs.

Despite these risks, we must still remember rightly and truth-fully, for otherwise one may misuse certain memories for selfish or

28. Luke 22:19.

29. For a useful analysis of Metz's *memoria passionis,* see Frede-Wenger, "'Good' Friday after Auschwitz?" 137–49.

30. Baldwin, *Notes of a Native Son,* 30.

31. Booth, *Communities of Memory,* 138.

immoral ends or exaggerate certain wrongs that were committed.[32] In being guided by a commitment for justice, truth, and mercy, theological memory also calls an individual to cross the societal divides of class, ethnicity, religion, race, and other identity markers. Thus, we must strive to overcome denial and face those truths that challenge the stability and "orthodoxy" of our beliefs, identity, and history. To quote Baldwin again: "[W]hat the memory repudiates controls the human being. What one does not remember dictates who one loves or fails to love . . . What one does not remember contains the only hope, danger, trap, inexorability, of love—only love can help you recognize what you do not remember."[33]

Overcoming denial is an act of love. It admits the possibility that a damaging truth may be recovered through remembering, yet courageously perseveres. What we "choose" to forget or not remember could be the difference of life or death, if not of our own lives than of others whom we are also responsible for in some way.[34] Overcoming denial should be the mantra that encapsulates much of our religious practice and our engagement in a deeper, more critical assessment of our familial, religious, cultural, and national histories; in short, all the multiple strands that make up our identities. Such a commitment not only may reveal difficult truths but also may unearth past connections and similarities between groups previously thought to be "eternal" enemies. It may empower actions that heal our broken world and so reinforce the viability of a theodicy. Theologically, such a commitment to remember is to look unflinchingly with the victims of horrific crimes or at one's own prejudice, inaction, miseries, and major setbacks—and still seek the strength, faith, and courage to sing the praises of God. In this way one is also forced to confront any lingering elements of one's hesitancy to confront honestly and embrace fully the Other, who, ironically, forms parts of one's identity by being labelled enemy, infidel, or heretic.

32. Volf, *End of Memory*, 56.

33. Baldwin, *Evidence of Things Not Seen*, xiv. See also Schwab, *Haunting Legacies*, 84.

34. John Donne's "Meditation 17" poignantly portrays our interconnectedness.

Are We Responsible if We Forget? Overcoming Denial

In this embrace of the Other, is Baldwin right in claiming that we are responsible for what we remember or forget? Cees Nooteboom, for example, quips in *Rituals*, "Memory is like a dog that lies down where it pleases."[35] As anyone can attest, even with the best intentions, our commitment to remember can easily falter amidst the humdrum or hectic pace of our daily lives. Nevertheless, I agree with Booth, who states: "Memory's guarding of moral outrage, the core of resentment and of the thirst for vengeance or retribution, is at the heart of doing justice . . . Memory helps to ensure that time does not prematurely heal all wounds, because healing of that kind would deny justice its due."[36] Aware of how memory can be capricious and knowing the dangers that forgetting or remembering erroneously can inflict, I also want to locate a means to nurture a theological memory that can orient a person to do what is good and just. To sidestep such an admittedly complex task is to ignore a fundamental absence in many theoretical theodicies: how to minimize unjust, human-wrought suffering. Hannah Arendt, seeking a similar goal, evaluated the educative merits of Socrates' 2-in-1[37] and Kant's categorical imperative.[38] Others may look to Rawls's difference principle[39] or place one's hope in the power and beauty of literature, as Julia Kristeva does in *Powers of Horror*[40] and as Amos Oz advocates on account of literature's ability to make the reader encounter the Other.[41] I agree with Oz, but there also needs to be a sound moral and/or theological value system to guide our reading to identify how and why we imagine the Other. To try to empathize and understand the Other is imperative, but without the means to judge, whom I should emulate is another matter entirely. To repeat: the goal here is to develop a way to inculcate in all of us the capacity to be less susceptible to committing the acts that not only cause so much harm but also denigrate the meaning and value of this

---

35. Draaisma, *Why Life Speeds Up*, 1.

36. Booth, *Communities of Memory*, 122–23.

37. Arendt, *Responsibility and Judgment*, 157.

38. Kant, *Grounding for the Metaphysics of Morals*, 40 (434) and 44 (440).

39. Rawls, *Theory of Justice*, 65–73.

40. Kristeva, *Powers of Horror*, 210.

41. Oz, "Devil's Progress," 4–5.

world, and so the possibility for a viable theodicy. Such a task can only be hinted at here, but one path could be particularly fruitful.

Prayerful Commitment

John Roth has written: "If prayer is to be recognized as prayer . . . it is not desirable to separate prayer from either questions of theodicy or questions about theodicy."[42] In this work, I have argued that a commitment to remember the stories of victims of mass atrocity and horrendous suffering is a means of purification or self-examination. Here I want to argue that a theodicy must emphasize the value of incorporating such a commitment within one's prayer (or spiritual) life. This will not only help purify and challenge one's theological and theodic language but also support the praxis emphasized in Criterion Four. It is to look at the potential muck and sin of one's own life before blaming and castigating others, or even God. While prayer needs further theoretical and systematic analysis in light of mass atrocity, it remains that space and nexus to bridge some of the gap between God and ourselves. As Mark O'Keefe writes: "God's self-giving love, which is the model and foundation of all loving, seeks reciprocity, mutuality, return . . . On our part, then, every act of prayer is an act of giving ourselves in return, surrendering to the one who first gave himself to us."[43] In conjunction with my other criteria and in light of the definition of prayer above and the one given in the previous chapter, it is the practice I promote as the best means to develop and sustain moral renewal and conversion. In particular, this spiritual practice may be especially helpful for those who have so far been protected from radical evil. While it is easy to reduce these despondent accounts to a historical anomaly, the knock on the door, as Solzhenitsyn writes, always comes unexpectedly.

The crux is how one reads these texts so that one's prayer can be a genuine means to reach a state of solidarity with such victims. Thus, memory—through the language of prayer—can be the conduit for a person to engage the burden of past (and present) injustice and encounter it at one's deepest, most intimate level, whether in those private moments when an individual is alone in meditation or prayer or when participating with a community through a liturgical,

---

42. Roth, "Response to Grob and Manemann," 270.

43. O'Keefe, "Prayer and Conversion," 268.

sacramental, meditative, or other praxic act. Such a theological practice works on various levels, recalling God's promises and the stories of saints and believers healed while also remembering the tales of the broken, forsaken, and despondent. Such memories and the contemplation of such memories are meant to fuel and guide one's thoughts and attitudes towards performing good actions.[44] It is, thus, an integral means to honor the lives of such victims and to examine one's own actions and thoughts by allowing the sacredness of one's prayer life to trespass on the more sacred ground of the stories of victims of atrocity.

Further comprehensive analysis is needed here,[45] but let me offer some salient points and questions. First, I agree with Avishai Margalit's remark that "it is hard to carry the memory of isolated and unconnected events and people, taken from very different histories,"[46] not to mention the impossibility of remembering the sheer number of such events.[47] Second, if one tries to incorporate these images within one's prayer life there is also the danger of turning them into a fetish instead of seeking an encounter with such lives as sacred and bearing responsibility. Third, there is the possibility to be so overwhelmed that one simply becomes numb to such horrific accounts.[48] Fourth, when one reads explicit testimonies of suffering as depicted in a work like Iris Chang's *The Rape of Nanking*,[49] how can one even begin allowing such worlds to be transfixed in memory, to slither into the sacred life and language of one's private prayers?[50] Fifth, if one agrees that such

44. Origen also notes the value of remembering God and one's obligations to God ("Prayer," 83).

45. Two good places to start would be Booth, *Communities of Memory*, and Blustein, *Moral Demands of Memory*.

46. Margalit, *Ethics of Memory*, 80.

47. Ibid., 32.

48. Always lurking is the risk of overexposure, which can lead to our accepting these realities as quasi-normative. Iris Chang, in *The Rape of Nanking*, quotes war correspondent John Gillepsie: "I think I have said enough of these horrible cases—there are hundreds of thousands of them. Seeing so many of them finally makes the mind dulled so that you cease to be shocked anymore" (155).

49. We read, for example, how "Chinese witnesses saw Japanese soldiers rape girls under ten years of age in the streets and then slash them in half by the sword. In some cases, the Japanese sliced open the vaginas of preteen girls in order to ravish them more effectively" (Chang, *Rape of Nanking*, 91).

50. Eva Hoffman writes in *After Such Knowledge*: "The injunction 'to remember' repeated frequently and hypnotically enough can become precisely a summons not to make the effort of thought, not to consider what we are remembering or how

a commitment to remember the victims is obligatory, does one then choose the specific memories or try to remember as many as one can? Lastly, does such a need cease if such exposure fuels an awareness that seems to make one less likely to commit such a wrong, or in theodic terms, ensures the necessary humility, hesitation, and reflection needed before asserting a theodic argument?

"Memory," as Margaret MacMillan writes, "is not only selective, it is malleable."[51] It seems this prayer-practice is part of such a tenuous, ongoing project, with the gaps of memory so prominent, with the "heat of the moment" so falsely palliative, that for such an injunction to bear any weight, it must be sustained like the old refrain "to pray ceaselessly." I would contend that Christians who have been fortunate to escape debilitating travails, for example, should read the Bible or a meditative reflection alongside an account of mass atrocity, as a means to listen to those who endured such struggles and to think and pray on the matter to come to understanding and judgment to aid one's actions. Such a practice will be jarring and challenging and so should only be followed periodically and, ideally, in the context of a supportive community. A Muslim would juxtapose the Qur'an and a survivor testimony, and so on, for those of other faith or secular traditions.

Contemplating such stories is not without precedent in Christianity with its long spiritual tradition of meditating upon Christ's wounds or reflecting on the lives of the saints, many of whom were martyred. Catholics, for example, partake in the Stations of the Cross and pray the Sorrowful Mysteries of the Rosary, which call on the believer to contemplate the scourging at the pillar or the crowning of thorns. Ignatian spirituality also entails believers imagining themselves in the various scenes of Christ's passion. There is, then, not only a rich spiritual practice to build upon, but also a way to connect further the life of Christ with these victims. The difference is that some of these stories will offer no hope or reason to maintain one's theological and theodic positions without gaps and fractures. However, just as contemplating Christ's passion is a means to spur the believer to good words and deeds, so, too, can the contemplation of these testimonies provide the same impetus for good actions while purging (and

---

difficult such a feat really is" (176).

51. MacMillan, *Dangerous Games*, 44.

reinforcing) one's theodic language. It is to answer the call the victims so courageously invoke.

Criterion Four: Orients and Sustains a Devoted Praxis

Spurred in part by prayer, one's committed, moral praxis is not only the key response to evil, but is also an essential piece of any theodicy that aims to theorize about—and help sustain—the beauty and goodness of the world. As Rabbi Shai Held writes: "Since evil and suffering are the biggest obstacles to human recognition of the divine, the elimination (or, at least, the dramatic mitigation) of the former makes the latter more possible."[52]

Any theodicy divorced of a praxic-concern seems deserving of the acerbic language often heaped upon it. As Kenneth Surin writes: "To regard theodicy as a purely theoretical and scholarly exercise is to provide—albeit unwittingly—a tacit sanction of the myriad evils that exist on this planet."[53]

Praxis is a synthesis of our thoughts, intentions, deliberations, statements, judgments, and actions. Practically, in confronting evil and suffering, praxis in the form of serving others may be the best means to rediscover the goodness of life, especially as embodied by selfless people in the world who quietly commit acts of kindness and love. Such praxis is also a calling to remove any barriers that keep individuals marginalized. Any moral or ethical system must acknowledge the fragility and vulnerability of the human condition, acknowledge one's own sins and the failures of one's religious and civic institutions, and strive to reach out with compassion and mercy to the most ostracized and devalued. Such a commitment will also be shared by many antitheodicists and so is another means to close the gap between theodicists and antitheodicists. Again, Sobrino reminds us that to find God, we need to find humanity; and through service to one another—especially towards the most defenseless—humanity can often be found.[54] Through such praxis, one may encounter that deep, loving presence of God that had seemed remote, hidden—*Deus absconditus*. It is difficult to disavow all goodness in the world when you know people who strive to make this world better. Once you leave

---

52. Held, "Living and Dreaming with God," 20.
53. Surin, *Theology and the Problem of Evil*, 50.
54. Sobrino, *No Salvation outside the Poor*, 97.

yourself open to seeing this goodness, a space develops for the grace of God to be felt (again). The hope of promoting such a space, as my final criterion argues, is in part why all theodicies must also integrate theological protest and radical forgiveness.

Criterion Five: Integrates Theological Protest and Radical Forgiveness

Bruce Barber writes: "In this modern paradigm, evil is assumed to be a 'problem,' such that we must ask God to justify himself/itself to us. In light of the cross of Christ, this question must *always* be regarded as a blasphemous question."[55] Jewish theologians Berger and Patterson, moreover, remark: "And, with faith theologically understood as acceptance, Christians have not generally encouraged questioning or arguing with God."[56]

Hopefully, this work has disproved the contention of the former quote and shown why the latter quote should be challenged.[57] Because protest and forgiveness have been examined in previous chapters, here I want to show how to integrate them. In simple terms, protest and forgiveness purify each other. Forgiveness without protest may be seen as "cheap forgiveness," a failure to confront the evil and suffering within one's midst. In forgiveness, one absolves the person who has committed the atrocity but rails against the offense committed, decries it, and clamors for such acts never to be repeated. Thus, forgiveness both heals and loves—and condemns and curses. Protest without forgiveness may become embittered and weighed down by a sense of privilege and entitlement. Protest must have a means of closure and healing or it will eventually consume all in its path. Forgiveness rightly focuses and directs one's legitimate anger and resentment toward an injustice. Thus, they are intertwined and are essential to stress in forming a viable theodic position.

55. Barber, "Theodicy, Eschatology, and Postmodernity," 203.

56. Berger and Patterson, *Jewish-Christian Dialogue*, 108.

57. On the related issue of dissent and the Catholic Church, Paul Valadier writes: "It is too often forgotten that 'dissent' is not necessarily the fruit of disobedience on the part of believers or theologians. In many cases it is the by-product of an authoritarianism that is incapable of offering a theological justification of its positions" ("Has the Concept of *Sensus Fidelium* Fallen into Desuetude?" 190). See also Curran and McCormick, *Dissent in the Church*, and my "Nurturing Theological Dissent."

For example, in one of the most noteworthy psalms of affliction in the Bible, we read: "But I am a worm, less than human; / scorned by men, despised by people . . . [Yet] You drew me from the womb; / made me secure at my mother's breast. / I became your charge at birth; / from my mother's breast, you have been my God."[58] In prayer, meditating on Christ's life and suffering—and the many disciples who walked and walk a similar path—along with a commitment to remember and meditate upon this world's innocent victims, may help guide one through those inevitable dark nights. Within this struggle is also where theological protest can be such an invaluable aid. As argued in chapter 8, protest can be a prayer to purge ourselves of misconceptions about God and our adherence to false and potentially damaging expectations. It thus encourages a disinterested (or other-centered) faith. Recall, for example, Jesus's cry on the cross before he died and his quoting of Ps 22 (which, as seen above, is ultimately a poignant prayer of trust in God amidst horrible suffering). In essence, one blends together and inhabits the same theological space of "My God, my God, why have you forsaken me?"[59] and "Father, into your hands I commend my spirit."[60]

Advocating protest is also a crucial point in common between theodicy and antitheodicy. Antitheodicists argue that no justification for the ills of this world is possible. They protest the magnitude of the injustice. For them, no reasons can ever explain such agony. But a theodicist should also protest. And within such protest and because of one's dialogue and commitment to remember the excessive trials of so

---

58. Ps 22:7–11.

59. Mark 15:34; Matt 27:46.

60. Luke 23:46. In Luke, one can also read: "Father, forgive them; they know not what they do" (23:33). While not Jesus's last words, and not the oldest words in the papyrus manuscripts of Luke, they are nevertheless the most important words on the cross and ones that should have guided a Christian's theological relationship with the Jewish people, especially in challenging views that erroneously blame Christ's death on "the Jews." See Benedict XVI, *Jesus of Nazareth: Holy Week*, 183–200. As a theologian of a liberationist, postcolonial, and postmodern bent, I would obviously disagree with Benedict's minimizing of the deeply political thrust of Jesus's ministry, but it is important that he blames Jesus's death predominantly on the "Temple aristocracy" and not the Jews, as such. Still, his failure to see Jesus as a threat to Rome remains perplexing in light of the many (Catholic) martyrs who have similarly fallen because their lives and words challenged the totalitarian nature of an occupying (or undemocratic) State.

many others, one knows there are limits, walls, barriers to one's proclamations and the need for tact, nuance, and measured language.[61]

Hopefully, such protest can be enriching, which is why one ideally is being nourished in one's prayer life and guided by a tradition in dialogue with a community. If one protests in isolation, then such a practice could be all-consuming, inhibiting one's relationship with God. Ideally, protest should promote positive, moral action—the desire to seek and implement change—which is why memory, protest, and praxis are so intertwined and are elemental to most Jewish thinkers and liberation theologians. The practice of radical forgiveness is one way to bring these three strands together.

While forgiveness does not curtail judgment, it means one judges with love and mercy, never in retaliation or vindictiveness. Is everyone called to forgive, however, and is forgiveness always a means of healing for the victims? Often, practical concerns take priority in some contexts. In *The Witnesses: War Crimes and the Promise of Justice in The Hague*, Eric Stover interviews "Jusa," a Muslim who had returned to his village where Bosnian Croat troops (with neighborhood support or acquiescence) had attacked him and his fellow Muslims. His ancestral home had been torched and his wife was killed in the fire. Two sons were shot to death. When asked how he got along again with his Croat neighbors, Jusa replied that if he saw an individual Croat he might wave, but if there was a group, "they just pass by and nobody says a thing. There's bad blood here. And it's not going to change soon. Still, if I ever rebuild my house I'm going to have to make some form of peace with them, if only to reconnect my sewage and water lines."[62]

Langer, moreover, challenges the notion that forgiveness is always morally cleansing: "I have never encountered a single Holocaust testimony supporting the conclusion that compassion for those guilty of mass murder is 'deeply therapeutic and restorative.'"[63] Such a claim

---

61. Rabbi Marc Ellis, while praising liberation theology, also rebukes some liberation theologians for not recognizing how "theological reflections of the Jewish community after the Holocaust do not resonate with triumphal language in the theological realm" (*Towards a Jewish Theology of Liberation*, 73); and also Cohn-Sherbok, *As It Is in Heaven*; and Maduro, ed., *Judaism, Christianity, and Liberation*.

62. Stover, *Witnesses*, 95.

63. Langer, *Using and Abusing the Holocaust*, 91. He is quoting from Gobodo-Madikizela, *A Human Being Died that Night*. See also Saunders, "Questionable Associations."

needs continued analysis, especially in light of Christian tradition, but as noted in the previous chapter, meaningful forgiveness entails both the forgiver and the forgiven freely coming together in an unthreatening and stable environment. In a Holocaust context or as in the Balkans, this is often impossible because many of the victims have been murdered and their perpetrators continue to live as if nothing has changed.

According to Charles Griswold, six conditions should be met for the offended party to renounce "resentment, or at least, [give] up the judgment that the wrong-doer warrants continued resentment."[64] First, the individual must take responsibility for her actions. Second, she must renounce and condemn the actions she committed. Noting that "forgiveness is in part a communicative act,"[65] Griswold's third criterion is that "the wrong-doer must experience and express regret at having caused that particular injury to that particular person . . . Fourth, the offender must commit to becoming the sort of person who does not inflict injury, and that commitment must be shown through deeds as well as words . . . Fifth, the offender must show that she understands, from the injured person's perspective, the damage done by the injury."[66] Griswold also adds a sixth condition: the offender must, as clearly as possible, offer a true narrative and context for why and how the wrong-doer committed this offense, answering questions the "injured party" asks, such as "who is this person, such that she could have injured me thus? Such that she warrants forgiveness?"[67]

The six conditions above cannot be applied in every case, especially in instances of mass atrocity. Should the possibility of forgiveness be permanently closed? Innocent Rwililiza, a teacher whose wife and son were murdered in the Rwandan genocide, speaks of "humanitarian organizations importing forgiveness to Rwanda, and they wrap it in lots of dollars to win us over . . . As for us, we speak of forgiveness to earn their good opinion—and because the subsidies can be lucrative. But when we talk among ourselves, the word *forgiveness* has no place; I mean that it's oppressive . . . It's outside of nature."[68]

64. Griswold, *Forgiveness*, 49.

65. Ibid., 50.

66. Ibid., 50–51.

67. Ibid., 51.

68. Hatzfeld, *Strategy of Antelopes*, 18.

Recall also the observation of Langer above, and Wiesel's prayer for God never to forgive the perpetrators of the Holocaust. Holocaust survivor William Benson, moreoever, remarks: "I teach my children, you never forgive, you never forget. And they should teach their children about Germany never to forget, never to forgive, never as long as our children can teach their children and keep on teaching their children. I don't want them to forgive, ever. This is something you don't forgive."[69]

Benson and Rwandan genocide survivor Immaculée Ilibagiza present two human but extreme responses towards their perpetrators. I accept the limitations and problems of certain kinds of forgiveness in certain contexts, but I obstinately remain unconvinced that the possibility of forgiveness can be permanently renounced without detrimental effects to the victim. Would not such pain and bitterness, while understandable, incessantly threaten, if not actually succeed in, consuming such a victim's outlook and worldview? Testimonial accounts give no definitive, universal answer. In some versions, forgiveness is viewed as an obstacle to peace of mind and the possibility of enduring. Perhaps one can accept the reality and devastating loss of atrocities without forgiveness and still make a commitment not to let these losses pervade and debilitate the rest of one's life. While keeping open the possibility for forgiveness (under the proper conditions Griswold sets out) would seem to place one in a better position to cope and live with such trauma and loss, this may not be desirable or plausible in every case for every individual. Because I have argued that even in the postmortem state there remains the possibility for a perpetrator to refuse the need for repentance, reconciliation may never be complete in every instance, but the desire to forgive can still aid the victim's process of healing. It would (likely) entail admitting one's own faults and the need for healing and the willingness and courage to be ready to forgive one's self, other human beings, and God, even if the latter is ultimately not to blame. Such forgiveness, which must be all-embracing, and so radical, is also linked with disinterested faith. For in such a disinterested state, one is already imbued with the gift of forgiveness, not expecting to live a life here free of any suffering or affliction.

Regardless of how divine justice is enacted, candid protest should lead to rectifying some problem or preventing its reoccurrence on earth. We can see this position in many testimonies of mass atrocity.

69. William Benson, as interviewed by Johnson and Reuband, *What We Knew*, 7.

They write so that the world will know. After his escape from the gulags of North Korea, Kang Chol-Hwan testifies: "I was worried that Japanese or Korean papers might write about my case. What then would happen to my family? I tried to take comfort in the fact that whatever damage there might be was probably already done. There was no turning back. And I'd won on at least two counts: I was safe and sound, and I would be able to tell the world about life in the North Korean camps."[70] Such a protest can fuel praxis because one is spurred to act on account of one's anger at injustice. Forgiveness opens a space for that same praxis, a space for healing, reconciliation, and renewal.

SUMMARY OF THE FIVE CRITERIA

These criteria are meant to reinforce each other and to curtail any excesses that could be detrimental to one's faith stance. Thus, for example, a disinterested faith balances a calling for theological protest, while a calling to promote and highlight the goodness of our world is continually challenged and checked by the ongoing commitment to see this world with the sense of fragmentation and skepticism of a post-Holocaust perspective. These criteria are also intended to serve as a means to develop a viable theodic position and to be used to critique other theodicies and antitheodicies. In the spirit of this work, however, these criteria remain open to further revisions or additions, but it is hoped that many of these features, having been well tested over time, will continue to have relevance to one's moral and spiritual needs.

Mass atrocity and horrendous suffering assault the credibility of a theodicy and so one's theological beliefs. However, as argued throughout this work, a theodicy that acknowledges its failures and limitations—and so one's ultimate dependence on faith and the grace given by God—is in a better position to persevere amidst valid reasons to doubt and cry out. In seeking a viable theodicy, one is always aware that it remains a fractured theodicy. All theistic belief in this world must necessarily be fractured so long as injustice and the groans of the tortured and maligned are with us. Such a stance is better aligned to develop a meaningful response to articulate why a fractured, but still viable faith is not only plausible but necessary for there to be enduring meaning in the world and for the hope of redemption to be fully realized. These criteria are a means to begin to formulate and develop such a position.

70. Chol-Hwan, *Aquariums of Pyongyang*, 218.

Epilogue

Salvaging Faith amidst the Rubble: A Fractured, but Viable Theodicy

She was bitten all over, that compañera. She had no ears. All of them were missing part of the tongue or had their tongues split apart.[1]

The ghastly testimony above from Rigoberta Menchu's autobiography speaks of torture of the body, of tongue and ears that would have made the acts of speech and listening impaired, if not impossible. These victims, however, were also later burned alive. While theodicists must be cautious of speaking for such victims, they must assess how such survivor testimonies impact a theodicy's intentions and purported values.

This attempt at seeking a viable theodic position has sought to graft such stories within one's theological memory and theodic arguments. It has sought to listen to and reflect upon the stories of these victims of horrific suffering and carefully to consider how their words and experiences bear upon any theodic and theistic claims. Often, as many questions as "answers" were raised, which should be expected with such a task and method. As Darrell Fasching writes: "It is doubt and questioning that always lures me on to broader horizons and deeper insights through an openness to the infinite that leaves me *contentedly discontent*."[2] With Fasching and Wiesel, I agree with the value

1. Menchú, *I, Rigoberta Menchú*, 178.
2. Fasching, *Ethical Challenge of Auschwitz and Hiroshima*, 7.

and necessity of questions and the need to acknowledge the fragments and gaps in many of our "answers." Nevertheless, seeking to articulate answers is still important, as such a process, even if it raises deeper and more fundamental problems, is an essential step to move closer towards the aims and positions one ultimately aspires to reach.

One key question is whether only a fragmentary *Tikkun* is possible, as Emil Fackenheim writes. The examination of radical evil assaults one's religious faith with a sense of abrasion, erasure, gaps, and conflict. It seems to desiccate all theodic arguments and so the vitality of one's religious belief. While I yearn to speak of hope and goodness, the theodic position I advocate—like Metz's *memoria passionis*—entails a commitment to try to remain in the presence of young Benja dunked violently in the well; with Esther and her baby on their death march to the crematoria; with Little Eleanora in the gulags; with the anonymous boy of Plaszow forced to eat his own diarrhea; with Partnoy's husband, amidst torture, trying to think of singing "*El sapito*" to his daughter; with the young anonymous girl raped in Sudan; and with the woman in the ditch, scratching the ground at Auschwitz—so many victims; too many, perhaps, as a poet might say, for even God to remember. These testimonies never dispel all darkness and doubt. They call for a theodic language that is humble, flexible, and honest. They ensure that the threat of despair shadows one's theological hope.

For those of us who have been fortunately shielded from radical evil, it has been my contention that avoiding, concealing, or rationalizing such injustices points to an anemic faith position and misrepresents the truth claims that one's religious faith advocates. Such denial or avoidance thus inevitably distorts one's identity and integrity. As Rowan Williams comments in the context of the writings of Dostoyevsky: "The credibility of faith is in its freedom to let itself be judged and grow."[3] Turning to these victims is certainly a potent means for one's faith to be judged and to mature. Such possibility for development demands a faith position that admits its contradictions, weaknesses, and limitations (and when linked with a Church or religious institution, its historical "sins"[4]). Such steps are crucial for any hope towards forming a viable

---

3. Williams, *Dostoevsky*, 10.

4. What words can express the anguish and hopelessness amidst the pervasive child abuse scandal in the Catholic Church? See my "From Disgraced to Grace"; and Shorto, "Irish Affliction."

theodic language, even as that language inevitably incorporates a sense of fissure, discontinuity, mystery, and brokenness.

Thus, viable theodic language knowingly lacks complete certitude and is marked in some fashion by failure, uncertainty, and questioning. To borrow again Metz's term: for a Christian, a theodic language should be a "Holy Saturday language." It is fractured and in need of healing. It awaits resurrection, as hope in the mercy and justice of God in the afterlife becomes essential. In the meantime, formed by one's religious tradition and community of faith and engaged in dialogue with multiple discourses, disciplines, and religions, such theodic language can nevertheless illumine or point to a position and belief that seems viable and reasonable. This is in part because it strives to maintain an open and reflective position that acknowledges its potential to be confused, opaque, or simply wrong while aiming to reflect critically on how and why one's positions can be maintained and defended. This tendency keeps such a position from becoming static and ossified. It maintains that a *Tikkun* can be "whole" and "complete" even if such "wholeness" involves an acceptance of loss and fragments.

In his act of witnessing to the devastating 2010 earthquake in Haiti, photojournalist Gerard Straub writes: "Here God is hidden in the suffering, hidden in the rubble of our lives, hidden in great and small acts of resistance, hidden in truly inexhaustible mystery."[5] Straub identifies himself more as a spiritual seeker than a believer: but he could not deny a sense of hope in Haiti despite all the rubble and misery. A hidden God does not bring much comfort: it is an image I can do without. But there is something about simple, let alone heroic acts of mercy that call forth God's presence.[6] While we must listen closely to those victims who testify to a godless world, we must also heed those who see a glimmer of the divine.

"I yearn to merge with you in prayer," the Yiddist poet Peretz Markish wrote after the pogroms in the Ukraine. "And yet my heart, my lips are moved only to blasphemies and curses."[7] While Markish's words maintain a longing for God, I touched upon misotheism in

---

5. Straub, *Hidden in the Rubble*, 2.

6. Hans Keilson's novel, *Comedy in a Minor Key*, subtly testifies to those individuals in the Netherlands (represented by Marie and Wim) who helped to save a Jewish person (Nico) out of pragmatic, egotistical, even unreflective motives (20, 84).

7. Quoted in Ochs, "God of Jews and Christians," 253

chapter 9. The notion of hating God is too repellent for me to consider advocating—even amidst all the senseless destruction in our world—and yet, I also fear that complacency, timidity, and my own good fortune inhibit me from taking this leap, one that may even be prescribed and moral in certain contexts. The Tasmanian Aboriginal theologian, Lee Miena Skye, notes how many aboriginal women, "in spite of the legacy of a violent Christology and the multilayered oppression these women experience . . . have found a gentle Christ . . ."[8] There is a tinge of the miraculous here, but who could rebuke those who could not accept Christ because of those who "preached" him?

Ultimately, with a fractured faith that must struggle and thrive amidst life's swelter, confusion, and desperation, a theodicist must work within this world's fragile, fragmentary space, and ultimately must trust in—or be open to—the God he or she wants to justify and, ultimately, love and serve. Navigating such dual, divergent aims necessarily leads to gaps and fragmentary assertions, also necessitating the requirement to incorporate or acknowledge grace and hope, two of the bedrocks of one's faith, which steer one's theodicy as much as one's theodicy steers one's faith. Theodic positions, therefore, remain fragile and fractured, but still illumine a horizon for connection, solidarity, and intimacy with God. To repeat: a fractured theodicy can still be viable, especially if the postmortem embrace of God is desired and expected. Without this embrace, however, theodicy is not merely fractured, it is useless and immoral, deserving all the slanders that have been heaped upon it.

The Incarnation, however, enfolding the life of Christ as a fellow sufferer and journeyer in this world, enfleshes an empathetic God who can respond in love, solidarity, and tenderness, with the prerequisite divine qualities to heal and redeem.[9] Those of us with a Christian faith, in the midst of such overbearing darkness, may turn to the gospel stories of healing, and so remain adamant that if Jesus did not assuage such victims in this life, he will surely do so in the next. Of course, countless lives—as numerable as the stars in the sky and the sands on the seashore—hang upon that word *surely*—as does

---

8. Skye, "Australian Aboriginal Women's Christologies," 195.

9. How one interprets Christ's suffering, whether one ascribes to it any meaning or purpose, becomes imperative. See my "Healing the Distorted Face," 302–17.

faith, as do countless theodicies and antitheodicies. And yet, for many, even that word *surely* is not enough. It is too late: no longer welcome.

While under captivity by the Janjaweed militias in the Sudan, Halima Bashir, a Muslim doctor, prayed: "*At least God, let me die quickly. Please God, let it be painless. Please God, don't let them torture my soul.*"[10]

Bashir is later gang raped, slashed with blades, and burned with cigarettes. "'You know what we decided to do with you?' [one of her attackers later] announced quietly. 'We're not going to kill you. Get it? Not die. Not die. Live.'"[11] The man boasts he is keeping her alive as a further punishment. Bashir writes: "I was in a faraway place where my god had taken me . . . It wasn't death, which I'd asked for and begged for and prayed for. But it was the next best thing—the next best thing that my god could do for me in the circumstances."[12]

We come back again to a powerless God, a kenotic, suffering one—a God in the rubble—but a God present nonetheless, perhaps alleviating, perhaps intervening though in a more subtle, seemingly insignificant way. Insignificant? Bashir lives, survives, finds love and new life in England. Hers is another triumphant story, but one that still must compete with the silenced ones, the drowned, those who saw the Gorgon's head; the unsaved, the ones seemingly lost in elipses . . . and god knows what else.

"Our concern," Eliezer Berkovits pens, "is with the question of whether the affirmations of faith may be made meaningfully, notwith-standing God's terrible silence during the Holocaust."[13] There is, really, no tidy, clean way to say it: the notwithstanding clause.

Sympathetic to the sway of doubt and the deadness of unanswer-able questions, one can perhaps still speak of a fractured, but viable theodic faith. Such a faith clings to the hope that those children mas-sacred and abused in our world today—and all the victims of unjust suffering—will finally encounter the loving God who has promised so much, and they will be satisfied, will be healed, will finally, finally be at peace. It is this hope that may be all we have—the only position, after sifting among the rubble, which ultimately seems viable, and the only one we can live and die with in any meaningful sense.

10. Bashir, *Tears of the Desert*, 223.

11. Ibid., 227.

12. Ibid., 227.

13. Berkovits, *Essential Essays*, 332.

Bibliography

Abuelaish, Izzeldin. *I Shall Not Hate: A Gaza Doctor's Journey on the Road to Peace and Human Dignity*. New York: Walker, 2012.

Ackerman, Diane. *An Alchemy of the Mind: The Marvel and the Mystery of the Brain*. New York: Scribner, 2004.

Adams, Marilyn McCord. Afterword to *Encountering Evil: Live Options in Theodicy*, edited by Stephen T. Davis. Louisville: Westminster John Knox, 2001.

———. *Christ and Horrors: The Coherence of Christology*. Cambridge: Cambridge University Press, 2006.

———. *Horrendous Evils and the Goodness of God*. Ithaca: Cornell University Press, 1999.

———. *Wrestling for Blessing*. London: Darton, Longman & Todd, 2005.

Adeney, Frances S., and Arvind Sharma, editors. *Christianity and Human Rights: Influences and Issues*. Albany: State University of New York Press, 2007.

Addis, Mark. "D. Z. Phillips' Fideism." In *Wittgenstein's Mirror*, edited by Robert L. Arrington and Mark Addis, 85–100. London: Routledge, 2001.

Admirand, Peter. "'All lost! To prayers, to prayers! All lost': Why Postmodernity, Religious Pluralism, and Interreligious Dialogue Need to Be Embraced." In *Redefining Modernism and Postmodernism*, edited by Sebnem Toplu and Hubert Zapf, 79–98. Newcastle: Cambridge Scholars, 2010.

———. "Amidst Fractured Faith and the Fragility of Reason." *New Blackfriars* 92:1039 (2011) 268–84.

———. "Destructive, Concrete Evil as Absence: A Reevaluation of *Privatio Boni* in the Context of Mass Atrocity." In *Uneasy Humanity: Perpetual Wrestling with Evils*, edited by Colette Balmain and Nanette Norris, 41–51. Oxford: Interdisciplinary Press, 2009.

———. "Dirt, Collapse, and Eco-responsibility: 'Natural' Evils and the Eager Longing for Eco-justice." *Worldviews: Global Religions, Culture, and Ecology* 15 (2011) 1–24.

———. "Embodying an 'Age of Doubt, Solitude, and Revolt': Christianity Beyond 'Excarnation' in *A Secular Age*." *Heythrop Journal* 51:6 (2010) 905–20.

———. "From Disgraced to Grace: The Paedophile Scandal and its Impact on Catholic Intra- and Inter-religious Dialogue," unpublished paper.

———. "Healing the Distorted Face: Doctrinal Reinterpretation(s) and the Christian Response to the Other." *One in Christ* 42 (2008) 302–17.

———. "How Not to Raise Children: From Adam to David, a Contemporary Theological Perspective." In *Text, Theology, and Trowel: Recent Research into the Hebrew Bible*, edited by Jason M. Silverman and Lidia D. Matassa, 169–81. Eugene, OR: Pickwick, 2011.

————. "Interfaith Dialogue as Presence, Gift and Obligation." *Teaching Religious Education* 4 (2009) 4–7. Online: http://www.slss.ie/resources/c/1233/Teaching RE%20Issue%204.pdf.

————. "Jesus and Yeshua: Jewish Interpretations of the Gospels and Its Impact on Jewish-Christian Dialogue." In *A Land Like Your Own: Traditions of Israel and Their Reception*, edited by Jason Silverman and Amy Daughton, 101–13. Eugene, OR: Pickwick, 2010.

————. "Mission in Remission: Mission and Interreligious Dialogue in a Postmodern, Postcolonial Age." *Concilium: International Journal for Theology* 1 (2011) 95–104.

————. "'My Children Have Defeated Me!': Finding and Nurturing Theological Dissent." *Irish Theological Quarterly*, forthcoming.

————. "The Other as Oneself within Judaism: A Catholic Interpretation." *Journal of Inter-Religious Dialogue* 3 (2010) 113–24. Online: http://irdialogue.org/wp-content/uploads/2010/03/JIRD-3-Admirand.pdf.

————. "Overcoming 'Mere Oblivion': Mission Encountering Dialogue." *Search: A Church of Ireland Journal* 34:1 (2011) 30–38.

————. Review of *The Disenchantment of Secular Discourse*, by Steven D. Smith. *The Heythrop Journal*, forthcoming.

————. Review of *The Future of Liberation Theology: An Argument and Manifesto*, by Ivan Petrella. *The International Journal of Public Theology* 1 (2008) 133–34.

————. Review of *The Secular Outlook: In Defense of Moral and Political Secularism*, by Paul Cliteur. *The Heythrop Journal* 52:3 (2011) 536–37.

————. Review of *Stricken by God? Nonviolent Identification and the Victory of Christ*, edited by Brad Jersak and Michael Hardin. *Theological Book Review* 20:2 (2007) 88.

————. "'Scripture Speak[ing] Fictitious Words': Jusef as a Model for Interfaith Reconciliation." *Revista Dionysiana* 4 (2010).

————. "Testimonies of Mass Atrocity and the Search for a Viable Theodicy." *Bulletin ET* 18 (2007) 88–99.

————. "Theological Memory in the Face of Tragedy and Mass Atrocity." In *Facing Tragedies*, edited by Christopher Hamilton et al., 129–38. Berlin: Lit-Verlag, 2009.

————. "Traversing Towards the Other (Mark 7:24-30): The Syrophoenician Woman amidst Voicelessness and Loss." In *The Bible: Culture, Community and Society*, edited by Angus Paddison and Neil Messer. London: T&T Clark International, forthcoming.

Agamben, Giorgio. *Remnants of Auschwitz: The Witness and the Archive*. Translated by Daniel Heller-Roazen. New York: Zone, 2008.

Aguilar, Mario I. *Theology, Liberation and Genocide: Reclaiming Liberation Theology*. London: SCM Press, 2009.

Althaus-Reid, Marcella. "From Liberation Theology to Indecent Theology." In *Latin American Liberation Theology: The Next Generation*, edited by Ivan Petralla, 20–38. Maryknoll, NY: Orbis, 2005.

Améry, Jean. *At the Mind's Limits: Contemplations by a Survivor on Auschwitz and Its Realities*. Translated by Sidney Rosenfeld and Stella P. Rosenfeld. Bloomington: Indiana University Press, 1994.

Anderson, Gary A. *Sin: A History*. New Haven: Yale University Press, 2009.

Anselm. *Monologion and Proslogion with the Replies of Gaunilo and Anselm.* Translated by Thomas Williams. Indianapolis: Hackett, 2005.

Appelfeld, Aharon. "After the Holocaust." Translated by Jeffrey M. Green. In *Writing and the Holocaust,* edited by Berel Lang, 83–91. New York: Holmes & Meier, 1988.

———. *The Story of a Life.* Translated by Aloma Halter. London: Hamilton, 2005.

Applebaum, Anne. *Gulag: A History.* New York: Anchor, 2003.

Aquinas, Thomas. "One Way of Understanding God Talk." In B. Davies, *Philosophy of Religion,* 162–64.

———. *Selected Philosophical Writings.* Translated by Timothy McDermott. Oxford: Oxford University Press, 2008.

———. *Summa Theologica.* Edited by Anton C. Pagis. New York: Modern Library, 1948.

———. "Why Think of God as Omnipotent?" In B. Davies, *Philosophy of Religion,* 415–21.

Arendt, Hannah. *Eichmann in Jerusalem: A Report on the Banality of Evil.* New York: Penguin, 1976.

———. *The Human Condition.* Chicago: University of Chicago Press, 1958.

———. *Responsibility and Judgment.* New York: Schocken, 2003.

Aristotle. *Nicomachean Ethics.* In *Introduction to Aristotle,* translated and edited by Richard McKeon, 298–543. New York: McGraw-Hill, 1947.

Armstrong, Karen. *The Bible: A Bibliography.* London: Atlantic, 2008.

———. *The Great Transformation: The World in the Time of Buddha, Socrates, Confucius and Jeremiah.* London: Atlantic, 2007.

Ateek, Naim Stifan. *A Palestinian Cry for Reconciliation.* Maryknoll, NY: Orbis, 2009.

Augustine. *City of God.* Translated by Henry Bettenson. Edited by David Knowles. Middlesex: Penguin, 1980.

———. *Confessions.* Translated by Henry Chadwick. Oxford: Oxford University Press, 1992.

Azevedo, Marcello de Carvalho. "Basic Ecclesial Communities." Translated by Margaret D. Wilde. In Ellacuría and Sobrino, *Mysterium Liberationis,* 636–53.

The Babylonian Talmud: Tractate Berakoth Soncino Talmud. Edited by Isidore Epstein. BN, 2006.

Bailey, Kenneth E. *Jesus through Middle Eastern Eyes: Cultural Studies in the Gospels.* Downers Grove, IL: InterVarsity, 2008.

Balakian, Peter. *Black Dog of Fate: An American Son Uncovers His Armenian Past.* New York: Broadway, 1998.

Baldwin, James. *The Evidence of Things Not Seen.* New York: Holt, 1995.

———. "If Black Language Isn't a Language, Then Tell Me, What Is?" In *The Price of the Ticket: Collected Nonfiction, 1948–1985,* 649–52. London: Michael Joseph, 1985.

Barber, Bruce. "Afterword: Theodicy, Eschatology, and Postmodernity." In Barber and Neville, *Theodicy and Eschatology,* 201–5.

Barber, Bruce, and David Neville, editors. *Theodicy and Eschatology.* Hindmarsh: ATF, 2005.

Barker, Gregory A., editor. *Jesus in the World's Faiths: Leading Thinkers from Five Religions Reflect on His Meaning.* Maryknoll, NY: Orbis, 2005.

Barry, Sebastian. *A Long, Long Way.* London: Faber & Faber, 2005.

Bashir, Halima, with Damien Lewis. *Tears of the Desert: A Memoir of Survival in Darfur*. New York: One World, 2008.

Bau, Joseph. *Dear God, Have You Ever Gone Hungry?* Translated by Shlomo Yurman. New York: Arcade, 1998.

Baum, Gregory. *Compassion and Solidarity: The Church for Others*. Montreal: CBC, 1987.

Beah, Ishmael. *A Long Way Gone: Memoirs of a Boy Soldier*. New York: Sara Crichton, 2007.

Bearak, Barry. "The Day the Sea Came." *The New York Times Sunday Magazine*, 27 November 2005. Online: http://www.nytimes.com/2005/11/27/ magazine/27tsunami1.html?_r=1&pagewanted=print.

Becker, Karl J., and Ilaria Morali, editors. *Catholic Engagement with World Religions: A Comprehensive Study*. Maryknoll, NY: Orbis, 2010.

Benedict XVI (Ratzinger, Joseph). *Jesus of Nazareth: From the Baptism in the Jordan to the Transfiguration*. Translated by Adrian J. Walker. New York: Doubleday, 2007.

———. *Jesus of Nazareth: Holy Week: From the Entrance into Jerusalem to the Resurrection*. Translated by Philip J. Whitmore. New York: Paulist, 2011.

———. *Pilgrim Fellowship of Faith. The Church as Communion*. Translated by Henry Taylor. San Francisco: Ignatius, 2005.

Berger, Alan L., and David Patterson, editors. *Jewish-Christian Dialogue: Drawing Honey from the Rock*. St. Paul: Paragon House, 2008.

Bergmann, Michael, et al., editors. *Divine Evil?: The Moral Character of the God of Abraham*. Oxford: Oxford University Press, 2011.

Berkovits, Eliezer. *Essential Essays on Judaism*, edited by David Hazony. Jerusalem: Shalem, 2003.

———. *Faith after the Holocaust*. New York: KTAV, 1973.

Bernard of Clairvaux. "On Loving God." In McGinn, *Essential Writings of Christian Mysticism*, 435–37.

Bernstein, Richard J. "Evil and the Temptation of Theodicy." In *The Cambridge Companion to Levinas*, edited by Simon Critchley and Robert Bernasconi, 252–67. Cambridge: Cambridge University Press, 2002.

———. *Radical Evil: A Philosophical Investigation*. Cambridge: Polity, 2003.

Berry, Thomas. "Christianity's Role in the Earth Project." In *Christianity and Ecology: Seeking the Well-Being of Earth and Humans*, edited by Dieter T. Hessel and Rosemary Radford Ruether, 127–34. Cambridge: Harvard University Press, 2000.

Berry, Wendell. "Christianity and the Survival of Creation." In *Earth and Word: Classic Sermons on Saving the Planet*, edited by David Rhoads, 47–61. New York: Continuum, 2007.

Beste, Jennifer. "Challenges of Interpersonal Harm for a Theology of Freedom and Grace." In *God and the Victim: Traumatic Intrusions on Grace and Freedom*, 3–16. Oxford: Oxford University Press, 2007.

Bettenson, Henry Scowcroft. *The Early Christian Fathers: A Selection of Writings from the Fathers from St. Clement of Rome to St. Athanasius*. London: Oxford University Press, 1956.

Beverley, John. "The Margin at the Center: On *Testimonio*." In Gugelberger, *The Real Thing*, 23–41.

Bhagavad-Gita. Translated by Barbara Stoler Miller. New York: Bantam, 1986.

Biggar, Nigel. *Aiming to Kill: The Ethics of Suicide and Euthanasia*. London: Darton, Longman, & Todd, 2004.

———, editor. *Burying the Past: Making Peace and Doing Justice after Conflict*. Washington, DC: Georgetown University Press, 2003.

Bijlert, Victor A. van. "The Struggle with Evil: The Theology of Evil in the Bhagavad Gita and the Devimahatmya." In Gort, *Probing the Depths of Evil and Good*, 57–71.

Bitton-Jackson, Livia. *I Have Lived a Thousand Lives: Growing Up in the Holocaust*. London: Pocket, 2000.

Bloom, Harold. *Jesus and Yahweh: The Names Divine*. New York: Penguin, 2005.

Blumenthal, David R. "Auschwitz and Hiroshima: Icons of Our Century." In Frey, *Genocidal Temptation*, 241–56.

———. "Cross-Disciplinary Notes: Four Questions for Teaching the Shoah." In Goldenberg and Millen, *Testimony, Tensions, and Tikkun*, 160–71.

———. "Despair and Hope in Post-Shoah Jewish Life." In Frey, *Genocidal Temptation*, 173–86.

———. *Facing the Abusing God: A Theology of Protest*. Louisville: Westminster John Knox, 1993.

Blustein, Jeffrey. *The Moral Demands of Memory*. Cambridge: Cambridge University Press, 2008.

Bonhoeffer, Dietrich. *Letters and Papers from Prison*. Translated by Reginald Fuller and Frank Clark. Edited by Eberhard Bethge. New York: Touchstone, 1997.

Boo, Katherine. *Behind the Beautiful Forevers: Life, Death, and Hope in a Mumbai Undercity*. New York: Random House, 2012.

Booth, W. James. *Communities of Memory: On Witness, Identity, and Justice*. Ithaca: Cornell University Press, 2006.

Borowski, Tadeusz. *This Way to the Gas, Ladies and Gentlemen*. Translated by Barbara Vedder. New York: Penguin, 1976.

Boys, Mary C. "Redeeming 'Gospel Feminism' from Anti-Judaism." In *The Wisdom of Creation*, edited by Edward Foley and Robert Schreiter, 24–36. Collegeville, MN: Liturgical, 2004.

Brackley, Dean. *The Call to Discernment in Troubled Times: New Perspectives on the Transformative Wisdom of Ignatius of Loyola*. New York: Crossroad, 2004.

Braiterman, Zachary. *(God) After Auschwitz: Tradition and Change in Post-Holocaust Jewish Thought*. Princeton: Princeton University Press, 1998.

Brenner, Reeve. *The Faith and Doubt of Holocaust Survivors*. New York: Free Press, 1980.

Breznitz, Shlomo. "The Advantages of Delay: A Psychological Perpsective on Memoirs of Trauma." In Katz and Rosen, *Obliged by Memory*, 43–51.

Brown, David. "Noncommunicable Diseases May Prove Harder to Control than Other Ailments." *The Washington Post*. 20 September 2011. Online: http://www.washingtonpost.com/national/health-science/noncommunicable-diseases-may-prove-harder-to-control-than-other-ailments/2011/09/06/gIQAzZ9agK_story.html.

Browning, Christopher. *Ordinary Men: Reserve Police Battalion 101 and the Final Solution in Poland*. New York: Harper, 1998.

———. *Remembering Survival: Inside a Nazi Slave-Labor Camp*. New York: Norton, 2011.

Bruce, Steve. *Secularization*. Oxford: Oxford University Press, 2011.

Bruteau, Beatrice, editor. *Jesus through Jewish Eyes: Rabbis and Scholars Engage an Ancient Brother in a New Conversation.* Maryknoll, NY: Orbis, 2003.

Burnett, Joel S. *Where Is God? Divine Absence in the Hebrew Bible.* Minneapolis: Fortress, 2010.

Burrell, David B. *Deconstructing Theodicy: Why Job Has Nothing to Say to the Puzzle of Suffering.* Grand Rapids: Brazos, 2008.

———. *Knowing the Unknowable God: Ibn-Sina, Maimonides, Aquinas.* Notre Dame: University of Notre Dame Press, 2001.

———. *Towards a Jewish-Christian-Muslim Theology.* Oxford: Wiley-Blackwell, 2011.

Camus, Albert. *The Plague.* Translated by Stuart Gilbert. New York: Vintage, 1975.

Caputo, John D., and Michael J Scanlon, editors. *God, the Gift, and Postmodernism.* Bloomington: Indiana University Press, 1999.

Caputo, John D., Mark Dooley, and Michael J. Scanlon, editors. *Questioning God.* Bloomington: Indiana University Press, 2001.

Card, Claudia. *The Atrocity Paradigm: A Theory of Evil.* Oxford: Oxford University Press, 2002.

———. *Confronting Evils: Terrorism, Torture, Genocide.* Cambridge: Cambridge University Press, 2010.

Cardenal, Ernesto. *The Gospel in Solentiname.* Translated by Donald D. Walsh. Maryknoll, NY: Orbis, 2010.

Cargas, Harry James, editor. *Problems Unique to the Holocaust.* Lexington: University Press of Kentucky, 1999.

Cartledge, Mark J., and David Cheetham, editors. *Intercultural Theology: Approaches and Themes.* London: SCM, 2011.

Caruth, Cathy. *Unclaimed Experience: Trauma, Narrative, and History.* Chapel Hill: University of North Carolina Press, 1996.

Casas, Bartolomé de las. *A Short Account of the Destruction of the Indies.* Translated by Nigel Griffin. London: Penguin, 1992.

Catechism of the Catholic Church. New York: Doubleday, 1995.

Catherine of Sienna. *The Dialogue.* In *Catherine of Sienna: The Dialogue.* Translated by Suzanne Noffke. New York: Paulist, 1980.

Cenkner, William. "Introduction." In Cenkner, *Evil and the Response of World Religions*, i–ix.

———, editor. *Evil and the Response of World Religions.* St. Paul: Paragon House, 1997.

Chang, Iris. *The Rape of Nanking.* New York: Penguin, 1997.

Chang, Jung, and Jon Halliday. *Mao: The Unknown Story.* London: Jonathan Cape, 2005.

Chol-Hwan, Kang. *The Aquariums of Pyongyang: Ten Years in the North Korean Gulag.* Translated by Yair Reiner. New York: Basic, 2000.

Chuang Tzu. *The Book of Chuang Tzu.* Translated by Martin Palmer et al. London: Penguin, 2006.

Chung, Paul S., et al., editors. *Asian Contextual Theology for the Third Millenium: Theology of Minjung in Fourth-Eye Formation.* Eugene, OR: Pickwick, 2007.

Cicero, Marcus Tullius. *The Nature of the Gods.* Translated by Horace C. P. McGregor. London: Penguin, 1972.

Claus, Hugo. *The Sorrow of Belgium.* Translated by Arnold J. Pomerans. Woodstock, NY: Overlook, 2002.

Clendinnen, Inga. *Reading the Holocaust*. Cambridge: Cambridge University Press, 1999.

Clifford, Anne M., and Anthony J. Godzieba, editors. *Christology, Memory, Inquiry, Practice*. Maryknoll, NY: Orbis, 2003.

Cliteur, Paul. *The Secular Outlook: In Defense of Moral and Political Secularism*. Oxford: Wiley-Blackwell, 2010.

Cobb, John B., and Christopher Ives, editors. *The Emptying God: A Buddhist-Jewish-Christian Conversation*. Eugene, OR: Wipf & Stock, 2005.

Cobb, John B., and Ward M. McAfee, editors. *The Dialogue Comes of Age: Christian Encounters with Other Traditions*. Minneapolis: Fortress, 2010.

Cohen, Arthur A. *The Tremendum*. New York: Continuum, 1980.

Cohn-Sherbok, Dan. *On Earth as It Is in Heaven: Jews, Christians, and Liberation Theology*. Maryknoll, NY: Orbis, 1986.

———, editor. *Holocaust Theology: A Reader*. New York: New York University Press, 2002.

Colijn, G. Jan, and Marcia Sachs Littell, editors. *Confronting the Holocaust: A Mandate for the Twenty-First Century*. Studies in the Shoah 19–20. Lanham, MD: University Press of America, 1997.

Comblin, José. "Grace." Translated by Dinah Livingstone. In Ellacuría and Sobrino, *Mysterium Liberationis*, 522–32.

———. "Holy Spirit." Translated by Robert R. Barr. In Ellacuría and Sobrino, *Mysterium Liberationis*, 462–82.

Cook, M. A. *A Brief History of the Human Race*. New York: Norton, 2003.

Cook, Michael J. *Modern Jews Engage the New Testament: Enhancing Jewish Well-Being in a Christian Environment*. Woodstock, VT: Jewish Lights, 2008.

Cooper, Terry D. *Dimensions of Evil: Contemporary Perspectives*. Minneapolis: Fortress, 2007.

Corkery, James. "Joseph Ratzinger on Liberation Theology: What Did He Say? Why Did He Say It? What Can Be Said about It?" In *Movement or Moment? Assessing Liberation Theology Forty Years after Medellín*, edited by Patrick Claffey and Joe Egan, 183–200. Bern: Peter Lang, 2009.

Cornille, Catherine. *The Im-possibility of Interreligious Dialogue*. New York: Crossroads, 2008.

Cosgrove, Elliot J., editor. *Jewish Theology in Our Time: A New Generation Explores the Foundations & Future of Jewish Belief*. Woodstock, VT: Jewish Lights, 2010.

Craig, Mary. *Tears of Blood: A Cry for Tibet*. Washington, DC: Counterpoint, 1999.

Cubilié, Anne. *Women Witnessing Terror: Testimony and the Cultural Politics of Human Rights*. New York: Fordham University Press, 2005.

Cunningham, Philip A., et al., editors. *The Catholic Church and the Jewish People: Recent Reflections from Rome*. New York: Fordham University Press, 2007.

Curran, Charles E., editor. *Change in Official Catholic Moral Teachings*. Readings in Moral Theology 13. New York: Paulist, 2003.

Curran, Charles E., and Richard A. McCormick, editors. *Dissent in the Church*. Readings in Moral Theology 6. New York: Paulist, 1988.

Dalai Lama. *Beyond Religion: Ethics for a Whole World*. Translated by Thupten Jinpa Langri. Boston: Houghton Mifflin Harcourt, 2011.

———. Foreword to *Fire under the Snow: Testimony of a Tibetan Prisoner*, by Palden Gyatso. London: Harvill, 1997.

————. *The Good Heart: A Buddhist Perspective on the Teachings of Jesus.* Edited by Robert Kiely. Translated by Geshe Thupten Jinpa. Boston: Wisdom, 1998.

Dalrymple, William. *From the Holy Mountain: A Journey among the Christians of the Middle East.* New York: Henry Holt, 1999.

Danner, Mark. *The Massacre at El Mozote.* New York: Vintage, 1993.

Dante. *The Inferno.* Translated by John Ciardi. New York: Penguin, 1982.

Davies, Brian. "Introduction." In Davies, *Philosophy of Religion,* 135–40.

————. *The Reality of God and the Problem of Evil.* London: Continuum, 2006.

————, editor. *Philosophy of Religion: A Guide and Anthology.* Oxford: Oxford University Press, 2000.

Davies, Paul. "Sincerity and the End of Theodicy: Three Remarks on Levinas and Kant." In *The Cambridge Companion to Levinas,* edited by Simon Critchley and Robert Bernasconi, 161–87. Cambridge: Cambridge University Press, 2002.

Davis, Norman. *Europe: A History.* Oxford: Oxford University Press, 1996.

Davis, Stephen T., editor. *Encountering Evil: Live Options in Theodicy.* Louisville: Westminster John Knox, 2001.

Davis, Stephen T., Daniel Kendall, and Gerald O'Collins, editors. *The Trinity: An Interdisciplinary Symposium on the Trinity.* Oxford: Oxford University Press, 2004.

Day, Abby. *Believing in Belonging: Belief and Social Identity in the Modern World.* Oxford: Oxford University Press, 2011.

D'Costa, Gavin, editor. *Christian Uniqueness Reconsidered: The Myth of a Pluralistic Theology of Religions.* Maryknoll, NY: Orbis, 1990.

————. "The Descent into Hell as a Solution for the Problem of the Fate of Unevangelized Non-Christians: Balthasar's Hell, the Limbo of the Fathers and Purgatory." *International Journal of Systematic Theology* 11:2 (2009) 146–71.

Delbo, Charlotte. *Auschwitz and After.* Translated by Rosette C. Lamont. New Haven: Yale University Press, 1995.

Delio, Ilia. *The Emergent Christ: Exploring the Meaning of Catholic in an Evolutionary Universe.* Maryknoll, NY: Orbis, 2011.

————. *A Franciscan View of Creation: Learning to Live in a Sacramental World.* Mansfield, OH: The Franciscan Institute, 2003.

Dempsey, Judy. "German Women Seized during World War II Seek Recognition." *The International Herald Tribune,* 15 June 2007. Online: http://www.iht.com/articles/2007/06/15/news/letter.php.

Deng, Alephonsion, Benson Deng, and Benjamin Ajak, with Judy A. Bernstein. *They Poured Fire on Us from the Sky: The True Story of Three Lost Boys from Sudan.* New York: PublicAffairs, 2005.

Des Pres, Terrence. *The Survivor: An Anatomy of Life in the Death Camps.* Oxford: Oxford University Press, 1980.

The Dhammapada. Translated by Juan Mascaró. London: Penguin, 1973.

Diamant, Anita. *The Red Tent.* New York: Picador, 1997.

Diamond, Jared. *Collapse: How Societies Choose to Fail or Succeed.* New York: Penguin, 2006.

————. *Guns, Germs, and Steel: The Fates of Human Societies.* New York: Norton, 1999.

Di Giovanni, Janine. *The Place at the End of the World: Essays from the Edge.* London: Bloomsbury, 2006.

Domning, Daryl O., with Monika K. Hellwig. *Original Selfishness: Original Sin and Evil in the Light of Evolution.* Aldershot: Ashgate, 2006.

Donat, Alexander. "Voice from the Ashes: Wanderings in Search of God." In Katz et al., *Wrestling with God*, 275–86.

Doniger, Wendy. *The Hindus: An Alternative History.* New York: Penguin 2009.

Dostoyevsky, Fyodor. *The Brothers Karamazov.* Translated by Constance Garnett. New York: Signet, 1986.

———. *The House of the Dead.* Translated by David McDuff. Middlesex: Penguin, 1985.

Draaisma, Douwe. *Why Life Speeds Up as You Get Older: How Memory Shapes Our Past.* Translated by Arnold and Erica Pomerans. Cambridge: Cambridge University Press, 2004.

Drakulic, Slavenka. *The Balkan Express: Fragments from the Other Side of War.* New York: Norton, 1993.

Dressler, Markus, and Arvind-Pal S. Mandair, editors. *Secularism and Religion-Making.* Oxford: Oxford University Press, 2011.

Duffy, Regis A. "Sacraments in General." In Fiorenza and Galvin, *Systematic Theology*, 183–210.

Dulles, Avery Cardinal. *A History of Apologetics.* San Francisco: Ignatius Press, 2005.

Dunson, Donald H. *Child, Victim, Soldier: The Loss of Innocence in Uganda.* Maryknoll, NY: Orbis, 2008.

Eagleton, Terry. *On Evil.* New Haven: Yale University Press, 2010.

Echeverria, Eduardo J. "The Gospel of Redemptive Suffering: Reflections on John Paul II's *Salvifici Doloris.*" In Van Inwagen, *Christian Faith and the Problem of Evil*, 111–47.

Eckardt, Alice L., and A. Roy Eckardt. *Long Night's Journey into Day: A Revised Retrospective on the Holocaust.* Detroit: Wayne State University Press, 1988.

Eckhart, Meister. "Sermon 2." In McGinn, *Essential Writings of Christian Mysticism*, 36–40.

Eiseley, Loren. *The Star Thrower.* New York: Harvest, 1979.

Ellacuría, Ignacio. "The Crucified People." Translated by Philip Berryman and Robert R. Barr. In Ellacuría and Sobrino, *Mysterium Liberationis*, 580–603.

———. "The Historicity of Christian Salvation." Translated by Margaret D. Wilde. In Ellacuría and Sobrino, *Mysterium Liberationis*, 251–89.

———. "Utopia and Prophecy in Latin America." Translated by James R. Brockman. In Ellacuría and Sobrino, *Mysterium Liberationis*, 289–328.

Ellacuría, Ignacio, and Jon Sobrino, editors. *Mysterium Liberationis: Fundamental Concepts of Liberation Theology.* Maryknoll, NY: Orbis, 1993.

Ellis, Marc H. *Toward a Jewish Theology of Liberation.* Maryknoll, NY: Orbis, 1987.

Enns, Elaine, and Ched Myers. *Ambassadors of Reconciliation.* Vol. 2, *Diverse Christian Practices of Restorative Justice and Peacemaking.* Maryknoll, NY: Orbis, 2009.

Euripedes. *The Bacchae and Other Plays.* Translated by Philip Vellacott. Middlesex: Penguin, 1986.

Evans, Gareth. *The Responsibility to Protect: Ending Mass Atrocity Crimes Once and for All.* Washington, DC: The Brookings Institution, 2008.

Fackenheim, Emil, "The 614th Commandment Reconsidered." In *Jewish Philosophers and Jewish Philosophy*, edited by Michael L. Morgan, 193–94. Bloomington: Indiana University Press, 1996.

———. *To Mend the World: Foundations of Post-Holocaust Jewish Thought.* Bloomington: Indiana University Press, 1994.

Fasching, Darrell J. *The Ethical Challenge of Auschwitz and Hiroshima: Apocalypse or Utopia?* Albany: State University of New York Press, 1993.

———. "Ethics after Auschwitz and Hiroshima." In Frey, *Genocidal Temptation*, 1–24.

———. *Narrative Theology after Auschwitz: From Ethics to Alienation.* Minneapolis: Fortress, 1992.

Fassin, Didier, and Richard Rechtman. *The Empire of Trauma: An Inquiry into the Conditions of Victimhood.* Translated by Rachel Gomme. Princeton: Princeton University Press, 2009.

Faust, Drew Gilpin. *This Republic of Suffering: Death and the American Civil War.* New York: Vintage, 2009.

Feinstein, Edward, editor. *Jews and Judaism in the Twenty-First Century: Human Responsibility, the Presence of God, and the Future of the Covenant.* Woodstock, VT: Jewish Lights, 2007.

Felman, Shoshana, and Dori Laub. *Testimony: Crises of Witnessing in Literature, Psychoanalysis, and History.* New York: Routledge, 1992.

Finlayson, Clive. *The Humans Who Went Extinct: Why Neanderthals Died Out and We Survived.* Oxford: Oxford University Press, 2009.

Fiorenza, Francis Schüssler, and John P. Galvin, editors. *Systematic Theology: Roman Catholic Perspectives.* Vol. 2. Minneapolis: Fortress, 1991.

Foley, Elena Procario. "Heir or Orphan: Theological Evolution and Devolution before and after *Nostra Aetate.*" In *Vatican II Forty Years Later*, edited by William Madges, 308–39. Maryknoll, NY: Orbis, 2006.

Fonrobert, Charlotte Elisheva, and Martin S. Jaffee, editors. *The Cambridge Companion to the Talmud and Rabbinic Literature.* Cambridge: Cambridge University Press, 2007.

Fonseca, Isabel. *Bury Me Standing: The Gypsies and Their Journey.* London: Vintage, 2009.

Forbes, Peter. *Dazzled and Deceived: Mimicry and Camouflage.* New Haven: Yale University Press, 2009.

Forché, Carolyn, editor. *Against Forgetting: Twentieth-Century Poetry of Witness.* New York: Norton, 1993.

Frankl, Victor E. *Man's Search for Meaning.* Translated by Ilse Lasch. New York: Washington Square, 1985.

Frede-Wenger, Britta. "'Good' Friday after Auschwitz?" In Patterson and Roth, *Fire in the Ashes*, 137–49.

Fredericks, James L. *Faith among Faiths: Christian Theology and Non-Christian Religions.* New York: Paulist, 1999.

Fredriksen, Paula. *Augustine and the Jews: A Christian Defense of Jews and Judaism.* New York: Doubleday, 2008.

Freud, Sigmund. *Beyond the Pleasure Principle.* Translated by James Strachey. New York: Norton, 1989.

Frey, Robert S., editor. *The Genocidal Temptation: Auschwitz, Hiroshima, Rwanda, and Beyond.* Dallas: University Press of America, 2004.

Friedländer, Saul. "*Facing the Shoah*: Memory and History." In Singer, *Humanity at the Limit*, 1–11.

Fromm, Erich. *Escape from Freedom.* New York: Henry Holt, 1994.

Frymer-Kensky, Tikva et al., editors. *Christianity in Jewish Terms*. Boulder, CO: Westview, 2000.

Funkenstein, Amos. "Theological Interpretations of the Holocaust." In Katz et al., *Wrestling with God*, 639–47.

Galvin, John P. "Sin and Grace." In Fiorenza and Galvin, *Systematic Theology*, 75–141.

Gaudium et Spes. Online: http://www.vatican.va/archive/hist_councils/ii_vatican_council/documents/vat-ii_cons_19651207_gaudium-et-spes_en.html.

Gebara, Ivone. *Out of the Depths: Women's Experience of Evil and Suffering*. Translated by Ann Patrick Ware. Minneapolis: Fortress, 2002.

Geddes, Jennifer L. "Religious Rhetoric in Responses to Atrocity." In *The Religious in Responses to Mass Atrocity: Interdisciplinary Perspectives*, edited by Thomas Brudholm and Thomas Cushman, 21–37. Cambridge: Cambridge University Press, 2009.

Gerald of Wales. *The History and Topography of Ireland*. Translated by John O'Meara. London: Penguin, 1982.

Gettleman, Jeffrey, and Josh Kron. "U.N. Report on Congo Massacres Draws Anger." *New York Times*, 2 October 2010. Online: http://www.nytimes.com/2010/10/02/world/africa/02congo.html.

Gillis, Chester. *Pluralism: A New Paradigm for Theology*. Leuven: Peeters, 1998.

Gillman, Neil. "Judaic Doctrines of Death and Afterlife." In *The Encyclopaedia of Judaism*, 2nd ed., vol. 1, A–E, edited by Jacob Neusner et al., 593–609. Leiden: Brill, 2005.

Ginzburg, Eugenia Semyonovna. *Journey into the Whirlwind*. Translated by Paul Stevenson and Max Hayward. San Diego: Harvest 1995.

Gira, Dennis. "A Buddhist Approach to the Question of 'Evil.'" *Concilium* 1 (2009) 100–107.

Girard, René. *I See Satan Fall Like Lightning*. Translated by James G. Williams. Maryknoll, NY: Orbis, 2008.

Glatzer, Nahum, editor. *The Judaic Tradition*. West Orange: Behrman, 1969.

Glover, Jonathan. *Humanity: A Moral History of the Twentieth Century*. London: Pimlico, 2001.

Goldenberg, Myrna, and Rochelle L. Millen, editors. *Testimony, Tensions, and Tikkun: Teaching the Holocaust in Colleges and Universities*. Seattle: University of Washington Press, 2007.

Goldhagen, Daniel Jonah. *Worse than War: Genocide, Eliminationism, and the Ongoing Assault on Humanity*. New York: PublicAffairs, 2009.

Goldstein, Elyse, editor. *New Jewish Feminism: Probing the Past, Forging the Future*. Woodstock, VT: Jewish Lights, 2009.

Gobodo-Madikizela, Pumla. *A Human Being Died That Night: A South African Story of Forgiveness*. Boston: Houghton Mifflin, 2003.

Gort, Jerald D., et al., editors. *Probing the Depths of Evil and Good: Multireligious Views and Case Studies*. Amsterdam: Rodopi, 2007.

Gourevitch, Philip. *We Wish to Inform You That Tomorrow We Will Be Killed with Our Families: Stories from Rwanda*. New York: Farrar, Straus, & Giroux, 1998.

Green, Arthur. *Radical Judaism: Rethinking God and Tradition*. New Haven: Yale University Press, 2010.

Greenberg, Gershon, "Between Holocaust and Redemption: Silence, Cognition, and Eclipse." In Katz, *The Impact of the Holocaust on Jewish Theology*, 110–31.

————. "Introduction" [to "Part I: Ultra-Orthodox Responses during and following the War"]. In Katz et al., *Wrestling with God*, 11–38.

Greenberg, Irving. "Cloud of Smoke, Pillar of Fire: Judaism, Christianity and Modernity after the Holocaust." In Katz et al., *Wrestling with God*, 499–523.

————. Foreword to *Long Night's Journey into Day: A Revised Retrospective on the Holocaust,* by Alice L. Eckardt and A. Roy Eckardt, 9–11. Detroit: Wayne State University Press, 1988.

————. *For the Sake of Heaven and Earth: The New Encounter between Judaism and Christianity.* Philadelphia: Jewish Publication Society, 2004.

————. "From Destruction to Redemption." In *Jews and Judaism in the Twenty-First Century: Human Responsibility, the Presence of God, and the Future of the Covenant,* edited by Edward Feinstein, 41–56. Woodstock, VT: Jewish Lights, 2007.

Greenberg, Yudit Kornberg. "Hindu-Jewish Summits (2007–2008): A Postmodern Religious Encounter." *Interreligious Insight* 7:1 (2009) 26–39.

Griswold, Charles L. *Forgiveness: A Philosophical Exploration.* Cambridge: Cambridge University Press, 2007.

Grob, Leonard, and John K. Roth, editors. *Anguished Hope: Holocaust Scholars Confront the Palestinian-Israeli Conflict.* Grand Rapids: Eerdmans, 2008.

Grossman, Vassily. *Life and Fate.* Translated by Robert Chandler. New York: New York Review of Books, 2006.

Gugelberger, Georg M. "Introduction: Institutionalization of Transgression: Testimonial Discourse and Beyond." In Gugelberger, *The Real Thing*, 1–19.

————, editor. *The Real Thing: Testimonial Discourse and Latin America.* Durham, NC: Duke University Press, 1996.

Gula, Richard. *Reason Informed by Faith.* New York: Paulist, 1989.

Gutiérrez, Gustavo. *On Job: God-Talk and the Suffering of the Innocent.* Translated by Matthew J. O'Connell. Maryknoll, NY: Orbis, 2002.

————. "Option for the Poor." Translated by Robert R. Barr. In Ellacuría and Sobrino, *Mysterium Liberationis*, 235–50.

————. *A Theology of Liberation.* Translated by Caridad Inda and John Eagleson. Maryknoll, NY: Orbis, 1988.

Gyatso, Palden. *Fire under the Snow: Testimony of a Tibetan Prisoner.* Translated by Tsering Shakya. London: Harvill, 1997.

Haas, Andrew, et al., editors. *The Oxford Handbook of English Literature and Theology.* Oxford: Oxford University Press, 2009.

Haas, Peter J. "Forgiveness, Reconciliation, and Jewish Memory after Auschwitz." In Patterson and Roth, *After-Words: Post-Holocaust Struggles with Forgiveness*, 5–15.

————. "In Response to Didier Pollefeyt." In Patterson and Roth, *Fire in the Ashes*, 234–37.

————. "Judaism in Protestant Encounters with the Shoah" In Patterson and Roth, *Fire in the Ashes*, 59–70.

————. "Science and the Determination of the Good." In Roth, *Ethics after the Holocaust*, 49–59.

Haight, Roger. *The Future of Christology.* New York: Continuum, 2007.

Halberstam, David. *War in a Time of Peace: Bill Clinton and the Generals.* London: Jersey Yellow, 2001.

Hallisey, Charles. "Buddhism." In Neusner, *Evil and Suffering*, 36–66.

Hammer, Jill. "To Her We Shall Return: Jews Turning to the Goddess, the Goddess Turning to Jews." In *New Jewish Feminism: Probing the Past, Forging the Future*, edited by Elyse Goldstein, 22–34. Woodstock, VT: Jewish Lights, 2009.

Hammer, Reuven, editor and translator. *The Classic Midrash: Tannaitic Commentaries on the Bible*. New York: Paulist, 1995.

Hanh, Thich Nhat. *Living Buddha, Living Christ*. London: Rider, 1995.

Hanje, Kim. "The Theodicy of Unificationsim." *Journal of the Korean Academy of New Religions* (2010) 219–234.

Harlow, Barbara. *Resistance Literature*. New York: Methuen, 1987.

Harrowitz, Nancy. "The Grey Zone of Scientific Invention: Primo Levi and the Omissions of Memory." In Katz and Rosen, *Obliged by Memory*, 83–103.

Hart, David Bentley. "Tsunami and Theodicy." *First Things*. Republished 8 May 2008. Online: http://www.firstthings.com/onthesquare/2008/05/tsunami-and-theodicy.

Hartman, Geoffrey. "Elie Wiesel and the Morality of Fiction." In Katz and Rosen, *Obliged by Memory*, 107–16.

Harvey, Peter. *An Introduction to Buddhism: Teachings, History, and Practices*. Cambridge: Cambridge University Press, 1995.

Hatley, James. *Suffering Witness: The Quandary of Responsibility after the Irreparable*. Albany: State University of New York Press, 2000.

Hatzfeld, Jean. *Machete Season: The Killers in Rwanda Speak*. Translated by Linda Coverdale. New York: Picador, 2006.

———. *The Strategy of Antelopes: Living in Rwanda after the Genocide: A Report*. Translated by Linda Coverdale. London: Serpent's Tail, 2009.

Heck, Alfons. *A Child of Hitler: Germany in the Days when God Wore a Swastika*. Frederick, CO: Renaissance, 1988.

Heike, Irmtraud. "Female Concentration Camp Guards as Perpetrators: Three Case Studies." In *Ordinary People as Mass Murderers: Perpetrators in Comparative Perspectives*, edited by Olaf Jensen and Claus-Christian W. Szejnmann, 121–42. Palgrave: Balingstoke, 2008.

Held, Shai. "Living and Dreaming with God." In *Jewish Theology in Our Time: A New Generation Explores the Foundations and Future of Jewish Belief*, edited by Elliot J. Cosgrove, 17–22. Woodstock, VT: Jewish Lights, 2010.

Hellwig, Monika K. "Eschatology." In Fiorenza and Galvin, *Systematic Theology*, 347–72.

Helmick, Raymond G., and Rodney Petersen, editors. *Forgiveness and Reconciliation*. Philadelphia: Templeton Foundation Press, 2002.

Herman, Judith Lewis. "Afterword: The Dialectic of Trauma Continues." In *Trauma and Recovery: The Aftermath of Violence—From Domestic Abuse to Political Terror*, 237–45. New York: Basic, 1997.

Hick, John. *Death and Eternal Life*. Louisville: Westminster John Knox, 1994.

———. *Evil and the God of Love*. London: Macmillan, 1977.

Hick, John, and Paul F. Knitter, editors. *The Myth of Christian Uniqueness: Toward a Pluralistic Theology of Religions*. Maryknoll, NY: Orbis, 1997.

Him, Chanrithy. *When Broken Glass Floats: Growing Up under the Khmer Rouge*. London: Norton, 2001.

Himes, Kenneth R., editor. *Modern Catholic Social Teaching: Commentaries and Interpretations*. Washington, DC: Georgetown University Press, 2004.

Hirsch, David H. "Critique by David Hirsch" [of "The Kafkaesque World of the Holocaust"]. In Roth, *Ethics after the Holocaust*, 252–60.

―――. "The Gray Zone or the Banality of Evil." In Roth, *Ethics after the Holocaust*, 90–107.

Hirsch, Roslyn. "Translator's Foreword." In Nomberg-Przytyk, *True Tales from a Grotesque Land*. Chapel Hill: University of North Carolina Press, 1985.

Hochschild, Adam. *King Leopold's Ghost: A Story of Greed, Terror, and Heroism in Colonial Africa*. London: Papermac, 2000.

Hoffman, Eva. *After Such Knowledge: Memory, History, and the Legacy of the Holocaust*. New York: PublicAffairs, 2004.

Hogan, Linda, editor. *Applied Ethics in a World Church: The Padua Conference*. Maryknoll, NY: Orbis, 2008.

Homer. *The Iliad*. Translated by E. V. Rieu. Baltimore: Penguin, 1968.

―――. *The Odyssey*. Translated by Robert Fitzgerald. London: David Campbell, 1992.

Howard, Thomas Albert. *God and the Atlantic: America, Europe, and the Religious Divide*. Oxford: Oxford University Press, 2011.

Ignatius of Antioch. "The Epistle to the Romans." Translated by Andrew Louth. In *Early Christian Writings: The Apostolic Fathers*, 85–89. Penguin: London, 1987.

Ignatius of Loyola. *The Spiritual Exercises of Saint Ignatius*. Translated by Anthony Mottola. New York: Doubleday, 1989.

Ilibagiza, Immaculée, with Steve Erwin. *Left to Tell: Discovering God amidst the Rwandan Holocaust*. Carlsbad, CA: Hay House, 2006.

Inati, Shams C. *The Problem of Evil: Ibn Sînâ's Theodicy*. Binghamton, NY: Global Productions, 2000.

Isenberg, Sheldon R. "From Myth to Psyche to Mystic Psychology: The Evolution of the Problem of Evil in Judaism." In Cenkner, *Evil and the Response of World Religions*, 16–31.

Jal, Emmanuel, with Megan Lloyd Davies. *War Child: A Child Soldier's Story*. London: Abacus, 2009.

Jenkins, Philip. *The Lost History of Christianity: The Thousand-Year Golden Age of the Church in the Middle East, Africa, and Asia—and How It Died*. Oxford: Lion, 2008.

Jersak, Brad, and Michael Hardin, editors. *Stricken by God? Nonviolent Identification and the Victory of Christ*. Grand Rapids: Eerdmans, 2007.

John Paul II. *Memory and Identity: Personal Reflections*. London: Weidenfeld & Nicolson, 2005.

―――. *Salvifici Doloris*. Online: http://www.vatican.va/holy_father/john_paul_ii/apost_letters/documents/hf_jp-ii_apl_11021984_salvifici-doloris_en.html.

Johnson, Elizabeth A. "Losing and Finding Creation in the Christian Tradition." In *Christianity and Ecology: Seeking the Well-Being of Earth and Humans*, edited by Dieter T. Hessel and Rosemary Radford Ruether, 3–21. Cambridge: Harvard University Press, 2000.

―――. *Quest for the Living God: Mapping Frontiers in the Theology of God*. New York: Continuum, 2011.

Johnson, Eric A., and Karl-Heinz Reuband. *What We Knew: Terror, Mass Murder, and Everyday Life in Nazi Germany: An Oral History*. Cambridge: Basic, 2006.

Jonas, Hans. "The Concept of God after Auschwitz: A Jewish Voice." In *Mortality and Morality: A Search for the Good after Auschwitz*, edited by Lawrence Vogel, 131–43. Evanston, IL: Northwestern University Press, 1996.

Junker-Kenny, Maureen. "Ethics, the Hermeneutics of Memory, and the Concept of God." In *Naming and Thinking God in Europe Today: Theology in Global Dialogue*, edited by Norbert Hintersteiner, 211–31. Amsterdam: Rodopi, 2007.

The Kabbalah. Translated by Daniel C. Matt. New York: Quality Paperback Book Club, 1998.

Kant, Immanuel. *Grounding for the Metaphysics of Morals*. Translated by James W. Ellington. 3rd ed. Indianapolis: Hackett, 1993.

———. *Religion within the Boundaries of Mere Reason*. Translated by Allen Wood. Cambridge: Cambridge University Press, 1998.

Kaplan, Robert D. *Monsoon: The Indian Ocean and the Future of American Power*. New York: Random House, 2011.

Katz, Steven T. "Introduction" [to "Part 3: European and American Responses during and following the War"]. In Katz et al., *Wrestling with God*, 355–69.

———. "The Issue of Confirmation and Disconfirmation in Jewish Thought after the Shoah." In Katz, *The Impact of the Holocaust on Jewish Theology*, 13–60.

———. *Post-Holocaust Dialogues: Critical Studies in Modern Jewish Thought*. New York: New York University Press, 1985.

———, editor. *The Impact of the Holocaust on Jewish Theology*. New York: New York University Press, 2005.

Katz, Steven T., and Alan Rosen, editors. *Obliged by Memory: Literature, Religion, Ethics*. Syracuse: Syracuse University Press, 2006.

Katz, Steven T., Shlomo Biderman, and Gershon Greenberg, editors. *Wrestling with God: Jewish Theological Responses during and after the Holocaust*. Oxford: Oxford University Press, 2007.

Keenan, James, editor. *Catholic Theological Ethics in the World Church*. New York: Continuum, 2007.

Keilson, Hans. *Comedy in a Minor Key*. Translated by Damion Searls. London: Hesperus, 2010.

Keller, Catherine, et al., editors. *Postcolonial Theologies: Divinity and Empire*. St. Louis: Chalice, 2004.

Kelly, Maria. *The Great Dying: The Black Death in Dublin*. Stroud, Gloucestershire: Tempus, 2003.

Kendall, Daniel, and Gerald O'Collins, editors. *In Many and Diverse Ways: In Honor of Jacques Dupuis*. Maryknoll, NY: Orbis, 2003.

Kerr, Fergus. *Twentieth-Century Catholic Theologians*. Oxford: Blackwell, 2008.

Kessler, Edward. *An Introduction to Jewish-Christian Relations*. Cambridge: Cambridge University Press, 2010.

Khadra, Yasmina. *The Swallows of Kabul*. Translated by John Cullen. New York: Anchor, 2005.

Khalidi, Tarif, editor and translator. *The Muslim Jesus: Sayings and Stories in Islamic Literature*. Cambridge: Harvard University Press, 2003.

Kierkegaard, Søren. *Fear and Trembling*. Translated by Alastair Hannay. London: Penguin, 1985.

Kiernan, Ben. *Blood and Soil: A World History of Genocide and Extermination from Sparta to Darfur*. New Haven: Yale University Press, 2007.

Knight, Henry F. "The Face of Forgiveness in a Post-Holocaust World." In Patterson and Roth, *After-Words*, 28–40.

Knitter, Paul F., editor. *The Myth of Religious Superiority: A Multifaith Exploration.* Maryknoll, NY: Orbis, 2005.

Kogan, Michael S. *Opening the Covenant: A Jewish Theology of Christianity.* Oxford: Oxford University Press, 2008.

Kristeva, Julia. *Powers of Horror: An Essay on Abjection.* New York: Columbia University Press, 1982.

Kugel, James L. *How to Read the Bible: A Guide to Scripture Then and Now.* New York: Free Press, 2007.

Laato, Antti, and Johannes C. de Moor, editors. *Theodicy in the World of the Bible.* Leiden: Brill, 2003.

Lamdan, Neville, and Alberto Melloni, editors. *Nostra Aetate: Origins, Promulgation, Impact on Jewish-Catholic Relations.* Berlin: Lit Verlag, 2007.

Lampman, Lisa Barnes, editor. *God and the Victim: Theological Reflections on Evil, Victimization, Justice, and Forgiveness.* Grand Rapids: Eerdmans, 1999

Lane, Dermot A. *Stepping Stones to Other Religions: A Christian Theology of Inter-religious Dialogue.* Dublin: Veritas, 2011.

Lang, Berel. "Introduction." In Berel, *Writing and the Holocaust*, 1–15.

———, editor. *Writing and the Holocaust.* New York: Holmes & Meier, 1988.

Langer, Lawrence. *Admitting the Holocaust.* New York: Oxford University Press, 1995.

———. *Holocaust Testimonies: The Ruins of Memory.* New Haven: Yale University Press, 1991.

———. *Using and Abusing the Holocaust.* Bloomington: Indiana University Press, 2006.

Lara, María Pía, editor. *Rethinking Evil: Contemporary Perspectives.* Berkeley: University of California Press, 2001.

Larrimore, Mark, editor. *The Problem of Evil: A Reader.* Malden: Blackwell, 2004.

Laytner, Anson. *Arguing with God: A Jewish Tradition.* Northvale, NJ: Jason Aronson, 1990.

Lazarus, Neil, editor. *The Cambridge Companion to Postcolonial Literary Studies.* Cambridge: Cambridge University Press, 2004.

Lederach, John Paul, and Angela Jill Lederach. "When Mothers Speak." In *When Blood and Bones Cry Out: Journeys through the Soundscape of Healing and Reconciliation*, 147-69. St. Lucia: University of Queensland Press, 2010.

Lee, Dorothy. "'The Darkness Did Not Overcome It': Theodicy and Eschatology in John." In Barber and Neville, *Theodicy and Eschatology*, 43–65.

Lee, Soon Ok. *Eyes of the Tailless Animals: Prison Memoirs of a North Korean Woman.* Translated by Bahn-Suk Lee and Jin Young Choi. Bartlesville, OK: Living Sacrifice, 1999.

Legerwey, John. "Evil and Its Treatment in Early Taoism." In Gort, *Probing the Depths of Evil and Good*, 73–86.

Leibniz, G. W. *Theodicy: Essays on the Goodness of God, the Freedom of Man, and the Origin of Evil.* Translated by E. M. Huggard. La Salle, IL: Open Court, 1996.

Lengyel, Olga. *Five Chimneys: A Woman Survivor's True Story of Auschwitz.* Chicago: Academy Chicago Publishers, 1995.

Lerner, Natan. *Religion, Beliefs, and International Human Rights.* Maryknoll, NY: Orbis, 2000.

Levi, Primo. *The Drowned and the Saved.* Translated by Raymond Rosenthal. New York: Vintage, 1989.

———. *Moments of Reprieve: A Memoir of Auschwitz.* Translated by Ruth Feldman. Penguin: Middlesex, 1995.

———. *Survival in Auschwitz.* Translated by Stuart Woolf. New York: Touchstone, 1996.

Lévinas, Emmanuel. *Beyond the Verse: Talmudic Readings and Lectures.* Translated by Gary D. Mole. London: Continuum, 2007.

———. "Death of the Other and My Own." In *God, Death, and Time,* 16–22. Translated by Bettina Bergo. Stanford: Stanford University Press, 2000.

———. "Dialogue on Thinking-of-the-Other." In *Entre Nous: Thinking of the Other,* 201–6. Translated by Michael B. Smith and Barbara Hashev. London: Athlone, 1998.

———. *Difficult Freedom: Essays on Judaism.* Translated by Seán Hand. Baltimore: Johns Hopkins University Press, 1990.

———. *Ethics and Infinity: Conversations with Philippe Nemo.* Translated by Richard A. Cohen. Pittsburgh: Duquesne University Press, 2009.

———. "God and Philosophy." In *Collected Philosophical Papers,* 153–73. Translated by Alphonso Lingis. Dordrecht: Kluwer Academic, 1993.

———. *In the Time of Nations.* Translated by Michael B. Smith. London: Continuum, 2007.

———. *Nine Talmudic Readings.* Translated by Annette Aronowicz. Bloomington: Indiana University Press, 1994.

———. *Time and the Other.* Translated by Richard A. Cohen. Pittsburgh: Duquesne University Press, 1987.

———. "Transcendence and Evil." In *Collected Philosophical Papers,* 175–86. Translated by Alphonso Lingis. Dordrecht: Kluwer Academic, 1993.

———. "Useless Suffering." In *The Problem of Evil: A Reader,* edited by Mark Larrimore, 371–80. Malden, MA: Blackwell, 2004.

Levine, Amy-Jill. *The Misunderstood Jew: The Church and the Scandal of the Jewish Jesus.* New York: Harper, 2007.

Levine, Amy-Jill, and Marc Zvi Brettler, editors. *The Jewish Annotated New Testament.* Oxford: Oxford University Press, 2011.

Lewis. C. S. *The Problem of Pain.* San Francisco: Harper, 1996.

Leydesdorff, Selma. *Surviving the Bosnian Genocide: The Women of Srebrenica Speak.* Translated by Kay Richardson. Bloomington: Indiana University Press, 2011.

Leys, Ruth. *Trauma: A Genealogy.* Chicago: Chicago University Press, 2000.

Limón, Javier Jiménez. "Suffering, Death, Cross, and Martyrdom." Translated by Dinah Livingstone. In Ellacuría and Sobrino, *Mysterium Liberationis,* 702–15.

Locke, Hubert. "The Holocaust, Israel, and Jewish-Christian Relations." In Grob and Roth, *Anguished Hope,* 191–200.

Lohfink, Norbert. *The Covenant Never Revoked: Biblical Reflections on Christian-Jewish Dialogue.* Translated by John J. Scullion. New York: Paulist, 1991.

———. *Option for the Poor: The Basic Principle of Liberation Theology in the Light of the Bible.* Translated by Linda M. Maloney. N. Richland Hills: BIBAL, 1995.

Lopez, Donald S., editor. *Buddhist Scriptures.* London: Penguin, 2004.

Lower, Wendy. "Distant Encounter: An Auschwitz Survivor in the College Classroom." In *Approaching an Auschwitz Survivor: Holocaust Testimony and Its*

Transformations, edited by Jürgen Matthäus, 95–117. Oxford: Oxford University Press, 2009.

Lubin, Orly. "Holocaust Testimony, National Memory." In *Extremities: Trauma, Testimony, and Community*, edited by Nancy K. Miller and Jason Tougaw, 130–41. Urbana: University of Illinois Press, 2002.

Lycan, William G. "'Use' Theories." In *Philosophy of Language*, 88–99. New York: Routledge, 1999.

Lynch, Gordon. *The Sacred in the Modern World: A Cultural Sociological Approach.* Oxford: Oxford University Press, 2012.

MacCulloch, Diarmaid. *The Reformation: A History.* Penguin: New York: 2005.

Mackintosh-Smith, Tim. *Travels with a Tangerine: A Journey in the Footnotes of Ibn Battutah.* New York: Welcome Rain, 2001.

Maclure, Jocelyn, and Charles Taylor. *Secularism and Freedom of Conscience.* Translated by Jane Marie Todd. Cambridge: Harvard University Press, 2011.

MacMillan, Margaret. *Dangerous Games: The Uses and Abuses of History.* New York: Modern Library, 2009.

Madges, William, editor. *Vatican II: Forty Years Later.* Maryknoll, NY: Orbis, 2006.

Maduro, Otto, editor. *Judaism, Christianity, and Liberation: An Agenda for Dialogue.* Maryknoll, NY: Orbis, 1991.

Maimonides, Moses. *The Guide for the Perplexed.* Translated by M. Friedländer. New York: Dover, 1956.

———. *The Laws of Repentance.* Translated by Rabbi David Shure. Online: http://www.science-halacha.com/rambam/rambam_eng_contents.htm.

Malham, Joseph M. *By Fire into Light: Four Catholic Martyrs of the Nazi Camps.* Leuven: Peeters, 2002.

Mann, Charles C. *1491: New Revelations of the Americas before Columbus.* New York: Vintage, 2006.

———. *1493: How Europe's Discovery of the Americas Revolutionized Trade, Ecology and Life on Earth.* London: Granta, 2011.

Margalit, Avishai. *The Ethics of Memory.* Cambridge: Harvard University Press, 2002.

Markusen, Eric. "Reflections on the Holocaust and Hiroshima." In Frey, *Genocidal Temptation*, 25–39.

Marrujo, Olivia Ruiz. "The Gender of Risk: Sexual Violence against Undocumented Women." In *A Promised Land, A Perilous Journey: Theological Perspectives on Migration*, edited by Daniel G. Groody and Gioacchino Campese, 225–39. Notre Dame: University of Notre Dame Press, 2011.

Marty, Martin. *The Christian World: A Global History.* New York: Modern Library, 2009.

Matthäus, Jürgen, editor. *Approaching an Auschwitz Survivor: Holocaust Testimony and Its Transformations.* Oxford: Oxford University Press, 2009.

May, John D'Arcy. *After Pluralism: Towards an Interreligious Ethic.* Münster: Lit Verlag, 2000.

———. "Buddhists, Christians, and Ecology." In *Buddhism, Christianity, and the Question of Creation: Karmic or Divine?*, edited by Perry Schmidt-Leukel, 93–107. Aldershot: Ashgate, 2006.

———. "Catholic Fundamentalism? Some Implications of *Dominus Iesus* for Dialogue and Peacemaking." In *"Dominus Iesus": Anstössige Wahrheit oder anstössige Kirche?*, edited by Michael J. Rainer, 112–23. Münster: Lit Verlag, 2001.

———. "Nothingness-*qua*-Love? The Implications of Absolute Nothingness for Ethics." In Gort, *Probing the Depths of Evil and Good*, 135–50.

———. *Transcendence and Violence: The Encounter of Buddhist, Christian, and Primal Traditions*. New York: Continuum, 2003.

———. "What Do Socially Engaged Buddhists and Christian Liberation Theologians Have to Say to One Another?" *Dialogue* 21 (1994) 1–18.

———. "Whose Universality? Which Interdependence? Human Rights, Social Responsibility, and Ecological Integrity." In *Postcolonial Europe in the Crucible of Culture: Reckoning with God in a World of Conflicts*, edited by Jacques Haers et al., 193–211. Amsterdam: Rodopi, 2007.

———, editor. *Converging Ways? Conversion and Belonging in Buddhism and Christianity*. St. Otillien: Eos, 2007.

Maybaum, Ignaz. *Ignaz Maybaum: A Reader*, edited by Nicholas de Lange. New York: Berghan, 2001.

McCabe, Herbert. *God and Evil in the Theology of Thomas Aquinas*, edited by Brian Davies. London: Continuum, 2010.

———. *On Aquinas*, edited by Brian Davies. London: Continuum, 2008.

McCarthy, Cormac. *The Road*. New York: Vintage, 2007.

McClelland, Mac. "Aftershocks: Welcome to Haiti's Reconstruction Hell." *Mother Jones*. January/February 2011. Online: http://motherjones.com/politics/2011/01/haiti-rape-earthquake-mac-mcclelland.

McDonnell, Faith J. H., and Grace Akallo. *Girl Soldier: A Story of Hope for Northern Uganda's Children*. Grand Rapids: Chosen, 2007.

McFague, Sallie. "An Ecological Christology: Does Christianity Have It?" In *Christianity and Ecology: Seeking the Well-Being of Earth and Humans*, edited by Dieter T. Hessel and Rosemary Radford Ruether, 29–45. Cambridge: Harvard University Press, 2000.

McGinn, Bernard, editor. *The Essential Writings of Christian Mysticism*. New York: Modern Library, 2006.

McNally, Richard. "The Politics of Trauma." In *Remembering Trauma*, 1–26. Cambridge: Belknap, 2003.

McWilliams, Warren. *Where Is the God of Justice? Biblical Perspectives on Suffering*. Peabody, MA: Hendrickson, 2005.

Meier, Christian. *A Culture of Freedom: Ancient Greece and the Origins of Europe*. Translated by Jefferson Chase. Oxford: Oxford University Press, 2011.

Melville, Herman. *Moby-Dick*. Ware, Hertfordshire: Wordsworth, 2002.

Menchú, Rigoberta. *I, Rigoberta Menchú: An Indian Woman in Guatemala*. Translated by Ann Wright. Edited by Elisabeth Burgos-Debray. London: Verso, 1984.

Mencius. *Mencius*. Translated by D. C. Lau. London: Penguin, 2004.

Meredith, Martin. *The Fate of Africa: A History of Fifty Years of Independence*. New York: PublicAffairs, 2005.

Merli, Claudia "Context-Bound Islamic Theodicies: The Tsunami as Supernatural Retribution vs. Natural Catastrophe in Southern Thailand." *Religion* 40:2 (2010): 104–11.

Metz, Johannes Baptist. *The Emergent Church*. Translated by Peter Mann. New York: Crossroad, 1986.

———. "Facing the Jews: Christian Theology after Auschwitz." Translated by John Griffiths. In *Johann-Baptist Metz and Jürgen Moltmann, Faith and the Future:*

Essays on Theology, Solidarity, and Modernity, 38–48. Nijmegan: The Concilium Foundation, 1995.

———. "The Future in the Memory of Suffering." Translated by John Griffiths. In Johann-Baptist Metz and Jürgen Moltmann, *Faith and the Future: Essays on Theology, Solidarity, and Modernity*, 3–16. Nijmegan: The Concilium Foundation, 1995.

Meyer, Marvin, and Charles Hughes, editors. *Jesus Then and Now: Images of Jesus in History and Christology.* Harrisburg, PA: Trinity, 2001.

Miller, Nancy K., and Jason Tougaw. "Introduction: Extremities." In *Extremities: Trauma, Testimony, and Community*, edited by Nancy K. Miller and Jason Tougaw, 1–23. Urbana: University of Illinois Press, 2002.

Milton, John. *Paradise Lost.* In *The Norton Anthology of English Literature.* 6th ed. Vol. 1. Edited by M. H. Abrams, 1475–1610. New York: Norton, 1993.

Moltmann, Jürgen. *Coming of God: Christian Eschatology.* Translated by Margaret Kohl. Minneapolis: Fortress, 2004.

———. *The Crucified God.* Translated by R. A. Wilson and John Bowden. Minneapolis: Fortress, 1993.

———. "God Is Unselfish Love." In *The Emptying God: A Buddhist-Jewish-Christian Conversation*, edited by John B. Cobb and Christopher Ives, 116–124. Eugene, OR: Wipf & Stock, 1990.

Montgomery, David R. *Dirt: The Erosion of Civilizations.* Berkeley: University of California Press, 2007.

Moorhead, Caroline. *Human Cargo: A Journey among Refugees.* New York: Picador, 2006.

Moreno, Juan Ramón. "Evangelization." Translated by Phillip Berryman. In Ellacuría and Sobrino, *Mysterium Liberationis*, 564–80.

Mostert, Christiaan. "Theodicy and Eschatology." In Barber and Neville, *Theodicy and Eschatology*, 97–120.

Moyaert, Marianne, and Didier Pollefeyt, editors. *Never Revoked: Nostra Aetate as Ongoing Challenge for Jewish-Christian Dialogue.* Leuven: Peeters, 2010.

Müller, Filip. *Eyewitness Auschwitz: Three Years in the Gas Chambers.* Edited and translated by Susanne Flatauer. Chicago: Dee, 1999.

Myers, Ched. *Binding the Strong Man: A Political Reading of Mark's Story of Jesus.* Anniversary ed. Maryknoll, NY: Orbis, 2010.

———. "The Cedar Has Fallen! The Prophetic Word versus Imperial Clear-Cutting." In *Earth and Word: Classic Sermons on Saving the Planet*, edited by David Rhoads, 211–23. New York: Continuum, 2007.

———. *"Say to This Mountain": Mark's Story of Discipleship.* Maryknoll, NY: Orbis, 1996.

———. *Who Will Roll Away the Stone? Discipleship Queries for First World Christians.* Maryknoll, NY: Orbis, 1994.

Myers, Ched, and Elaine Enns. *Ambassadors of Reconciliation.* Vol. 1, *New Testament Reflections on Restorative Justice and Peacemaking.* Maryknoll, NY: Orbis, 2009.

Nance, Kimberly A. *Can Literature Promote Justice? Trauma Narrative and Social Action in Latin American Testimonio.* Nashville: Vanderbilt University Press, 2006.

National Conference of US Catholic Bishops. *Economic Justice for All: A Pastoral Letter on Catholic Social Teaching and the U.S. Economy.* Washington, DC: NCCC, 1996.

Neibuhr, Reinhold. *The Nature and Destiny of Man*. New York: Scribner, 1964.

Neiman, Susan. *Evil in Modern Thought: An Alternative History of Philosophy*. Princeton: Princeton University Press, 2002.

Némirovsky, Iréne. *Suite Française*. Translated by Sandra Smith. New York: Knopf, 2006.

Neufeldt, Ronald. "Hindu Views of Jesus." In *Hindu-Christian Dialogue: Perspectives and Encounters*, edited by Harold Coward, 162–75. Maryknoll, NY: Orbis, 1990.

Neuffer, Elizabeth. *The Key to My Neighbor's House: Seeking Justice in Bosnia and Rwanda*. New York: Picador, 2001.

Neumann-Buber, Margarete. *Milena: The Tragic Story of Kafka's Great Love*. Translated by Ralph Manheim. New York: Arcade, 1988.

Neusner, Jacob. *A Midrash Reader*. Minneapolis: Fortress, 1990.

———. *A Rabbi Talks with Jesus*. Rev. ed. Montreal: McGill-Queen's University Press, 2007.

———. "Theodicy in Judaism." In *Theodicy in the World of the Bible*, edited by Antti Laato and Johannes C. de Moor, 685–727. Leiden: Brill, 2003.

———, editor. *Evil and Suffering*. Cleveland: Pilgrim, 1998.

———, editor and translator. *Genesis Rabbah: The Judaic Commentary to the Book of Genesis: A New American Translation*. Atlanta: Scholars, 1985.

Neusner, Jacob, and Bruce Chilton, editors. *The Golden Rule: The Ethics of Reciprocity in World Religions*. London: Continuum, 2008.

Neville, David. "God's Presence and Power: Christology, Eschatology, and 'Theodicy' in Mark's Crucifixion Narrative." In Barber and Neville, *Theodicy and Eschatology*, 19–41.

Nietzsche, Friedrich. *The Anti-Christ*. Translated by R. J. Hollingdale. New York: Penguin, 1978.

———. *On the Genealogy of Morals* and *Ecce Homo*. Translated by Walter Kaufman. New York: Vintage, 1989.

———. *Thus Spoke Zarathustra*. Translated by Walter Kaufmann. New York: Penguin, 1978.

Nomberg-Przytyk, Sara. *Auschwitz: True Tales from a Grotesque Land*. Translated by Roslyn Hirsch. Edited by Eli Pfefferkorn and David H. Hirsch. Chapel Hill: University of North Carolina Press, 1985.

Nossiter, Adam. "Gabon's Capital: A Legacy of 'Ill-Acquired Goods.'" *The International Herald Tribune*, September 15, 2009.

Ochs, Peter. "The God of Jews and Christians." In *Christianity in Jewish Terms*, edited by Tikva Frymer-Kensky et al., 49–69. Boulder, CO: Westview, 2000.

———. "The Renewal of Jewish Theology Today: Under the Sign of Three." In *The Blackwell Companion to Postmodern Theology*, edited by Graham Ward, 324–48. Oxford: Blackwell, 2005.

O'Connell, Daniel. Foreword to *By Fire into Light: Four Catholic Martyrs of the Nazi Camps*, by Joseph M Malham. Leuven: Peeters, 2002.

O'Grady, John, and Peter Scherle, editors. *Ecumenics from the Rim: Explorations in Honour of John D'Arcy May*. Berlin: Lit, 2007.

O'Keefe, Mark. "Prayer and Conversion." In *The Tradition of Catholic Prayer*, edited by Christian Raab and Harry Hagan, 263–74. Collegeville: Liturgical, 2007.

Oldridge, Darren. *Strange Histories: The Trial of the Pig, the Walking Dead, and Other Matters of Fact from the Medieval and Renaissance Worlds*. New York: Routledge, 2005.

O'Neill, Maura. *Mending a Torn World: Women in Interreligious Dialogue*. Maryknoll, NY: Orbis, 2007.

O'Neill, Tom. "Escape from North Korea." *National Geographic Magazine*, February 2009, 77–99.

Origen, "Prayer." In McGinn, *Essential Writings of Christian Mysticism*, 81–85.

———. *Origen: An Exhortation to Martyrdom, Prayer, and Selected Works*. Translated by Rowan A. Greer. New York: Paulist, 1979.

Osiel, Mark. *Making Sense of Mass Atrocity*. Cambridge: Cambridge University Press, 2011.

Ovid. *Metamorphoses*. Translated by Rolfe Humpries. Bloomington: Indiana University Press, 1983.

Oz, Amos. "The Devil's Progress." *The Guardian*, September 3, 2005, Review.

Ozick, Cynthia. "The Rights of History and the Rights of Imagination." In Katz and Rosen, *Obliged by Memory*, 3–18.

Parkin, David, editor. *The Anthropology of Evil*. Oxford: Blackwell, 1985.

Parry, Robin A., and Christopher Hugh Partridge, editors. *Universal Salvation: The Current Debate*. Carlisle: Paternoster, 2003.

Partnoy, Alicia. *The Little School: Tales of Survival and Disappearance*. Translated by Alicia Partnoy with Lois Athey and Sandra Braunstein. San Francisco: Cleis, 1998.

Pascal, Blaise. *Penseés*. Translated by A. J. Krailsheimer. Middlesex: Penguin, 1970.

Patterson, David, and John K. Roth, editors. *After-Words: Post-Holocaust Struggles with Forgiveness, Reconciliation, Justice*. Seattle: University of Washington Press, 2004.

———. *Fire in the Ashes: God, Evil, and the Holocaust*. Seattle: University of Washington Press, 2005.

Patterson, Michael C. "Forgiveness through Post-traumatic Growth." In *Forgiving and Remembering in Northern Ireland: Approaches to Conflict Resolution,* edited by Graham Spencer, 187–98. London: Continuum, 2011.

Paulson, Ronald. *Sin and Evil: Moral Values in Literature*. New Haven: Yale University Press, 2007.

Pawlikowski, John T. *Christ in the Light of the Christian-Jewish Dialogue*. New York: Paulist Press, 1982.

———. "Divine and Human Responsibilty in the Light of the Holocaust." In Singer, *Humanity at the Limit*, 15–25.

———. *Jesus and the Theology of Israel*. Wilmingon: Michael Glazer, 1989.

———. "Jews and Christians: Their Covenantal Relationship in the American Context." In *Two Faiths, One Covenant? Jewish and Christian Identity in the Presence of the Other*, edited by Eugene B. Korn and John T. Pawlikowski, 155–65. Lanham, MD: Rowman & Littlefield, 2005.

———. "The Search for a New Paradigm for the Christian-Jewish Relationship: A Response to Michael Singer." In *Reinterpreting Revelation and Tradition: Jews and Christians in Conversation*, edited by John T. Pawlikowski and Hayim Goren Perelmuter, 25–48. Franklin, WI: Sheed & Ward, 2000.

———. "Uniqueness and Universality in the Holocaust: The Need for a New Language." In Colijn and Littell, *Confronting the Holocaust*, 51–62.

Pears, Angie. *Doing Contextual Theology*. London: Routledge, 2010.

Petrella, Ivan. *The Future of Liberation Theology: An Argument and Manifesto*. London: SCM, 2006.

————, editor. *Latin American Liberation Theology: The Next Generation*. Maryknoll, NY: Orbis, 2005.

Phan, Peter C. *Being Religious Interreligiously: Asian Perspectives on Interfaith Dialogue*. Maryknoll, NY: Orbis, 2004.

————. "Prophecy and Contemplation: The Language of Liberation Theology against Evil." In Cenkner, *Evil and the Response of World Religions*, 183–98.

Philbrick, Nathaniel. *Mayflower: A Story of Courage, Community, and War*. New York: Penguin, 2007.

Phillips, D. Z. *The Problem of Evil and the Problem of God*. Minneapolis: Fortress, 2005.

————. "Theism without Theodicy." In Davis, *Encountering Evil*, 145–61.

Pieris, Aloysius. *Fire and Water: Basic Issues in Asian Buddhism and Christianity*. Maryknoll, NY: Orbis, 1996.

Pinker, Steven. *The Better Angels of Our Nature: Why Violence Has Declined*. New York: Viking, 2011.

Pinnock, Sarah K. *Beyond Theodicy: Jewish and Christian Continental Thinkers Respond to the Holocaust*. Albany: State University of New York Press, 2002.

Plantinga, Alvin. *God, Freedom, and Evil*. Grand Rapids: Eerdmans, 1977.

Plato. *The Republic*. Translated by Desmond Lee. London: Penguin, 2003.

Pocock, David. "Unruly Evil." In Parkin, *The Anthropology of Evil*, 42–56.

Pogge, Thomas. "World Poverty and Human Rights." In *Ethics and International Affairs*, 3rd ed, edited by Joel H. Rosenthal and Christian Barry, 307–315. Washington, DC: Georgetown University Press, 2009.

Pollefeyt, Didier. "Between a Dangerous Memory and a Memory in Danger: The Israeli-Palestinian Struggle from a Christian Post-Holocaust Perspective." In Grob and Roth, *Anguished Hope*, 135–46.

————. "Christology after Auschwitz: A Catholic Perspective." In Meyer, *Jesus Then and Now*, 229–48.

————. "The Church and the Jews: Unsolvable Paradox or Unfinished Story?" In *Nostra Aetate: Origins, Promulgation, Impact on Jewish-Catholic Relations*, edited by Neville Lamdan and Alberto Melloni, 131–44. Berlin: Lit Verlag, 2007.

————. "Critique" [of "Emmanuel Levinas and the Primacy of Ethics in Post-Holocaust Philosophy"]. In Roth, *Ethics after the Holocaust*, 30–38.

————. "Developing Criteria for Religious and Ethical Teaching of the Holocaust." In Goldenberg and Millen, *Testimony, Tensions, and Tikkun*, 172–87.

————. "Ethics, Forgiveness and the Unforgiveable." In *Incredible Forgiveness: Christian Ethics between Fanaticism and Reconciliation*, edited by Didier Pollefeyt, 121–160. Leuven: Peeters, 2004.

————. "Forgiveness after the Holocaust." In Patterson and Roth, *After-Words*, 55–69.

————. "*Horror Vacui*: God and Evil in/after Auschwitz." In Patterson and Roth, *Fire in the Ashes*, 219–31.

————. "In Response to Britta Frede-Wenger and Peter J. Haas." In Patterson and Roth, *Fire in the Ashes*, 238–42.

————. "In Response to Peter J. Haas and Juergen Manemann." In Patterson and Roth, *After-Words*, 75–80.

————. *Jews and Christians: Rivals or Partners for the Kingdom of God? In Search of an Alternative for the Theology of Substitution*. Louvain: Peeters, 1997.

————. "The Kafkaesque World of the Holocaust: Paradigmatic Shifts in the Ethical Interpretation of the Nazi Genocide." In Roth, *Ethics after the Holocaust*, 210–42.

———. "Pollefeyt's Response to Critiques." In Roth, *Ethics after the Holocaust*, 273–79.

———. "The Significance of Nazi Ethics for Medical Ethics Today." In Singer, *Humanity at the Limit*, 250–58.

———. "Victims of Evil or Evil of Victims?" In *Problems Unique to the Holocaust*, edited by Harry James Cargas, 67–82. Lexington: University Press of Kentucky, 1999.

———, editor. *Incredible Forgiveness: Christian Ethics Between Fanaticism and Reconciliation*. Leuven: Peeters, 2004.

Pope, Stephen L. "Proper and Improper Partiality and the Preferential Option for the Poor." *Theological Studies* 54 (1993) 242–71.

Pope, Stephen L., and Charles Hefling, editors. *Sic et Non: Encountering Dominus Iesus*. Maryknoll, NY: Orbis, 2002.

Porter, Bill. *Road to Heaven: Encounters with Chinese Hermits*. San Francisco: Mercury House, 1993.

Pui-Lan, Kwok, editor. *Hope Abundant: Third World and Indigenous Women's Theology*. Maryknoll, NY: Orbis, 2010.

Queiruga, Andrés Torres. "From 'Ponerology' to Theodicy: Evil in Secular Culture." *Concilium* 1 (2009) 80–89.

The Qur'an. Translated by M. A. S. Abdel Haleem. Oxford: Oxford University Press, 2010.

Rahimi, Atiq. *Earth and Ashes*. Translated by Erdag M. Goknar. London: Vintage, 2003.

Rahner, Karl. "Why Does God Allow Us to Suffer?" In *Theological Investigations*. Vol. 19, 194–208. London: Darton, Longman, & Todd, 1961.

Raphael, Melissa. *The Female Face of God in Auschwitz: A Jewish Feminist Theology of the Holocaust*. London: Routledge, 2003.

———. "From Historiography to Theography: Reflections on the Role of Theological Aesthetics in *The Female Face of God in Auschwitz*." *Holocaust Studies: A Journal of Culture and History* 15:3 (2010) 47–56.

———. "The Gendering of Post-Holocaust Jewish Responses to War and Collective Violence." In *Religion and the Politics of Peace and Conflict*, edited by Linda Hogan and Dylan Lee Lehrke, 159–74. Eugene, OR: Wipf & Stock, 2009.

Ratushinskaya, Irina. *Grey Is the Color of Hope*. Translated by Alyona Kojevnikov. Vintage: New York, 1989.

Rawls, John. *A Theory of Justice*. Rev. ed. Cambridge: Belknap, 1999.

Rediker, Marcus. *The Slave Ship: A Human History*. New York: Viking, 2007.

Regan, Ethna. *Theology and the Boundary Discourse of Human Rights*. Washington, DC: Georgetown University Press, 2010.

Réjon, Francisco Moreno. "Fundamental Moral Theory in the Theology of Liberation." Translated by Robert R. Barr. In Ellacuría and Sobrino, *Mysterium Liberationis*, 210–21.

Ricoeur, Paul. *Essays on Biblical Interpretation*, edited by Lewis S. Mudge. Philadelphia: Fortress, 1980.

———. "Evil, a Challenge to Philosophy and Theology." In *Figuring the Sacred: Religion, Narrative, and Imagination*, edited by Mark I. Wallace, 249–61. Translated by David Pellauer. Minneapolis: Fortress, 1995.

Rieger, Joerg, editor. *Opting for the Margins: Postmodernity and Liberation in Christian Theology*. Oxford: Oxford University Press, 2003.

————. "Theology and the Power of the Margins in a Postmodern World." In *Opting for the Margins: Postmodernity and Liberation in Christian Theology*, edited by Joerg Rieger, 179–99. Oxford: Oxford University Press, 2003.

Rittner, Carol, et al., editors. *Genocide in Rwanda: Complicity of the Churches?* St. Paul: Paragon House, 2004.

Robinson, George. *Essential Judaism: A Complete Guide to Beliefs, Customs, and Rituals*. New York: Pocket, 2000.

Rohr, Richard. "The Franciscan Option." In *Stricken by God? Nonviolent Identification and the Victory of Christ*, edited by Brad Jersak and Michael Hardin, 206–12. Grand Rapids: Eerdmans, 2007.

Romero, Oscar. *The Violence of Love*. Translated by James R. Brockman. Maryknoll, NY: Orbis, 2004.

Rosenfeld, Alvin H. *The End of the Holocaust*. Bloomington: Indiana University Press, 2011.

Rosenthal, Joel H., and Christian Barry, editors. *Ethics and International Affairs*. 3rd ed. Washington, DC: Georgetown University Press, 2009.

Rosenzweig, Franz. *The Star of Redemption*. Translated by Barbara A. Galli. Madison: University of Wisconsin Press, 2005.

Roth, John K. *Ethics during and after the Holocaust: In the Shadow of Birkenau*. New York: Palgrave, 2007.

————. "In Response to Leonard Grob and Juergen Manemann." In Patterson and Roth, *Fire in the Ashes*, 265–71.

————. "Rejoinder." In Davis, *Encountering Evil*, 30–37.

————. "A Theodicy of Protest." In Davis, *Encountering Evil*, 1–20.

————, editor. *Ethics after the Holocaust: Perspectives, Critiques, and Responses*. St. Paul: Paragon House, 1999.

Roth, Philip. "A Conversation with Primo Levi." In Primo Levi, *Survival in Auschwitz*, 175–87. New York: Touchstone, 1996.

Rousseau, Jean-Jacques. *Social Contract*. Edited and translated by Maurice Cranston. London. Penguin, 1968.

Rubenstein, Richard L. *After Auschwitz: History, Theology, and Contemporary Judaism*. Baltimore: Johns Hopkins University Press, 1992.

Rubenstein, Richard L., and John K. Roth, editors. *Approaches to Auschwitz: The Holocaust and Its Legacy*. 2nd ed. Louisville: Westminster John Knox, 2003.

Ruether, Rosemary Radford. "Conclusion: Eco-Justice at the Center of the Church's Mission." In *Christianity and Ecology: Seeking the Well-Being of Earth and Humans*, edited by Dieter T. Hessel and Rosemary Radford Ruether, 603–13. Cambridge: Harvard University Press, 2000.

Rumi. *The Essential Rumi*. Translated by Coleman Barks. New York: Quality Paperback Book Club, 1998.

Runblom, Harald. Foreword to *The Genocidal Temptation: Auschwitz, Hiroshima, Rwanda, and Beyond*, edited by Robert S. Frey. Dallas: University Press of America, 2004.

Ruston, Roger. *Human Rights and the Image of God*. London: SCM, 2004.

Ryback, Timothy W. *The Last Survivor: Legacies of Dachau*. New York: Vintage, 1999.

Sacks, Rabbi Jonathan. *Future Tense: Jews, Judaism, and Israel in the Twenty-First Century*. New York: Schocken, 2009.

Saklani, Dinesh Prasad. "Maya as Evil: From Classical Hindu Thought to Bhakti Saints and Kabir. A Historical Exploration." In Gort, *Probing the Depths of Evil and Good*, 41–55.

Saunders, Rebecca. "Questionable Associations: The Role of Forgiveness in Transitional Justice." *The International Journal of Transitional Justice* 5 (2011) 119–41.

Scarry, Elaine. *The Body in Pain: The Making and Unmaking of the World*. New York: Oxford University Press, 1985.

Schaab, Gloria L. *The Creative Suffering of the Triune God: An Evolutionary Theology*. Oxford: Oxford University Press, 2007.

Schäfer, Peter. *Jesus in the Talmud*. Princeton: Princeton University Press, 2007.

Schanberg, Sydney H. *The Death and Life of Dith Pran*. New York: Penguin, 1985.

Schiff, Hilda, editor. *Holocaust Poetry*. New York: HarperCollins, 1985.

Schmidt-Leukel, Perry. "'Light and Darkness' or of 'Looking Through a Dim Mirror'? A Reply to Paul Williams from a Christian Perspective." In *Converging Ways? Conversion and Belonging in Buddhism and Christianity*, edited by John D'Arcy May, 67–88. St. Otillien: Eos, 2007.

———, editor. *Buddhism and Christianity in Dialogue: The Gerald Weisfeld Lectures 2004*. London: SCM, 2005.

———. *Buddhist Perceptions of Jesus*. St. Ottilien: Eos, 2001.

———. *War and Peace in World Religions: The Gerald Weisfeld Lectures 2003*. London: SCM, 2004.

Schmidt-Leukel, Perry, and Lloyd V. J. Ridgeon, editors. *Islam and Inter-Faith Relations: The Gerald Weisfeld Lectures 2006*. London: SCM, 2007.

Schreiter, Robert J., et al., editors. *Peacebuilding: Catholic Theology, Ethics, and Praxis*. Maryknoll, NY: Orbis, 2010.

Schrijver, Georges de. *Recent Theological Debates in Europe: Their Impact on Interreligious Dialogue*. Bangalore: Dharmaram, 2004.

Schwab, Gabriele. *Haunting Legacies: Violent Histories and Transgenerational Trauma*. New York: Columbia University Press, 2010.

Schweizer, Bernard. *Hating God: The Untold Story of Misotheism*. Oxford: Oxford University Press, 2011.

Segovia, Fernando F., and R. S. Sugirtharajah, editors. *A Postcolonial Commentary on the New Testament Writings*. London: T. & T. Clark, 2007.

Seneca. *Letters from a Stoic*. Translated by Robin Campbell. Middlesex: Penguin, 1982.

Senior, Donald. "Beloved Aliens and Exiles." In *A Promised Land, A Perilous Journey: Theological Perspectives on Migration*, edited by Daniel G. Groody and Gioacchino Campese, 20–34. Notre Dame: University of Notre Dame Press, 2011.

Shakespeare, William. *The Riverside Shakespeare*. Dallas: Houghton Mifflin, 1974.

———. *The Tragedy of King Richard the Third*. In Shakespeare, *Riverside Shakespeare*, 748–804.

———. *The Tragedy of Titus Andronicus*. In Shakespeare, *Riverside Shakespeare*, 1065–1100.

Shankman, Steven. *Other Others: Levinas, Literature, Transcultural Studies*. Albany: State University of New York Press, 2010.

Shorto, Russell. "The Irish Affliction." *New York Times Sunday Magazine*. 13 February 2011, 42–47, 51.

Singer, Michael A., editor. *Humanity at the Limit: The Impact of the Holocaust Experience on Jews and Christians.* Bloomington: Indiana University Press, 2000.

Sklodowska, Elzbieta. "Spanish American Testimonial Novel: Some Afterthoughts." In Gugelberger, *The Real Thing*, 84–100.

Skye, Lee Miena. "Australian Aboriginal Women's Christologies." In *Hope Abundant: Third World and Indigenous Women's Theology*, edited by Kwok Pui-Lan, 194–202. Maryknoll, NY: Orbis, 2010.

Smith, Steven D. *The Disenchantment of Secular Discourse.* Cambridge: Harvard University Press, 2010.

Snyder, Timothy. *Bloodlands: Europe between Hitler and Stalin.* New York: Basic, 2010.

Sobrino, Jon. "Central Position of the Reign of God in Liberation Theology." Translated by Robert R. Barr. In Ellacuría and Sobrino, *Mysterium Liberationis*, 350–88.

———. *Jesus the Liberator: A Historical-Theological Reading of Jesus of Nazareth.* Translated by Paul Burns and Francis McDonagh. Maryknoll, NY: Orbis, 1999.

———. *No Salvation outside the Poor: Prophetic-Utopian Essays.* Maryknoll, NY: Orbis, 2008.

———. *The Principle of Mercy: Taking the Crucified People from the Cross.* Maryknoll, NY: Orbis, 1993.

———. "Systematic Christology: Jesus Christ, the Absolute Mediator of the Reign of God." Translated by Robert R. Barr. In Ellacuría and Sobrino, *Mysterium Liberationis*, 440–61.

———. *Where Is God? Earthquake, Terrorism, Barbarity, and Hope.* Translated by Margaret D. Wilde. Maryknoll, NY: Orbis, 2004.

Sölle, Dorothee. "God's Pain and Our Pain: How Theology Has to Change after Auschwitz." In Maduro, *Judaism, Christianity, and Liberation,* 110–21.

———. *Suffering.* Translated by Everett R. Kalin. London: Darton, Longman & Todd, 1975.

Solomon, Norman. "Economics and Liberation: Can the Theology of Liberation Decide Economic Questions?" In Maduro, *Judaism, Christianity, and Liberation,* 122–39.

———, editor and translator. *The Talmud: A Selection.* London: Penguin, 2009.

Solzhenitsyn, Aleksandr. *The Gulag Archipelago 1918–1956.* Translated by Thomas P. Whitney. London: Harvill, 1995.

Song, Choan-Seng. *Third-Eye Theology: Theology in Formation in Asian Settings.* Maryknoll, NY: Orbis, 1990.

Sophocles. *Antigone.* In *Greek Tragedies: Volume 1,* edited by David Greene and Richmond Lattimore, 177–228. Translated by Elizabeth Wyckoff. Chicago: University of Chicago Press, 1960.

Southwold, Martin. "Buddhism and Evil." In Parkin, *The Anthropology of Evil,* 128–41.

Sperling, David S. "Jewish Perspectives on Jesus." In Meyer, *Jesus Then and Now,* 251–59.

Standiford, Les. *Washington Burning: How a Frenchman's Vision for Our Nation's Capital Survived Congress, the Founding Fathers, and the Invading British Army.* New York: Crown, 2008.

Staub, Ervin, and Laurie Anne Pearlman. "Healing, Reconciliation, and Forgiveness after Genocide and Other Collective Violence." In *Forgiveness and Reconciliation,* edited by Raymond G. Helmick and Rodney L. Petersen, 205–27. Philadelphia: Templeton Foundation Press, 2002.

Steele, Michael R. *Christianity, Tragedy, and Holocaust Literature.* Westport, CT: Greenwood, 1995.

Sternberg, Meir. *The Poetics of Biblical Narrative: Ideological Literature and the Drama of Reading.* Bloomington: Indiana University Press, 1987.

Stoeber, Michael. *Evil and the Mystics' God.* Houndmills: Macmillan, 1992.

———. *Reclaiming Theodicy: Reflections on Suffering, Compassion, and Spiritual Transformation.* Houndmills: Palgrave, 2005.

Stone, Norman. *World War One: A Short History.* London: Penguin, 2008.

Stover, Eric. *The Witnesses: War Crimes and the Promise of Justice in The Hague.* Philadelphia: University of Pennsylvania Press, 2007.

Straub, Gerard Thomas. *Hidden in the Rubble: A Haitian Pilgrimage to Compassion and Resurrection.* Maryknoll, NY: Orbis, 2010.

Sugirtharajah, R. S., editor. *Asian Faces of Jesus.* Maryknoll, NY: Orbis, 1993.

———, editor. *The Postcolonial Biblical Reader.* Oxford: Blackwell, 2006.

Suleiman, Susan Rubin. "The Advantages of Delay: A Psychological Perspective on Memoirs of Trauma." In Katz and Rosen, *Obliged by Memory*, 43–51.

———. "Do Facts Matter in Holocaust Memoirs? Wilkomirski/Wiesel." In Katz and Rosen, *Obliged by Memory*, 21–42.

Surin, Kenneth. *Theology and the Problem of Evil.* Eugene: Wipf & Stock, 1986.

Svendsen, Lars. *A Philosophy of Evil.* Translated by Kerri A. Pierce. Champaign: Dalkey Archive, 2010.

Sweeney, Marvin A. *Reading the Hebrew Bible after the Shoah: Engaging Holocaust Theology.* Minneapolis: Fortress, 2008.

Swidler, Leonard. *Jesus Was a Feminist: What the Gospels Reveal about His Revolutionary Perspective.* Lanham, MD: Sheed & Ward, 2007.

Swinburne, Richard. "Evil Does Not Show That There Is No God." In *Philosophy of Religion: A Guide and Anthology*, edited by Brian Davies, 599–613. Oxford: Oxford University Press, 2000.

———. *Is There a God?* Oxford: Oxford University Press, 1996.

———. *Providence and the Problem of Evil.* Oxford: Clarendon, 1998.

Tacitus. *The Annals of Imperial Rome.* Translated by Michael Grant. London: Penguin, 1989.

Tal, Kalí. *Worlds of Hurt: Reading the Literatures of Trauma.* Cambridge: Cambridge University Press, 1996.

Talbott, Thomas. "Christ Victorious." In Parry and Partridge, *Universal Salvation*, 15–31.

———. "Reply to My Critics." In Parry and Partridge, *Universal Salvation*, 247–72.

Tao Te Ching. Translated by D. C. Lau. London: Penguin, 1963.

Tauler, John. "Sermon 3." In McGinn, *Essential Writings of Christian Mysticism*, 378–83.

Taylor, Charles. *A Secular Age.* Cambridge: Belknap, 2007.

Telushkin, Joseph. *Hillel: If Not Now, When?* New York: Schocken, 2010.

Thérèse of Lisieux. *The Autobiography of St. Thérèse of Lisieux: The Story of a Soul.* Translated by John Beevers. New York: Image, 1989.

Thomson, Susan, and Rosemary Nagy. "Law, Power, and Justice: What Legalism Fails to Address in the Functioning of Rwanda's Gacaca Courts." *The International Journal of Transitional Justice* 5 (2011) 11–30.

Thubron, Colin. *In Siberia.* London: Chatto & Windus, 1999.

———. *Shadow of the Silk Road.* London: Vintage, 2007.

———. *To a Mountain in Tibet*. New York: HarperCollins, 2011.

Tilley, Terrence W. *Evils of Theodicy*. Eugene, OR: Wipf & Stock, 2000.

Todorov, Tzvetan. *Facing the Extreme: Moral Life in the Concentration Camps*. Translated by Arthur Denner and Abigail Pollack. London: Weidenfeld & Nicolson, 1999.

Tolstoy, Leo. *A Confession*. Translated by David Patterson. New York: Norton, 1983.

———. *War and Peace*. Translated by Louise and Alymer Maude. New York: Simon & Schuster, 1942.

Traba, Marta. *Mothers and Shadows*. London: Readers International, 1993.

Tracy, David. *Dialogue with the Other: The Inter-Religious Dialogue*. Leuven: Peeters, 1990.

———. "Fragments: The Spiritual Situation of Our Times." In *God, the Gift and Postmodernism*, edited by John D. Caputo and Michael J. Scanlon, 170–84. Bloomington: Indiana University Press, 1999.

———. "On Tragic Wisdom." In *Wrestling with God and with Evil: Philosophical Reflections*, edited by Hendrik M. Vroom, 13–24. Amsterdam: Rodopi, 2007.

———. "Religious Values after the Holocaust: A Catholic View." In *Jews and Christians after the Holocaust*, edited by Abraham J. Peck, 87–107. Philadelphia: Fortress, 1982.

Trible, Phyllis, and Letty M. Russell, editors. *Hagar, Sarah, and Their Children: Jewish, Christian, and Muslim Perspectives*. Louisville: Westminster John Knox, 2006.

Troster, Lawrence. "Hearing the Outcry of Mute Things: Toward a Jewish Creation Theology." In *Ecospirit: Religions and Philosophies of the Earth*, edited by Laurel Kearns and Catherine Keller, 337–52. New York: Fordham University Press, 2007.

Tuhabonye, Gilbert, with Gary Brozek. *This Voice in My Heart: A Runner's Memoir of Genocide, Faith, and Forgiveness*. New York: Amistad, 2007.

Uchida, Yoshiko. *Desert Exile: The Uprooting of a Japanese-American Family*. Seattle: University of Washington Press, 1994.

Unna, Moshe. "Who Can Heal You?" In Katz et al., *Wrestling with God*, 288–92.

Unterman, Alan, editor and translator. *The Kabbalistic Tradition*. London: Penguin, 2008.

Vajiragnana, Medagama. "A Theoretical Explanation of Evil in Theravada Buddhism." In Cenkner, *Evil and the Response of World Religions*, 99–108.

Valadier, Paul. "Has the Concept of *Sensus Fidelium* Fallen into Desuetude?" In *Catholic Theological Ethics in the World Church*, edited by James Keenan, 187–92. New York: Continuum, 2007.

Vanhoozer, Kevin J., editor. *The Cambridge Companion to Postmodern Theology*. Cambridge: Cambridge University Press, 2009.

Van Inwagen, Peter. "The Argument from Evil." In Van Inwagen, *Christian Faith and the Problem of Evil*, 55–73.

———, editor. *Christian Faith and the Problem of Evil*. Grand Rapids: Eerdmans, 2004.

Verbin, Nehama. "Forgiving God: A Jewish Perspective on Evil and Suffering." In Gort, *Probing the Depths of Evil and Good*, 201–16.

Viret, Emmanuel. "Interahamwe." In *Online Encyclopedia of Mass Violence*. Online: www.massviolence.org/Interahamwe.

Virgil. *The Aeneid*. Translated by Robert Fitzgerald. London: David Campbell, 1992.

Volf, Miroslav. *The End of Memory: Remembering Rightly in a Violent World.* Grand Rapid: Eerdmans, 2006.

―――. *Exclusion and Embrace: A Theological Exploration of Identity, Otherness, and Reconciliation.* Nashville: Abingdon, 1996.

Vroom, Hendrik M. "Why Are We So Inclined to Evil?" In *Postcolonial Europe in the Crucible of Culture: Reckoning with God in a World of Conflicts,* edited by Jacques Haers et al., 163–75. Amsterdam: Rodopi, 2007.

Waldenfels, Hans. "Ecclesia in Asia." In Kendall and O'Collins, *In Many and Diverse Ways,* 194–208.

Ward, Graham "Postmodern Theology." In *The Modern Theologians: Introduction to Christian Theology since 1918,* edited by David Ford, 322–38. Malden: Blackwell, 2005.

Waxman, Zoë Vania. *Writing the Holocaust: Identity, Testimony, Representation.* Oxford: Oxford University Press, 2006.

Weil, Simone. *The Simone Weil Reader.* Edited by George A. Panichas. New York: David McKay, 1977.

Weinandy, Thomas G. *Does God Suffer?* Edinburgh: T. & T. Clark, 2000.

Welz, Claudia. "Reasons for Having No Reasons to Defend God: Kant, Kierkegaard, Levinas and Their Alternatives to Theodicy." In Vroom, *Wrestling with God and with Evil,* 167–86.

Wiesel, Elie. Afterword to *Obliged by Memory: Literature, Religion, Ethics,* by Steven T. Katz and Alan Rosen. Syracuse: Syracuse University Press, 2006.

―――. *All Rivers Run to the Sea: Memoirs.* Translated by Marion Wiesel. New York: Knopf, 1995.

―――. *And the Sea Is Never Full: Memoirs, 1969–.* Translated by Marion Wiesel. New York: Knopf, 1999.

―――. *The Elie Wiesel Trilogy.* New York: Hill & Wang, 1990.

―――. *Legends of Our Time.* Translated by Marion Wiesel. New York: Schocken, 1982.

―――. *Night.* Translated by Marion Wiesel. London: Penguin, 2006.

―――. *One Generation After.* Translated by Lily Edelman and Marion Wiesel. New York: Schocken, 2011.

―――. *Rashi: A Portrait.* Translated by Catherine Temerson. New York: Nextbook, 2009.

―――. *The Trial of God.* Translated by Marion Wiesel. New York: Schocken, 1986.

Wiesenthal, Simon. *The Sunflower: On the Possibilities and Limits of Forgiveness.* Edited by Harry James Cargas and Bonny V. Fetterman. New York: Schocken, 1998.

Wieviorka, Annette. *The Era of the Witness.* Translated by Jared Stark. Ithaca: Cornell University Press, 2006.

Wilkes, George R. "Legitimations and Limits of War in Jewish Tradition." In *Religion and the Politics of Peace and Conflict,* edited by Linda Hogan and Dylan Lee Lehrke, 3–24. Eugene, OR: Wipf & Stock, 2009.

Willett, Jincy, "Under the Bed." In *Fields of Reading, Motives for Writing,* edited by Nancy R. Comley et al., 654–61. 6th ed. New York: Bedford, 2003.

Williams, Rowan. *Dostoevsky: Language, Faith, and Fiction.* London: Continuum, 2009.

Wills, Garry. *What Paul Meant.* New York: Viking, 2006.

Wink, Walter. "Jesus' Third Way." In *The Powers That Be: Theology for a New Millennium*, 98–111. New York: Doubleday, 1998.

Wohlmuth, Josef. "Twentieth-Century Jewish Thought as a Challenge to Christian Theology." In *Naming and Thinking God in Europe Today: Theology in Global Dialogue*, edited by Norbert Hintersteiner, 389–409. Amsterdam: Rodopi, 2007.

Wolterstorff, Nicholas. *Justice: Rights and Wrongs*. Princeton: Princeton University Press, 2008.

Wright, N. T. *Evil and the Justice of God*. Downers Grove: InterVarsity, 2006.

Wu, Harry Hongada. *Bitter Winds*. New York: John Wiley, 1994.

———. *Troublemaker: One Man's Crusade against China's Cruelty*. New York: Times Books, 1996.

Wyschogrod, Michael. "Faith and the Holocaust." In Katz et al., *Wrestling with God*, 456–61.

Yerushalmi, Yosef Hayim. *Zakhor: Jewish History and Jewish Memory*. Seattle: University of Washington Press, 1996.

Young, James. "Holocaust Documentary Fiction: The Novelist as Eyewitness." In Berel, *Writing and the Holocaust*, 200–215.

———. *Writing and Rewriting the Holocaust: Narrative and the Consequences of Interpretation*. Bloomington: Indiana University Press, 1990.

Yúdice, George. "*Testimonio* and Postmodernism." In Gugelberger, *The Real Thing*, 42–57.

Žižek, Slavoj. *Living in the End of Times*. London: Verso, 2011.

Name Index

Subject Index

actions, 72n16, 238, 244; consequences of, 115–17, 259,
261; good, 284, 289, 290, 292,
293–94; judgments of, 70, 71–72;
moral, 84n63, 297; responsibility
for, 91–92, 174. *See also* evil(s);
speech acts

affliction. *See* suffering

Africa, atrocities in, xvii. *See also*
Rwandan genocide; Sierra Leone,
civil war in; Sudan, civil war in;
Uganda, child soldiers in

After Auschwitz (Rubenstein),
190–92

afterlife, 130, 161, 273; healing and
redemption in, 54, 69, 72–73,
109, 215, 223, 264–67, 270, 284;
Jewish thought on, 161n58, 197,
260n31; justice in, 81, 162, 216,
303; rejection of, 77, 78, 86, 155;
theism and, 244, 252. *See also*
eternal life; heaven; identity,
postmortem

agnosticism, 213, 251, 280

All Rivers Run to the Sea (Wiesel),
211–12

Amalekites, 30, 287n26

anger, 207, 208, 295; God's, 128–30

anthropodicy, 136–38, 141, 142,
149, 165, 178, 212, 284

anthropology, 93, 111, 115–17

antitheodicy, 16, 185; atheism and,
188, 189; theism and, 85, 187,

276, 277, 280. *See also Problem of
Evil and the Problem of God, The*
(Phillips); theodicy, antitheod-
icy's relationship to

apokatastasis, 254, 256. *See also*
universal salvation

apologetics, 241–42, 277

Argentina's Dirty War, 27, 46, 100,
137, 218n2, 248

*Arguing with God: A Jewish
Tradition* (Laytner), 169–83

Armenian genocide, 9, 34

Atcatl Battalion (El Salvador), 236

atheism, 11n30, 148, 165n1;
antitheodicy and, 188, 189;
purifying, 73, 80, 82–83; among
victims, 51, 52, 61, 234, 241, 251,
278–79. *See also* God, death of

atonement, 13n43, 268. *See also*
repentance

atrocities: definition of, 15, 137. *See
also* mass atrocities; testimonies
of mass atrocities

At the Mind's Limits (Améry), 57

Auschwitz (concentration camp),
28, 75n29, 97, 160, 267; aftermath of, xxn23, 7–8, 91–92,
185–89, 190–92, 197, 201–3,
229, 254; belief in God in, 217–
18, 226, 238; burning babies in,
6, 83, 205, 209n121; crematoria
at, 5–6, 100, 237, 275; guards
at, 34–35, 92; murders at, xviii,

Lightning Source UK Ltd.
Milton Keynes UK
UKOW030211111012

200368UK00001B/32/P